UNIX in a Nutshell

System V Edition

Revised and Expanded for SVR4 and Solaris 2.0

A Desktop Quick Reference

UNIX in a Nutshell

System V Edition
Revised and Expanded for SVR4 and Solaris 2.0

Daniel Gilly and
the staff of O'Reilly & Associates, Inc.

O'Reilly & Associates, Inc.
103 Morris Street, Suite A
Sebastopol, CA 95472

UNIX in a Nutshell System V Edition

Copyright © 1992 O'Reilly & Associates, Inc. All rights reserved.
Printed in the United States of America.

Editor: Mike Loukides

Printing History:

December 1986:	First edition.
September 1987:	Minor corrections.
February 1989:	Minor corrections.
October 1989:	Minor corrections.
May 1990:	Minor corrections.
June 1992:	Second edition. Revised and expanded for SVR4 and Solaris 2.0 by Daniel Gilly.
September 1992:	Minor corretions.

This book is printed on acid-free paper with 50% recycled content, 10-15% post-consumer waste. O'Reilly & Associates is committed to using paper with the highest recycled content available consistent with high quality.

ISBN: 1-56592-001-5

Table of Contents

Part II: Text Editing

Part IV: Software Development

Preface

It may be a cliche, but it's true: the second edition of *UNIX in a Nutshell* (for System V) really is "bigger and better." Besides having a whole new appearance, the book has been revised for SVR4 and Solaris 2.0. Major additions include:

- New SVR4 commands and options.
- Selected BSD-derived commands from the compatibility packages.
- Additional features specifically from Solaris 2.0.
- Coverage of the Korn shell.
- Sections on GNU Emacs and RCS (which aren't in standard SVR4).
- An index to the commands described in this book.
- Useful examples throughout the book.

Audience

This quick reference should be of interest to UNIX users and UNIX programmers, as well as to anyone (such as a system administrator) who might offer direct support to users and programmers. The presentation is geared mainly toward people who are familiar with the UNIX system—that is, you know what you want to do, and you even have some idea how to do it. You just need a reminder about the details. For example, if you want to remove the third field from a database, you might think, "*I know I can use the **cut** command, but what are the options?*" In many cases, specific examples are provided to show how a command is used.

This quick reference (or "quick ref") might also help people who are familiar with some aspects of UNIX but not with others. Many sections include an overview of the particular topic. While this isn't meant to be comprehensive, it's usually sufficient to get you started in unfamiliar territory.

And some of you may be coming from a UNIX system that runs the BSD or SunOS 4.1 version. To help with such a transition, SVR4 and Solaris 2.0 include a group of "compatibility" commands, many of which are presented in this guide.

Finally, if you're new to the UNIX operating system, and you're feeling bold, you might appreciate this book as a quick tour of what UNIX has to offer. The "Beginner's Guide" in Section 1 can point you to the most useful commands, and you'll find brief examples of how to use them, but take note: this book should not be used in place of a good beginner's tutorial on UNIX. This quick ref should be a *supplement*, not a substitute.

Scope of This Book

The quick ref is divided into five parts:

- Part I (Sections 1 through 5) describes the syntax and options for UNIX commands and for the Bourne, Korn, and C shells.

- Part II (Sections 6 through 11) presents various editing tools and describes their command set (alphabetically and by group). Part II begins with a review of pattern matching, including examples geared toward specific editors.

- Part III (Sections 12 through 16) describes the nroff/troff text formatting programs, related macro packages, and the preprocessors tbl, eqn, and pic.

- Part IV (Sections 17 through 20) summarizes the UNIX utilities for software development—SCCS, RCS, **make**, and program debuggers sdb and dbx.

- Part V contains two loose ends: a table of ASCII characters and equivalent values, and a command index to help you locate the commands presented in this book.

Conventions

The quick ref follows certain typographic conventions, outlined below:

Bold	is used for directories, filenames, commands, and options. All terms shown in bold are typed literally.
Italic	is used to show generic arguments and options; these should be replaced with user-supplied values. Italic is also used to highlight comments in examples.
Bold Italic	is used for headings.
`Constant Width`	is used to show the contents of files or the output from commands.
`Constant Bold`	is used in examples and tables to show commands or other text that should be typed literally by the user.

`Constant` `Italic`	is used in examples and tables to show generic text; these should be replaced with user-supplied values.
`%`, `$`	are used in some examples as the C shell prompt (`%`) and as the Bourne shell or Korn shell prompt (`$`).
[ ]	surround optional elements in a description of syntax. (The brackets themselves should never be typed.) Note that many commands show the argument [*files*]. If a filename is omitted, standard input (i.e., the keyboard) is assumed. End with an end-of-file character.
EOF	indicates the end-of-file character (normally CTRL-D).
		is used in syntax descriptions to separate items for which only one alternative may be chosen at a time.
→	is used at the bottom of a right-hand page to show that the current entry continues on the next page. The continuation is marked by a ←.

A final word about syntax. In many cases, the space between an option and its argument can be omitted. In other cases, the spacing (or lack of spacing) must be followed strictly. For example, **−w***n* (no intervening space) might be interpreted differently from **−w** *n*. It's important to notice the spacing used in option syntax.

Acknowledgments

Many people helped this book along the way. The first edition resulted from the efforts of the following staff members of O'Reilly & Associates: Jean Diaz, Dale Dougherty, Daniel Gilly, Linda Mui, Tim O'Reilly, Thomas Van Raalte, Linda Walsh, Sue Willing, and Donna Woonteiler.

The second edition has a new cover and new interior layout, designed by Edie Freedman. Arthur Saarinen drew the referee figures. Chris Reilley and Jeff Robbins assisted with graphics. The manuscript was formatted using troff macros that were implemented by Linda Mui and Lenny Muellner, and the manuscript was prepared through the efforts of Donna Woonteiler, Sue Willing, and especially Rosanne Wagger. Christine Kenney and Peter Mui were valuable resources, tracking down useful information and passing it along.

Special thanks to the technical reviewers for reading the drafts and fielding all kinds of questions; the book has profited greatly from the comments of Tan Bronson (Microvation Consultants), Peter van der Linden, and Mike Loukides (O'Reilly & Associates).

Part I

Commands and Shells

Part I presents a summary of UNIX commands of interest to users and programmers. It also describes the three major UNIX shells, including special syntax and built-in commands.

Section 1 - *Introduction*

Section 2 - *UNIX Commands*

Section 3 - *The UNIX Shell: An Overview*

Section 4 - *The Bourne Shell and Korn Shell*

Section 5 - *The C Shell*

Introduction

The UNIX operating system originated from AT&T (now USL) in the early 1970's. Because UNIX was able to run on different hardware from different vendors, this encouraged developers to modify UNIX and distribute it as their own value-added version of UNIX. Separate UNIX traditions evolved as a result: USL's System V, Berkeley Standard Distribution (BSD, from the University of California, Berkeley), Xenix, etc.

Merging the Traditions

Today, UNIX developers are trying to blend the different traditions back into a more standard version. (The ongoing work on POSIX, an international standard based on System V and BSD, is influencing this movement.) This quick reference describes two systems that offer what many people consider to be a "more standard" version of UNIX: System V Release 4 (SVR4) and Solaris 2.0.

SVR4, which was developed jointly by USL (a division of AT&T) and Sun Microsystems, has merged features from BSD and SVR3. This adds about two dozen BSD commands (plus some new SVR4 commands) to the basic UNIX command set. In addition, SVR4 provides a BSD Compatibility Package, a kind of "second string" command group. This package includes some of the most fundamental BSD commands, and its purpose is to help users of BSD-derived systems make the transition to SVR4.

Solaris 2.0 is a distributed computing environment from SunSoft (a division of Sun Microsystems). The history of Solaris 2.0 is more complicated.

Solaris 2.0 includes the SunOS 5.0 operating system plus additional features such as OpenWindows. SunOS 5.0, in turn, merges SunOS 4.1 and SVR4. Most of the new content comes from SVR4. As a result, Solaris 2.0 is based on SVR4 but contains additional BSD/SunOS features. To help in the transition from the old (largely BSD-based) SunOS, Solaris 2.0 provides the BSD/SunOS Compatibility Package and the Binary Compatibility Package.

Bundling

Another issue affecting UNIX systems is the idea of *bundling*. UNIX has many features—sometimes more than you need to use. Nowadays, UNIX systems are usually split, or bundled, into various component packages. Some components are included automatically in the system you buy; others are optional—you get them only if you pay extra. Bundling lets you to select only the components you need. Typical bundling includes the following:

Basic System	Basic commands and utilities.
Programming	Compilers, debuggers, and libraries.
Text Processing	Troff, macros, and related tools.
Networking	Utilities for connecting to remote machines, including commands like **rlogin**, **rcp**, etc.
Windowing	Graphical user interfaces such as OPEN LOOK and Motif.

Bundling depends on the vendor. For example, Solaris 2.0 is shipped with OpenWindows, a windowing environment based on OPEN LOOK; you don't have to buy it as a separate package. For other vendors, the windowing package may be an extra-cost option. Similarly, some vendors ship text processing tools or compilers, and others don't.

What's in the Quick Ref

This guide presents the major features of generic SVR4, plus a few extras from the compatibility packages and from Solaris 2.0. In addition, this guide presents sections on emacs and RCS. Although they are not part of the standard SVR4 distribution, they are found on many UNIX systems because they are useful add-ons.

But keep in mind: if your system doesn't include all the component packages, there will be commands in this quick ref that you won't be able to find on your system.

The summary of UNIX commands in Section 2 makes up a large part of this book. Only user/programmer commands are included; administrative commands are ignored. Section 2 describes the following set:

- Commands from SVR3.

- New commands and options in SVR4.

- Selected commands from the compatibility packages and from Solaris 2.0, such as **dbx** (the debugger) and **openwin** (the start-up program for OpenWindows).

SVR3 users should note that many commands listed in Section 2 are not in SVR3. These include:

apropos	face	iconv	mcs	rksh	users
atq	fmli	keylogin	mkmsgs	sccs	uudecode
atrm	fmt	keylogout	nawk	script	uuencode
chkey	fmtmsg	ksh	notify	soelim	uuglist
clear	fold	ldd	openwin	srchtxt	vacation
cof2elf	gcore	lpq	pic	strings	w
compress	gencat	lpr	printenv	talk	whatis
ctags	gettxt	lprm	printf	truss	which
dbx	gprof	lprof	ptx	tset	whoami
download	head	lptest	relogin	uncompress	whois
dpost	hostid	mailalias	reset	uptime	zcat
exstr	hostname				

Beginner's Guide

If you're just beginning to work on a UNIX system, the abundance of commands might prove daunting. To help orient you, the following tables present a small sampling of commands on various topics.

Communication

cu	Connect to UNIX system.
ftp	File transfer protocol.
login	Sign on to UNIX.
mailx	Read or send mail.
rlogin	Sign on to remote UNIX.
talk	Write to other terminals.
telnet	Connect to another system.
vacation	Respond to mail automatically.
write	Write to other terminals.

Comparisons

cmp	Compare two files.
comm	Compare items in files.
diff	Compare two files.
diff3	Compare three files.
dircmp	Compare directories.
sdiff	Compare two files, side by side.

File Management

cat	Join files or display them.
cd	Change directory.
chmod	Change access modes on files.
cp	Copy files.
csplit	Break files at specific locations.
file	Determine a file's type.
head	Show the first few lines of a file.
install	Set up system files.
ln	Create filename aliases.
ls	List files or directories.
mkdir	Create a directory.
more	Display files by screenful.
mv	Move or rename files or directories.
pwd	Print your working directory.
rcp	Copy files to remote system.
rm	Remove files.
rmdir	Remove directories.
split	Split files evenly.
tail	Show the last few lines of a file.
wc	Count lines, words, and characters.

Miscellaneous

banner	Make posters from words.
bc	Precision calculator.
cal	Display calendar.
calendar	Check for reminders.
clear	Clear the screen.
kill	Terminate a running command.
man	Get information on a command.
nice	Reduce a job's priority.
nohup	Preserve a job after logging out.
passwd	Set password.
script	Produce a transcript of your login session.
spell	. Report misspelled words.
su	Become a superuser.

Printing

cancel	Cancel a printer request.
lp	Send to the printer.
lpstat	Get printer status.
pr	Format and paginate for printing.

Programming

cb	C source code ``beautifier.''
cc	C compiler.
cflow	C function flowchart.
ctags	C function references.
ctrace	C debugger.
cxref	C cross-references.
lint	C debugger.
ld	Link editor.
lex	Lexical analyzer.
make	Execute commands in a specified order.
od	Dump input in various formats.
sdb	Symbolic debugger.
strip	Remove data from an object file.
truss	Trace signals and system calls.
yacc	Compiler used with lex.

Searching

egrep	Extended version of **grep**.
fgrep	Search files for literal words.
find	Search the system for filenames.
grep	Search files for text patterns.
strings	Search binary files for text patterns.

Shell Programming

echo	Repeat input on the output.
expr	Perform arithmetic and comparisons.
line	Read a line of input.
sleep	Pause during processing.
test	Test a condition.

Storage

compress	Compress files to free up space.
cpio	Copy archives in or out.
pack	Pack files to free up space.
pcat	Display contents of packed files.
tar	Tape archiver.
uncompress	Expand compressed (**.Z**) files.
unpack	Expand packed (**.z**) files.
zcat	Display contents of compressed files.

System Status

at	Execute commands later.
chgrp	Change file group.
chown	Change file owner.
crontab	Automate commands.
date	Display or set date.
df	Show free disk space.
du	Show disk usage.
env	Show environment variables.
finger	Point out information about users.
ps	Show processes.
ruptime	Show loads on working systems.
shutdown	Revert to single-user mode.
stty	Set or display terminal settings.
who	Show who is logged on.

Text Processing

cut   Select columns for display.
ex   Line-editor underlying vi.
fmt   Produce roughly uniform line lengths.
fold   Produce exactly uniform line lengths.
join   Merge different columns into a database.
nawk   New version of awk (pattern-matching language for database files).
paste   Merge columns or switch order.
sed   Noninteractive text editor.
sort   Sort or merge files.
tr   Translate (redefine) characters.
uniq   Find repeated or unique lines in a file.
vi   Visual text editor.
xargs   Process many arguments in manageable portions.

Troff

All but **deroff** are in the compatibility packages.

deroff   Remove troff codes.
eqn   Preprocessor for equations.
nroff   Formatter for terminal display.
pic   Preprocessor for line graphics.
tbl   Preprocessor for tables.
troff   Formatter for typesetting.

Guide for Users of BSD-derived Systems

Those of you making a transition to SVR4 from a BSD-derived system should note that BSD commands reside in your system's **/usr/ucb** directory. This is especially important when using certain commands, because the compatibility packages include several commands that have an existing counterpart in SVR4, and the two versions work slightly differently. If your PATH variable specifies **/usr/ucb** before the SVR4 command directories (e.g., **/usr**), you'll end up running the BSD version of the command. Check your PATH variable to make sure that you're getting what you want. The commands that have both BSD and SVR4 variants include:

basename	du	ln	sum
cc	echo	ls	test
chown	groups	ps	tr
deroff	install	shutdown	vacation
df	ld	stty	

This guide describes the SVR4 version of the above commands.

UNIX Commands

This section presents the UNIX commands of interest to users and programmers. Most of these commands appear in the "Commands" section of the *User's Reference Manual* and *Programmer's Reference Manual* for UNIX System V Release 4 (SVR4). This section describes additional commands from the compatibility packages; these commands are prefixed with **/usr/ucb**, the name of the directory in which they reside. With some exceptions, these commands are only in SVR4. Also included here are commands specific to Solaris 2.0, such as the debugger **dbx** and the start-up script for OpenWindows, **openwin**.

Each entry is labeled with the command name on the outer edge of the page. The syntax line is followed by a brief description and a list of all available options. (Obsolete options have been marked as "SVR3 only.") Many commands come with examples at the end of the entry. If you need only a quick reminder or suggestion about a command, you can skip directly to the examples.

Some options can be invoked only by a user with special system privileges. Such a person is often called a superuser. In this book we use the term *privileged user* instead.

Typographic conventions for describing command syntax are listed in the Preface. For additional help in locating commands, see the Command Index (Section 22) at the back of this guide.

Alphabetical Summary of Commands

admin	**admin** [*options*] *files* An SCCS command. See Section 17.
apropos	**/usr/ucb/apropos** *keywords* Look up one or more *keywords* in the on-line manual pages. Same as **man** −**k**. See also **whatis**.
ar	**ar** [−**V**] *key* [*args*] [*posname*] *archive* [*files*] Maintain a group of *files* that are combined into a file *archive*. Used most commonly to create and update library files as used by the link editor (**ld**). Only one key letter may be used, but each can be combined with additional *args* (with no separations between). *posname* is the name of a file in *archive*. When moving or replacing *files*, you can specify that they be placed before or after *posname*. See **lorder** for another example. −**V** prints the version number of **ar** on standard error.

Key

d	Delete *files* from *archive*.
m	Move *files* to end of *archive*.
p	Print *files* in *archive*.
q	Append *files* to *archive*.
r	Replace *files* in *archive*.
t	List the contents of *archive* or list the named *files*.
x	Extract contents from *archive* or only the named *files*.

Args

a	Use with **r** or **m** to place *files* in the archive after *posname*.
b	Same as **a** but before *posname*.
c	Create *archive* silently.
i	Same as **b**.
l	Place temporary files in local directory rather than **/tmp** (SVR3 only).
s	Force regeneration of *archive* symbol table (useful after running **strip** or **mcs**).
u	Use with **r** to replace only *files* that have changed since being put in *archive*.
v	Verbose; print a description.

Example

Replace **mylib.a** with object files from the current directory:

```
ar r mylib.a `ls *.o`
```

as [*options*] *files*

Generate an object file from each specified assembly language source *file*. Object files have the same root name as source files but replace the **.s** suffix with **.o**. There may be additional system-specific options. See also **dis**.

Options

    −m   Run **m4** on *file*.

    −n   Turn off optimization of long/short addresses.

    −o *objfile* Place output in object file *objfile* (default is *file*.**o**).

    −Q*c*   Put the assembler's version number in the object file (when *c* = **y**); default is not to put it (*c* = **n**).

    −R   Remove *file* upon completion.

    −T   Force obsolete assembler directives to be obeyed.

    −V   Display the version number of the assembler.

    −Y [*key*,] *dir*

        Search directory *dir* for the **m4** preprocessor (if *key* is **m**), for the file containing predefined macros (if *key* is **d**), or for both (if *key* is omitted).

at *options1 time* [*date*] [+ *increment*]
at *options2* [*jobs*]

Execute commands entered on standard input at a specified *time* and optional *date*. (See also **batch**.) End input with *EOF*. *time* can be formed either as a numeric hour (with optional minutes and modifiers) or as a keyword. *date* can be formed either as a month and date, as a day of the week, or as a special keyword. *increment* is a positive integer followed by a keyword. See below for details.

Options1

    −f *file* Execute commands listed in *file*.

    −m   Send mail to user after job is completed.

Options2

    −l   Report all jobs that are scheduled for the invoking user or, if *jobs* are specified, report only for those. See also **atq**.

    −r   Remove specified *jobs* that were previously scheduled. To remove a job, you must be a privileged user or the owner of the job. Use **−l** first to see the list of scheduled jobs. See also **atrm**.

→

Time

hh:mm [*modifiers*]

> Hours can have one digit or two (a 24-hour clock is assumed by default); optional minutes can be given as one or two digits; the colon can be omitted if the format is *h*, *hh*, or *hhmm*; e.g., valid times are 5, 5:30, 0530, 19:45. If modifier **am** or **pm** is added, *time* is based on a 12-hour clock. If the keyword **zulu** is added, times correspond to Greenwich Mean Time.

midnight | **noon** | **now**

> Use any one of these keywords in place of a numeric time. **now** must be followed by an *increment*.

Date

month num[, *year*]

> *month* is one of the 12 months, spelled out or abbreviated to their first three letters; *num* is the calendar date of the month; *year* is the four-digit year. If the given *month* occurs before the current month, **at** schedules that month next year.

day One of the seven days of the week, spelled out or abbreviated to their first three letters.

today | **tomorrow**

> Indicate the current day or the next day. If *date* is omitted, **at** schedules **today** when the specified *time* occurs later than the current time; otherwise, **at** schedules **tomorrow**.

Increment

> Supply a numeric increment if you want to specify an execution time or day *relative* to the current time. The number should precede any of the keywords **minute**, **hour**, **day**, **week**, **month**, or **year** (or their plural forms). The keyword **next** can be used as a synonym of **+ 1**.

Examples

> Note that the first two commands are equivalent:

```
at 1945 pm December 9
at 7:45pm Dec 9
at 3 am Saturday
at now + 5 hours
at noon next day
```

atq

atq [*options*] [*users*]

Print jobs created by the **at** command which are still in the queue. Normally, jobs are sorted by the order in which they will execute. Specify the *users* whose jobs you want to check. If no *users* are specified, the default is to display all jobs if you're a privileged user; otherwise, only your jobs are displayed.

-c   Sort the queue according to the time the **at** command was given.

-n   Print only the total number of jobs in queue.

---

atrm [*options*] [*users* | *jobIDs*]

Remove jobs queued with **at** that match the specified *jobIDs*. A privileged user may also specify the *users* whose jobs are to be removed.

Options

-a   Remove all jobs belonging to the current user. (A privileged user can remove *all* jobs.)

-f   Remove jobs unconditionally, suppressing all information regarding removal.

-i   Prompt for **y** (remove the job) or **n** (do not remove).

---

awk [*options*] [*program*] [*var=value* ...] [*files*]

Use the pattern-matching *program* to modify the specified *files*. **awk** has been replaced by **nawk** (there's also a GNU version called **gawk**). *program* instructions have the general form:

```
pattern { procedure }
```

pattern and *procedure* are each optional. When specified on the command line, *program* must be enclosed in single quotes to prevent the shell from interpreting its special symbols. Any variables specified in *program* can be assigned an initial value by using command-line arguments of the form *var=value*. See Section 11 for more information (including examples) on **awk**.

Options

-f *file*   Use program instructions contained in *file*, instead of specifying *program* on the command line.

-F*c*   Treat input *file* as fields separated by character *c*. Default input field separator is space or tab.

---

banner *characters*

Print *characters* as a poster on the standard output. Each word supplied must contain ten characters or less.

---

basename *pathname* [*suffix*]

Given a *pathname*, strip the path prefix and leave just the filename, which is printed on standard output. If specified, a filename *suffix* (e.g., **.c**) is removed also. **basename** is typically invoked via command substitution (` ` `) to generate a filename.

→

basename

←

See also **dirname**.

Example

Given the following fragment from a Bourne shell script:

```
prog_name="`basename $0`"
echo "$prog_name: QUITTING: can't open $ofile"\
    1>&2 ; exit 1
```

If the script is called **do_it**, then the following message would be printed on standard error:

```
do_it: QUITTING: can't open output_file
```

---

batch

batch

Execute commands entered on standard input. End with *EOF*. Unlike **at**, which will execute commands at a specific time, **batch** executes commands one after another (waiting for each one to complete). This avoids the high system load caused by running several background jobs at once. See also **at**.

Example

```
batch
sort in > out
troff -ms bigfile
EOF
```

---

bc

bc [*options*] [*files*]

Interactively perform arbitrary-precision arithmetic or convert numbers from one base to another. Input can be taken from *files* or read from the standard input. To exit, type **quit** or *EOF*.

Options

−c   Do not invoke **dc**; compile only. (Since **bc** is a preprocessor for **dc**, **bc** normally invokes **dc**.)

−l   Make available functions from the math library.

bc is a language (and compiler) whose syntax resembles that of C. **bc** consists of identifiers, keywords, and symbols, which are briefly described below. Examples follow at end.

Identifiers

An identifier is a single character, consisting of the lowercase letters a-z. Identifiers are used as names for variables, arrays, and functions. Within the same program you may name a variable, an array, and a function using the same letter. The following identifiers would not conflict:

x	Variable **x**.
x[*i*]	Element *i* of array **x**. *i* can range from 0 to 2047 and can also be an expression.
x(y,z)	Call function **x** with parameters **y** and **z**.

Input-output keywords

ibase, **obase**, and **scale** store a value. Typing them on a line by themselves displays their current value. More commonly, you would change their values through assignment. Letters A-F are treated as digits whose values are 10-15.

ibase = *n*	Numbers that are input (e.g., typed) are read as base *n* (default is 10).
obase = *n*	Numbers displayed are in base *n* (default is 10). Note: Once **ibase** has been changed from 10, use digit "A" to restore **ibase** or **obase** to decimal.
scale = *n*	Display computations using *n* decimal places (default is 0, meaning that results are truncated to integers). **scale** is normally used only for base-10 computations.

Statement keywords

A semicolon or a newline separates one statement from another. Curly braces are needed only when grouping multiple statements.

if (*rel-expr*) {*statements*}

Do one or more *statements* if relational expression *rel-expr* is true; for example:

```
if(x==y) i = i + 1.
```

while (*rel-expr*) {*statements*}

Repeat one or more *statements* while *rel-expr* is true; for example:

```
while(i>0) {p = p*n; q = a/b; i = i-1}
```

for (*expr1*; *rel-expr*; *expr2*) {*statements*}

Similar to **while**; for example, to print the first 10 multiples of 5, you could type:

```
for(i=1; i<=10; i++) i*5
```

break Terminate a **while** or **for** statement.

Function keywords

define *j*(*k*) { Begin the definition of function *j* having a single argument *k*. Additional arguments are allowed, separated by commas. Statements follow on successive lines. End with a }.

→

auto *x, y*   Set up *x* and *y* as variables local to a function definition, initialized to 0 and meaningless outside the function. Must appear first.

return(*expr*)   Pass the value of expression *expr* back to the program. Return 0 if (*expr*) is left off. Used in function definitions.

sqrt(*expr*)   Compute the square root of expression *expr*.

length(*expr*)   Compute how many digits are in *expr*.

scale(*expr*)   Same, but count only digits to the right of the decimal point.

Math library functions

These are available when **bc** is invoked with **−l**. Library functions set **scale** to 20.

s(*angle*)   Compute the sine of *angle*, a constant or expression in radians.

c(*angle*)   Compute the cosine of *angle*, a constant or expression in radians.

a(*n*)   Compute the arctangent of *n*, returning an angle in radians.

e(*expr*)   Compute **e** to the power of *expr*.

l(*expr*)   Compute natural log of *expr*.

j(*n, x*)   Compute Bessel function of integer order *n*.

Operators

These consist of operators and other symbols. Operators can be arithmetic, unary, assignment, or relational.

arithmetic	+ − * / % ^
unary	− ++ −−
assignment	=+ =− =* =/ =% =^ =
relational	< <= > >= == !=

Other symbols

/* */   Enclose comments.

( )   Control the evaluation of expressions (change precedence). Can also be used around assignment statements to force the result to print.

{ }   Used to group statements.

[ ]   Array index.

" *text* "   Use as a statement to print *text*.

Examples

Note below that when you type some quantity (a number or expression), it is evaluated and printed, but assignment statements produce no display.

```
ibase = 8        Octal input.
20               Evaluate this octal number.
16               Terminal displays decimal value.
obase = 2        Display output in base 2 instead of base 10.
20               Octal input.
10000            Terminal now displays binary value.
ibase = A        Restore base 10 input.
scale = 3        Truncate results to 3 places.
8/7              Evaluate a division.
1.001001000      Oops! Forgot to reset output base to 10.
obase=10         Input is decimal now, so "A" isn't needed.
8/7
1.142            Terminal displays result (truncated).
```

The following lines show the use of functions:

```
define p(r,n){   Function p uses two arguments.
  auto v         v is a local variable.
  v = r^n        r raised to the n power.
  return(v)}     Value returned.

scale=5
x=p(2.5,2)       x = 2.5 ^ 2
x                Print value of x.
6.25
length(x)        Number of digits.
3
scale(x)         Number of places right of decimal point.
2
```

bdiff *file1 file2* [*options*]

Compare *file1* with *file2* and report the differing lines. **bdiff** splits the files and then runs **diff**, allowing it to act on files that would normally be too large to handle. **bdiff** reads standard input if one of the files is −. See also **diff**.

Options

n   Split each file into *n*-line segments (default is 3500). This option must be listed first.

−s   Suppress error messages from **bdiff** (but not from **diff**).

bfs [*option*] *file*

Big file scanner. Read a large *file*, using ed-like syntax. This command is more efficient than ed for scanning very large files because the file is not read into a buffer. Files can be up to 1024K bytes. **bfs** can be used to view a large file and identify sections to be divided with **csplit**. Not too useful.

→

bfs ←	*Option* − Do not print the file size.
cal	**cal** [[*month*] *year*] With no arguments, print a calendar for the current month. Otherwise, print either a 12-month calendar (beginning with January) for the given *year* or a one-month calendar of the given *month* and *year*. *month* ranges from 1 to 12. *year* ranges from 1 to 9999. *Examples* ```\ncal 12 1994\ncal 1994 > year_file\n```
calendar	**calendar** [*option*] Read your **calendar** file and display all lines that contain the current date. The **calendar** file is like a memo board. You create the file and add entries like the following: ```\n5/4 meeting with design group at 2 pm\nmay 6 pick up anniversary card on way home\n``` When you run **calendar** on May 4, the first line is displayed. **calendar** can be automated by using **crontab** or **at** or by including it in your startup files **.profile** or **.cshrc**. *Option* − Allow a privileged user to invoke **calendar** for all users, searching each user's login directory for a file named **calendar**. Entries that match are sent to a user via mail.

cancel	**cancel** [*options*] [*printer*]
	
	Cancel print requests made with **lp**. The request can be specified by its ID, by the *printer* on which it is currently printing, or by the username associated with the request (only privileged users can cancel another user's print requests). Use **lpstat** to determine either the *id* or the *printer* to cancel.
	
	Options
	
	    id Cancel print request *id*.
	    −u *user* Cancel request associated with *user*.

cat	**cat** [*options*] [*files*] Read one or more *files* and print them on standard output. Read standard input if no *files* are specified or if − is specified as one of the files; end input with *EOF*. You can use the > operator to

combine several files into a new file; use >> to append files to an existing file.

cat

Options

- **−e**   Print a $ to mark the end of each line. Must be used with **−v**.

- **−s**   Suppress messages about nonexistent files. (Note: In the BSD version, **−s** squeezes out extra blank lines.)

- **−t**   Print each tab as ˆI and each form feed as ˆL. Must be used with **−v**.

- **−u**   Print output as unbuffered (default is buffered in blocks or screen lines).

- **−v**   Display control characters and other nonprinting characters.

Examples

```
cat ch1                  Display a file.
cat ch1 ch2 ch3 > all    Combine files.
cat note5 >> notes       Append to a file.
cat > temp1              Create file at terminal; end with EOF.
cat > temp2 << STOP      Create file at terminal; end with STOP.
```

---

cb [*options*] [*files*]

cb

C program "beautifier" that formats *files* using proper C programming structure.

Options

- **−j**   Join split lines.
- **−l** *length*   Split lines longer than *length*.
- **−s**   Standardize code to style of Kernighan and Ritchie in *The C Programming Language*.
- **−V**   Print the version of **cb** on standard error.

Example

```
cb -l 70 calc.c > calc_new.c
```

---

cc [*options*] *files*

cc

Compile one or more C source files (*file*.**c**), assembler source files (*file*.**s**), or preprocessed C source files (*file*.**i**). **cc** automatically invokes the link editor **ld** (unless **−c** is supplied). In some cases, **cc** generates an object file having a **.o** suffix and a corresponding root name. By default, output is placed in **a.out**. **cc** accepts additional system-specific options.

Note: This command runs the ANSI C compiler; use **/usr/bin/cc** if you want to run the compiler for Kernighan and Ritchie's C.

→

UNIX Commands

2-11

Options

–#   Show when each compiler tool is invoked. Solaris 2.0 only.

–A *name*[(*tokens*)]
          Supply an **#assert** directive, assigning *name* with optional *tokens* as parameters.

–A –   Ignore predefined assertions and macros.

–B *mode* Use with one or more **–l** options to tell **ld** what type of library files to search. When *mode* is **dynamic**, libraries are shared, meaning that library files ending in both **.so** and **.a** are searched. When *mode* is **static**, only **.a** files are searched. To restore the previous search mode for additional **–l** options, supply **–B** again and change its *mode*.

–C   Do not strip comments during preprocessing.

–c   Suppress link editing and keep any object files that were produced.

–D *name*[=*def*]
          Supply a **#define** directive, defining *name* to be *def* or, if no *def* is given, the value **1**.

–dc Tell **ld** to link dynamically when c is **y** (the default) or to link statically when c is **n**.

–dalign Produce double load/store instructions to improve performance. Solaris 2.0 only.

–E   Run only the macro preprocessor, sending results to standard output.

–fast   Use **cc** options that give fastest compilation. Solaris 2.0 only.

–flags   Briefly describe available options. Solaris 2.0 only.

–fnonstd Produce SIGFPE signals for floating-point overflows and division by zero. Solaris 2.0 only.

–fsingle Evaluate float expressions as single-precision. Solaris 2.0 only.

–G   Produce a shared object instead of a dynamically linked executable.

–g   Generate more symbol-table information needed for debuggers **dbx** (Solaris) or **sdb** (SVR4).

–H   List (on standard error) the pathnames of header files used in C *files*.

–I *dir*   Search for include files in directory *dir* (in addition to standard locations). Supply a **–I** for each new *dir* to be searched.

–K *word* If *word* is **PIC**, produce position-independent code; if *word* is **minabi**, compile with the minimum dynamic linking that preserves ABI conformance.

–keeptmp
>Don't delete temporary files. Solaris 2.0 only.

–L *dir*   Like **–I**, but search *dir* for library archives.

–l *name*   Link source *file* with library files **lib***name***.so** or **lib-***name***.a**.

–O
>Optimize object code (produced by **.c** or **.i** files).

–o *file*   Send object output to *file* instead of to **a.out**.

–P
>Run only the preprocessor and place the result in *file***.i**.

–p
>Generate benchmark code to count the times each routine is called. File **mon.out** is created, so **prof** can later be used to produce an execution profile.

–Q*c*
>List in the output (*c* = **y**) or do not list (*c* = **n**) information about the compilation tools invoked. Default is to list.

–ql
>Invoke the basic block analyzer and produce code to count the times each source line is executed. Use **lprof** to list the counts.

–qp   Same as **–p**.

–S
>Compile (and optimize, if **–O** is supplied), but don't assemble or link; assembler output is placed in *file***.s**.

–U *name* Remove definition of name, as if through an **#undef** directive.

–V   Print version information for compiler tools.

–v
>Check semantics strictly, and allow some **lint** constructs to work.

–W[**p02abl**],*arg1*[,*arg2* . . .]
>Each comma-separated argument is a command-line token (option, parameter) from **cc**. **–W** hands off these arguments to allow separate processing by a particular compiler tool. **p** or **0** specifies the compiler; **2**, optimizer; **b**, basic block analyzer; **a**, assembler; **l**, link editor.

–X*c*   Set *c* as the level of ANSI C compliance:

>**t** Transition (default). Source code must comply with pre-ANSI features.
>
>**a** ANSI. Code must comply with ANSI features, but doesn't warn about new escape sequences or trigraphs.
>
>**c** Conformance. More rigorous than **a**.
>
>**s** Code is allowed to be old Sun C. Solaris 2.0 only.

–xpg
>Like **–p**, but produce file **gmon.out**; use **gprof** to produce an execution profile. Solaris 2.0 only.

–xsb
>Produce symbol-table data for Source Code Browser. Solaris 2.0 only.

→

cc
←
	−xsbfast Same as **−xsb**, but don't actually compile. Solaris 2.0 only.
	−xstrconst
	    Add string literals to text segment, not data segment. Solaris 2.0 only.
	−Y*c,dir* Specify that item *c* is searched in directory *dir*. *c* can be **p**, **0**, **2**, **a**, **b**, or **l**, as explained under **−W**. *c* can also be:
	    I Include files to search last for (see **−I**).
	    P Libraries; *dir* is a list of directories, separated by a colon (see **−L**).
	    S Startup object files.
	
	Example
	Compile **xpop.c** and link it to the X libraries:
	
	`cc -o xpop xpop.c -lXaw -lXmu -lXt -lX11`

cd	**cd** [*dir*] Change directory. **cd** is actually a built-in shell command. See Section 4 or 5.
cdc	**cdc −r***sid* [*option*] *files* An SCCS command. See Section 17.

cflow	**cflow** [*options*] *files*
	
	Produce an outline (or flowchart) of external function calls for the C, lex, yacc, assembler, or object *files*. **cflow** also accepts the **cc** options **−D**, **−I**, and **−U**.
	
	Options
	    −d*n* Stop outlining when nesting level *n* is reached.
	    −i_ Include functions whose names begin with _.
	    −ix Include external and static data symbols.
	    −r Invert the listing; show the callers of each function and sort in lexographical order by callee.

chgrp	**chgrp** [*options*] *newgroup files* Change the ownership of one or more *files* to *newgroup*. *newgroup* is either a group ID number or a group name located in **/etc/group**. You must own the file or be a privileged user to succeed with this command.

−h   Change the group on symbolic links. Normally, **chgrp** acts on the file *referenced* by a symbolic link, not on the link itself.

−R   Recursively descend through the directory, including subdirectories and symbolic links, setting the specified group ID as it proceeds.

---

chkey

Prompt for login password and use it to encrypt a new key. See also **keylogin** and **keylogout**.

---

chmod [*option*] *mode files*

Change the access *mode* of one or more *files*. Only the owner of a file or a privileged user may change its mode. Create *mode* by concatenating the characters from *who, opcode,* and *permission. who* is optional (if omitted, default is **a**); choose only one *opcode.*

Option

−R   Recursively descend directory arguments while setting modes.

Who

u   User
g   Group
o   Other
a   All (default)

Opcode

+   Add permission
−   Remove permission
=   Assign permission (and remove permission of the unspecified fields)

Permission

r   Read
w   Write
x   Execute
s   Set user (or group) ID
t   Sticky bit; save text (file) mode or prevent removal of files by nonowners (directory)
u   User's present permission
g   Group's present permission
o   Other's present permission
l   Mandatory locking

$\rightarrow$

---

chmod	Alternatively, specify permissions by a 3-digit sequence. The first digit designates owner permission; the second, group permission; and the third, others permission. Permissions are calculated by adding the following octal values:

←

4	Read
2	Write
1	Execute

Note: A fourth digit may precede this sequence. This digit assigns the following modes:

4	Set user ID on execution
2	Set group ID on execution or set mandatory locking
1	Set sticky bit

Examples

Add execute-by-user permission to *file*:

```
chmod u+x file
```

Either of the following will assign read-write-execute permission by owner (7), read-execute permission by group (5), and execute-only permission by others (1) to *file*:

```
chmod 751 file
chmod u=rwx,g=rx,o=x file
```

Any one of the following will assign read-only permission to *file* for everyone:

```
chmod =r file
chmod 444 file
chmod a-wx,a+r file
```

Set the user ID, assign read-write-execute permission by owner, and assign read-execute permission by group and others:

```
chmod 4755 file
```

---

chown

chown [*options*] *newowner files*

Change the ownership of one or more *files* to *newowner*. (Note: The BSD version lets you change the group as well.) *newowner* is either a user ID number or a login name located in **/etc/passwd**.

Options

−h	Change the owner on symbolic links. Normally, **chown** acts on the file *referenced* by a symbolic link, not on the link itself.
−R	Recursively descend through the directory, including subdirectories and symbolic links, resetting the ownership ID.

clear

Clear the terminal display.

cmp [*options*] *file1 file2*

Compare *file1* with *file2*. Use standard input if *file1* is –. See also **comm** and **diff**.

Options

–l   For each difference, print the byte number in decimal and the differing bytes in octal.

–s   Work silently; print nothing, but return exit codes:
      0   Files are identical.
      1   Files are different.
      2   Files are inaccessible.

Example

Print a message if two files are the same (exit code is 0):

```
cmp -s old new && echo 'no changes'
```

cof2elf [*options*] *files*

Convert one or more COFF *files* to ELF format, overwriting the original contents. Input can be object files or archives.

Options

–i   Ignore unrecognized data; do the conversion anyway.

–q   Quiet mode; suppress messages while running.

–Q*c*   Print information about **cof2elf** in output (if *c* = **y**) or suppress information (if *c* = **n**, the default).

–s*dir*   Save the original files to an existing directory *dir*.

–V   Print the version of **cof2elf** on standard error.

col [*options*]

A postprocessing filter that handles reverse linefeeds and escape characters, allowing output from tbl (or nroff, occasionally) to appear in reasonable form on a terminal.

Options

–b   Ignore backspace characters; helpful when printing man pages.

–f   Process half-line vertical motions, but not reverse line motion. (Normally, half-line input motion is displayed on the next full line.)

–p   Print unknown escape sequences (normally ignored) as regular characters. This option can garble output, so its use is not recommended.

→

col
←
	−x Normally, **col** saves printing time by converting sequences of spaces to tabs. Use **−x** to suppress this conversion.
	
	Examples
	Run *file* through tbl and nroff, then capture output on screen by filtering through **col** and **more**:
	
	    tbl *file* **| nroff | col | more**
	
	Save man page output in *file*.**print**, stripping out backspaces (which would otherwise appear as ˆH):
	
	    man *file* **| col -b >** *file*.**print**

comb	**comb** [*options*] *files* An SCCS command. See Section 17.

comm	**comm** [*options*] *file1 file2*
	
	Compare lines common to the sorted files *file1* and *file2*. Three-column output is produced: lines unique to *file1*, lines unique to *file2*, and lines common to both *files*. **comm** is similar to **diff** in that both commands compare two files. But **comm** can also be used like **uniq**; that is, **comm** selects duplicate or unique lines between *two* sorted files, whereas **uniq** selects duplicate or unique lines within the *same* sorted file.
	
	Options
	  − Read the standard input.
	  −1 Suppress printing of column 1.
	  −2 Suppress printing of column 2.
	  −3 Suppress printing of column 3.
	  −12 Print only lines in column 3 (lines common to *file1* and *file2*).
	  −13 Print only lines in column 2 (lines unique to *file2*).
	  −23 Print only lines in column 1 (lines unique to *file1*).
	
	Example
	Compare two lists of top-ten movies, and display items that appear in both lists:
	
	    comm -12 siskel_top10 ebert_top10

compress	**compress** [*options*] [*files*] Reduce the size of one or more *files* using adaptive Lempel-Ziv coding, and move to *file*.**Z**. Restore with **uncompress** or **zcat**. *Compress −c filename >> /u0?/oradata/filename*

−b*n*	Limit the number of bits in coding to *n*; *n* is 9-16, and 16 is the default. A lower *n* produces a larger, less densely compressed file.
−c	Write to the standard output (do not change files).
−f	Compress unconditionally; i.e., do not prompt before overwriting files.
−v	Print the resulting percentage of reduction for *files*.

cp [*options*] *file1 file2*   **cp**
cp [*options*] *files directory*

Copy *file1* to *file2*, or copy one or more *files* to the same names under *directory*. If the destination is an existing file, the file is overwritten; if the destination is an existing directory, the file is copied into the directory (the directory is *not* overwritten).

Options

−i	Prompt for confirmation (**y** for yes) before overwriting an existing file.
−p	Preserve the modification time and permission modes for the copied file. (Normally **cp** supplies the permissions of the invoking user.)
−r	Recursively copy a directory, its files, and its subdirectories to a destination *directory*, duplicating the tree structure. (This option is used with the second command-line format when at least one of the source *file* arguments is a directory.)

Example

Copy two files to their parent directory (keep the same names):

```
cp outline memo ..
```

cpio *flags* [*options*]   **cpio**

Copy file archives in from or out to tape or disk, or to another location on the local machine. Each of the three flags **−i**, **−o**, or **−p** accepts different options.

cpio −i [*options*] [*patterns*]

Copy in (extract) files whose names match selected *patterns*. Each pattern can include filename metacharacters from the Bourne shell. (Patterns should be quoted or escaped so they are interpreted by **cpio**, not by the shell.) If no pattern is used, all files are copied in. During extraction, existing files are not overwritten by older versions in the archive (unless **−u** is specified).

→

cpio −o [*options*]

Copy out a list of files whose names are given on the standard input.

cpio −p [*options*] *directory*

Copy files to another directory on the same system. Destination pathnames are interpreted relative to the named *directory*.

Comparison of valid options

Options available to the **−i**, **−o**, and **−p** flags are shown respectively in the first, second, and third row below. (The − is omitted for clarity.)

```
i: 6    b B c C d E f H I k   m M   r R s S t u v V
o: a A    B c C       H     L   M O             v V
p: a          d           l L m       R         u v V
```

Options

−a Reset access times of input files.

−A Append files to an archive (must use with **−O**).

−b Swap bytes and half-words. Words are 4 bytes.

−B Block input or output using 5120 bytes per record (default is 512 bytes per record).

−c Read or write header information as ASCII characters; useful when source and destination machines are of differing types.

−C *n* Like **B**, but block size can be any positive integer *n*.

−d Create directories as needed.

−E *file* Extract filenames listed in *file* from the archives.

−f Reverse the sense of copying; copy all files *except* those that match *patterns*.

−H *format*

Read or write header information according to *format*. Values for format are **crc** (ASCII header containing expanded device numbers), **odc** (ASCII header containing small device numbers), **ustar** (IEEE/P1003 Data Interchange Standard header), or **tar** (tar header).

−I *file* Read *file* as an input archive.

−k Skip corrupted file headers and I/O errors.

−l Link files instead of copying.

−L Follow symbolic links.

−m Retain previous file modification time.

−M *msg*

Print *msg* when switching media. Use variable **%d** in the message as a numeric ID for the next medium. **−M** is valid only with **−I** or **−O**.

−O *file* Direct the output to *file*.

−r	Rename files interactively.
−R *ID*	Reassign file ownership and group information to the user's login *ID* (privileged users only).
−s	Swap bytes.
−S	Swap half-words.
−t	Print a table of contents of the input (create no files). When used with the **−v** option, resembles output of **ls −l**.
−u	Unconditional copy; old files can overwrite new ones.
−v	Print a list of filenames.
−V	Print a dot for each file read or written (this shows **cpio** at work without cluttering the screen).
−6	Process a UNIX 6th Edition archive format file.

Examples

Generate a list of old files using **find**; use list as input to **cpio**:

```
find . -name "*.old" -print | cpio -ocBv\
   > /dev/rst8
```

Restore from a tape drive all files whose name contains "save" (subdirectories are created if needed):

```
cpio -icdv "save" < /dev/rst8
```

To move a directory tree:

```
find . -depth -print | cpio -padm /mydir
```

---

crontab [*file*]
crontab *flags* [*user*]

Run **crontab** on your current crontab file, or specify a crontab *file* to add to the crontab directory. A privileged user can run **crontab** for another user by supplying a *user* after any of the flags. A crontab file is a list of commands, one per line, that will execute automatically at a given time. Numbers are supplied before each command to specify the execution time. The numbers appear in five fields, as follows:

Minute	0-59
Hour	0-23
Day of month	1-31
Month	1-12
Day of week	0-6, with 0 = Sunday

Use a comma between multiple values, a hyphen to indicate a range, and an asterisk to indicate all possible values. For example, assuming the crontab entries below:

```
3 59 * * 5    find / -print | backup_program
0 0 1,15 * *  echo "Timesheets due" | mail user
```

→

crontab
←
	The first command backs up the system files every Friday at 3:59 a.m., and the second command mails a reminder on the 1st and 15th of each month.
	
	Flags
	
	  −e Edit the user's current crontab file (or create one).
	  −l List the user's file in the crontab directory.
	  −r Delete the user's file in the crontab directory.

crypt	**crypt** [*password*] < *file* > *encryptedfile* Encrypt a *file* to prevent unauthorized access. *password* is either a string of characters you choose or the flag **−k**, which assigns the value of environment variable CRYPTKEY as the password. The same *password* is used to encrypt a file or to decrypt an encrypted file. If no password is given, **crypt** prompts for one. **crypt** is available only in the United States (due to export restrictions).
cscope	**cscope** [*options*] *files* Interactive utility for finding code fragments in one or more C, lex, or yacc source *files*. **cscope** builds a symbol cross-reference (named **cscope.out** by default) and then calls up a menu. The menu prompts the user to search for functions, macros, variables, preprocessor directives, etc. Type **?** to list interactive commands. Subsequent calls to **cscope** rebuild the cross-reference if needed (i.e., if filenames or file contents have changed). Source filenames can be stored in a file **cscope.files**. This file can then be specified instead of *files*. Options **−I**, **−p**, and **−T** are also recognized when placed in **cscope.files**.

Options

    −b   Build the symbol cross-reference only.

    −C   Ignore uppercase/lowercase differences in searches.

    −c   Create output in ASCII (don't compress data).

    −d   Don't update the cross-reference.

    −e   Don't show the CTRL-E prompt between files.

    −f *out* Name the cross-reference file *out* instead of **cscope.out**.

    −I *dir*   Search for include files in *dir* before searching the default (**/usr/include**). **cscope** searches the current directory, then *dir*, then the default.

    −i *in*   Check source files whose names are listed in *in* rather than in **cscope.files**.

    −L   Use with *−n pat* to do a single search.

    −l   Run in line mode; useful from within a screen editor.

−P *path* Use with **−d** to prepend *path* to filenames in existing cross-reference. This lets you run **cscope** without changing to directory where cross-reference was built.

−p *n* Show the last *n* parts of the filename path. Default is 1 (filename); use 0 to suppress the filename.

−s *dir* Look for source files in directory *dir* instead of in current directory.

−T Match only the first eight characters of C symbols.

−U Ignore file timestamps (assume no files changed).

−u Build cross-reference unconditionally (assume all files changed).

−V Print the **cscope** version on first line of screen.

−n pat Go to field *n* of input (starting at 0), then find *pat*.

---

csh [*options*] [*arguments*]

Command interpreter that uses syntax resembling C. **csh** (the C shell) executes commands from a terminal or a file. See Section 5 for information on the C shell, including command-line options.

---

csplit [*options*] *file arguments*

Separate *file* into sections and place sections in files named **xx00** through **xx***n* ($n < 100$), breaking *file* at each pattern specified in *arguments*. See also **split**.

Options

−f *file* Name new files *file***00** through *filen* (default is **xx00** through **xx***n*).

−k Keep newly created files, even when an error occurs (which would normally remove these files). This is useful when you need to specify an arbitrarily large repeat argument, {*n*}, and you don't want the "out of range" error to remove the new files.

−s Suppress all character counts.

Arguments

Any one or a combination of the following expressions. Arguments containing blanks or other special characters should be surrounded by single quotes.

/expr/ Create file from the current line up to the line containing the regular expression *expr*. This argument takes an optional suffix of the form +*n* or −*n*, where *n* is the number of lines below or above *expr*.

%*expr*% Same as */expr/* except no file is created for lines previous to line containing *expr*.

→

num	Create file from current line up to line number *num*.
{*n*}	Repeat argument *n* times. May follow any of the above arguments. Files will split at instances of *expr* or in blocks of *num* lines.

Examples

Create up to 20 chapter files from the file **novel**:

```
csplit -k -f chap. novel '%CHAPTER%' '{20}'
```

Create up to 100 address files (**xx00** through **xx99**), each four lines long, from a database named **address_list**:

```
csplit -k address_list 4 {99}
```

---

ctags

ctags [*options*] *files*

Create a list of function and macro names that are defined in the specified C, Pascal, FORTRAN, yacc, or lex source *files*. The output list (named **tags** by default) contains lines of the form:

　name　　*file*　　　*context*

where *name* is the function or macro name, *file* is the source file in which *name* is defined, and *context* is a search pattern that shows the line of code containing *name*. After the list of tags is created, you can invoke vi on any file and type:

```
:set tags=tagsfile
:tag name
```

This switches the vi editor to the source file associated with the *name* listed in *tagsfile* (which you specify with **−f**).

Options

−a	Append tag output to existing list of tags.
−B	*context* uses backward search patterns.
−F	*context* uses forward search patterns (default).
−f*tagsfile*	
	Place output in *tagsfile* (default is **tags**).
−t	Include typedefs as tags.
−u	Update tags file to reflect new locations of functions (e.g., when functions are moved to a different source file). Old tags are deleted; new tags are appended.
−v	Produce a listing (index) of each function, source file, and page number (1 page = 64 lines). **−v** is intended to create a file for use with **vgrind**, which is available in the BSD compatibility package.
−w	Suppress warning messages.
−x	Produce a listing of each function, its line number, source file, and context.

Examples

Store tags in **Taglist** for all C programs:

```
ctags -f Taglist *.c
```

Update tags and store in **Newlist**:

```
ctags -u -f Newlist *.c
```

ctrace [*options*] [*file*]

Debug a C program. **ctrace** reads the C source *file* and writes a modified version to standard output. Common options are **−f** and **−v**. **ctrace** also accepts the **cc** options **−D**, **−I**, and **−U**.

Options

−b	Trace only the basic C functions (SVR3 only).
−e	Print variables as floating point.
−f *functions*	
	Trace only the specified *functions*.
−l *n*	Follow a statement loop *n* times (default is 20).
−o	Print variables in octal.
−p '*s*'	Print trace output via function *s* (default is **printf**).
−P	Run the C preprocessor before tracing.
−Q*c*	Print information about **ctrace** in output (if *c* = **y**) or suppress information (if *c* = **n**, the default).
−r*file*	Change the trace function package to *file* (default is **runtime.c**).
−s	Suppress certain redundant code.
−t*n*	Trace *n* variables per statement (default is 10; maximum is 20).
−u	Print variables as unsigned.
−v *functions*	
	Do not trace the specified *functions*.
−V	Print version information on standard error.
−x	Print variables as floating point.

cu [*options*] [*destination*]

Call up another UNIX system or a terminal via a direct line or a modem. A non-UNIX system can also be called.

Options

−b*n*	Process lines using *n*-bit characters (7 or 8).
−c*name*	
	Search UUCP's **Devices** file and select the local area network that matches *name* (this assumes connection to a system).

→

-d   Print diagnostics.

-e   Send even-parity data to remote system.

-h   Emulate local **echo** and support calls to other systems
        expecting terminals to use half duplex mode.

-l*line* Communicate on *line* device (e.g., **/dev/tty001**).

-n   Prompt user for a telephone number.

-o   Use odd parity (opposite of -e).

-s*n*   Set transmission rate to *n* (e.g., 1200, 2400, 9600 bps).
        Default is **Any**.

-t   Dial an ASCII terminal that has auto answer set.

Destination

telno   The telephone number of the modem to connect to.

system Call the *system* known to **uucp** (run **uuname** to list
        valid system names).

addr   An address specific to your local area network.

cu runs as two processes: transmit and receive. Transmit reads
from standard input and passes lines to the remote system; receive
reads data from the remote system and passes lines to standard
output. Lines that begin with a tilde (˜) are treated as commands
and are not passed.

Transmit options

˜.   Terminate the conversation.

˜!   Escape to an interactive shell on the local system.

˜!*cmd*... Run command on local system (via **sh -c**).

˜$*cmd*...

        Run command locally; send output to remote sys-
        tem.

˜%cd   Change directory on the local system.

˜%take *file* [*target*]

        Copy *file* from remote system to *target* on the local
        system. If *target* is omitted, *file* is used in both
        places.

˜%put *file* [*target*]

        Copy *file* from the local system to *target* on the
        remote system. If *target* is omitted, *file* is used in
        both places.

˜ ˜ ...   Use two tildes when you want to pass a line that
        begins with a tilde. This lets you issue commands to
        more than one system in a **cu** chain. For example,
        use ˜˜. to terminate the conversation on a second
        system **cu**'d to from the first.

˜%b   Send a BREAK sequence to remote system.

˜%d   Turn debug mode on or off.

˜t   Print termio structure for local terminal.

˜l	Print termio structure for communication line.
˜%ifc	Turn on/off the DC3/DC1 XON/XOFF control protocol (characters ^S, ^Q) for the remainder of the session (formerly **˜%nostop**, which is still valid).
˜%ofc	Set output flow control either on or off.
˜%divert	Allow/prevent diversions not specified by **˜%take**.
˜%old	Allow/prevent old-style syntax for diversions received.

Examples

Connect to terminal line **/dev/ttya** at 1200 baud:

```
cu -s1200 -l/dev/ttya
```

Connect to modem with phone number 555-9876:

```
cu 5559876
```

Connect to system named **usenix**:

```
cu usenix
```

---

cut *options* [*files*]

Select a list of columns or fields from one or more *files*. Option **−c** or **−f** must be specified. *list* is a sequence of integers. Use a comma between separate values and a hyphen to specify a range (e.g., 1-10,15,20 or 50-). See also **paste**, **join**, and **newform**.

Options

−c*list*	Cut the column positions identified in *list*.
−d*c*	Use with **−f** to specify field delimiter as character *c* (default is tab); special characters (e.g., a space) must be quoted.
−f*list*	Cut the fields identified in *list*.
−s	Use with **−f** to suppress lines without delimiters.

Examples

Extract usernames and real names from **/etc/passwd**:

```
cut -d: -f1,5 /etc/passwd
```

Find out who is logged on, but list only login names:

```
who | cut -d" " -f1
```

Cut characters in the fourth column of *file*, and paste them back as the first column in the same file:

```
cut -c4 file | paste - file
```

cxref

cxref [*options*] *files*

Build a cross-reference table for each of the C source *files*. The table lists all symbols, providing columns for the name and the associated function, file, and line. In the table, symbols are marked by = if assigned, – if declared, or * if defined. **cxref** also accepts the **cc** options **–D**, **–I**, and **–U**.

Options

–c	Report on all files in a single table.
–C	Don't execute the second pass of **cxref**; save output from first pass in **.cx** files. (Like **–c** in **lint** and **cc**.)
–d	Simplify report by omitting print declarations.
–F	Print files using full pathname, not just the filename.
–l	Don't print local variables.
–L[*n*]	Limit the "LINE" field to *n* columns (default is 5).
–o *file*	Send output to *file*.
–s	Silent mode; don't print input filenames.
–t	Format for 80-column listing.
–V	Print version information on standard error.
–w[*n*]	Format for maximum width of *n* columns (default is 80; *n* must be more than 50).

–W*n1,n2,n3,n4*

Set the width of each (or any) column to *n1*, *n2*, *n3*, or *n4* (respective defaults are 15, 13, 15, and 20). Column headings are NAME, FILE, FUNCTION, and LINE, respectively.

---

date

date [*option*] [*+format*]
date [*options*] [*string*]

In the first form, print the current date and time, specifying an optional display *format*. In the second form, a privileged user can set the current date by supplying a numeric *string*. *format* can consist of literal text strings (blanks must be quoted) as well as field descriptors, whose values will appear as described below (the listing shows some logical groupings).

Format

%n	Insert a newline.
%t	Insert a tab.
%m	Month of year (01-12).
%d	Day of month (01-31).
%y	Last two digits of year (00-99).
%D	Date in **%m/%d/%y** format.
%b	Abbreviated month name.

%e	Day of month (1-31); pad single digits with a space.
%Y	Four-digit year (e.g., 1996).
%h	Same as **%b**.
%B	Full month name.
%H	Hour in 24-hour format (00-23).
%M	Minute (00-59).
%S	Second (00-61); 61 permits leap seconds.
%R	Time in **%H:%M** format.
%T	Time in **%H:%M:%S** format.
%I	Hour in 12-hour format (01-12).
%p	String to indicate a.m. or p.m. (default is AM or PM).
%r	Time in **%I:%M:%S %p** format.
%a	Abbreviated weekday.
%A	Full weekday.
%w	Day of week (Sunday = 0).
%U	Week number in year (00-53); start week on Sunday.
%W	Week number in year (00-53); start week on Monday.
%j	Julian day of year (001-366).
%Z	Time zone name.
%x	Country-specific date format.
%X	Country-specific time format.
%c	Country-specific date and time format (default is **%a %b %e %T %Z %Y**; e.g., Mon Feb 1 14:30:59 EST 1993).

The preceding country-specific formats, as well as language names (e.g., for month and weekday) are defined in a file given by **strftime**(4).

Options

—a *s.f* (Privileged user only.) Gradually adjust the system clock until it drifts *s* seconds away from what it thinks is the "current" time. (This allows continuous micro-adjustment of the clock while the system is running.) *f* is the fraction of seconds by which time drifts. By default, the clock speeds up; precede *s* by a — to slow down.

—u Display or set the time using Greenwich Mean Time.

Strings for setting date

A privileged user can set the date by supplying a numeric *string*. *string* consists of time, day, and year concatenated in one of three ways: *time* or [*day*]*time* or [*day*]*time*[*year*]. Note: You don't type the brackets.

time A two-digit hour and two-digit minute (*HHMM*); *HH* uses 24-hour format.

→

date

←

	day	A two-digit month and two-digit day of month (*mmdd*); default is current day and month.
	year	The year specified as either the full four digits or just the last two digits; default is current year.

Examples

Set the date to July 1 (**0701**), 4 a.m. (**0400**), 1995 (**95**):

```
date 0701040095
```

The command:

```
date +"Hello%t Date is %D %n%t Time is %T"
```

produces a formatted date as follows:

```
Hello        Date is 05/09/93
             Time is 17:53:39
```

---

dbx

/usr/ucb/dbx [*options*] [*objfile* [*corefile*]]

Solaris 2.0 only. A source code debugger for programs written in C, C++, Pascal, and FORTRAN. Programs compiled with the **–g** option of **cc** (and other compilers) produce *objfile*, an object file that includes a symbol table. *corefile* contains the core image produced when *objfile* is executed. **a.out** is the default object file, and core is the default *corefile*. Dbx commands can be stored in a start-up **.dbxinit** file that resides in the current directory or in the user's home directory. Dbx executes these commands just before reading the symbol table. See Section 20 for more information on dbx.

Options

–c *cmd*	Run dbx *cmd* after initialization.
–C	Collect profile data for debugged program.
–e	Echo input commands on standard output.
–i	Act as if standard input is a terminal.
–I *dir*	Add *dir* to the directory search path. The dbx command **use** resets the search path.
–kbd	Debug a program that puts the keyboard in up-down translation mode.
–P *file_des*	
	Pipe output to the **debugger** command via file descriptor *file_des*. **debugger** passes this option automatically.
–q	Suppress messages during loading (useful during auto-traceback).
–r	Execute *objfile* right away, then wait for user response from the keyboard.
–s *file*	Read initialization commands from start-up *file*.

–sr *tmp* Like **–s**, but then delete start-up file (*tmp*).	**dbx**
– *pid* Debug a currently running program whose process ID is *pid* (used mainly for auto-traceback).	

---

dc [*file*]

An interactive desk calculator program that performs arbitrary-precision integer arithmetic (input may be taken from a *file*). Normally you don't run **dc** directly, since it's invoked by **bc** (see **bc**). **dc** provides a variety of one-character commands and operators that perform arithmetic; **dc** works like a Reverse Polish calculator; therefore, operators and commands follow the numbers they affect. Operators include + – / * % ^ (as in C); some simple commands include:

p   Print current result.

q   Quit **dc**.

c   Clear all values on the stack.

v   Take square root.

i   Change input base; similar to **bc**'s **ibase**.

o   Change output base; similar to **bc**'s **obase**.

k   Set scale factor (number of digits after decimal); similar to **bc**'s **scale**.

!   Remainder of line is a UNIX command.

Examples

```
3 2 ^ p    Evaluate 3 squared, then print result.
9
8 * p      Current value (9) times 8, then print result.
72
47 – p     Subtract 47 from 72, then print result.
25
v p        Square root of 25, then print result.
5
2 o p      Display current result in base 2.
101
```

Note: Spaces are not needed except between numbers.

---

dd [*option=value*]

Make a copy of an input file (**if=**) using the specified conditions, and send the results to the output file (or standard output if **of** is not specified). Any number of options can be supplied, although **if** and **of** are the most common and are usually specified first. Because **dd** can handle arbitrary block sizes, it is useful when converting between raw physical devices.

dc

dd

→

Options

   bs=*n*   Set input and output block size to *n* bytes; this option supersedes **ibs** and **obs**.

   cbs=*n*   Set the size of the conversion buffer (logical record length) to *n* bytes. Use only if the conversion *flag* is **ascii**, **ebcdic**, **ibm**, **block**, or **unblock**.

   conv=*flags* Convert the input according to one or more (comma-separated) *flags* listed below. The first five *flags* are mutually exclusive.

ascii	EBCDIC to ASCII.
ebcdic	ASCII to EBCDIC.
ibm	ASCII to EBCDIC with IBM conventions.
block	Variable-length records (i.e., those terminated by a newline) to fixed-length records.
unblock	Fixed-length records to variable-length.
lcase	Uppercase to lowercase.
ucase	Lowercase to uppercase.
noerror	Continue processing when errors occur (up to 5 in a row).
swab	Swap all pairs of bytes.
sync	Pad input blocks to **ibs**.

   count=*n*   Copy only *n* input blocks.

   files=*n*   Copy *n* input files (e.g., from magnetic tape), then quit.

   ibs=*n*   Set input block size to *n* bytes (default is 512).

   if=*file*   Read input from *file* (default is standard input).

   obs=*n*   Set output block size to *n* bytes (default is 512).

   of=*file*   Write output to *file* (default is standard output).

   iseek=*n*   Seek *n* blocks from start of input file (like **skip** but more efficient for disk file input).

   oseek=*n*   Seek *n* blocks from start of output file.

   seek=*n*   Same as **oseek** (retained for compatibility).

   skip=*n*   Skip *n* input blocks; useful with magnetic tape.

You can multiply size values (*n*) by a factor of 1024, 512, or 2 by appending the letter **k**, **b**, or **w**, respectively. You can use the letter **x** as a multiplication operator between two numbers.

Examples

Convert an input file to all lowercase:

```
dd if=caps_file of=small_file conv=lcase
```

Retrieve variable-length data; write it as fixed-length to **out**: *data_retrieval_cmd* | **dd of=out conv=sync,block**	**dd**

delta [*options*] *files*

An SCCS command. See Section 17.

---

deroff [*options*] [*files*]

Remove all nroff/troff requests and macros, backslash escape sequences, and **tbl** and **eqn** constructs from the named *files*.

Options

    −mm   Suppress text that appears on macro lines (i.e., paragraphs will print but headings might be stripped).

    −ml   Same as **−mm**, but also deletes lists created by **mm** macros; e.g., .BL/.LE, .VL/.LE constructs. (Nested lists are handled poorly.)

    −w   Output the text as a list, one word per line. See also example under **xargs**.

---

df [*options*] [*name*]

Report the number of free disk blocks and inodes available on all mounted file systems or on the given *name*. (Unmounted file systems are checked with **−F**.) *name* can be a device name (e.g., **/dev/dsk/0s9**), the directory name of a mounting point (e.g., **/usr**), a directory name, or a remote resource name (e.g., an RFS/NFS resource). Besides the options listed, there are additional options specific to different file system types or **df** modules.

Options

    −b   Print only the number of free kilobytes.

    −e   Print only the number of free files.

    −f   Report free blocks but not free inodes (SVR3 only).

    −F *type*   Report on an unmounted file system specified by *type*. Available *types* can be seen in the file **/etc/vfstab**.

    −g   Print the whole **statvfs** structure (overriding other print options).

    −k   Print allocation in kilobytes (typically used without other options).

    −l   Report only on local file systems.

    −n   Print only the file system *type* name; with no other arguments, **−n** lists the types for all mounted file systems.

    −o *suboptions*

        Supply a comma-separated list of *type*-specific *suboptions*.

→

df	−t	Report total allocated space as well as free space.
←	−v	Echo command line but do not execute command.

diff

diff [*options*] [*diroptions*] *file1 file2*

diff reports lines that differ between *file1* and *file2*. Output consists of lines of context from each file, with *file1* text flagged by a < symbol and *file2* text, by a > symbol. Context lines are preceded by the ed command (**a**, **c**, or **d**) that would be used to convert *file1* to *file2*. If one of the files is −, standard input is read. If one of the files is a directory, **diff** locates the filename in that directory corresponding to the other argument (e.g., **diff my_dir junk** is the same as **diff my_dir/junk junk**). If both arguments are directories, **diff** reports lines that differ between all pairs of files having equivalent names (e.g., **olddir/program** and **newdir/program**); in addition, **diff** lists filenames unique to one directory, as well as subdirectories common to both. See also **sdiff** and **cmp**.

Options

	−b	Ignore repeating blanks and end-of-line blanks; treat successive blanks as one.
	−c	Produce output in alternate format, with three lines of context.
	−C*n*	Like −**c**, but produce *n* lines of context.
	−D *def*	Merge *file1* and *file2* into a single file containing conditional C preprocessor directives (**#ifdef**). Defining *def* and then compiling will yield *file2*; compiling without defining *def* yields *file1*.
	−e	Produce a script of commands (**a**, **c**, **d**) to recreate *file2* from *file1* using the ed editor.
	−f	Produce a script to recreate *file1* from *file2*; the script is in the opposite order, so it isn't useful to ed.
	−h	Do a half-hearted comparison; complex differences (e.g., long stretches of many changes) may not show up; −**e** and −**f** are disabled.
	−i	Ignore uppercase and lowercase distinctions.
	−n	Like −**f**, but counts changed lines. **rcsdiff** works this way.
	−t	Expand tabs in output lines; useful for preserving indentation changed by −**c** format.
	−w	Like −**b** but ignores all spaces and tabs; e.g., **a + b** is the same as **a+b**.

Options −**c**, −**C**, −**D**, −**e**, −**f**, −**h**, and −**n** cannot be combined with each other (they are mutually exclusive). The following *diroptions* are valid only when both file arguments are directories.

Diroptions

−l   Long format; output is paginated by **pr** so that **diff** list-
      ings for each file begin on a new page; other compari-
      sons are listed afterward.

−r   Run **diff** recursively for files in common subdirectories.

−s   Report files that are identical.

−S*file* Begin directory comparisons with *file*, skipping files
          whose names are alphabetically before *file*.

---

diff3 [*options*] *file1 file2 file3*

Compare three files and report the differences with the following
codes:

====   All three files differ.

====1   *file1* is different.

====2   *file2* is different.

====3   *file3* is different.

Options

−e   Create an ed script to incorporate into *file1* all differ-
      ences between *file2* and *file3*.

−E   Same as −**e**, but mark with angle brackets any lines that
      differ between all three files.

−x   Create an ed script to incorporate into *file1* all differ-
      ences between all three files.

−X   Same as −**x**, but mark with angle brackets any lines that
      differ between all three files.

−3   Create an ed script to incorporate into *file1* differences
      between *file1* and *file3*.

/usr/ucb/diffmk *oldfile newfile markedfile*

A useful program for reviewing changes between drafts of a document. **diffmk** compares two versions of a file (*oldfile* and *newfile*)
and creates a third file (*markedfile*) that contains troff "change
mark" requests. When *markedfile* is formatted with nroff or troff,
the differences between the two files will be marked in the margin
(via the **.mc** request). **diffmk** uses a | to mark changed lines and
a * to mark deleted lines. Note that change marks are produced
even if the changes are inconsequential (e.g., extra blanks, different input line lengths).

→

diffmk
←
	Example
	To run **diffmk** on multiple files, it's convenient to set up directories in which to keep the old and new versions of your files, and to create a directory in which to store the marked files:
	
	```\n$ mkdir OLD NEW CHANGED\n```
	
	Move your old files to **OLD** and your new files to **NEW**. Then use this rudimentary Bourne shell script:
	
	```\n$ cat do.mark\nfor file\ndo\necho "Running diffmk on $file ..."\ndiffmk ../OLD/$file $file ../CHANGED/$file\ndone\n```
	
	You must run the script in the directory of new files:
	
	```\n$ cd NEW\n$ do.mark Ch*\n```

---

dircmp

dircmp [*options*] *dir1 dir2*

Compare the contents of *dir1* and *dir2*. See also **diff** and **cmp**.

Options

    −d   Execute **diff** on the files which differ.

    −s   Don't report files that are identical.

    −w*n*   Change the output line length to *n* (default is 72).

---

dirname

dirname *pathname*

Print *pathname* excluding last level. Useful for stripping the actual filename from a pathname. See also **basename**.

---

dis

dis [*options*] *files*

Disassemble the object or archive *files*. See also **as**.

Options

    −d *section*   Disassemble only the specified *section* of data, printing its offset.

    −D *section*   Same as **−d**, but print the data's actual address (formerly **−da**).

    −F *func*   Disassemble only the specified function; reuse **−F** for additional functions.

    −l *string*   Disassemble only the library file *string* (e.g., *string* would be *x* for **lib*x*.a**).

    −L   Look for C source labels in files containing debug information (e.g., files compiled with **cc −g**).

−o	Print octal output (default is hexadecimal).	**dis**
−t *section*	Same as **−d**, but print text output.	
−V	Print version information on standard error.	

download [*options*] [*files*]

Add a font to the beginning of one or more PostScript *files*. By adding a font name directly to a PostScript specification, this command can be used to make additional fonts available when printing a PostScript file. Fonts are added in the form of PostScript comments that begin with **%%DocumentFonts:**, followed by a list of PostScript font names. **download** loads the fonts whose names are listed in a map table. This table links PostScript names with the system file that contains the font definition. A map table for the Times font family might look like this:

```
Times-Bold     fonts/100dpi/timesbold.snf
Times-Italic   fonts/100dpi/timesitalic.snf
Times-Roman    fonts/100dpi/timesroman.snf
```

Options

− Read the standard input.

−f Search the entire PostScript file instead of just the header comments. Header comments such as **%%DocumentFonts: (atend)** will redirect **download** to the end of the file. Use this option when such comments aren't present.

−H *fontdir*
Use *fontdir* as the directory in which font definition files are to be searched (default is **/usr/lib/lp/post-script**).

−m *table*
Use map table specified by file *table*. A leading / in *table* indicates an absolute pathname; otherwise (as in example above), the filename is appended to the *fontdir* specified by **−H**.

−p *printer*
Normally, **download** loads fonts that reside on the host machine. With this option, **download** will first check for fonts that reside on *printer* (by looking at **/etc/lp/printers/***printer***/residentfonts**).

dpost [*options*] [*files*]

A postprocessor that translates troff-formatted *files* into PostScript for printing.

→

dpost
←

Options

−   Read the standard input.

−c *n*   Print *n* copies of each page (default is 1).

−e 0 | 1 | 2
    Set text encoding to 0 (default), 1, or 2. Higher encoding reduces the output size and speeds printing, but may be less reliable.

−F *dir* Set the font directory to *dir* (default is **/usr/lib/font**).

−H *dir* Set the host-resident font directory to *dir*. Files there must describe PostScript fonts and have filenames corresponding to a two-character troff font.

−L *file* Set the PostScript prologue to *file* (default is **/usr/lib/postscript/dpost.ps**).

−m *scale*
    Increase (multiply) the size of logical pages by factor *scale* (default is 1.0).

−n *n*   Print *n* logical pages on each sheet of output (default is 1).

−o *list* Print only pages contained in comma-separated *list*. A page range is specified by *n-m*.

−O   Omit PostScript pictures from output. Useful when running in a networked environment.

−p *layout*
    Specify *layout* to be either **portrait** (long side is vertical; also the default) or **landscape** (long side is horizontal). *layout* can be abbreviated to **p** or **l**.

−T *device*
    Use *device* to best describe available PostScript fonts. Default is **post**, with **dpost** reading binary files in **/usr/lib/font/devpost**. Use of **−T** is discouraged.

−w *n* Draw troff graphics (e.g., pic, tbl) using lines that are *n* points thick (default is 0.3).

−x *n* Offset the x-coordinate of the origin *n* inches to the right (if *n* is positive).

−y *n* Offset the y-coordinate of the origin *n* inches down (if *n* is positive). Default origin is the upper-left corner of the page.

Example

```
pic file | tbl | eqn | troff -ms -Tpost | dpost -c2
```

du

du [*options*] [*directories*]

Print disk usage; i.e., the number of 512-byte blocks used by each named directory and its subdirectories (default is current directory).

Options

−a   Print usage for all files, not just subdirectories.

−r   Print "cannot open" message if a file or directory is inaccessible.

−s   Print only the grand total for each named directory.

echo [−n] [*string*]

This is the **/bin/echo** command. **echo** also exists as a command built into the C shell and Bourne shell (see Sections 4 and 5). **/bin/echo** is the same as the Bourne shell version with one exception: the **−n** option to **/bin/echo** works only when the user's PATH variable lists **/usr/ucb** before **/usr/bin**. The C-shell version does not support escape characters.

Examples

```
echo "testing printer" | lp
echo "TITLE\nTITLE" > file ; cat doc1 doc2 >> file
echo "Warning: ringing bell \07"
```

ed [*options*] [*file*]

The standard text editor. If the named *file* does not exist, **ed** creates it; otherwise, the existing *file* is opened for editing. As a line editor, ed is generally no longer used because vi and ex have superseded it. Some utilities, such as **diff**, continue to make use of ed. Encryption can be used only in the United States.

Options

−C   Same as **−x**, but assume *file* began in encrypted form.

−p *string*

   Set *string* as the prompt for commands (default is *****). The **P** command turns the prompt display on and off.

−s   Suppress character counts, diagnostics, and the **!** prompt for shell commands.

−x   Supply a key to encrypt or decrypt *file* using **crypt**.

edit [*options*] [*file*]

A line-oriented text editor that runs a simplified version of ex for novice users. The **set** variables **report**, **showmode**, and **magic** are preset to report editing changes, to display edit modes (when in **:vi** mode), and to require literal search patterns (no metacharacters allowed), respectively. (Encryption is not supported outside the United States.)

→

edit ←	*Options*
	–C Same as **–x**, but assume files are already encrypted.
	–r Recover file after a system crash or editor crash.
	–x Encrypt file when it is written.

egrep	**egrep** [*options*] [*regexp*] [*files*]

Search one or more *files* for lines that match a regular expression *regexp*. **egrep** doesn't support the regular expressions \(, \), \n, \<, \>, \{, or \}, but does support the other expressions, as well as the extended set +, ?, |, and ( ). Remember to enclose these characters in quotes. Regular expressions are described in Section 6. Exit status is 0 if any lines match, 1 if not, and 2 for errors. See also **grep** and **fgrep**. **egrep** typically runs faster than those.

Options

    –b   Precede each line with its block number.

    –c   Print only a count of matched lines.

    –e *regexp*   Use this if *regexp* begins with **-**.

    –f *file*   Take expression from *file*.

    –h   List matched lines but not filenames (inverse of **–l**).

    –i   Ignore uppercase and lowercase distinctions.

    –l   List filenames but not matched lines.

    –n   Print lines and their line numbers.

    –v   Print all lines that *don't* match *regexp*.

Examples

Search for occurrences of *Victor* or *Victoria* in *file*:

```
egrep 'Victor(ia)*' file
egrep '(Victor|Victoria)' file
```

Find and print strings such as *old.doc1* or *new.doc2* in *files*, and include their line numbers:

```
egrep -n '(old|new)\.doc?' files
```

env	**env** [*option*] [*variable=value* ...] [*command*]

Display the current environment or, if environment *variables* are specified, set them to a new *value* and display the modified environment. If *command* is specified, execute it under the modified environment.

Option

    –   Ignore current environment entirely.

/usr/ucb/eqn [*options*] [*files*]　　　　　　　　　　**eqn**

Equation preprocessor for troff. See Section 16.

---

ex [*options*] *files*　　　　　　　　　　**ex**

A line-oriented text editor; a superset of ed and the root of vi. See Sections 8 and 9 for more information.

Options

  −c*command*

      Begin edit session by executing the given ex *command* (usually a search pattern or line address). If *command* contains spaces or special characters, enclose it in single quotes to protect it from the shell. For example, *command* could be **':set list'** (show tabs and newlines) or /*word* (search for *word*) or **'$'** (show last line). (Note: **−c***command* was formerly +*command*.)

  −L　　List filenames that were saved due to an editor or system crash.

  −r *file*　Recover and edit *file* after an editor or system crash.

  −R　　Edit in read-only mode to prevent accidental changing of files.

  −s　　Suppress status messages (e.g., errors, prompts); useful when running an ex script. (**−s** was formerly the − option.)

  −t *tag*　Edit the file containing *tag*, and position the editor at its definition (see **ctags** for more information).

  −v　　Invoke vi. Running vi directly is simpler.

  −x　　Supply a key to encrypt or decrypt *file* using **crypt**.

  −C　　Same as **−x** but assume that *file* began in encrypted form.

Examples

  Either of the following examples will apply the ex commands in **exscript** to text file **doc**:

```
ex -s doc < exscript
cat exscript | ex -s doc
```

---

expr *arg1 operator arg2* [*operator arg3* ...]　　　　　　　　　　**expr**

Evaluate arguments as expressions and print the result. Arguments and operators must be separated by spaces. In most cases, an argument is an integer, typed literally or represented by a shell variable. There are three types of operators: arithmetic, relational, and logical. Exit status for **expr** is 0 (expression is nonzero and nonnull), 1 (expression is 0 or null), or 2 (expression is invalid).

→

expr

←

Arithmetic operators

Use these to produce mathematical expressions whose results are printed.

+   Add *arg2* to *arg1*.
–   Subtract *arg2* from *arg1*.
*   Multiply the arguments.
/   Divide *arg1* by *arg2*.
%   Take the remainder when *arg1* is divided by *arg2*.

Addition and subtraction are evaluated last, unless they are grouped inside parentheses. The symbols *, (, and) have meaning to the shell, so they must be escaped (preceded by a backslash or enclosed in single quotes).

Relational operators

Use these to compare two arguments. Arguments can also be words, in which case comparisons assume **a** < **z** and **A** < **Z**. If the comparison statement is true, the result is 1; if false, the result is 0. Symbols > and < must be escaped.

=   Are the arguments equal?
!=   Are the arguments different?
>   Is *arg1* greater than *arg2*?
>=   Is *arg1* greater than or equal to *arg2*?
<   Is *arg1* less than *arg2*?
<=   Is *arg1* less than or equal to *arg2*?

Logical operators

Use these to compare two arguments. Depending on the values, the result can be *arg1* (or some portion of it), *arg2*, or 0. Symbols | and **&** must be escaped.

| Logical OR; if *arg1* has a non-zero (and non-null) value, the result is *arg1*; otherwise, the result is *arg2*.

&   Logical AND; if both *arg1* and *arg2* have a non-zero (and non-null) value, the result is *arg1*; otherwise, the result is 0.

:   Sort of like **grep**; *arg2* is a pattern to search for in *arg1*. *arg2* must be a regular expression in this case. If the *arg2* pattern is enclosed in \(\), the result is the portion of *arg1* that matches; otherwise, the result is simply the number of characters that match. A pattern match always applies to the beginning of the argument (the ˆ symbol is assumed by default).

Division happens first; result is 10:

```
expr 5 + 10 / 2
```

Addition happens first; result is 7 (truncated from 7.5):

```
expr \( 5 + 10 \) / 2
```

Add 1 to variable **i**; this is how variables are incremented in shell scripts:

```
i=`expr $i + 1`
```

Print 1 (true) if variable **a** is the string "hello":

```
expr $a = hello
```

Print 1 (true) if **b** plus 5 equals 10 or more:

```
expr $b + 5 \>= 10
```

In the examples below, variable **p** is the string "version.100". This command prints the number of characters in **p**:

```
expr $p : '.*'          Result is 11
```

Match all characters and print them:

```
expr $p : '\(.*\)'      Result is "version.100"
```

Print the number of lowercase letters matched:

```
expr $p : '[a-z]*'      Result is 7
```

Match a string of lowercase letters:

```
expr $p : '\([a-z]*\)'   Result is "version"
```

Truncate **$x** if it contains five or more characters; if not, just print **$x**. (Logical OR uses the second argument when the first one is 0 or null; i.e., when the match fails.)

```
expr $x : '\(.....\)' \| $x
```

In a shell script, rename files to their first five letters:

```
mv $x `expr $x : '\(.....\)' \| $x`
```

(To avoid overwriting files with similar names, use **mv −i.**)

---

exstr [*options*] *file*   **exstr**

Extract strings from C source files, so that they can be stored in a database and retrieved at application run-time using the **gettxt** system call. With no options, **exstr** produces a **grep**-type list showing only filename and strings. **exstr** is one of several commands to use when customizing applications for international use.

→

Typical use involves three steps:

1. Specify −e and the C source file, and redirect the output to a file. This creates a database of text strings and identifying information.

2. Edit this database by adding information that was previously returned by the **mkmsgs** command.

3. Specify −r and the C source file, using the edited database as input. This replaces hardcoded text strings with calls to **gettxt**. **gettxt** lets you access translated versions of text strings. (The strings reside in a directory specified by environment variable LC_MESSAGES.)

Options

−e   Extract text strings from *file*. (−e is not used with other options.) The information appears in this format:

file:line:field:msg_file:msg_num:string

file	C source file from the command-line.
line	Line number on which the string is found in *file*.
field	In-line numerical position of the string's beginning.
msg_file	Initially null, but later filled in when you edit the database. *msg_file* is the name of the list of message strings that you create by running the **mkmsgs** command.
msg_num	Initially null but filled in later. It corresponds to the order of the strings in *msg_file*.

−r   Replace strings in the source file with calls to **gettxt**.

−d   Use with −r to give the **gettxt** call a second argument, the original text string. This string will be printed as the fallback in case the **gettxt** call fails.

Example

Assume a C source file named **proverbs.c**:

```
main() {
        printf("Haste makes waste\n");
        printf("A stitch in time\n");
}
```

1. First issue the command:

```
% exstr -e proverbs.c > proverb.list
```

proverb.list might look something like this:

```
proverbs.c:3:8:::Haste makes waste\n
proverbs.c:4:8:::A stitch in time\n
```

2. Run **mkmsgs** to create a message file (e.g., **prov.US**) that can be read by the **gettxt** call. If the two proverbs strings above are listed ninth and tenth in **prov.US**, then you would edit **proverb.list** as follows:

```
proverbs.c:3:8:prov.US:9:Haste makes waste\n
proverbs.c:4:8:prov.US:10:A stitch in time\n
```

3. Finally, specify **−r** to insert **gettxt** calls:

```
% exstr -rd proverbs.c < proverb.list > Prov.c
```

The international version of your program, **Prov.c**, now looks like this:

```
extern char *gettxt();
main() {
  printf(gettxt("prov.US:9", "Haste makes\
      waste\n"));
  printf(gettxt("prov.US:10", "A\
      stitch in time\n"));
}
```

---

face [*options*] [*files*]

Invoke the Framed Access Command Environment Interface and open *files*. By convention, each filename must be of the form **Menu.***string*, **Form.***string*, or **Text.***string*, depending on the type of object being opened. If no *files* are specified, **face** opens the FACE menu along with the default objects specified by the environment variable LOGINWIN.

Options

−a *afile*   Load the list of pathname aliases specified in the file *afile*. Entries have the form *alias=pathname*. Once this file is loaded, you can use the shorthand notation $*alias* to refer to a long pathname.

−c *cfile*   Load the list of command aliases specified in the file *cfile*. This file allows you to modify the default behavior of FACE commands or create new commands.

−i *ifile*   Load file *ifile*, which specifies startup features such as the introductory frame, banner information, screen colors, and labels.

factor	**factor** [*num*] Produce the prime factors of *num* or wait for input.
false	**false** A null command that returns an unsuccessful (nonzero) exit status. Normally used in Bourne shell scripts. See also **true**. *Example* ``` while false do commands done ```
fgrep	**fgrep** [*options*] [*pattern*] [*files*] Search one or more *files* for lines that match a literal, text-string *pattern*. Because **fgrep** does not support regular expressions, it is faster than **grep** (hence **fgrep**, for fast **grep**). Exit status is 0 if any lines match, 1 if not, and 2 for errors. See also **egrep** and **grep**.

Can use grep options.

Options

−b	Precede each line with its block number.
−c	Print only a count of matched lines.
−e *pat*	Use this if pattern *pat* begins with − .
−f*file*	Take a list of patterns from *file*.
−h	Print matched lines but not filenames (inverse of **−l**).
−i	Ignore uppercase and lowercase distinctions.
−l	List filenames but not matched lines.
−n	Print lines and their line numbers.
−v	Print all lines that *don't* match *pattern*.
−x	Print lines only if *pattern* matches the entire line.

−s -

Examples

Print lines in *file* that don't contain any spaces:

```
fgrep -v ' ' file
```

Print lines in *file* that contain the words in **spell_list**:

```
fgrep -f spell_list file
```

file	**file** [*options*] *files* Classify the named *files* according to the type of data they contain. **file** checks the magic file (usually **/etc/magic**) to identify some file types.

Options

  −c   Check the format of the magic file (*files* argument is
           invalid with **−c**).
  −f*list*   Run **file** on the filenames in *list*.
  −h   Do not follow symbolic links.
  −m*file* Use *file* as the magic file instead of **/etc/magic**.

Many file types are understood. Output lists each filename, followed by a brief classification such as:

```
ascii text
c program text
c-shell commands
data
empty
iAPX 386 executable
directory
[nt]roff, tbl, or eqn input text
shell commands
symbolic link to ../usr/etc/arp
```

Example

List all files that are deemed to be troff/nroff input:

```
file * | grep roff
```

---

find *pathname(s) condition(s)*

An extremely useful command for finding particular groups of files
(numerous examples follow this description). **find** descends the
directory tree beginning at each *pathname* and locates files that
meet the specified *conditions*. At least one *pathname* and one
condition must be specified. The most useful conditions include
−print (which must be explicitly given to display any output),
−name and **−type** (for general use), **−exec** and **−size** (for
advanced users), and **−mtime** and **−user** (for administrators).

Conditions may be grouped by enclosing them in \(\) (escaped
parentheses), negated with ! (use \! in the C shell), given as alter-
natives by separating them with **−o**, or repeated (adding restrictions to the match; usually only for **−name, −type, −perm**).

Conditions

  −atime +*n* | −*n* | *n*

           Find files that were last accessed more than *n* (+*n*),
           less than *n* (−*n*), or exactly *n* days ago. Note that
           find will change the access time of directories sup-
           plied as *pathnames.*
  −cpio *dev* Take matching files and write them on device *dev,*
           using **cpio**. (SVR3 only.)

−ctime +*n* | −*n* | *n*

Find files that were changed more than *n* (+*n*), less than *n* (−*n*), or exactly *n* days ago. Change refers to modification, permission or ownership changes, etc.; therefore, **−ctime** is more inclusive than **−atime** or **−mtime**.

−depth   Descend the directory tree, skipping directories and working on actual files first (and *then* the parent directories). Useful when files reside in unwritable directories (e.g., when using **find** with **cpio**).

−exec *command* { } \;

Run the UNIX *command* on each file matched by **find**, (provided *command* executes successfully on that file; i.e., returns a 0 exit status). When *command* runs, the argument { } substitutes the current file. Follow the entire sequence with an escaped semicolon (\;).

−follow   Follow symbolic links and track the directories visited (don't use this with **−type l**).

−fstype *type*

Find files that reside on file system *type*.

−group *gname*

Find files belonging to group *gname*. *gname* can be a group name or a group ID number.

−inum *n*   Find files whose inode number is *n*.

−links *n*   Find files having *n* links.

−local   Find files that physically reside on the local system.

−mount   Search for files that reside only on the same file system as *pathname*. (Use **−xdev** on BSD systems.)

−mtime +*n* | −*n* | *n*

Find files that were last modified more than *n* (+*n*), less than *n* (−*n*), or exactly *n* days ago.

−name *pattern*

Find files whose names match *pattern*. Filename metacharacters may be used, but should be escaped or quoted.

−newer *file*

Find files that have been modified more recently than *file*; similar to **−mtime**.

−nogroup Find files belonging to a group *not* in **/etc/group**.

−nouser   Find files owned by a user *not* in **/etc/passwd**.

−ok *command* { } \;

Same as **−exec**, but user must prompt (with a **y**) before *command* is executed.

−perm *nnn*

Find files whose permission flags (e.g., **rwx**) match octal number *nnn* exactly (e.g., 664 matches **−rw−rw−r−−**). Use a minus sign to make a "wildcard" match of any specified bit (e.g., **–perm –600** matches **–rw–*********, where * can be any mode).

–print   Print the matching files and directories, using their full pathnames.

–prune   "Prune" the directory tree of unwanted directory searches; that is, skip the directory most recently matched.

–size *n*[**c**] Find files containing *n* blocks, or if **c** is specified, *n* characters long.

–type *c*   Find files whose type is *c*. *c* can be **b** (**b**lock special file), **c** (**c**haracter special file), **d** (**d**irectory), **p** (fifo or named **p**ipe), **l** (symbolic **l**ink), or **f** (plain file).

–user *user*
     Find files belonging to a *user* name or ID.

Examples

List all files (and subdirectories) in your home directory:

```
find $HOME -print
```

List all files named **chapter1** in the **/work** directory:

```
find /work -name chapter1 -print
```

List "memo" files owned by **ann**:

```
find /work /usr -name 'memo*' -user ann -print
```

Search the file system (begin at root) for manpage directories:

```
find / -type d -name 'man*' -print
```

Search the current directory, look for filenames that *don't* begin with a capital letter, and send them to the printer:

```
find . \! -name '[A-Z]*' -exec lp {} \;
```

Find and compress files whose names *don't* end with **.Z**:

```
compress `find . \! -name '*.Z' -print`
```

Remove all empty files on the system (prompting first):

```
find / -size 0 -ok rm {} \;
```

Skip RCS directories, but list remaining read-only files:

```
find . -name RCS -prune -o -perm 444 -print
```

→

find ←	Search the system for files that were modified within the last two days (good candidates for backing up): `find / -mtime -2 -print` Recursively **grep** for a pattern down a directory tree: `find /book -print	xargs grep '[Nn]utshell'`
finger	**finger** [*options*] *users* Display data about one or more *users*, including information listed in the files **.plan** and **.project** in *user*'s home directory. You can specify each *user* either as a login name (exact match) or as a first or last name (display information on all matching names). Networked environments recognize arguments of the form *user@host* and *@host*. **Options** **−b** Omit user's home directory and shell from display. **−f** Used with **−s** to omit heading that normally displays in short format. **−h** Omit **.project** file from display. **−i** Show "idle" format, a terse format (like **−s**). **−l** Force long format (default). **−m** *users* must match usernames exactly, instead of also searching for a match of first or last names. **−p** Omit **.plan** file from display. **−q** Show "quick" format, the tersest of all (requires an exact match of username). **−s** Show short format. **−w** Used with **−s** to omit user's full name that normally displays in short format.
fmli	**fmli** [*options*] *files* Invoke the Form and Menu Language Interpreter and open *files*. By convention, each filename must be of the form **Menu.***string*, **Form.***string*, or **Text.***string*, depending on the type of object being opened. **Options** **−a** *afile* Load the list of pathname aliases specified in the file *afile*. Entries have the form *alias=pathname*. Once this file is loaded, you can use the shorthand notation $*alias* to refer to a long pathname. **−c** *cfile* Load the list of command aliases specified in the file *cfile*. This file allows you to modify the default behavior of FMLI commands or create new commands.

−**i** *ifile*   Load file *ifile*, which specifies startup features such as the introductory frame, banner information, screen colors, and labels.

fmt [*options*] [*files*]

Fill and join text, producing lines of roughly the same length. (Unlike nroff, the lines are not justified.) **fmt** ignores blank lines and lines beginning with a dot (**.**) or with "From:". The emacs editor uses **ESC-q** to join paragraphs, so **fmt** is useful for other editors, such as vi. The following vi command fills and joins the remainder of the current paragraph:

```
!}fmt
```

Options

−**c**   Don't adjust the first two lines; align subsequent lines with the second line. Useful for paragraphs that begin with a hanging tag.

−**s**   Split long lines but leave short lines alone. Useful for preserving partial lines of code.

−**w** *n*   Create lines no longer than *n* columns wide. Default is 72. (Can also be invoked as −*n* for compatibility with BSD.)

fmtmsg [*options*] *text*

Print *text* as part of a formatted error message on stderr (or on system console). *text* must be quoted as a single argument. **fmtmsg** is used in shell scripts to print messages in a standard format. Messages display as follows:

```
label:    severity:    text
TO FIX:   action       tag
```

You can define the MSGVERB variable to select which parts of the message to print. Each part is described with the options below.

Options

−**a** *action*   A string describing the first action to take in recovering the error. The string "TO FIX:" precedes the *action* string.

−**c** *source*   The source of the problem, where *source* is one of **hard** (hardware), **soft** (software), or **firm** (firmware).

−**l** *label*   Identify the message source with a text *label*, often of the form *file:command*.

−**s** *severity*   How serious the condition is. *severity* is one of **halt**, **error**, **warn**, or **info**.

→

fmtmsg	−**t** *tag*	Another string identifier for the message.
←	−**u** *types*	Classify the message as one or more *types* (separated by commas). *types* can be one of the keywords **appl**, **util**, or **opsys** (meaning that the problem comes respectively from an application, utility, or the kernel), either of the keywords **recov** or **nrecov** (application will or won't recover), **print** (message displays on *stderr*), and **console** (message displays on system console).

fold

fold [*option*] [*files*]

Break the lines of the named *files* so that they are no wider than the specified width. **fold** breaks lines exactly at the specified width, even in the middle of a word.

Option

−**w** *n*   Create lines having width *n* (default is 80). (Can also be invoked as −*n* for compatibility with BSD.)

ftp

ftp [*options*] [*hostname*]

Transfer files to and from remote network site *hostname*. **ftp** prompts the user for a command. Type **help** to see a list of known commands.

Options

−**d**   Enable debugging.

−**g**   Disable filename globbing.

−**i**   Turn off interactive prompting.

−**n**   No auto-login upon initial connection.

−**v**   Verbose on. Show all responses from remote server.

gcore

gcore [*option*] *process_ids*

Create ("get") a core image of each running process specified. The core image can be used with debugging utilities such as **sdb**.

Option

−**o** *file*   Create core file named *file.process_id* (default is **core.***process_id*).

gencat

gencat [*option*] *database msgfiles*

Append (or merge) messages contained in one or more *msgfiles* with the formatted message *database* file. If *database* doesn't exist, it is created. Each message in *msgfile* is preceded by a numerical identifier. Comment lines can be added by using a dollar sign at the beginning of a line, followed by a space or tab.

 —m   Build a single *database* that is backward-compatible
           with databases created by earlier versions of **gencat**.

---

get [*options*] *files*   **get**

An SCCS command. See Section 17.

---

getopts *string name* [*arg*]   **getopts**

Same as built-in Bourne shell command **getopts**. See Section 4.

---

gettxt *msgfile*:*msgnum* [*default_message*]   **gettxt**

Obtain the message that resides in file *msgfile* and whose message
ID is *msgnum*. *msgnum* is a number from 1 to *n*, where *n* is the
number of messages in *msgfile*. **gettxt** searches for *msgfile* in
directory **/usr/lib/locale/***locale***/LC_MESSAGES**, where *locale* is
the language in which the message strings have been written. The
value of *locale* is set by environment variable LC_MESSAGES, or
failing that, the LANG environment variable. If neither is set, *locale*
defaults to a directory named **C**. If **gettxt** fails, it displays
default_message or (if none is specified) the string, "Message not
found!!"

---

gprof [*options*] [*objfile* [*pfile*]]   **gprof**

Solaris 2.0 only. Display call-graph profile data of C programs.
Programs compiled with the **—pg** option of **cc** (and other compilers) produce a call-graph profile file *pfile*, whose default name is
gmon.out. The specified object file *objfile* (**a.out** by default) contains a symbol table that is read and correlated with *pfile*. See also
prof and **lprof**

Options

 —a   Don't print statically declared functions.
 —b   Brief; don't print field descriptions in the profile.
 —c   Find the program's static call-graph. Call counts of 0
             indicate static-only parents or children.
 —e *name* Don't print the graph profile entry for the routine
             name. **—e** may be repeated.
 —E *name* Like **—e** above. In addition, during time computa-
             tions, omit the time spent in *name*.
 —f *name* Print the graph profile entry only for routine *name*.
             —f may be repeated.
 —F *name* Like **—f** above. In addition, during time computa-
             tions, use only the times of the printed routines. **—F**
             may be repeated, and it overrides **—E**.

→

gprof ←	**−s**	With this option you supply one or more existing *pfiles*. Sum the information in all specified profile files and send it to a profile file called **gmon.sum**. Useful for accumulating data across several runs.
	−z	Show routines that have zero usage. Useful with **−c** to find out which routines were never called.

---

grep

grep [*options*] *regexp* [*files*]

Search one or more *files* for lines that match a regular expression *regexp*. Regular expressions are described in Section 6. Exit status is 0 if any lines match, 1 if not, and 2 for errors. See also **egrep** and **fgrep**.

Options

−b	Precede each line with its block number.
−c	Print only a count of matched lines.
−h	Print matched lines but not filenames (inverse of **−l**).
−i	Ignore uppercase and lowercase distinctions.
−l	List filenames but not matched lines.
−n	Print lines and their line numbers.
−s	Suppress error messages for nonexistent or unreadable files.
−v	Print all lines that *don't* match *regexp*.

Examples

List the number of users who use the C shell:

```
grep -c /bin/csh /etc/passwd
```

List header files that have at least one #include directive:

```
grep -l '^#include' /usr/include/*
```

List files that don't contain *pattern*:

```
grep -c pattern files | grep :0
```

---

groups

groups [*user*]

Show the groups that *user* belongs to (default is your groups). Groups are listed in **/etc/passwd** and **/etc/group**.

---

head

head [−*n*] [*files*]

Print the first few lines of one or more *files*. Use −*n* to print the first *n* lines (default is 10).

Examples

Display the first 20 lines of **phone_list**:

```
head -20 phone_list
```

Display the first ten phone numbers having a 202 area code:

```
grep '(202)' phone_list | head
```

---

help [*commands* | *error_codes*]

An SCCS command. See Section 17.

/usr/ucb/hostid

Print the hexadecimal ID number of the host machine.

/usr/ucb/hostname [*newhost*]

Print the name of the host machine. Often the same as **uname**. A privileged user can change the host name to *newhost*.

---

iconv −**f** *from_encoding* −**t** *to_encoding* [*file*]

Convert the contents of *file* from one character set (*from_encoding*) to another (*to_encoding*). If the destination character set provides no equivalent for a character, it is converted to an underscore (_). Supported conversion sets are listed in the directory **/usr/lib/iconv**.

---

id [−**a**]

List user and group IDs; list all groups with −**a**.

---

install [*options*] *file* [*directories*]

Used primarily in makefiles to update files. **install** tries to locate an old version of *file* by searching user-supplied *directories* (or default directories such as **/bin** or **/etc**). *file* is then copied to the directory, overwriting the older version. Normally, if no older *file* exists, **install** does nothing.

Options

−**c** *dir*   Conditional copy; if *file* already exists in *dir*, do nothing; otherwise, copy *file* to *dir*.

−**f** *dir*   Forced copy; copy *file* to *dir*, whether or not *file* is already there.

−**g** *group*   Set group ID of new file to *group* (privileged users only).

→

install	**−i**	When searching for *file*, ignore default directories but search specified *directories*. Normally, both sets are searched (with user-supplied directories searched before defaults). **−c** and **−f** are invalid with **−i**.
←	**−m** *mode*	Set permissions of new file to *mode*.
	−n *dir*	Place *file* in *dir* if it's not in any of the default directories.
	−o	Save old version of *file* in **OLD***file* instead of overwriting it.
	−s	Suppress all messages except error messages.
	−u *user*	Set owner of new file to *user*.

---

ipcrm

ipcrm [*options*]

Remove a message queue, semaphore set, or shared memory identifier as specified by the *options*. **ipcrm** is useful for freeing shared memory left behind by programs that failed to de-allocate the space. Use **ipcs** first to list items to remove.

Options

−m *shmid*	Remove shared memory identifier *shmid*.
−M *shmkey*	Remove *shmid* created with key *shmkey*.
−q *msqid*	Remove message queue identifier *msqid*.
−Q *msgkey*	Remove *msqid* created with key *msgkey*.
−s *semid*	Remove semaphore identifier *semid*.
−S *semkey*	Remove *semid* created with key *semkey*.

---

ipcs

ipcs [*options*]

Print data about active interprocess communication facilities.

Options

−m	Report on active shared memory segments.
−q	Report on active message queues.
−s	Report on active semaphores.

With the **−m**, **−q**, or **−s** options, only the specified interprocess facility is reported on. Otherwise information about all three is printed.

−a	Use all of the print options (short for **−bcopt**).
−b	Report maximum allowed number of message bytes, segment sizes, and number of semaphores.
−c	Report the creator's login name and group.
−C*file*	Read status from *file* instead of from **/dev/kmem**.
−N*list*	Use the argument for the named *list* instead of **/stand/unix**.

−o	Report outstanding usage.
−p	Report process numbers.
−t	Report time information.

ismpx [*option*]

Test whether standard input is running under **layers**. (Command name comes from "**Is** the **m**ultiple**x**or running?") Output is either **yes** (exit status 0) or **no** (exit status 1). Useful for shell scripts that send programs to a windowing terminal or depend on screen size.

Option

−s   Suppress output and return exit status only.

Example shell script

```
if ismpx -s
then jwin
fi
```

join [*options*] *file1 file2*

Join the common lines of sorted *file1* and sorted *file2*. (Read standard input if *file1* is −.) The output contains the common field and the remainder of each line from *file1* and *file2*. In the options below, *n* can be 1 or 2, referring to *file1* or *file2*.

Options

−a*n*	List unpairable lines in file *n* (or both if *n* is omitted).
−e *s*	Replace any empty output field with the string *s*.
−j*n m*	Join on the *m*th field of file *n* (or both files if *n* is omitted).
−o *n.m*	Each output line contains fields specified by file number *n* and field number *m*. The common field is suppressed unless requested.
−t*c*	Use character *c* as field separator for input and output.

Examples

Assuming the following input files:

```
% cat score
olga     81      91
rene     82      92
zack     83      93
% cat grade
olga     B       A
rene     B       A
```

$\rightarrow$

join ←	List scores followed by grades, including unmatched lines: ``` % join -a score grade olga 81 91 B A rene 82 92 B A zack 83 93 ``` Pair each score with its grade: ``` % join -o 1.1 1.2 2.2 1.3 2.3 score grade olga 81 B 91 A rene 82 B 92 A ```
jsh	**jsh** [*options*] [*arguments*] Job control version of **sh** (the Bourne shell). This provides control of background and foreground processes for the standard shell. See Section 4.
jterm	**jterm** Reset layer of windowing terminal after a program changes the terminal attributes of the layer. Used only under **layers**. Returns 0 on success; 1 otherwise.
jwin	**jwin** Print size of current window in bytes. Used only under **layers**.
keylogin	**keylogin** Prompt user for a password, then use it to decrypt the person's secret key. This key is used by secure network services (e.g., NFS). **keylogin** is needed only if the user was not prompted for a password upon logging in. See also **chkey** and **keylogout**.
keylogout	**keylogout** [*option*] Revoke access to (delete) the secret key used by secure network services (e.g., NFS). See also **chkey** and **keylogin**. *Option* **−f** Forget the root key. If specified on a server, NFS security will be broken. Use with care.
kill	**kill** [*options*] *IDs* Terminate one or more process *IDs*. You must own the process or be a privileged user. This command is similar to the **kill** command that is built into the Bourne, Korn, and C shells. A minus sign before an *ID* specifies a process group ID. (The built-in version doesn't allow process group IDs, but it does allow job IDs.)

Options

  −l   List the signal names. (Used by itself.)
  −*signal*   The signal number (from **ps −f**) or name (from **kill −l**). With a signal number of 9, the kill is absolute.

---

ksh [*options*] [*arguments*]

Korn shell command interpreter. See Section 4 for more information, including command-line options.

---

layers [*options*] [*layers_program*]

A layer multiplexor for windowing terminals. **layers** manages asynchronous windows on a windowing terminal. *layers_program* is a file containing a firmware patch that **layers** downloads to the terminal (before layers are created or startup *commands* are executed).

Options

  −**d**   Print sizes of the text, data, and bss portions of a downloaded firmware patch on standard error.
  −**D**   Print debugging messages on standard error.
  −**f** *file*   Initialize **layers** with a configuration given by *file*. Each line of *file* is a layer to be created and has the format *x1 y1 x2 y2 commands*, specifying the origin, the opposite corner, and start up commands. E.g.:

```
10 10 800 240 date; who; exec $SHELL
```

  −**h** *list*   Supply a comma-separated *list* of STREAMS modules to push onto a layer.
  −**m** *size*   Set data part of **xt** packets to maximum *size* (32-252).
  −**p**   Print downloading protocol statistics and a trace of a downloaded firmware patch on standard error.
  −**s**   Report protocol statistics on standard error after exiting **layers**.
  −**t**   Turn on **xt** driver packet tracing and produce a trace dump on standard error after exiting **layers**.

---

ld [*options*] *objfiles*

Combine several *objfiles*, in the specified order, into a single executable object module (**a.out** by default). **ld** is the link editor and is often invoked automatically by compiler commands such as **cc**.

Options

  −**a**   Force default behavior for static linking (generate an object file and list undefined references). Do not use with −**r**.

→

−b   Ignore special processing for shared reference symbols (dynamic linking only); output becomes more efficient but less sharable.

−B *mode* See description under **cc**.

−B symbolic

In dynamic linking, bind a symbol to its local definition, not to its global definition.

−d[*c*]   Link dynamically (*c* is **y**) or statically (*c* in **n**); dynamic linking is the default.

−e *symbol*

Set *symbol* as the address of the output file's entry point.

−G   In dynamic linking, create a shared object and allow undefined symbols.

−h *name* Use *name* as the shared object file to search for during dynamic linking (default is UNIX object file).

−I *name* Use *name* as the pathname of the loader (interpreter) to write into the program header. Default is none (static) or **/usr/lib/libc.so.1** (dynamic).

−l*x*   Search a library named **lib***x***.so** or **lib***x***.a** (the placement of this option on the line affects when the library is searched).

−L *dir*   Search directory *dir* before standard search directories (this option must precede **−l**).

−m   List a memory profile for input/output sections.

−M *mapfile*

Invoke **ld** directives from *mapfile* (**−M** messes up the output and is discouraged).

−N   Put the data section immediately after the text section. (SVR3 only.)

−o*file*   Send the output to *file* (default is **a.out**).

−Q*c*   List version information about **ld** in the output (*c* = **y**, the default) or do not list (*c* = **n**).

−r   Allow output to be subject to another **ld**.

−s   Remove symbol table and relocation entries.

−t   Suppress warning about multiply-defined symbols of unequal size.

−u *symbol*

Enter *symbol* in symbol table; useful when loading from an archive library. *symbol* must precede the library that defines it (so **−u** must precede **−l**).

−V   Print the version of **ld**.

−YP, *dirlist*

Specify a comma-separated list of directories to use in place of the default search directories (see also **−L**).

−z defs | nodefs | text
> Specify **nodefs** to allow undefined symbols. The default, **defs**, treats undefined symbols as a fatal error. Use **text** to produce an error when there are nonwritable relocations.

---

ldd [*option*] *file*

List dynamic dependencies; that is, list shared objects that would be loaded if *file* were executed. (If a valid *file* needs no shared objects, **ldd** succeeds but produces no output.) In addition, **ldd**'s options can be used to show unresolved symbol references that would result from running *file*. Specify only one option.

Options

−d	Check references to data objects only.
−r	Check references to data objects and to functions.

---

lex [*options*] [*files*]

Generate a lexical analysis program (named **lex.yy.c**) based on the regular expressions and C statements contained in one or more input *files*. See also **yacc** and the Nutshell Handbook *lex & yacc*.

Options

−c	*file*'s program statements are in C (default).
−n	Suppress the output summary.
−Qc	Print version information in **lex.yy.c** (if c = **y**) or suppress information (if c = **n**, the default).
−t	Write program to standard output, not **lex.yy.c**.
−v	Print a summary of machine-generated statistics.
−V	Print version information on standard error.

---

line

Read the next line from standard input and write it to standard output. Exit status is 1 upon *EOF*. Typically used in shell scripts to read from the terminal.

Example

Print the first two lines of output from **who**:

```
who | ( line ; line )
```

---

lint [*options*] *files*

Detect bugs, portability problems, and other possible errors in the specified C programs. By default, **lint** uses definitions in the C library **llib-lc.ln**. If desired, output from **.c** files can be saved in "object files" having a **.ln** suffix. A second **lint** pass can be invoked on **.ln** files and libraries for further checking. **lint** also

→

lint

←

accepts the **cc** options **−D**, **−I**, **−U**, and **−X**. See also the Nutshell Handbook, *Checking C Programs with lint*.

Note: This command checks programs written in ANSI C; use **/usr/ucb/lint** if you want to check programs written in Kernighan and Ritchie's C. Note also that options **−a**, **−b**, **−h**, and **−x** have exactly the opposite meaning in the versions for BSD and System V.

Options

−a	Ignore long values assigned to variables that aren't long.
−b	Ignore break statements that cannot be reached.
−c	Don't execute the second pass of **lint**; save output from first pass in **.ln** files. (Same as BSD **−i** option.)
−F	Print files using full pathname, not just the filename.
−h	Don't test for bugs, bad style, or extraneous information.
−k	Re-enable warnings that are normally suppressed by directive **/* LINTED** [*message*] ***/**, and print the additional *message* (if specified).
−L*dir*	Search for **lint** libraries in directory *dir* before searching standard directories.
−l*x*	Use library **llib−l***x***.ln** in addition to **llib−lc.ln**.
−m	Ignore **extern** declarations that could be **static**.
−n	Do not check for compatibility.
−o *lib*	
	Create a **lint** library named **llib−l.***lib***.ln** from the output of the first pass of **lint**.
−p	Check for portability to variants of C.
−R*file*	Place **.ln** output (from a **.c** file) in *file*, for use by **cxref**.
−s	Produce short (one-line) diagnostics. Solaris 2.0 only.
−u	Ignore functions or external variables that are undefined or unused.
−v	Ignore unused arguments within functions; same as specifying the directive **/* ARGSUSED */**.
−V	Print product name and release on standard error.
−W*file*	
	Same as **−R**, except *file* is prepared for **cflow**.
−x	Ignore unused variables referred to by **extern** declarations.
−y	Same as using the directive **/* LINTLIBRARY */**, which is the same as supplying options **−v** and **−x**.

ln

ln [*options*] *file1 file2*
ln [*options*] *files directory*

Create pseudonyms (links) for files, allowing them to be accessed by different names. In the first form, link *file1* to *file2*, where *file2* is usually a new filename. If *file2* is an existing file, it is overwritten; if *file2* is an existing directory, a link named *file1* is created in

that directory. In the second form, create links in *directory*, each
link having the same name as the file specified.

Options

> **−f** Force the link to occur (don't prompt for overwrite per-
> mission).
>
> **−n** Do not overwrite existing files.
>
> **−s** Create a symbolic link. This lets you link across file
> systems and also see the name of the link when you
> run **ls −l** (otherwise there's no way to know the name
> that a file is linked to).

ln

login

login [*options*]

Sign on and identify yourself to the system. At the beginning of
each terminal session, the system prompts you for your username
and, if relevant, a password. The options are usually not used.

Options

> *user* Sign on as *user* (instead of being prompted).
>
> **−d***tty* Specify the pathname of the *tty* that serves as the login
> port.
>
> *var=value*
>   When specified after the username, assign a *value* to
> one or more environment variables. PATH and SHELL
> can't be changed.)

logname

logname

Display your login name. (Print the value of the LOGNAME environment variable located in **/etc/profile**.)

lorder *objfiles*

lorder

Take object filenames (e.g., files with **.o** suffix) and output a list of
related pairs. The first file listed includes references to external
identifiers that are defined in the second. **lorder** output can be
sent to **tsort** to make link editing of an archive more efficient.

Example

> To produce an ordered list of object files, and replace them in
> the library **program_arch** (provided they are newer):

```
ar cru program_arch `lorder *.o | tsort`
```

lp [*options*] [*files*]

lp

Send *files* to the printer. To send standard input, specify − as one
of the *files*.

→

Options

−c Copy *files* to print spooler; if changes are made to *file* while it is still queued for printing, the printout is unaffected.

−d *dest* Send output to destination printer named *dest*.

−d any Used after **−f** or **−S** to print the request on any printer that supports the given *name*.

−f *name* Print request on preprinted form *name*. *name* references printer attributes set by the administrative command **lpforms**.

−H *action* Print according to the named *action*: **hold** (notify before printing), **resume** (resume a held request), **immediate** (print next; privileged users only).

−i *IDs* Override **lp** options used for request *IDs* currently in the queue; specify new **lp** options after **−i**. For example, change the number of copies sent.

−m Send mail after *files* are printed.

−n *number* Specify the *number* of copies to print.

−o *options* Set one or more printer-specific *options*. Standard options include:

nobanner	Omit banner page (separator) from request.
nofilebreak	Suppress formfeeds between files.
cpi=n	Print n characters per inch. n can also be **pica**, **elite**, or **compressed**.
lpi=n	Print n lines per inch.
length=n	Print pages n units long; e.g., 11i (inches), 66 (lines).
width=n	Print pages n units wide; e.g., 8.5i (inches) 72 (columns).
stty=$list$	Specify a quoted *list* of **stty** options.

−P *list* Print only the page numbers specified in *list*.

−q n Print request with priority level n (39 = lowest).

−r Don't adapt request if *content* isn't suitable; reject instead. (Obscure; used only with **−T**.)

−s Suppress messages.

−S *name* Use the named print wheel or character set for printing.

−t *title* Use *title* on the printout's banner page.

−T *content* Send request to a printer that supports *content* (default is **simple**; an administrator sets *content* via **lpadmin** **−I**).

−**w**   Write a terminal message after *files* are printed (same as −**m** if user isn't logged on). Confirm the printing with a message on the user's terminal.

−**y** *mode*   Print according to locally-defined *modes*.

Examples

Send mail after printing five copies of **report**:

```
lp -n 5 -m report
```

Format and print **thesis**; print **title** too:

```
nroff -ms thesis | lp - title
```

/usr/ucb/lpq [*options*] [*job#s*] [*users*]

Show the printer queue. Standard SVR4 uses **lpstat**.

/usr/ucb/lpr [*options*] [*files*]

Send *files* to the printer. Standard SVR4 uses **lp**.

/usr/ucb/lprm [*options*] [*job#s*] [*users*]

Remove requests from printer queue. Standard SVR4 uses **cancel**.

---

lprof [*options*]
lprof −**m** *files* [−**T**] −**d** *out*

Display a program's profile data on a line-by-line basis. Data includes a list of source files, each source code line (with line numbers), and the number of times each line was executed. By default, **lprof** interprets the profile file *prog*.**cnt**. This file is generated by specifying **cc** −**ql** when compiling a program or when creating a shared object named *prog* (default is **a.out**). The PROFOPTS environment variable can be used to control profiling at run time. See also **prof** and **gprof**.

Options

−**c** *file*   Read input profile *file* instead of *prog*.**cnt**.

−**d** *out*   Store merged profile data in file *out*. Must be used with −**m**.

−**I** *dir*   Search for include files in *dir* as well as in the default place (**/usr/include**).

−**m** *files* Merge several profile *files* and total the execution counts. *files* are of the form *f1*.**cnt**, *f2*.**cnt**, *f3*.**cnt** , etc., where each file contains the profile data from a different run of the same program. Used with −**d**.

→

lprof ←	**−o** *prog* Look in the profile file for a program named *prog* instead of the name used when the profile file was created. **−o** is needed when files have been renamed or moved.
	−p Print the default listing; useful with **−r** and **−s**.
	−r *list* Used with **−p** to print only the source files given in *list*.
	−s For each function, print the percentage of code lines that are executed.
	−T Ignore timestamp of executable files being profiled. Normally, times are checked to insure that the various profiles were made from the same version of an executable.
	−V Print the version of **lprof** on standard error.
	−x Omit execution counts. For lines that executed, show only the line numbers; for lines that didn't execute, print the line number, the symbol [U], and the source line.

---

lpstat

lpstat [*options*]

Print the **lp** print queue status. With options that take a *list* argument, omitting the list produces all information for that option. *list* can be separated by commas or, if enclosed in double quotes, by spaces.

Options

−a [*list*]   Show whether the *list* of printer or class names is accepting requests.

−c [*list*]   Show information about printer classes named in *list*.

−d   Show the default printer destination.

−D   Use after **−p** to show a brief printer description.

−f [*list*]   Verify that the *list* of forms is known to **lp**.

−l   Use after **−f** to describe available forms, after **−p** to show printer configurations, or after **−S** to describe printers appropriate for the specified character set or print wheel.

−o [*list*]   Show the status of output requests. *list* contains printer names, class names, or request IDs.

−p [*list*]   Show the status of printers named in *list*.

−r   Show whether the print scheduler is on or off.

−R   Show the job's position in the print queue.

−s   Summarize the print status (shows almost everything).

−S [*list*]   Verify that the *list* of character sets or print wheels is known to **lp**.

–t	Show all status information (reports everything).
–u [*list*]	Show request status for users on *list*. *list* can be:

user	*user* on local machine.
all	All users on local machine.
*host***!***user*	*user* on machine *host*.
*host***!all**	All users on *host*.
all! *user*	*user* not on local machine.
all!all	All users not on local machine.

–v [*list*]	Show device associated with each printer named in *list*.

/usr/ucb/lptest [*length* [*n*]]

Display all 96 printable ASCII characters on the standard output. Characters are printed in each position, forming a "ripple pattern." You can specify the output line *length* (default is 79) and display *n* lines of output (default is 200). **lptest** is useful for testing printers and terminals or for running shell scripts with dummy input.

---

ls [*options*] [*names*]

If no *names* are given, list the files in the current directory. With one or more *names*, list files contained in a directory *name* or that match a file *name*. *names* can include filename metacharacters. The options let you display a variety of information in different formats. The most useful options include **–F**, **–R**, **–l**, and **–s**. Some options don't make sense together; e.g., **–u** and **–c**.

Options

–a	List all files, including the normally hidden . files.
–b	Show nonprinting characters in octal.
–c	List files by creation/modification time.
–C	List files in columns (the default format).
–d	List only the directory name, not its contents.
–f	Interpret each *name* as a directory (files are ignored).
–F	Flag filenames by appending **/** to directories, ***** to executable files, and **@** to symbolic links.
–g	Like **–l**, but omit owner name (show **g**roup).
–i	List the inode for each file.
–l	Long format listing (includes permissions, owner, size, modification time, etc.).
–L	List the file or directory referenced by a symbolic link rather than the link itself.
–m	Merge the list into a comma-separated series of names.
–n	Like **–l**, but use GID and UID numbers instead of owner and group names.

→

ls	**−o**	Like **−l**, but omit group name (show **o**wner).
←	**−p**	Mark directories by appending **/** to them.
	−q	Show nonprinting characters as **?**.
	−r	List files in reverse order (by name or by time).
	−R	Recursively list subdirectories as well as current directory.
	−s	Print size of the files in blocks.
	−t	List files according to modification time (newest first).
	−u	List files according to the file access time.
	−x	List files in rows going across the screen.
	−1	Print one entry per line of output.

Examples

List all files in the current directory and their sizes; use multiple columns and mark special files:

```
ls -asCF
```

List the status of directories **/bin** and **/etc**:

```
ls -ld /bin /etc
```

List C source files in the current directory, the oldest first:

```
ls -rt *.c
```

Count the files in the current directory:

```
ls | wc -1
```

---

m4

m4 [*options*] [*files*]

Macro processor for RATFOR, C, and other program *files*.

Options

−B*n*
Set push-back and argument collection buffers to *n* (default is 4,096).

−D*name*[=*value*]
Define *name* as *value* or, if *value* is not specified, define *name* as null.

−e Operate interactively, ignoring interrupts.

−H*n* Set symbol table hash array to *n* (default is 199).

−s Enable line-sync output for the C preprocessor.

−S*n* Set call stack size to *n* (default is 100 slots).

−T*n* Set token buffer size to *n* (default is 512 bytes).

−U*name* Undefine *name*.

mail [*options*] [*users*]

Read mail (if no *users* listed), or send mail to other *users*. Type ?
for a summary of commands. Esoteric debugging options exist
(not listed) for system administrators.

Options for sending mail

−m *type*	Print a "Message-type:" line at the heading of the letter, followed by *type* of message.
−t	Print a "To:" line at the heading of the letter, showing the names of the recipients.
−w	Force mail to be sent to remote users without waiting for remote transfer program to be completed.

Options for reading mail

−e	Test for the existence of mail without printing it. Exit status is 0 if mail exists; otherwise 1.
−f *file*	Read mail from alternate mailbox *file*.
−F *names*	Forward all incoming mail to recipient *names*.
−h	Display a window of messages rather than the latest message.
−p	Print all messages without pausing.
−P	Print messages with all header lines displayed.
−q	Terminate on an interrupt.
−r	Print oldest messages first.

mailalias [*options*] *names*

Display the e-mail addresses associated with one or more alias
names. **mailalias** displays addresses that are listed in the files
/var/mail/*name*, **$HOME/lib/names**, and in the files pointed to
by the list in **/etc/mail/namefiles**. **mailalias** is called by **mail**.

Options

−s	Suppress *name*; show only corresponding mail address.
−v	Verbose mode; show debugging information.

mailx [*options*] [*users*]

Read mail, or send mail to other *users*. For a summary of commands, type ? in command mode (e.g., when reading mail) or ~?
in input mode (e.g., when sending mail). The start-up file **.mailrc**
in the user's home directory is useful for setting display variables
and for defining alias lists.

→

mailx ←	*Options*	
	-d	Set debugging.
	-e	Test for the existence of mail without printing it. Exit status is 0 if mail exists; otherwise 1.
	-f [*file*]	Read mail in alternate *file* (default is **mbox**).
	-F	Store message in a file named after the first recipient.
	-h *n*	Stop trying to send after making *n* network connections, or "hops" (useful for avoiding infinite loops).
	-H	Print mail headers only.
	-i	Ignore interrupts (useful on modems); same as **ignore** environment variable.
	-I	Use with **-f** when displaying saved news articles; newsgroup and article-ID headers are included.
	-n	Do not read the startup **mailx.rc** file.
	-N	Don't print mail headers.
	-r *address*	Specify a return *address* for mail you send.
	-s *sub*	Print string *sub* in the subject header field.
	-T *file*	Record message IDs and article IDs (of news articles) in *file*.
	-u *user*	Read *user*'s mail.
	-U	Convert **uucp**-type addresses to Internet format.
	-V	Print version number of **mailx** and exit.

make	**make** [*options*] [*targets*]

Update one or more *targets* according to dependency instructions in a description file in the current directory. By default, this file is called **makefile** or **Makefile**. See Section 19 for more information on **make**. See also the Nutshell Handbook, *Managing Projects with make*.

Options

-e	Override **makefile** assignments with environment variables.
-f *makefile*	
	Use *makefile* as the description file; a filename of **-** denotes standard input.
-i	Ignore command error codes (same as **.IGNORE**).
-k	Abandon the current entry when it fails, but keep working with unrelated entries.
-n	Print commands but don't execute (used for testing).
-p	Print macro definitions and target descriptions.
-q	Query; return 0 if file is up-to-date; nonzero otherwise.

−r Do not use "default" rules.

−s Do not display command lines (same as **.SILENT**).

−t Touch the target files, causing them to be updated.

make

---

makekey

makekey

Improve encryption schemes by creating a more difficult key. **makekey** is available only in the United States (due to export restrictions).

(side tab) **UNIX Commands**

/usr/ucb/man [options] [[section] subjects]

man

Display information from the on-line reference manuals. Each *subject* is usually the name of a command from Section 1 of the on-line manuals, unless you specify an optional *section* from 1 to 8. If you don't specify a *subject*, you must supply either a keyword (for **−k**) or a file (for **−f**). No options except **−M** can be used with **−k** or **−f**. The MANPATH environment variable defines the directory in which **man** searches for information (default is **/usr/share/man**). PAGER defines how output is sent to the screen (default is **more −s**). Note: In Solaris 2.0, *section* must be preceded by **−s**.

Options

− Pipe output through **cat** instead of **more −s**.

−a Show all pages matching *subject*. Solaris 2.0 only.

−d Debug; evaluate the **man** command but don't execute. Solaris 2.0 only.

−F Search MANPATH directories, not windex database. Solaris 2.0 only.

−f *files* Display a one-line summary of one or more reference *files*. Same as **whatis**.

−k *keywords*
Display any header line that contains one of the specified *keywords*. Same as **apropos**.

−l Like **−a**, but only list the pages. Solaris 2.0 only.

−M *path*
Search for on-line descriptions in directory *path* instead of default directory. **−M** overrides MANPATH.

−r Reformat but don't display manual page. Same as **−t**. Solaris 2.0 only.

−t Format the manual pages with troff.

−T *mac*
Display information using macro package *mac* instead of **tmac.an** (the *man* macros).

→

Examples

Save documentation on the **mv** command (strip backspaces):

```
man mv | col -b > Move.doc
```

Display commands related to linking and compiling:

```
man -k link compile | more
```

Display a summary of all **intro** files:

```
man -f intro
```

Look up the page for **nice**, as well as the **intro** page from Section 3M:

```
man nice 3m intro          In SVR4
man nice -s 3m intro        In Solaris 2.0
```

---

mcs

mcs [*options*] *files*

Manipulate the comment section. **mcs** is used to add to, compress, delete, or print a section of one or more ELF object *files*. The default section is **.comment**. If any input file is an archive, **mcs** acts on each component file and removes the archive symbol table (unless **−p** was the only option specified). Use **ar s** to regenerate the symbol table. At least one option must be supplied.

Options

−a *string* Append *string* to the comment section of *files*.

−c Compress the comment section of *files* and remove duplicate entries.

−d Delete the comment section (including header).

−n *name* Act on section *name* instead of **.comment**.

−p Print the comment section on standard output.

−V Print the version of **mcs** on standard error.

Example

```
mcs -p kernel.o          Print the comment section of kernel.o
```

---

mesg

mesg [*options*]

Change the ability of other users to send **write** messages to your terminal. With no options, display the permission status. On System V, a hyphen can precede the options.

Options

n Forbid **write** messages.

y Allow **write** messages (the default).

mkdir [options] directories

Create one or more *directories*. You must have write permission in
the parent directory in order to create a directory. See also **rmdir**.

Options

−m *mode* Set the access *mode* for new directories.

−p Create intervening parent directories if they don't
exist.

Examples

Create a read-only directory named **personal**:

```
mkdir -m 444 personal
```

The following sequence:

```
mkdir work; cd work
mkdir junk; cd junk
mkdir questions; cd ../..
```

could be accomplished by typing this:

```
mkdir -p work/junk/questions
```

mkmsgs [options] string_file msg_file

Convert *string_file* (a list of text strings) into *msg_file* (the file
whose format is readable by **gettxt**). The created *msg_file* is also
used by the commands **exstr** and **srchtxt**.

Options

−i *locale* Create *msg_file* in directory:

```
/usr/lib/locale/locale/LC_MESSAGES
```

For example, if *string_file* is a collection of error
messages in German, you might specify *locale* as
german.

−o Overwrite existing *msg_file*.

more [options] [files]

Display the named *files* on a terminal, one screenful at a time.
After each screen is displayed, press RETURN to display the next
line or press the spacebar to display the next screenful. Press **h** for
help with additional commands, **q** to quit, **/** to search, or **:n** to go
to the next file. **more** can also be invoked using the name **page**.

Options

−c Page through the file by clearing each window
instead of scrolling. This is sometimes faster.

→

more	**−d**	Display the prompt *Press space to continue, 'q' to quit*.
←	**−f**	Count logical rather than screen lines. Useful when long lines wrap past the width of the screen.
	−l	Ignore formfeed (^L) characters.
	−r	Force display of control characters, in the form *^x*.
	−s	Squeeze; display multiple blank lines as one.
	−u	Suppress underline characters and backspace (^H).
	−w	Wait for a user keystroke before exiting.
	−n	Use *n* lines for each window (default is a full screen).
	+num	Begin displaying at line number *num*.
	+/pattern	Begin displaying two lines before *pattern*.

Examples

Page through *file* in "clear" mode, and display prompts:

```
more -cd file
```

Format **doc** to the screen, removing underlines:

```
nroff doc | more -u
```

View the man page for the **grep** command; begin near the word "BUGS" and compress extra white space:

```
man grep | more +/BUGS -s
```

---

mv

mv [*options*] *sources target*

Basic command to move files and directories around on the system or to rename them. **mv** works as follows:

Source	*Target*	*Result*
File	*name*	Rename file as *name*.
File	Existing file	Overwrite existing file with source file.
Directory	*name*	Rename directory as *name*.
Directory	Existing directory	Move directory to be a subdirectory of existing directory.
One or more files	Existing directory	Move files to directory.

Options

−−	Use this when one of the names begins with a −.
−f	Force the move, even if *target* file exists; suppress messages about restricted access modes.
−i	Inquire; prompt for a **y** (yes) response before overwriting an existing target.

nawk [*options*] ['*program*'] [*files*] [*variable=value*]

New version of awk, with additional capabilities. Nawk is a pattern-matching language useful for manipulating data. See Section 11 for more information on nawk.

Options

−f *file*   Read program instructions from *file* instead of supplying *program* instructions on command line.

−F *regexp*
      Separate fields using regular expression *regexp*.

−v *variable=value*
      Assign *value* to *variable* before executing '*program*'. If specified at the end of the command line, assignment occurs after opening *files*.

---

newform [*options*] *files*

Format *files* according to the options specified. **newform** resembles **cut** and **paste** and can be used to filter text output. Options can appear more than once and can be interspersed between *files* (except for **−s**, which must appear first).

Options

−a[*n*]   Append *n* characters to the end of each line or, if *n* isn't specified, append characters until each line has the length specified by **−l**.

−b[*n*]   Delete *n* characters from beginning of each line or, if *n* isn't specified, delete characters until each line has the length specified by **−l**.

−c*m*   Use character *m* (instead of a space) when padding lines with **−a** or **−p**;

−e[*n*]   Same as **−b** but delete from the end. **−c** must precede **−a** or **−p**.

−f   Display *tabspec* format used by last **−o** option.

−i'*tabspec*'
      Expand tabs to spaces using *tabspec* conversion (default is 8 spaces); *tabspec* is one of the options listed under **tabs**.

−l[*n*]   Use line length *n* (default is 72). If **−l** is not specified, default line length is 80. **−l** usually precedes other options that modify line length (**−b**, **−e**, **−c**, **−a**, or **−p**).

−o'*tabspec*'
      Turn spaces into tabs using *tabspec* conversion.

−p[*n*]   Same as **−a** but pad beginning of line.

−s   Strip leading characters from each line (up to and including first tab); the first seven characters are moved to the end of the line (without the tab). All lines must contain at least one tab.

→

newform ←	*Example* Remove sequence numbers from a COBOL program: `newform -11 -b7 file`
newgrp	**newgrp** [−] [*group*] Log in to *group*. If *group* name is not specified, your original group is reinstated. If − is given, log in using the same environment as when logging in as *group*.
news	**news** [*options*] [*item_files*] Consult the news directory for information on current events. With no arguments, **news** prints all current *item_files*. Items usually reside in **/usr/news** or **/var/news**. *Options* −**a** Print all news items, whether current or not. −**n** Print names of news items, but not their contents. −**s** Report the number of current news items.
nice	**nice** [*option*] *command* [*arguments*] Execute a *command* and *arguments* with lower priority (i.e., be "nice" to other users). *Option* −*n* Run *command* with a niceness of *n* (1-19); default is 10. Higher *n* means lower priority. A privileged user can raise priority by specifying a negative *n* (e.g., −5).

nl	**nl** [*options*] [*file*]
	
	Number the lines of *file* in logical page segments. Numbering resets to 1 at the start of each page.
	
	Options
	
	−**b***type* Number lines according to *type*. Values are:
	        a All lines.
	        n No lines.
	        t Text lines only (the default).
	        p"*exp***"** Lines containing *exp* only.
	−**d***xy* Use characters *xy* to delimit logical pages (default is \:).
	−**f***type* Like −**b** but number footer (default *type* is **n**).
	−**h***type* Like −**b** but number header (default *type* is **n**).
	−**i***n* Increment each line number by *n* (default is 1).

−l*n*	Count *n* consecutive blank lines as one line.
−n*format*	Set line number *format*. Values are:
	ln Left justify, omit leading zeros.
	rn Right justify, omit leading zeros (default).
	rz Right justify.
−p	Do not reset numbering at start of pages.
−s*c*	Separate text from line number with character(s) *c* (default is a tab).
−v*n*	Number each page starting at *n* (default is 1).
−w*n*	Use *n* columns to show line number (default is 6).

Examples

List the current directory, numbering files as 1), 2), etc.:

```
ls | nl -w3 -s') '
```

Number C source code and save it:

```
nl prog.c > print_prog
```

Number only lines that begin with #include:

```
nl -bp"^#include" prog.c
```

---

nm [*options*] *objfiles*

Print the symbol table (name list) in alphabetical order for one or more object files (usually ELF or COFF files). Output includes each symbol's value, type, size, name, etc. A key letter categorizing the symbol can also be displayed.

Options

−e	Report only external and static symbols; obsolete.
−f	Report all information; obsolete.
−h	Suppress the header.
−l	Use with **−p**; indicate WEAK symbols by appending an asterisk (*****) to key letters.
−n	Sort the external symbols by name.
−o	Report values in octal.
−p	Precede each symbol with its key letter (used for parsing).
−r	Report the object file's name on each line.
−T	Truncate the symbol name in the display; obsolete.
−u	Report only the undefined symbols.
−v	Sort the external symbols by value.
−V	Print **nm**'s version number on standard error.
−x	Report values in hexadecimal.

→

nm ←	*Key letters* **A** Absolute symbol. **C** Common symbol. **D** Data object symbol. **F** File symbol. **N** Symbol with no type. **S** Section symbol. **T** Text symbol. **U** Undefined symbol.
nohup	**nohup** *command* [*arguments*] **&** Continue to execute the named *command* and optional command *arguments* after you log out (make command immune to hangups; i.e., **no h**ang**up**). In the C shell, **nohup** is built in. In the Bourne shell, **nohup** allows output redirection; output goes to **nohup.out** by default.
notify	**notify** [*options*] Inform user when new mail arrives. With no options, indicate whether automatic notification is enabled or disabled. *Options* **−m** *file* Save mail messages to *file* (default is **$HOME/.mailfile**). Applies only when automatic notification is enabled (**−y** option). **−n** Disable mail notification. **−n** is used alone. **−y** Enable mail notification.
nroff	**/usr/ucb/nroff** [*options*] [*files*] Format documents to line printer or to screen. See Section 12.
od	**od** [*options*] [*file*] [[+] *offset*[**.** | **b**]] Octal dump; produce a dump (normally octal) of the named *file*. *file* is displayed from its beginning, unless you specify an *offset* (normally in octal bytes). In the descriptions below, a "word" is a 16-bit unit. *Options* **−b** Display bytes as octal. **−c** Display bytes as ASCII. **−d** Display words as unsigned decimal. **−D** Display 32-bit words as unsigned decimal. **−f** Display 32-bit words as floating point.

−F	Display 64-bit words as extended precision.
−o	Display words as unsigned octal (the default).
−O	Display 32-bit words as unsigned octal.
−s	Display words as signed decimal.
−S	Display 32-bit words as signed decimal.
−v	Verbose; show all data.
−x	Display words as hexadecimal.
−X	Display 32-bit words as hexadecimal.
+	Required before *offset* if *file* isn't specified.

Modifiers for offset

.	*offset* value is decimal.
b	*offset* value is 512-byte blocks.

openwin [*options*]

Solaris 2.0 only. **openwin** is the shell script that sets up OpenWindows, the windowing environment based on the OPEN LOOK graphical user interface. OpenWindows provides application programs that let you edit, print, or delete files, send and receive mail, make icons and screen dumps, schedule activities on a calendar, etc. Online help is included. To access OpenWindows, your environment variable OPENWINHOME must be set to the directory in which the OpenWindows software resides. The description below presents a "roadmap" of OpenWindows' Workspace menu, including a summary of the available programs and utilities.

Options

openwin accepts all options that are valid for **xnews**, along with some additional options specific to **openwin**. Most of these options are used to initialize the display format of the OpenWindows environment. The display format is usually initialized automatically, so command-line options are rarely used (see the Save Workspace utility). For more information, see the online reference pages for **openwin** or **xnews**.

Workspace menu

Programs
Submenu from which to select the DeskSet applications. Individual programs are summarized below.

Utilities
Submenu from which to select OpenWindows utilities. Individual utilities are summarized below.

Properties
Window from which you can set background colors, icon locations, scrollbar placement, and other properties of the Workspace environment.

→

Help
Window that provides menu-based help on the features of OpenWindows.

Desktop Intro
Window that provides novice users with a basic introduction (e.g., how to use the mouse, how to use the help facility).

Exit
Menu item that quits OpenWindows.

Programs submenu
This submenu provides access to the DeskSet applications, of which the most essential are File Manager, Text Editor, Mail Tool, and Command Tool. The applications are summarized below, in the order they appear in the Programs submenu.

Command Tool
Open a terminal window for entering UNIX commands at a system prompt. Because the window is scrollable by default, you can review (and even edit) previous commands.

Text Editor
Open a text editor on new or existing files. Editor functions include searching, replacing, moving, and copying.

File Manager
Manipulate files and directories. Tasks include creating, moving, deleting, and printing. Files can be listed using different sorting methods, as icons, etc.

Mail Tool
Read or send electronic mail.

Calendar Manager
A month-at-a-glance window that lets you set appointments and receive automatic reminders.

Clock
Display a clock. You can customize the clock display by selecting various features from the Properties window. (To bring up this window, move the pointer inside the Clock, then press the MENU button on the mouse.)

Calculator
Display a calculator that can perform mathematical operations. Enter input using either mouse-button presses or keyboard typing. Important Calculator buttons include:

Keys	Label the buttons of the calculator keypad with their keyboard equivalents.
Base	Display values in octal, hex, binary, or decimal (the default).

Mode	Pop up a window containing buttons for special functions. Modes include Financial, Logical, or Scientific.
Display	Display values in notations such as fixed-point or scientific.

Print Tool

Send print requests, select a printer, check the queue, or stop a print request.

Audio Tool

Record and play audio files.

Tape Tool

Copy files to a tape cartridge.

Binder

Change the default association (that is, binding) between icons and DeskSet applications (e.g., you can change an icon's color). Also useful for binding a new icon to its associated application. See "Icon Editor" below.

Snapshot

Create raster-image files or view existing ones. For example, you can "take a picture" of all or part of your screen, then store it as a raster-image file (for later viewing or printing).

Icon Editor

Create or modify icon images or pointers. Useful for graphically labeling file types that are displayed by the File Manager application.

Performance Meter

Display graphs (or dials) to monitor various aspects of system and network performance.

Shell Tool

Same as Command Tool except that scrolling is initially disabled by default.

Demos

A list of OpenWindows demonstration programs you can run. In order for the system to locate these programs, you must specify the **–includedemo** option when running **openwin**.

Utilities submenu

This submenu provides access to OpenWindows utilities, of which the most essential are Save Workspace and Refresh. The utilities are summarized below, in the order they appear in the Utilities submenu.

Refresh

Redraw the Workspace. Useful if applications leave distracting visual remnants after being closed.

$\rightarrow$

Reset Input

Make keyboard input readable again. (Input is sometimes garbled by running an incompatible application at the same time as OpenWindows.)

Function Keys

(Currently unsupported.) Display the function keys and show the operation that they would perform while using the current application. This utility will allow support for international keyboards.

Window Controls

Manipulate the active application window (open, close, resize, or move in front of or behind another window). This utility duplicates the operations available to most applications from their window menu (which is pulled down from the application header).

Save Workspace

Store the appearance of your Workspace. Once you have customized the size and position of your applications, use Save Workspace to store this appearance. Now, each time you start up OpenWindows, your applications will automatically appear the way you previously saved them.

Lock Screen

Cover the Workspace with a moving pattern. Useful when you are away from your screen. Lock Screen hides your applications (providing added security) and prevents phosphor burnout of the screen. To unlock the screen, press any key or mouse button, then type your password.

Console

Provide a terminal window in which to view any error messages or system messages you receive.

Online help

There are four types of online help: the Desktop tutorial, the Help handbooks, Spot Help, and manpages. The Desktop tutorial and Help handbooks are accessed from the Workspace menu as described above.

Spot Help is available by moving the pointer to a specific place on the Workspace (e.g., a menu item). If you now press the keyboard's Help key, an information window pops up to describe the spot where the pointer is.

Manpages are reference pages that you call up by typing the **man** command at a UNIX prompt. To view manpages, you don't need to be running OpenWindows, but you do need to define the MANPATH variable to include the directory where the OpenWindows manpages are located. By default, this directory is:

```
$OPENWIN/share/man
```

So, for example, you could define a few search directories for **man** by placing the following line in your **.cshrc** file:

```
setenv MANPATH /usr/man:$OPENWIN/share/man
```

After sourcing **.cshrc**, you could browse OpenWindows topics by typing either of these commands:

```
man -k openwin
man file
```

Here's a list of the most useful manpage *files* you might want to find out about:

audiotool	install_cmgr	snapshot
binder	mailtool	tapetool
calctool	olwm	textedit
clock	pageview	xfontsel
cm	perfmeter	xlsfonts
cmdtool	printtool	xmodmap
filemgr	reservecolors	xrdb
iconedit	shelltool	xset

---

pack [*options*] *files*

Compact each *file* and place the result in *file*.**z**. The original file is replaced. To restore packed *files* to their original form, see **pcat** and **unpack**.

Options

—   Print number of times each byte is used, relative frequency, and byte code.

−**f**   Force the **pack** even when disk space isn't saved.

---

page [*options*] [*files*]

Same as **more**.

---

passwd [*options*] [*user*]

Create or change a password associated with a *user* name. Only the owner or a privileged user may change a password. Owners need not specify their *user* name.

Option

−**s**   Display password information:
1. *user* name.
2. Password status (**NP** for no password, **PS** for password, **LK** for locked).

$\rightarrow$

---

passwd
←

3. The last time the password was changed (in *mm/dd/yy* format).
4. Number of days that must pass before *user* can rechange the password.
5. Number of days before the password expires.
6. Number of days prior to expiration that *user* is warned of impending expiration.

Options (privileged users only)

−a   Use with **−s** to display password information for all users. *user* should not be supplied.

−d   Delete password; *user* is no longer prompted for one.

−f   Force expiration of *user*'s password; *user* must change password at next login.

−l   Lock *user*'s password; mutually exclusive with **−d**.

−n   Set item 4 of *user*'s password information. Usually used with **−x**.

−w   Set item 6 for *user*.

−x   Set item 5 for *user*. Use −1 to disable password aging, 0 to force expiration like **−f**.

---

paste

paste [*options*] *files*

Merge corresponding lines of one or more *files* into vertical columns, separated by a tab. See also **cut**, **join**, **newform**, and **pr**.

Options

−   Replace a filename with the standard input.

−d'*char***'**   Separate columns with *char* instead of a tab. *char* can be any regular character or the following escape sequences:

    \n   Newline
    \t   Tab
    ****   Backslash
    \0   Empty string

    Note: You can separate columns with different characters by supplying more than one *char*.

−s   Merge subsequent lines from one file.

Examples

Create a three-column *file* from files *x*, *y*, and *z*:

```
paste x y z > file
```

List users in two columns:

```
who | paste - -
```

Merge each pair of lines into one line: **paste**

```
paste -s -d"\t\n" list
```

pcat *files*   **pcat**

Display (as with **cat**) one or more packed *files*. See also **pack** and
unpack.

pg [*options*] [*files*]   **pg**

Display the named *files* on a terminal, one page at a time. After
each screen is displayed, you are prompted to display the next
page by pressing the RETURN key. Press **h** for help with additional
commands; press **q** to quit. See also **more**.

Options

−c	Clear screen (same as **−c** of **more**).
−e	Do not pause between files.
−f	Do not split long lines.
−n	Issue a **pg** command without waiting for a carriage return (**more** works this way).
−p*str*	Use string *str* for the command prompt. The special variable **%d** displays the page number.
−r	Restricted mode; shell escapes aren't allowed.
−s	Display messages in standout mode (reverse video).
−n	Use *n* lines for each window (default is a full screen).
+*num*	Begin displaying at line number *num*.
+/*pat*	Begin displaying at first line containing pattern *pat*.

Example

```
pg -p 'Page %d :' file
```

/usr/ucb/pic [*options*] [*files*]   **pic**

Preprocessor for nroff/troff line pictures. See Section 16.

pr [*options*] [*files*]   **pr**

Format one or more *files* according to *options* to standard output.
Each page includes a heading that consists of the page number,
filename, date, and time.

Options

−a	Multi-column format; list items in rows going across.
−d	Double-spaced format.
−e*cn*	Set input tabs to every *n*th position (default is 8), and use *c* as field delimiter (default is a tab).

→

−f	Separate pages using formfeed character (^L) instead of a series of blank lines.
−F	Fold input lines (avoids truncation by **−a** or **−m**).
−h_str_	Replace default header with string _str_.
−ic_n_	For output, replace white space with field delimiter _c_ (default is a tab) every _n_th position (default is 8).
−l_n_	Set page length to _n_ (default is 66).
−m	Merge files, printing one in each column (can't be used with −_n_ and −**a**). Text is chopped to fit. See also **paste**.
−nc_n_	Number lines with numbers _n_ digits in length (default is 5), followed by field separator _c_ (default is a tab). See also **nl**.
−o_n_	Offset each line _n_ spaces (default is 0).
−p	Pause before each page.
−r	Suppress messages for files that can't be found.
−s_c_	Separate columns with _c_ (default is a tab).
−t	Omit the page header and trailing blank lines.
−w_n_	Set line width to _n_ (default is 72).
+_num_	Begin printing at page _num_ (default is 1).
−_n_	Produce output having _n_ columns (default is 1); tabs are expanded as with −**i**.

Examples

Print a side-by-side list, omitting heading and extra lines:

```
pr -m -t list.1 list.2 list.3
```

Alphabetize a list of states; number the lines in five columns:

```
sort states_50 | pr -n -5
```

---

printenv

/usr/ucb/printenv [_variable_]

Print values of all environment variables or, optionally, only the specified _variable_. The SVR4 alternative **env** doesn't let you view just one variable, but it lets you redefine them.

---

printf

printf _formats_ [_strings_]

Print _strings_ using the specified _formats_. _formats_ can be ordinary text characters, C-language escape characters, or more commonly, a set of conversion _arguments_ listed below.

Arguments

%s	Print the next _string_.
%_n_**$s**	Print the _n_th _string_.

%[−]*m*[.*n*]**s**   Print the next *string*, using a field that is *m* characters wide. Optionally limit the field to print
only the first *n* characters of *string*. Strings are
right-adjusted unless the left-adjustment flag − is
specified.

Examples

```
printf '%s %s\n' "My files are in" $HOME
printf '%-25.15s %s\n' "My files are in" $HOME
```

---

prof [*options*] [*object_file*]

Display the profile data for an object file. The file's symbol table is
compared with profile file **mon.out** (previously created by the
monitor function). Choose only one of the sort options −**a**, −**c**,
−**n**, or −**t** . See also **lprof** and **gprof**.

Options

−**a**	List output by symbol address.
−**c**	List output by decreasing number of calls.
−**g**	Include non-global (static) function symbols.
−**h**	Suppress the report heading.
−**l**	Exclude non-global function symbols (the default).
−**m***pf*	Use *pf* as the input profile file instead of **mon.out**.
−**n**	List by symbol name.
−**o**	Show addresses in octal (invalid with −**x**).
−**s**	Print a summary on standard error.
−**t**	List by decreasing total time percentage (the default).
−**V**	Print version information on standard error.
−**x**	Show addresses in hexadecimal (invalid with −**o**).
−**z**	Include zero usage calls.

---

prs [*options*] *files*

An SCCS command. See Section 17.

---

ps [*options*]

Report on active processes. In options, *list* arguments should
either be separated by commas or put in double quotes. In comparing the amount of output produced, note that −**e** > −**d** > −**a** and
−**l** > −**f**. In the BSD version, options work much differently; you
can also display data for a single process.

Options

−**a**	List all processes except group leaders and processes not associated with a terminal.

→

−c	List scheduler data set by **priocntl**.
−d	List all processes except session leaders.
−e	List all processes.
−f	Produce a full listing.
−g_list_	List data only for specified _list_ of group leader ID numbers (i.e., processes with same ID and group ID).
−j	Print the process group ID and session ID.
−l	Produce a long listing.
−n_list_	Use the alternate _list_ of names (default is **/unix**); obsolete as of Release 4.
−p_list_	List data only for process IDs in _list_.
−s_list_	List data only for session leader IDs in _list_.
−t_list_	List data only for terminals in _list_ (e.g., **tty1**).
−u_list_	List data only for usernames in _list_.

ptx

ptx [_options_] [_infile_ [_outfile_]]

Solaris 2.0 only. Generate a permuted index from _infile_ and send output to _outfile_. (Standard input and output are the defaults.) To print the index, format the output file using the **−mptx** option to nroff or troff.

Options

−b _file_	In addition to using tab, space, and newline, use the characters in _file_ as word separators.
−f	Fold uppercase and lowercase; i.e., ignore case when sorting keywords.
−g _n_	Set column gaps in output to _n_ characters.
−i _file_	Ignore keywords listed in _file_. Default _file_ is **/usr/lib/eign**.
−o _file_	Use only the words in _file_ as keywords (inverse of **−i**).
−r	Use the first field of _infile_ as a reference ID. This field does not get permuted but appears as the last field of the output.
−t	Prepare output for phototypesetting (default line length is 100 characters).
−w _n_	Produce output lines _n_ characters wide (default is 72).

Example

Given a three-line input file **ptx.in**:

```
ar(1) ar: archive and library maintainer
at(1) at: execute commands at a later time
awk(1) awk: pattern scanning language
```

A permuted index could be generated as follows:

```
ptx -f -i ignore -w 80 -r ptx.in > ptx.out
troff -mptx options ptx.out | spooler
```

In this case, **ptx** merges uppercase and lowercase (**–f**) ignores a list of keywords (**–i**), uses 80-character output lines (**–w**), and appends the first word (the command name) as a section reference (**–r**).

pwd

Print the full pathname of the current directory. Note: The built-in versions **pwd** (Bourne and Korn shells) and **dirs** (C shell) are faster, so you might want to define the following C-shell alias:

```
alias pwd dirs -1
```

rcp [options] sources target

Copy files between machines. Both *sources* and *target* are filename specifications of the form *host:pathname*, where *host:* can be omitted for a file on the local machine. If no *pathname* is included in *target*, source files are placed in your home directory. If you have a different username on the remote host, specify the form *username@hostname:file*

Options

–p   Preserve in copies the modification times, access times, and modes of the source files.

–r   If *target* and *sources* are both directories, copy each subtree rooted at *source*.

Examples

Copy the local files **junk** and **test** to your home directory on machine **hermes**:

```
rcp junk test hermes:
```

Copy the local **bin** directory and all subdirectories to the **/usr/tools** directory on machine **diana**:

```
rcp -r /bin diana:/usr/tools
```

Copy all files in your home directory on machine **hera**, and put them in local directory **/usr/daniel** with times and modes unchanged:

```
rcp -p "hera:*" /usr/daniel
```

Quote the first argument to prevent filename expansion from occurring on the local machine.

red	**red** [*options*] [*file*] Restricted version of ed. With **red**, only files in the current working directory can be edited. Shell commands using **!** are not allowed.
regcmp	**regcmp** [–] *files* Stands for "regular expression compile." Compile the regular expressions in one or more *files* and place output in *file*.**i** (or in *file*.**c** if – is specified). The output is C source code, while the input entries in *files* are of the form: `C variable    "regular expression"`
relogin	**relogin** [*option*] [*terminal*] Change the login entry to reflect the current window running under **layers**. This ensures that commands like **who** and **write** use the correct login information. **layers** calls **relogin** automatically, but you may sometimes want to use **relogin** to change the destination window for **write** messages. *terminal* is the filename of the terminal to change; e.g., **ttyp0**. *Option* **–s** Don't print error messages.
reset	**/usr/ucb/reset** [*options*] [*type*] Clear terminal settings. **reset** disables CBREAK mode, RAW mode, output delays, and parity checking. **reset** also restores undefined special characters and enables processing of newlines, tabs, and echoing. This command is useful when a program aborts in a way that leaves the terminal confused (e.g., keyboard input might not echo on the screen). To enter **reset** at the keyboard, you may need to use a linefeed instead of a carriage return. **reset** uses the same command-line arguments as **tset**.
rksh	**rksh** [*options*] [*arguments*] Restricted version of **ksh** (the Korn shell), used in secure environments. **rksh** prevents you from changing out of the directory or from redirecting output. See Section 4.
rlogin	**rlogin** [*options*] *host* Connect terminal on current local host system (i.e., login) to a remote *host* system. The **.rhosts** file in your home directory (on the remote host) lists the hostnames that you're allowed to connect to without giving a password.

−8   Allow 8-bit data to pass, instead of 7-bit data.

−e *c*   Use escape character *c* (default is ˜). You can type ˜ **.** to disconnect from remote host, though you'll exit more "cleanly" by logging out.

−l *user*   Log in to remote host as *user*, instead of using the name on the local host.

−L   Allow **rlogin** to run in litout mode.

---

rm [*options*] *files*   **rm**

Delete one or more *files.* To remove a file, you must have write permission in the directory that contains the file, but you need not have permission on the file itself. If you do not have write permission on the file, you will be prompted (**y** or **n**) to override.

Options

−f   Remove write-protected files without prompting.

−i   Prompt for **y** (remove the file) or **n** (do not remove the file).

−r   If *file* is a directory, remove the entire directory and all its contents, including subdirectories. Be forewarned: use of this option can be dangerous.

−−   Mark the end of options (**rm** still accepts −, the old form). Use this when you need to supply a filename beginning with −.

---

rmdel −**r***sid files*   **rmdel**

An SCCS command. See Section 17.

---

rmdir [*options*] *directories*   **rmdir**

Delete the named *directories* (the name itself, not the contents). *directories* are deleted from the parent directory and must be empty (if not, **rm −r** can be used instead). See also **mkdir**.

Options

−p   Remove *directories* and any intervening parent directories that become empty as a result; useful for removing subdirectory trees.

−s   Suppress standard error messages caused by **−p**.

---

rsh   **rsh**

Restricted version of **sh** (the Bourne shell) that is intended to be used where security is important. **rsh** prevents you from changing out of the directory or from redirecting output. See Section 4.

rsh	**rsh** [*options*] *host* [*command*]
	A BSD-derived command to invoke a remote shell. This command is usually found in **/usr/ucb** and should not be confused with **rsh**, the restricted shell.
	rsh connects to *host* and executes *command*. If *command* is not specified, **rsh** allows you to **rlogin** to *host*. If shell metacharacters need to be interpreted on the remote machine, enclose them in quotes. This command is sometimes called **remsh**.
	Options
	−l *user* Connect to *host* with a login name of *user*.
	−n Divert input to **/dev/null**. Sometimes useful when piping **rsh** to a command that reads standard input but that might terminate before **rsh**.
ruptime	**ruptime** [*options*]
	Show the status of local networked machines (similar to **uptime**).
	Options
	−a Include users even if they've been idle for more than one hour. Normally such users are not counted.
	−l Sort by load average.
	−r Reverse the sort order.
	−t Sort by uptime.
	−u Sort by number of users.
rwho	**rwho** [*option*]
	Report who is logged on for all machines on the local network (similar to **who**).
	Option
	−a List users even if they've been idle for more than one hour.
sact	**sact** *files*
	An SCCS command. See Section 17.
sccs	**/usr/ucb/sccs** [*options*] *command* [*SCCS_flags*] [*files*]
	A user-friendly interface to SCCS. See Section 17.
sccsdiff	**sccsdiff** **−r***sid1* **−r***sid2* [*options*] *files*
	An SCCS command. See Section 17.

script [*option*] [*file*]

script

Create a record of your login session, storing in *file* everything that displays on your screen. The default file is called **typescript**. **script** records non-printing characters as control characters and includes prompts. This command is useful for beginners or for saving output from a time-consuming command.

Option

–a	Append the **script** record to *file*.

UNIX Commands

sdb [*options*] [*objfile* [*corefile* [*dir_list*]]]

sdb

A C and FORTRAN symbolic debugging program used to look at "core" files resulting from aborted programs. *objfile* contains an executable program, and *corefile* contains the core image produced when *objfile* was executed. **a.out** is the default *objfile*. **core** is the default *corefile*. The *dir_list* argument specifies the source directory for the files compiled to create *objfile*. See Section 20 for more information on **sdb**.

Options

–e	Ignore symbolic data; treat addresses as file offsets.
–s *n*	Don't stop processes that receive signal number *n*. See the **signal** system call for values of *n*. **–s** may be used more than once.
–V	Print version information (exit if no *objfile* is given).
–w	Make *objfile* and *corefile* writable.
–W	Suppress warning messages about older files.

sdiff [*options*] *file1 file2*

sdiff

Produce a side-by-side comparison of *file1* with *file2*. Output is:

text text	Identical lines.
text <	Line exists only in *file1*.
> *text*	Line exists only in *file2*.
text | *text*	Lines are different.

Options

–l List only lines of *file1* that are identical.

–o *outfile* Send identical lines of *file1* and *file2* to *outfile*; print line differences and edit *outfile* by entering, when prompted, the following commands:

e	Edit an empty file.
e b	Edit both left and right columns.
e l	Edit left column.
e r	Edit right column.
l	Append left column to outfile.
q	Exit the editor.

→

sdiff	**r**	Append right column to outfile.
←	**s**	Silent mode; do not print identical lines.
	v	Turn off "silent mode."

−s   Do not print identical lines.

−w*n*   Set line length to *n* (default is usually 130).

Example

Show differences using 80 columns, and ignore identical lines:

```
sdiff -s -w80 list.1 list.2
```

---

sed

sed [*options*] [*files*]

Stream editor—edit one or more *files* without user interaction. See Section 10 for more information on **sed**.

Options

−e '*instruction*'
        Apply the editing *instruction* to the files.

−f *script*   Apply the set of instructions from the editing *script*.

−n   Suppress default output.

---

sh

sh [*options*] [*arguments*]

The standard command interpreter (or Bourne shell) that executes commands from a terminal or a file. See Section 4 for more information on the Bourne shell, including command-line options.

---

shl

shl

Control more than one shell (layer) from a single terminal. From the **shl** prompt level, you can issue the commands listed below (abbreviating them to any unique prefix if desired). The *name* text string should not exceed eight characters. See also **layers**.

block *name* [*name2* ...]
        Block the output for each layer *name* (same as **stty loblk**).

create [*name*]
        Create the layer *name* (no more than seven total).

delete *name* [*name2* ...]
        Delete the layer *name*.

help or **?**   Provide **shl** command syntax.

layers [−l] [*name* ...]
        Print information about layers. **−l** provides a **ps**-like display.

name   Make layer *name* be the current level.

quit Exit **shl** and kill all the layers.	**shl**

resume [*name*]

         Return to latest layer or to layer *name*.

toggle   Flip back to the previous layer.

unblock *name* [*name2* . . .]

         Do not block output for each layer *name* (same as **stty –loblk**).

/usr/sbin/shutdown [*options*]

Allow a privileged user to change system state. Default behavior is to terminate user processes, taking system down from multi-user state (state 2) to single-user state. That is, only the system console provides access. **shutdown** sends a warning message, waits 60 seconds, sends a final message, waits another 60 seconds, and finally prompts for confirmation. **shutdown** is the SVR4 alternative to **halt** or **reboot**.

Options

  –g*n*   Use a grace-period of *n* seconds instead of 60.

  –i*k*   Tell the **init** command to place system in state *k*.

     s   Single-user state (the default).
     0   Shutdown for safe power-off.
     1   Like **s**, but mount multi-user file systems.
     5   Stop system; go to firmware mode.
     6   Stop system and then reboot.

  –y   Suppress the default prompt for confirmation.

---

size [*options*] [*objfile* . . .]

Print the (decimal) number of bytes of each *objfile*. If *objfile* is not specified, **a.out** is used.

Options

  –f   Print sizes, names, and total size for allocatable sections.

  –F   Print sizes, permission flags, and total size for loadable segments.

  –n   Print sizes for nonallocatable sections or for nonloadable segments.

  –o   Print output in octal.

  –V   Report the **size** program version number.

  –x   Print output in hexadecimal.

---

sleep *seconds*

Wait a specified number of *seconds* before executing another command. Often used in shell scripts.

soelim

/usr/ucb/soelim [*files*]

A preprocessor that reads nroff/troff input *files*, resolving and then eliminating .so requests. That is, input lines such as

```
.so header
```

are replaced by the contents of the file **header**. Normally, .so requests are resolved by nroff or troff. Use **soelim** whenever you are preprocessing the input (e.g., passing it through tbl or sed) and the complete text is needed prior to formatting.

Example

Run a sed script on (all) input before formatting:

```
soelim file | sed -e 's/--/\\(em/' | nroff | lp
```

---

sort

sort [*options*] [*files*]

Sort the lines of the named *files*, typically in alphabetical order. See also **uniq, comm, join**.

Options

−b	Ignore leading spaces and tabs.
−c	Check whether *files* are already sorted, and if so, produce no output.
−d	Sort in dictionary order (ignore punctuation).
−f	"Fold"; ignore uppercase/lowercase differences.
−i	Ignore nonprinting characters (those outside ASCII range 040-176).
−m	Merge sorted input files.
−M	Compare first three characters as months.
−n	Sort in arithmetic order.
−o*file*	Put output in *file*.
−r	Reverse the order of the sort.
−t*c*	Separate fields with *c* (default is a tab).
−u	Identical lines in input file appear only one (*u*nique) time in output.
−y*kmem*	Adjust the amount of memory **sort** uses. If *kmem* is not specified, allocate the maximum memory.
−z*recsz*	Provide the maximum number of bytes for any one line in the file. This option prevents abnormal termination of **sort** in certain cases.
+*n* [**−***m*]	Skip *n* fields before sorting, and sort up to field position *m*. If *m* is missing, sort to end of line. Positions take the form *a*. *b*, which means character *b* of field *a*. If . *b* is missing, sort at the first character of the field.

Examples

List files by decreasing number of lines:

```
wc -l * | sort -r
```

Alphabetize a list of words, remove duplicates, and print the frequency of each word:

```
sort -fd wordlist | uniq -c
```

Sort the password file numerically by the third field (user ID):

```
sort +2n -t: /etc/passwd
```

---

spell [*options*] [*files*]

Compare the words of one or more named *files* with the system dictionary and report all misspelled words. System files for **spell** reside in **/usr/lib/spell**.

Options

- **−b**   Check for British spelling.
- **−i**   Ignore files included with the nroff or troff .so request (SVR3 only).
- **−l**   Follow *all* included files (files named in .so or .nx requests); default is to ignore files that begin with **/usr/lib**.
- **−v**   Include words that are derived from dictionary list but are not literal entries.
- **−x**   Show every possible word stem (on standard error).
- **+***wordlist*
  Use the sorted *wordlist* file as a local dictionary to add to the system dictionary; words in *wordlist* are not treated as misspelled.

Example

Run the first pass of **spell**:

```
spell file1 file2 > jargon
```

After editing the **jargon** file, use it as a list of special terms. The second pass of **spell** produces genuine misspellings:

```
spell +jargon file[12] > typos
```

---

split [*option*] [*infile*] [*outfile*]

Split *infile* into a specified number of line segments. *infile* remains unchanged, and the results are written to *outfile***aa**, *outfile***ab**, etc. (default is **xaa**, **xab**, etc.). If *infile* is − (or missing), standard input is read. See also **csplit**.

→

split
←
	Option
	    −*n* Split *infile* into *n* line segments (default is 1000).
	
	Examples
	Break *bigfile* into 1000-line segments:
	
	    `split bigfile`
	
	Join four files, then split them into ten-line files named **new.aa**, **new.ab**, etc. Note that without the –, **new.** would be treated as a nonexistent input file:
	
	    `cat list[1-4]
		split -10 - new.`

srchtxt	**srchtxt** [*options*] [*regexp*] A **grep**-like utility to search message files for text strings that match regular expression *regexp*. **srchtxt** is one of the message manipulation commands like **gettxt** and **mkmsgs**. If no *regexp* is used, **srchtxt** displays all message strings from the specified files. *Options* −**l** *locale* Search files that reside in the directory **/usr/lib/locale/***locale***/LC_MESSAGES**, where *locale* is the language in which the message strings have been written. The default *locale* is set by environment variable LC_MESSAGES or LANG. If neither is set, **srchtxt** searches directory **/usr/lib/locale/C/LC_MESSAGES**. −**m** *msgfiles* Search for strings in one or more comma-separated *msgfiles*. Specifying a pathname for *msgfiles* overrides the −**l** option. −**s** Don't print message numbers for strings.
strings	**strings** [*options*] *files* Search object or binary *files* for sequences of four or more printable characters that end with a newline or null. See also **od**. *Options* −**a** Search entire *file*, not just the initialized data portion of object files. Can also specify this option as −. −**o** Display the string's offset position before the string. −**n** *n* Minimum string length is *n* (default is 4). Can also specify this option as −*n*.
strip	**strip** [*options*] *files* Remove information from ELF object *files* or archive *files*, thereby reducing file sizes and freeing disk space. The following items can be removed:

1) Symbol table.
2) Debugging information.
3) Line number information.
4) Static symbol information.
5) External symbol information.
6) Block delimiters.
7) Relocation bits.

Options

−b   Don't strip items 4, 5, and 6.

−l   Strip only item 3 (line number information).

−r   Don't strip items 4, 5, and 7.

−V   Print the version number of **strip** on standard error.

−x   Strip only items 2 and 3.

stty [*options*] [*modes*]

Set terminal I/O options for the current device. Without options, **stty** reports the terminal settings, where a ^ indicates the CONTROL key and ^^ indicates a null value. Most modes can be switched using an optional − (shown in brackets). The corresponding description is also shown in brackets. As a privileged user, you can set or read settings from another device using the syntax:

```
stty [options] [modes] < device
```

Options

−a   Report all option settings.

−g   Report current settings.

Control modes

0   Hang up phone.

n   Set terminal baud rate to *n* (e.g., 2400).

[−]**clocal**   [Enable]disable modem control.

[−]**cread**   [Disable]enable the receiver.

cs*n*   Select character size (5-8).

[−]**cstopb**   [One]two stop bits per character.

[−]**hup**   [Do not]hang up connection on last close.

[−]**hupcl**   Same as previous.

ispeed *n*   Set terminal input baud rate to *n*.

[−]**loblk**   [Do not]block layer output.

ospeed *n*   Set terminal output baud rate to *n*.

[−]**parenb**   [Disable]enable parity generation and detection.

→

[–]**parext**	[Disable]enable extended parity generation and detection for mark and space parity.
[–]**parodd**	Use [even]odd parity.

Input modes

[–]**brkint**	[Do not]signal INTR on break.
[–]**icrnl**	[Do not]map CR to NL on input.
[–]**ignbrk**	[Do not]ignore break on input.
[–]**igncr**	[Do not]ignore CR on input.
[–]**ignpar**	[Do not]ignore parity errors.
[–]**imaxbel**	[Do not]echo BEL when input line is too long.
[–]**inlcr**	[Do not]map NL to CR on input.
[–]**inpck**	[Disable]enable input parity checking.
[–]**istrip**	[Do not]strip input characters to seven bits.
[–]**iuclc**	[Do not]map uppercase to lowercase on input.
[–]**ixany**	Allow [XON]any character to restart output.
[–]**ixoff**	[Do not]send START/STOP characters when queue is nearly empty/full.
[–]**ixon**	[Disable]enable START/STOP output control.
[–]**parmrk**	[Do not]mark parity errors.

Output modes

bs_n_	Select style of delay for backspaces (0 or 1).
cr_n_	Select style of delay for carriage returns (0-3).
ff_n_	Select style of delay for formfeeds (0 or 1).
nl_n_	Select style of delay for linefeeds (0 or 1).
[–]**ocrnl**	[Do not]map CR to NL on output.
[–]**ofdel**	Set fill character to [NULL]DEL.
[–]**ofill**	Delay output with [timing]fill characters.
[–]**olcuc**	[Do not]map lowercase to uppercase on output.
[–]**onlcr**	[Do not]map NL to CR-NL on output.
[–]**onlret**	[Do not]perform CR after NL.
[–]**onocr**	[Do not]output CRs at column zero.
[–]**opost**	[Do not]postprocess output; ignore all other output modes.
tab_n_	Select style of delay for horizontal tabs (0-3).
vt_n_	Select style of delay for vertical tabs (0 or 1).

Local modes

[–]**echo**	[Do not]echo every character typed.
[–]**echoctl**	[Do not]echo control characters as ^*char*, delete as ^?.
[–]**echoe**	[Do not]echo ERASE character as BS-space-BS string.
[–]**echok**	[Do not]echo NL after KILL character.

[–]**echoke**	[Do not]BS-SP-BS erase entire line on line kill.
[–]**echonl**	[Do not]echo NL.
[–]**echoprt**	[Do not]echo erase character as character is "erased."
[–]**flusho**	Output is [not] being flushed.
[–]**icanon**	[Disable]enable canonical input (ERASE and KILL processing).
[–]**iexten**	[Disable]enable extended functions for input data.
[–]**isig**	[Disable]enable checking of characters against INTR, QUIT, and SWITCH.
[–]**noflsh**	[Enable]disable flush after INTR, QUIT, or SWITCH.
[–]**pendin**	[Do not]retype pending input at next read or input character.
[–]**stappl**	[Line]application mode on a synchronous line.
[–]**stflush**	[Disable]enable flush on synchronous line.
[–]**stwrap**	[Enable]disable truncation on synchronous line.
[–]**tostop**	[Do not]send SIGTTOU when background processes write to the terminal.
[–]**xcase**	[Do not]change case on local output.

Control assignments

ctrl–char c	Set control character to *c*. *ctrl-char* is: **ctab, discard, dsusp, eof, eol, eol2, erase, intr, kill, lnext, quit, reprint, start, stop, susp, swtch, werase**.
min, time *n*	Set min or time to *n*.
line *i*	Set line discipline to *i* (1-126).

Combination modes

async	Set normal asynchronous communications.
cooked	Same as **–raw**.
[–]**evenp**	Same as [–]**parenb** and **cs[8]7**.
ek	Reset ERASE and KILL characters to # and @.
[–]**lcase**	[Un]set **xcase, iuclc**, and **olcuc**.
[–]**LCASE**	Same as [–]**lcase**.
[–]**markp**	[Disable]enable **parenb, parodd**, and **parext** and set **cs[8]7**.
[–]**nl**	[Un]set **icrnl** and **onlcr**. **–nl** also unsets **inlcr, igncr, ocrnl**, and **onlret**.
[–]**oddp**	Same as [–]**parenb**, [–]**parodd**, and **cs7[8]**.
[–]**parity**	Same as [–]**parenb** and **cs[8]7**.
[–]**raw**	[Disable]enable raw input and output (no ERASE, KILL, INTR, QUIT, EOT, SWITCH, or output post-processing).

→

sane	Reset all modes to reasonable values.	
[−]**spacep**	[Disable]enable **parenb** and **parext** and set **cs[8]**7.	
[−]**tabs**	[Expand to spaces]preserve output tabs.	
term	Set all modes suitable for terminal type *term* (**tty33**, **tty37**, **vt05**, **tn300**, **ti700**, or **tek**).	

Hardware flow control modes

[−]**rtsxoff**	[Disable]enable RTS on input.
[−]**ctsxon**	[Disable]enable CTS on output.
[−]**dtrxoff**	[Disable]enable DTR on input.
[−]**cdxon**	[Disable]enable CD on output.
[−]**isxoff**	[Disable]enable isochronous on input.

Clock modes

[**x**	**r**]**cibrg**	Get the transmit I receive clock from internal baud rate generator.
[**x**	**r**]**ctset**	Get the transmit I receive clock from transmitter timing-lead, circuit 114, pin 15.
[**x**	**r**]**crset**	Get the transmit I receive clock from receiver timing-lead, circuit 115, pin 17.

For modes beginning with **t**, *pin* is transmitter timing-lead, circuit 113, pin 24. For modes beginning with **r**, *pin* is receiver timing-lead, circuit 128, no pin.

[**t**	**r**]**setcoff**	No transmitter I receiver timing clock.
[**t**	**r**]**setcrbrg**	Send receive baud rate generator to *pin*.
[**t**	**r**]**setctbrg**	Send transmit baud rate generator to *pin*.
[**t**	**r**]**setctset**	Send transmitter timing to *pin*.
[**t**	**r**]**setcrset**	Send receiver timing to *pin*.

Window size

columns *n*	Set size to *n* columns.
rows *n*	Set size to *n* rows.
xpixels *n*	Set size to *n* pixels across.
ypixels *n*	Set size to *n* pixels up and down.

su

su [*option*] [*user*] [*shell_args*]

Create a shell with the effective user ID of another *user* (that is, login as *user*). If no *user* is specified, create a shell for a privileged user (that is, become a superuser). Enter *EOF* to terminate. You can run the shell with particular options by passing them as *shell_args* (e.g., if the shell runs **sh**, you can specify −**c** *command* to execute *command* via **sh**, or −**r** to create a restricted shell).

–   Go through the entire login sequence (i.e., change to *user*'s environment).

---

sum [*option*] *file*   **sum**

Calculate and print a checksum and the number of (512-byte) blocks for *file*. Useful for verifying data transmission.

Option

–r   Use an alternate checksum algorithm; this produces the same results as the BSD version of **sum**.

---

tabs [*tabspec*] [*options*]   **tabs**

Set terminal tab stops according to *tabspec*. The default *tabspec*, –8, gives the standard UNIX tab settings. Specify *tabspec* as a predefined set of tab stops for particular languages, for example: **a** (IBM assembler), **c** (COBOL), **f** (FORTRAN), **p** (PL/1), **s** (SNO-BOL), and **u** (UNIVAC). *tabspec* can also be a repeated number, arbitrary numbers, or called from a file.

Tabspec

–*n*   Repeat tab every *n* columns (e.g., 1+*n*, 1+2**n*, etc.).

n1,n2,...

        Arbitrary ascending values. If *n* is preceded by +, it is added (i.e., tab is relative to previous position).

–a   1, 10, 16, 36, 72.

–a2   1, 10, 16, 40, 72.

–c   1, 8, 12, 16, 20, 55.

–c2   1, 6, 10, 14, 49.

–c3   1, 6, 10, 14, 18, 22, 26, 30, 34, 38, 42, 46, 50, 54, 58, 62, 67.

–f   1, 7, 11, 15, 19, 23.

–p   1, 5, 9, 13, 17, 21, 25, 29, 33, 37, 41, 45, 49, 53, 57, 61.

–s   1, 10, 55.

–u   1, 12, 20, 44.

––*file* Read first line of *file* for tabs.

Options

+m*n*   Set left margin to *n* (default is 10).

–T*type* Set terminal *type* (default is TERM).

---

tail [*options*] [*file*]   **tail**

Print the last ten lines of the named *file*. Use only one of **–f** or **–r**.

→

---

tail

←

Options

−f   Don't quit at the end of file; "follow" file as it grows. End with a BREAK (CTRL-C).

−r   Copy lines in reverse order.

−n[k]   Begin printing at nth item from end of file. k specifies the item to count: **l** (lines, the default), **b** (blocks), or **c** (characters).

−k   Same as previous, but use the default count of 10.

+n[k]   Like **−n**, but start at nth item from beginning of file.

+k   Like **−k**, but count from beginning of file.

Examples

Show the last 20 lines containing instances of .Ah:

```
grep '.Ah' file | tail -20
```

Continually track the latest **uucp** activity:

```
tail -f /usr/spool/uucp/LOGFILE
```

Show the last ten characters of variable **name**:

```
echo "$name" | tail -c
```

Reverse all lines in **list**:

```
tail -r list
```

---

talk

talk *user* [**@***hostname*] [*tty*]

Exchange typed communication with another *user* who is on the local machine or on machine *hostname*. **talk** might be useful when you're logged in via modem and need something quickly, making it inconvenient to telephone or send e-mail. **talk** splits your screen into two windows. When connection is established, you type in the top half while *user*'s typing appears in the bottom half. Type CTRL-L to redraw the screen and CTRL-D (or interrupt) to exit. If *user* is logged in more than once, use *tty* to specify the terminal line.

---

tar

tar [*options*] [*files*]

Copy *files* to or restore *files* from tape. If any *files* are directories, **tar** acts on the entire subtree. Options need not be preceded by −. Note that options are supplied as one group, with any arguments placed afterward in corresponding order.

Function options (choose one)

c   Create a new tape.

r   Append *files* to tape.

t	Print the names of *files* if they are stored on the tape (if *files* not specified, print names of all files).
u	Add files if not on tape or if modified.
x	Extract *files* from tape (if *files* not specified, extract all files).

Options

b *n*	Use blocking factor *n* (default is 1; maximum is 20).
f *arch*	Store files in or extract files from archive *arch*; *arch* is usually a device name (default is **/dev/mt0**). If *arch* is –, standard input or output is used as appropriate (e.g., when piping a **tar** archive to a remote host).
l	Print error messages about links it can't find.
L	Follow symbolic links.
m	Do not restore file modification times; update them to the time of extraction.
o	Change ownership of extracted files to that of user running program.
v	Print function letter (*x* for extraction or *a* for archive) and name of files.
w	Wait for user confirmation (**y**).
n[*c*]	Select tape drive *n* and use speed *c*. *n* is 0-7 (default is 0); *c* is **l** (low) **h** (high) **m** (medium, the default). Used to modify *arch*.

Examples

Create an archive of **/bin** and **/usr/bin** (**c**), show the command working (**v**), and store on the tape in **/dev/rmt0**:

```
tar cvf /dev/rmt0 /bin /usr/bin
```

List the tape's contents in a format like **ls –l**:

```
tar tvf /dev/rmt0
```

Extract the **/bin** directory:

```
tar xvf /dev/rmt0 /bin
```

Create an archive of the current directory, and store it in a file **backup.tar** on the system.

```
tar cvf - `find . -print` > backup.tar
```

(The – tells **tar** to store the directory on standard output, which is then redirected.)

/usr/ucb/tbl [*options*] [*files*]   **tbl**

Preprocessor for nroff/troff tables. See Section 16.

tee	**tee** [*options*] [*files*] Duplicate the standard input; send one copy to standard output and another copy to *files*. ***Options*** **−a** Append output to *files*. **−i** Ignore all interrupts. ***Examples*** Display a **who** listing on the screen, and store it in two files: `who	tee userlist ttylist`  Display misspelled words, and add them to existing **typos**:     `spell ch02	tee -a typos`
telnet	**telnet** [*host* [*port*]] Communicate with another *host* using the TELNET protocol. *host* may be either a name or an Internet address (dot format). **telnet** has a command mode (indicated by the **telnet>** prompt) and an input mode (usually a login session on the *host* system). If no *host* is given, **telnet** defaults to command mode. You can also enter command mode from input mode by typing the escape character CTRL-]. In command mode, type **?** or **help** to list the available commands.
test	**test** *expression* or **[** *expression* **]** Evaluate an *expression* and, if its value is true, return a zero exit status; otherwise, return a nonzero exit status. In shell scripts, you can use the alternate form **[** *expression* **]**. This command is generally used with conditional constructs in shell programs. See Section 4 for more information on **test**.
time	**time** *command* [*arguments*] Execute a *command* with optional *arguments* and print the total elapsed time, execution time, process execution time, and system time of the process (all in seconds).
timex	**timex** [*options*] *command* [*arguments*] Execute a *command* with optional *arguments* and print information specified by the **time** command. Report process data with various options.

Options

−o   Show total number of blocks and characters used.

−p *suboptions*

    Show process accounting data with possible *suboptions*.

−s   Show total system activity (similar to output from the **sar** command).

Suboptions for **−p**

−f   Include fork/exit flag and system exit status.

−h   Show "hog" factor (fraction of CPU time used) instead of mean memory size.

−k   Show total kcore-minutes instead of memory size.

−m   Show mean core size (this is the default behavior).

−r   Show CPU use computation.

−t   Show user and system CPU times.

---

touch [*options*] [*date*] *files* touch

For one or more *files*, update the access time and modification time (and dates) to the current time and date, or update to the optional *date*. *date* is a date and time in the format *mmddhhmm*[*yy*]. **touch** is useful in forcing other commands to handle files a certain way; e.g., the operation of **make**, and sometimes **find**, relies on a file's access and modification time.

Options

−a   Update only the access time.

−c   Do not create nonexistent files.

−m   Update only the modification time.

---

tput [*options*] *capname* [*arguments*] tput

Print the value of the terminal capability *capname* (and its associated numeric or string *arguments*) from the **terminfo** database. *capname* is a **terminfo** capability such as **clear** or **col**. (See the Nutshell Handbook, *termcap & terminfo*.) The last four options are mutually exclusive and are not used when specifying a *capname*. Exit statuses are: 0 when a Boolean *capname* is set to true or when a string *capname* is defined; 1 when a Boolean is false or when a string is undefined; 2 for usage errors; 3 for unknown terminal *type*; 4 for unknown *capname*.

Options

−T*type*   Print the capabilities of terminal *type* (default is the terminal in use).

−S   Read *capname* from standard input (this allows **tput** to evaluate more than one *capname*).

→

tput ←	**init** Print initialization strings and expand tabs. **reset** Print reset strings if present; act like **init** if not. **longname** Print the terminal's long name.

Examples

Show the number of columns for the **xterm** window:

```
tput -Txterm cols
```

Define shell variable **restart** to reset terminal characteristics:

```
restart=`tput reset`
```

---

tr

tr [*options*] [*string1* [*string2*]]

Copy standard input to standard output, performing substitution of characters from *string1* to *string2* or deletion of characters in *string1*.

Options

−c   Complement characters in *string1* with ASCII 001-377.

−d   Delete characters in *string1* from output.

−s   Squeeze out repeated output characters in *string2*.

Examples

Change uppercase to lowercase in a file:

```
cat file | tr '[A-Z]' '[a-z]'
```

Turn spaces into newlines (ASCII code 012):

```
tr ' ' '\012' < file
```

Strip blank lines from **file** and save in **new.file** (or use \011 to change successive tabs into one tab):

```
cat file | tr -s "" "\012" > new.file
```

Delete colons from **file**; save result in **new.file**:

```
tr -d : < file > new.file
```

---

troff

/usr/ucb/troff [*options*] [*files*]

Document formatter for laser printer or typesetter. See Section 12.

---

true

true

A null command that returns a successful (zero) exit status. Normally used in Bourne shell scripts. See also **false**.

---

truss

truss [*options*] *arguments*

Trace system calls, signals, and machine faults while executing *arguments*. *arguments* is either a UNIX command or, if **−p** is specified, a list of process IDs representing the processes to run. The options **−m**, **−t**, **−v**, **−x**, **−s**, **−r**, and **−w** accept a comma-separated list of arguments. A **!** reverses the sense of the list, telling **truss** to ignore those elements of the list during the trace. (In the C shell, use a backslash before **!**.) The optional **!** and corresponding description are shown in brackets.

Options

−a   Display parameters passed by each **exec** call.

−c   Count the traced items rather than listing them.

−e   Display values of environment variables passed by each **exec** call.

−f   Follow child processes. Useful for tracing shell scripts.

−i   List sleeping system calls only once, upon completion.

−m[**!**]*faults*
Trace [exclude from trace] the list of machine *faults*. *faults* are names or numbers, as listed in **<sys/fault.h>** (default is **−mall −m!fltpage**).

−o *outfile*
Send trace output to *outfile*, not standard error.

−p   Trace one or more process IDs instead of a command.

−r[**!**]*file_descriptors*
Display [don't display] the I/O buffer of **read** system calls for *file_descriptors* (default is **−r!all**).

−s[**!**]*signals*
Trace [exclude from trace] the list of *signals*. *signals* are names or numbers, as listed in **<sys/signal.h>** (default is **−sall**).

−t[**!**]*system_calls*
Trace [exclude from trace] the list of *system_calls*. *system_calls* are names or numbers, as listed in Section 2, "System Calls," of the *UNIX Programmer's Reference Manual* (default is **−tall**).

−v[**!**]*system_calls*
Verbose mode. Same as **−t**, but list also the contents of any structures passed to *system_calls* (default is **−v!all**).

−w[**!**]*file_descriptors*
Display [don't display] the I/O buffer of **write** system calls for *file_descriptors* (default is **−w!all**).

−x[**!**]*system_calls*
Same as **−t**, but display the system call arguments as raw code (hexadecimal) (default is **−x!all**).

Examples

Trace system calls **open** and **close** for **lp** command:

```
truss -t open,close lp files > truss.out
```

→

truss ←	Trace the **make** command, including its child processes, and store the output in **make.trace**: `truss -f -o make.trace make` *target*
tset	**/usr/ucb/tset** [*options*] [*type*] Set terminal modes. Without arguments, the terminal is reinitialized according to the TERM environment variable. **tset** is typically used in startup scripts (**.profile** or **.login**). *type* is the terminal type; if preceded by a **?**, **tset** prompts the user to enter a different type, if needed. Press RETURN to use the default value, *type*. See also **reset**. *Options* — Print terminal name on standard output; useful for passing this value to TERM. **−e***c* Set erase character to *c*; default is ^H (backspace). **−i***c* Set interrupt character to *c* (default is ^C). **−I** Do not output terminal initialization setting. **−k** *c* Set line-kill character to *c* (default is ^U). **−m**[*port*[*baudrate*]**:***tty*] Declare terminal specifications. *port* is the port type (usually **dialup** or **plugboard**). *tty* is the terminal type; it can be preceded by **?** as above. *baudrate* checks the port speed and can be preceded by any of these characters: **>** Port must be greater than *baudrate*. **<** Port must be less than *baudrate*. **@** Port must transmit at *baudrate*. **!** Negate a subsequent **>**, **<**, or **@** character. **−n** Initialize new tty driver modes. Useless because of redundancy with **stty new**. **−Q** Do not print "Erase set to" and "Kill set to" messages. **−r** Report the terminal type. **−s** Return the values of TERM assignments to shell environment. This is a commonly done via **eval `tset −s`** (in the C shell, you would surround this with the commands **set noglob** and **unset noglob**). *Examples* Set TERM to **wy50**: `eval `tset -s wy50``  Prompt user for terminal type (default will be **vt100**):  `eval `tset -Qs -m '?vt100'``

Similar to above, but the baudrate must exceed 1200:

```
eval `tset -Qs -m '>1200:?xterm'`
```

Set terminal via modem; the **?$TERM** checks that the terminal type is set (C shell only):

```
eval `tset -s -m dialup:'?vt100' "?$TERM"`
```

---

tsort [*file*]

Perform a topological sort on *file*. Typically used to reorganize an archive library for more efficient handling by **ar** or **ld**. Not very useful.

Example

Find the ordering relationship of all object files, and sort them for access by **ld**:

```
lorder *.o | tsort
```

---

tty [*options*]

Print the device name of your terminal. This is useful for shell scripts and often for commands that need device information.

Options

-l   Print the synchronous line number.

-s   Return only the codes: 0 (a terminal), 1 (not a terminal), 2 (invalid options used).

---

umask [*value*]

Print the current value of the file creation mode mask, or set it to *value*, a three-digit octal code specifying the read-write-execute permissions to be turned off. This is the opposite of **chmod**. Usually used in **.login** or **.profile**. **umask** is available as a built-in command in the Bourne and C shells (see Sections 4 and 5).

umask Number	File Permission	Directory Permission
0	rw-	rwx
1	rw-	rw-
2	r--	r-x
3	r--	r--
4	-w-	-wx
5	-w-	-w-
6	---	--x
7	---	---

→

umask ←	*Examples*
	Turn off write permission for others:
	umask 002 *Produces file permission* -rw-rw-r--
	Turn off all permissions for group and others:
	umask 077 *Produces file permission* -rw-------
	Note that you can omit leading zeroes.

---

uname

uname [*options*]

Print the current UNIX system name.

Options

−a	Report all of the following information:
−m	The hardware name.
−n	The node name (the default).
−p	The host's processor type.
−r	The operating system release.
−s	The system name.
−v	The operating system version.

---

uncompress

uncompress [*option*] [*files*]

Restore the original file compressed by **compress**. The **.Z** extension is implied, so it can be omitted when specifying *files*.

Option

−c	Same as **zcat** (write to standard output without changing *files*).

---

unget

unget [*options*] *files*

An SCCS command. See Section 17.

---

uniq

uniq [*options*] [*file1* [*file2*]]

Remove duplicate adjacent lines from sorted *file1*, sending one copy of each line to *file2* (or to standard output). Often used as a filter. Specify only one of **−c**, **−d**, or **−u**. See also **comm** and **sort**.

Options

−c	Print each line once, counting instances of each.
−d	Print duplicate lines once, but no unique lines.
−u	Print only unique lines (no copy of duplicate entries is kept).

$-n$ Ignore first n fields of a line. Fields are separated by spaces or by tabs.

$+n$ Ignore first n characters of a field.

Examples

Send one copy of each line from **list** to output file **list.new**:

```
uniq list list.new
```

Show which names appear more than once:

```
sort names | uniq -d
```

Show which lines appear exactly three times:

```
sort names | uniq -c | grep "3 "
```

---

units

Interactively supply a formula to convert a number from one unit to another. The file **/usr/lib/units** gives a complete list of the units. Use *EOF* to exit.

---

unpack *files*

Expand one or more *files*, created with **pack**, to their original form. See **pcat** and **pack**.

/usr/ucb/uptime

Print the current time, amount of time logged in, number of users logged in, and the system load averages. This output is also produced by the first line of the **w** command.

/usr/ucb/users [*file*]

Display the currently logged-in users as a space-separated list. Same as **who −q**. Information is read from a system *file* (default is **/var/adm/utmp**).

---

uucp [*options*] [*source*!]*file* [*destination*!]*file*

Copy a file (or group of files) from the source to the destination. The *source* and *destination* can be remote systems. The destination file can be a directory.

Options

−c   Do not copy files to the spool directory (the default).

−C   Copy files to the spool directory for transfer.

−d   Make directories for the copy when they don't exist (the default).

$\rightarrow$

uucp	**–f**	Do not make directories when they don't exist.
←	**–g**x	Set grade (priority) of job. x is typically a single letter or digit, where **a** and **1** give the highest transfer priority. Use **uuglist** to show values for x.
	–j	Print the **uucp** job number.
	–m	When copy is complete, send mail to person who issued **uucp** command.
	–n_user_	When copy is complete, send mail to _user_.
	–r	Queue job, but don't start transfer program (**uucico**).
	–s_file_	Send transfer status to _file_ (a full pathname); overrides **–m**.
	–xn	Debug at level n (0-9); higher numbers give more output.

Example

This shell script sends a compressed file to system **orca**:

```
cat send_it
compress $1
uucp -C -n$2 -m $1.Z orca\!/usr/spool/uucppublic
uncompress $1
```

With **–C**, the transfer is made on a copy in the spool directory. (Normally, **uucp** gets the file from its original location, so you couldn't rename it or uncompress it until the call goes through.) The script also notifies sender and recipient when the transfer finishes. Here's a sample run:

```
send_it chapter1 bob
```

---

uudecode

uudecode [_file_]

Read a uuencoded file and recreate the original file with the same mode and name (see **uuencode**).

---

uuencode

uuencode [_file_] _name_ | **mail** _remotesys_!_usr_

Convert a binary _file_ to a form which can be sent to _usr_ via **mail**. The encoding uses only printing ASCII characters and includes the mode and _name_ of the file. When _file_ is reconverted via **uudecode** on the remote system, output will be sent to _name_. (Therefore, when saving the encoded mail message to a file on the remote system, *don't* store it in a file called _name_ or you'll overwrite it!) Note that **uuencode** can take standard input, so a single argument will be taken as the name to be given to the file when it is decoded.

uuglist [*option*]

List all service grades available for use with the **–g** option of **uux** and **uucp**. Service grades define the priority of data transferral; they are typically expressed as single characters or as a string.

Option

   –u   List grades available to the current user.

---

uulog [*options*]

Print information from the **uucp** or **uuxqt** log files, which reside in **/var/uucp/.Log** (down subdirectories **uucico** or **uuxqt**). See also **tail**.

Options

   –f*sys*   Issue a **tail –f** to print the most recent actions for a given system.

   –s*sys*   Print all actions for the given system.

   –u*user* Print commands issued by *user* (SVR3 only).

   –x   Check the **uuxqt** log file for the given system (used with **–f** or **–s**).

   –n   Execute a **tail** command of *n* lines (used with **–f**).

---

uuname [*options*]

Print the names of systems **uucp** knows about.

Options

   –c   Print system names known to **cu** (usually the same).

   –l   Print the local system's node name.

---

uupick [*option*]

Query the status of files sent to the user with **uuto**.

Option

   –s *system*   Search only for files sent from *system*.

Interactive responses

   a[*dir*]   Move all files sent from *system* to the named *directory*.

   d   Delete the entry.

   m[*dir*]   Move the file to the directory *dir*.

   p   Print the file.

   q   Quit **uupick**.

   *****   Print a command summary.

   !*cmd*   Execute the shell command *cmd*.

→

uupick	*EOF*	Quit **uupick**.
←	RETURN	Move to next entry.

uustat

uustat [*options*]

Provide information about **uucp** requests. This command can also be used to cancel **uucp** requests. Options **−a**, **−j**, **−k**, **−m**, **−p**, **−q**, and **−r** cannot be used with each other.

Options

−a	Report all queued jobs.
−c	When used with **−t**, report average time spent on queue instead of average transfer rate.
−dn	When used with **−t**, report averages for past n minutes instead of past hour.
−j	Report the total number of jobs displayed (use only with **−a** or **−s**).
−kn	Kill job request n; you must own it.
−m	Report accessibility of other systems.
−n	Suppress standard output but not standard error.
−p	Execute a **ps −flp** on active processes.
−q	Report the jobs queued for all systems.
−rn	Renew job n by issuing a **touch** on its associated files.
−ssystem	Report the status of jobs for *system*.
−Sx	Report status for jobs of type x:

c	Completed jobs
i	Interrupted jobs
q	Queued jobs
r	Running jobs

−tsystem	Report *system*'s average transfer rate (in bytes per second) over the past hour.
−uuser	Report the status of jobs for *user*.

uuto

uuto [*options*] *sourcefiles destination*

Send source files to a destination, where *destination* is of the form *system!user*. The user on the destination system can pick up the files with **uupick**.

Options

−m	Send mail when the copy is complete.
−p	Copy files to the spool directory.

uux [*options*] [[*sys*]!*command*]

Gather files from various systems and execute *command* on the specified machine *sys*. **uux** also recognizes the **uucp** options –**c**, –**C**, –**g**, –**r**, –**s**, and –**x**.

Options

–	Same as –**p** (pass standard input to *command*).
–a_user_	Notify *user* upon completion (see –**z**).
–b	Print the standard input when the exit status indicates an error.
–j	Print the **uux** job number.
–n	Do not send mail if *command* fails.
–p	Pass the standard input to *command*.
–z	Notify invoking user upon successful completion.

vacation [*options*]

Automatically return a mail message to sender announcing that you are on vacation. To disable this feature, type **mail –F " "**.

Options

–d	Append the date to *logfile*.
–F *user*	Forward mail to *user* when unable to send mail to *mailfile*.
–l *logfile*	Record in *logfile* the names of senders who received an automated reply (default is **$HOME/.maillog**).
–m *mailfile*	Save received messages in *mailfile* (default is **$HOME/.mailfile**).
–M *msg_file*	Use *msg_file* as the reply to mail automatically (default is **/usr/lib/mail/std_vac_msg**).

val [*options*] *file* . . .

An SCCS command. See Section 17.

vc [*options*] [*keyword=value* . . .]

Copy lines from standard input to standard output under control of the **vc** keywords and arguments within the standard input. This command is obsolete.

Options

–a	Replace control keywords in all lines, including text lines.
–c_k_	Use *k* instead of **:** as the control character.

→

UNIX
Commands

vc ←	−s Suppress warning messages. −t If any control characters are found before the first tab in the file, remove all characters up to the first tab.

vedit

vedit [options] [files]

Same as running vi, but with the **showmode** and **novice** flags set, the **report** flag set to 1, and **magic** turned off (metacharacters have no special meaning). Intended for beginners.

vi

vi [options] [files]

A screen-oriented text editor based on ex. See Sections 8 and 9 for more information on vi and ex. Options −c, −C, −L, −r, −R, and −t are the same as in ex.

Options

−c*command*
    Enter vi and execute the given vi *command*.

−l   Run in LISP mode for editing LISP programs.

−L   List filenames that were saved due to an editor or system crash.

−r*file*   Recover and edit *file* after an editor or system crash.

−R   Read-only mode. Files can't be changed.

−t *tag*   Edit the file containing *tag*, and position the editor at its definition (see **ctags** for more information).

−w*n*   Set default window size to *n*; useful when editing via a slow dial-up line.

−x   Supply a key to encrypt or decrypt *file* using **crypt**.

−C   Same as −x but assume *file* began in encrypted form.

+   Start vi on last line of file.

+*n*   Start vi on line *n* of file.

+/*pat*   Start vi on line containing pattern *pat*. This option fails if **nowrapscan** is set in your **.exrc**.

view

view [options] [files]

Same as **vi −R**.

w

/usr/ucb/w [options] [user]

Print summaries of system usage, currently logged-in users, and what they are doing. **w** is essentially a combination of **uptime**, **who**, and **ps −a**. Display output for one user by specifying *user*.

Options

   −h   Suppress headings and **uptime** information.

   −l   Display in long format (the default).

   −s   Display in short format.

---

wait [*n*]

                                                    wait

Wait for all background processes to complete, and report their termination status. Used in shell scripts. If *n* is specified, wait only for the process with process ID *n*.

---

wall   **wall**

message

Send a message to all users. End message with *EOF*. This is typically used by a privileged user to inform users of a system shutdown.

---

wc [*options*] [*files*]   **wc**

Print a character, word, and line count for *files*. If no *files* are given, read standard input. See other examples under **ls** and **sort**.

Options

   −c   Print character count only.

   −l   Print line count only.

   −w   Print word count only.

Examples

Count the number of users logged in:

```
who | wc -l
```

Count the words in three essay files:

```
wc -w essay.[123]
```

Count lines in variable **$file** (don't display filename):

```
wc -l < $file
```

---

what [*option*] *files*   **what**

An SCCS command. See Section 17.

/usr/ucb/whatis *commands*   **whatis**

Look up one or more *commands* in the on-line manual pages, and display a brief description. Same as **man −f**. See also **apropos**.

/usr/ucb/which [commands]

List which files would be executed if the named *commands* had been run as a command. **which** reads the user's **.cshrc** file, checking aliases and searching the **path** variable. Users of the Bourne or Korn shells can use the built-in **type** command as an alternative.

Example

```
which cc ls
/usr/ucb/cc
ls:      aliased to ls -sFC
```

who [options] [file]

Display information about the current status of the system. With no options, list the names of users currently logged in to the system. An optional system *file* (default is **/var/adm/utmp**) can be supplied to give additional information. **who** is usually invoked without options, but useful options include **am I** and **−u**. For more examples, see **cut**, **line**, **paste**, **tee**, and **wc**.

Options

−a	Use all options.
−b	Report information about the last reboot.
−d	Report expired processes.
−H	Print headings.
−l	Report inactive terminal lines.
−nx	Display *x* users per line (works only with **−q**).
−p	Report previously spawned processes.
−q	"Quick." Display only the usernames.
−r	Report the run level.
−s	List the name, line, and time fields (the default behavior).
−t	Report the last change of the system clock (via **date**).
−T	Report whether terminals are writable (+), not writable (−), or unknown (?).
−u	Report terminal usage (idle time). A dot (.) means less than one minute idle; **old** means more than 24 hours idle.
am i	Print the username of the invoking user.

Example

This sample output was produced at 8 a.m. on April 17:

```
who -uH
NAME     LINE    TIME            IDLE   PID   COMMENTS
martha   ttyp3   Apr 16 08:14   16:25   2240
george   ttyp0   Apr 17 07:33    .     15182
```

Since **martha** has been idle since yesterday afternoon (16 hours), it appears that Martha isn't at work yet. She simply left herself logged in. George's terminal is currently in use.

/usr/ucb/whoami

Print the effective username. This is usually the same as the standard SVR4 command **logname**. However, when you're running an **su** session as another user, **whoami** displays this user's name, but **logname** still displays your name.

whois [*option*] *name*

Search an Internet directory for the person, login, handle, or organization specified by *name*. Precede *name* with the modifiers !, ., or *, alone or in combination, to limit the search to either (1) the name of a person or of a username, (2) a handle, or (3) an organization.

Option

    −h *host*   Search on host machine *host*.

write *user* [*tty*]
message

Initiate or respond to an interactive conversation with *user*. A write session is terminated with *EOF*. If the user is logged in to more than one terminal, specify a *tty* number.

xargs [*options*] [*command*]

Execute *command* (with any initial arguments), but read remaining arguments from standard input instead of specifying them directly. **xargs** passes these arguments in several bundles to *command*, allowing *command* to process more arguments than it could normally handle at once. The arguments are typically a long list of filenames (generated by **ls** or **find**, for example) that get passed to **xargs** via a pipe.

Options

    −e*string*
        Stop passing arguments when argument *string* is encountered (default is underscore).

    −i   Pass arguments to *command*, replacing instances of { } on the command line with the current line of input.

    −l*n*   Execute *command* for *n* lines of arguments.

    −n*n*   Execute *command* with up to *n* arguments.

    −p   Prompt for a **y** to confirm each execution of *command*.

→

UNIX
Commands

xargs ←	**−s***n* Each argument list can contain up to *n* characters (470 is the default and the maximum value).
	−t Echo each *command* before executing.
	−x Exit if argument list exceeds *n* characters (from **−s**); **−x** takes effect automatically with **−i** and **−l**.

Examples

grep for *pattern* in all files on the system:

```
find / -print | xargs grep pattern > out &
```

Run **diff** on file pairs (e.g., **f1.a** and **f1.b**, **f2.a** and **f2.b** ...):

```
echo $* | xargs -n2 diff
```

The previous line would be invoked as a shell script, specifying filenames as arguments.

Display *file*, one word per line (same as **deroff −w**):

```
cat file | xargs -n1
```

Move files in **olddir** to **newdir**, showing each command:

```
ls olddir | xargs -i -t mv olddir/{ } newdir/{ }
```

yacc	**yacc** [*options*] *file*

Given a *file* containing context-free grammar, convert *file* into tables for subsequent parsing and send output to **y.tab.c**. This command name stands for **y**et **a**nother **c**ompiler-**c**ompiler. See also **lex** and the Nutshell Handbook *lex & yacc*.

Options

−d   Generate **y.tab.h**, producing **#define** statements that relate **yacc**'s token codes to the token names declared by the user.

−l   Exclude **#line** constructs from code produced in **y.tab.c**. (Use after debugging is complete.)

−Q*c*   Place version information about **yacc** in **y.tab.c** (if *c* = **y**) or suppress information (if *c* = **n**, the default).

−t   Compile runtime debugging code by default.

−v   Generate **y.output**, a file containing diagnostics and notes about the parsing tables.

−V   Print the version of **yacc** on standard error.

zcat	**zcat** [*files*]

Uncompress one or more **.Z** *files* to the standard output, leaving *files* unchanged. See **compress**.

The UNIX Shell: An Overview

For novice users, this section presents basic concepts about the UNIX shell. For advanced users, this section also summarizes the major similarities and differences between the Bourne, Korn, and C shells. Details on the three shells are provided in Sections 4 and 5.

The following topics are presented:

- Introduction to the shell

- Purpose of the shell

- Shell flavors

- Common features

- Differing features

Introduction to the Shell

Let's suppose that the UNIX operating system is a car. When you drive, you issue a variety of "commands": you turn the steering wheel, press the accelerator, or press the brake. But how does the car translate your commands into the action you want? Through the car's drive mechanism, which can be thought of as the car's user interface. Cars can be equipped with front-wheel drive, rear-wheel drive, four-wheel drive, and sometimes combinations of these.

The shell can be thought of as the user interface to UNIX, and by the same token, several shells are available in UNIX. Some systems provide only one shell. Many provide more than one for you to choose from. Each shell has different features, but all of them affect how commands will be interpreted and provide tools to create your UNIX environment.

The shell is simply a program that allows the system to understand your commands. (That's why the shell is often called a command interpreter.) For many users, the shell works invisibly—"behind the scenes." Your only concern is that the system do what you tell it to do; you don't care about the inner workings. In our car analogy, this is comparable to pressing the brake. Most of us don't care whether the "user interface" involves disk brakes or drum brakes, as long as the car stops.

Purpose of the Shell

There are three main uses for the shell:

- Interactive use

- Customization of your UNIX session

- Programming

Interactive Use

When the shell is used interactively, the system waits for you to type a command at the UNIX prompt. Your commands can include special symbols that let you abbreviate filenames or redirect input and output.

Customization of Your UNIX Session

A UNIX shell defines variables to control the behavior of your UNIX session. Setting these variables will tell the system, for example, which directory to use as your home directory, or the file in which to store your mail. Some variables are preset by the system; you can define others in start-up files that are read when you log in. Start-up files can also contain UNIX commands or special shell commands. These will be executed every time you log in.

Programming

UNIX shells provide a set of special (or built-in) commands that can be used to create programs called shell scripts. In fact, many built-in commands can be used interactively like UNIX commands, and UNIX commands are frequently used in shell scripts. Scripts are useful for executing a series of individual commands. This is similar to BATCH files in MS-DOS. Scripts can also execute commands repeatedly (in a loop) or conditionally (if-else), as in many high-level programming languages.

Shell Flavors

Many different UNIX shells are available. This quick reference describes the three most popular shells:

- The Bourne (or standard) shell, the most compact shell but also the simplest.

- The Korn shell, a superset of the Bourne shell that lets you edit the command line.

- The C shell, which uses C syntax and has many conveniences.

Most systems have more than one shell, and people will often use the Bourne shell for writing shell scripts and will use another shell for interactive use.

The **/etc/passwd** file determines which shell takes effect during your interactive UNIX session. When you log in, the system checks your entry in **/etc/passwd**. The last field of each entry calls a program to run as the default shell. For example:

If the program name is:	Your shell will be the:
/bin/sh	Bourne shell
/bin/rsh	Restricted Bourne shell
/bin/jsh	Bourne shell, including job control
/bin/ksh	Korn shell
/bin/rksh	Restricted Korn shell
/bin/csh	C shell

You can change to another shell by typing the program name at the command line. For example, to change from the Bourne shell to the C shell, type:

```
$ exec csh
```

Common Features

The table below is a sampling of features that are common to the Bourne, Korn, and C shells. Note that the Korn shell is an enhanced version of the Bourne shell; therefore, the Korn shell includes all features of the Bourne shell, plus some others. The commands **bg**, **fg**, **jobs**, **stop**, and **suspend** are available only on systems that support job control.

Symbol/ Command	Meaning/Action
>	Redirect output.
>>	Append to file.
<	Redirect input.
<<	``Here'' document (redirect input).
|	Pipe output.
&	Run process in background.
;	Separate commands on same line.
*	Match any character(s) in filename.
?	Match single character in filename.
[ ]	Match any characters enclosed.
( )	Execute in subshell.
` `	Substitute output of enclosed command.
" "	Partial quote (allows variable and command expansion).
' '	Full quote (no expansion).
\	Quote following character.
$var	Use value for variable.
$$	Process id.
$0	Command name.
$n	nth argument (0<n<9).
$*	All arguments as a simple word.
#	Begin comment.
bg	Background execution.
break	Break from loop statements.
cd	Change directories.
continue	Resume a program loop.
echo	Display output.
eval	Evaluate arguments.
exec	Execute a new shell.
fg	Foreground execution.
jobs	Show active jobs.
kill	Terminate running jobs.
newgrp	Change to a new group.
shift	Shift positional parameters.
stop	Suspend a background job.
suspend	Suspend a foreground job.
time	Time a command.
umask	Set or list file permissions.
unset	Erase variable or function definitions.
wait	Wait for a background job to finish.

Differing Features

The table below is a sampling of features that are different among the three shells.

sh	ksh	csh	Meaning/Action
$	$	%	Prompt.
		>!	Force redirection.
		>>!	Force append.
> file 2>&1	> file 2>&1	>& file	Combine stdout and stderr.
		{ }	Expand elements in list.
` `	$( )	` `	Substitute output of enclosed command.
$HOME	$HOME	$home	Home directory.
	~	~	Home directory symbol.
var=value	var=value	set var value	Variable assignment.
export var	export var=val	setenv var val	Set environment variable.
	${nn}		More than 9 args can be referenced.
"$@"	"$@"		All args as separate words.
$#	$#	$#argv	Number of arguments.
$?	$?	$status	Exit status.
$!	$!		Background exit status.
$-	$-		Current options.
. file	. file	source file	Read commands in file.
	alias x=y	alias x y	Name x stands for y.
case	case	switch/case	Choose alternatives.
	cd ~-	popd/pushd	Switch directories.
done	done	end	End a loop statement.
esac	esac	endsw	End case or switch.
exit [n]	exit [n]	exit [(expr)]	Exit with a status.
for/do	for/do	foreach	Loop through variables.
	print -r	glob	Ignore echo escapes.
hash	alias -t	hashstat	Display hashed commands (tracked aliases).
hash cmds	alias -t cmds	rehash	Remember command locations.
hash -r		unhash	Forget command locations.
	history	history	List previous commands.
	r	!!	Redo previous command.
	r str	!str	Redo command that starts with str.

sh	*ksh*	*csh*	*Meaning/Action*
	r *x=y cmd*	**!** *cmd* **:s/** *x* **/** *y* **/**	Edit command, then execute.
if [$i -eq 5]	**if ((i==5))**	**if ($i==5)**	Sample if statement.
fi	**fi**	**endif**	End if statement.
ulimit	**ulimit**	**limit**	Set resource limits.
pwd	**pwd**	**dirs**	Print working directory.
read	**read**	**$<**	Read from terminal.
trap 2	**trap 2**	**onintr**	Ignore interrupts.
	unalias	**unalias**	Remove aliases.
until	**until**		Begin until loop.
while/do	**while/do**	**while**	Begin while loop.

The Bourne Shell
and Korn Shell

This section presents the following topics:

- Overview of features
- Syntax
- Variables
- Arithmetic expressions (Korn shell only)
- Command history (Korn shell only)
- Built-in commands
- Job control
- Invoking the shell
- Restricted shells

Overview of Features

The Bourne shell is the standard shell and provides the following features:

- Input/output redirection.
- Wildcard characters (metacharacters) for filename abbreviation.
- Shell variables for customizing your environment.
- A built-in command set for writing shell programs.
- Job control (beginning in SVR4).

The Korn shell is a backward-compatible extension of the Bourne shell. Features that are valid only in the Korn shell are so indicated.

- Command-line editing (using vi or emacs).
- Access to previous commands (command history).
- Integer arithmetic.
- More ways to match patterns and substitute variables.
- Arrays and arithmetic expressions.
- Command name abbreviation (aliasing).

Syntax

This subsection describes the many symbols peculiar to the Bourne and Korn shell. The topics are arranged as follows:

- Special files
- Filename metacharacters
- Quoting
- Command forms
- Redirection forms
- Coprocesses (Korn shell only)

Special Files

`/etc/profile`	Executed automatically at login.
`$HOME/.profile`	Executed automatically at login.
`/etc/passwd`	Source of home directories for ~*name* abbreviations.
`$ENV`	Specifies the name of a file to read when a new Korn shell is created.

Filename Metacharacters

*	Match any string of zero or more characters.
?	Match any single character.
[abc...]	Match any one of the enclosed characters; a hyphen can be used to specify a range (e.g., a-z, A-Z, 0-9).
[!abc...]	Match any character *not* enclosed as above.

In the Korn shell:

?(pattern)	Match zero or one instance of *pattern*.
*(pattern)	Match zero or more instances of *pattern*.
+(pattern)	Match one or more instance of *pattern*.
@(pattern)	Match exactly one instance of *pattern*.
!(pattern)	Match any strings that don't contain *pattern*.
~	HOME directory of the current user.
~name	HOME directory of user *name*.
~+	Current working directory (PWD).
~-	Previous working directory (OLDPWD).

The *pattern* above can be a sequence of patterns separated by |, meaning that the match applies to any of the patterns. This extended syntax resembles that available to **egrep** and **awk**.

Examples

```
$ ls new*          List new and new.1.
$ cat ch?          Match ch9 but not ch10.
$ vi [D-R]*        Match files that begin with uppercase D through R.
$ cp !(Junk*|Temp*)*.c ..   Korn shell only. Copy C source files
                            except for Junk and Temp files.
```

Quoting

Quoting disables a character's special meaning and allows it to be used literally, as itself. The following characters have special meaning to the Bourne and Korn shells:

;	Command separator.
&	Background execution.
( )	Command grouping.
|	Pipe.
> < &	Redirection symbols.
* ? [ ] ~ + - @ !	Filename metacharacters.
" ' \	Used in quoting other characters.

`` ` ``	Command substitution.
`$`	Variable substitution (or command substitution).
`newline space tab`	Word separators.

The characters below can be used for quoting:

`" "`	Everything between `"` and `"` is taken literally, except for the following characters that keep their special meaning:

`$`	Variable substitution will occur.
`` ` ``	Command substitution will occur.
`"`	This marks the end of the double quote.

`' '`	Everything between `'` and `'` is taken literally except for another `'`.
`\`	The character following a `\` is taken literally. Use within `" "` to escape `"`, `$`, and `` ` ``. Often used to escape itself, spaces, or newlines.

Examples

```
$ echo 'Single quotes "protect" double quotes'
Single quotes "protect" double quotes

$ echo "Well, isn't that \"special\"?"
Well, isn't that "special"?

$ echo "You have `ls|wc -l` files in `pwd`"
You have       43 files in /home/bob

$ echo "The value of \$x is $x"
The value of $x is 100
```

Command Forms

`cmd &`	Execute *cmd* in background.
`cmd1 ; cmd2`	Command sequence; execute multiple *cmd*s on the same line.
`(cmd1 ; cmd2)`	Subshell; treat *cmd1* and *cmd2* as a command group.
`cmd1	cmd2`	Pipe; use output from *cmd1* as input to *cmd2*.
`cmd1 `cmd2``	Command substitution; use *cmd2* output as arguments to *cmd1*.
`cmd1 $(cmd2)`	Korn-shell command substitution; nesting is allowed.
`cmd1 && cmd2`	AND; execute *cmd1* and then (if *cmd1* succeeds) *cmd2*.
`cmd1 || cmd2`	OR; execute either *cmd1* or (if *cmd1* fails) *cmd2*.
`{ cmd1 ; cmd2 }`	Execute commands in the current shell.

Examples

`$ nroff file &`	*Format in the background.*
`$ cd; ls`	*Execute sequentially.*
`$ (date; who; pwd) > logfile`	*All output is redirected.*
`$ sort file	pr -3	lp`	*Sort file, page output, then print.*
`$ vi `grep -l ifdef *.c``	*Edit files found by grep.*

```
$ egrep '(yes|no)' `cat list`        Specify a list of files to search.
$ egrep '(yes|no)' $(cat list)       Korn shell version of previous.
$ egrep '(yes|no)' $(<list)          Same, but faster.
$ grep XX file && lp file            Print file if it contains the pattern,
$ grep XX file || echo "XX not found"    otherwise, echo an error message.
```

Redirection Forms

File Descriptor	Name	Common Abbreviation	Typical Default
0	Standard Input	stdin	Keyboard
1	Standard Output	stdout	Terminal
2	Standard Error	stderr	Terminal

The usual input source or output destination can be changed as follows:

Simple Redirection

cmd > *file*	Send output of *cmd* to *file* (overwrite).
cmd >> *file*	Send output of *cmd* to *file* (append).
cmd < *file*	Take input for *cmd* from *file*.
cmd << *text*	Read standard input up to a line identical to *text* (*text* can be stored in a shell variable). Input is usually typed on the screen or in the shell program. Commands that typically use this syntax include **cat**, **echo**, **ex**, and **sed**. (If <<– is used, leading tabs are ignored when comparing input with end-of-input *text* marker.) This command form is sometimes called a "Here" document.

Redirection Using File Descriptors

cmd >&*n*	Send *cmd* output to file descriptor *n*.
cmd *m*>&*n*	Same, except that output that would normally go to file descriptor *m* is sent to file descriptor *n* instead.
cmd >&–	Close standard output.
cmd <&*n*	Take input for *cmd* from file descriptor *n*.
cmd *m*<&*n*	Same, except that input that would normally come from file descriptor *m* comes from file descriptor *n* instead.
cmd <&–	Close standard input.

Multiple Redirection

cmd 2>*file*	Send standard error to *file*; standard output remains the same (e.g., the screen).
cmd > *file* 2>&1	Send both standard error and standard output to *file*.
(*cmd* > *f1*) 2>*f2*	Send standard output to file *f1*; standard error to file *f2*.
cmd | **tee** *files*	Send output of *cmd* to standard output (usually the terminal) and to *files*. (See the example in Section 2 under **tee**.)

No space should appear between file descriptors and a redirection symbol; spacing is optional in the other cases.

Examples

```
$ cat part1 > book
$ cat part2 part3 >> book
$ mail tim < report

$ sed 's/^/XX /g' << END_ARCHIVE
> This is often how a shell archive is "wrapped",
> bundling text for distribution.  You would normally
> run sed from a shell program, not from the command line.
> END_ARCHIVE
XX This is often how a shell archive is "wrapped",
XX bundling text for distribution.  You would normally
XX run sed from a shell program, not from the command line.
```

To redirect standard output to standard error:

```
$ echo "Usage error:  see administrator" 1>&2
```

The following command will send output (files found) to **filelist** and send error messages (inaccessible files) to file **no_access**:

```
$ (find / -print > filelist) 2>no_access
```

Coprocesses

Coprocesses are a feature of the Korn shell only.

cmd1 | *cmd2* |&	Coprocess; execute the pipeline in the background. The shell sets up a two-way pipe, allowing redirection of both standard input and standard output.
read -p *var*	Read coprocess input into variable *var*.
print -p *string*	Write *string* to the coprocess.
cmd <&p	Take input for *cmd* from the coprocess.
cmd >&p	Send output of *cmd* to the coprocess.

Examples

```
ed - memo |&          Start coprocess.
print -p /word/       Send ed command to coprocess.
read -p search        Read output of ed command into variable search.
print "$search"       Show the line on standard output.
A word to the wise.
```

Variables

This subsection describes the following:

- Variable substitution
- Built-in shell variables
- Other shell variables
- Arrays (Korn shell only)

Variable Substitution

No spaces should be used in the expressions below. The colon (`:`) is optional; if it's included, *var* must be non-null as well as set.

`var=value ...`	Set each variable *var* to a *value*.
`${var}`	Use value of *var*; braces are optional if *var* is separated.
`${var:-value}`	Use *var* if set; otherwise, use *value*.
`${var:=value}`	Use *var* if set; otherwise, use *value* and assign *value* to *var*.
`${var:?value}`	Use *var* if set; otherwise, print *value* and exit. If *value* isn't supplied, print the phrase "parameter null or not set."
`${var:+value}`	Use *value* if *var* is set; otherwise, use nothing.

In the Korn shell:

`${#var}`	Use the length of *var*.
`${#*}`	Use the number of positional parameters.
`${#@}`	Use the number of positional parameters.
`${var#pattern}`	Use value of *var* after removing *pattern* from the left. Remove the shortest matching piece.
`${var##pattern}`	Same as #*pattern*, but remove longest matching piece.
`${var%pattern}`	Use value of *var* after removing *pattern* from the right.
`${var%%pattern}`	Same as %*pattern*, but remove longest matching piece.

Examples

`$ u=up d=down blank=`	*Assign values to three variables (last is null).*
`$ echo ${u}root`	*Braces are needed here.*
`uproot`	
`$ echo ${u-$d}`	*Display value of* u *or* d; *since* u *is set, it is printed.*
`up`	
`$ echo ${tmp-`date`}`	*If* tmp *is not set, the* date *command is executed.*
`Thu Feb  4 15:03:46 EST 1993`	
`$ echo ${blank="no data"}`	blank *is set, so it is printed (a blank line).*
`$ echo ${blank:="no data"}`	blank *is set but null, so the string is printed*
`no data`	
`$ echo $blank`	blank *now has a new value*
`no data`	

Korn Shell Example

```
tail='${PWD##*/}'
```
Take the current directory name and
remove the longest character string ending with /.
This removes the leading pathname and leaves the tail.

Built-in Shell Variables

Built-in variables are automatically set by the shell and are typically used inside shell scripts. Built-in variables can make use of the variable substitution patterns shown above. Note that the **$** is not actually part of the variable name, although the variable is always referenced this way.

$#	Number of command-line arguments.
$-	Options currently in effect (arguments supplied to **sh** or to **set**).
$?	Exit value of last executed command.
$$	Process number of current process.
$!	Process number of last background command.
$0	First word; that is, command name.
$n	Individual arguments on command line (positional parameters). The Bourne shell allows only nine parameters to be referenced directly (n = 1-9); the Korn shell allows n to be greater than 9 if specified as **${$n}**.
$*	All arguments on command line ("**$1 $2** ... ").
"$@"	All arguments on command line, individually quoted ("**$1**" "**$2**" ...).

The Korn shell automatically sets these additional variables:

$_	Temporary variable; initialized to pathname of script or program being executed. Later, stores the last argument of previous command. Also stores name of matching MAIL file during mail checks.
ERRNO	Error number of last system call that failed.
LINENO	Current line number within the script or function.
OLDPWD	Previous working directory (set by **cd**).
OPTARG	Name of last option processed by **getopts**.
OPTIND	Numerical index of OPTARG.
PPID	Process number of this shell's parent.
PWD	Current working directory (set by **cd**).
RANDOM[=n]	Generate a new random number with each reference; start with integer n, if given.
REPLY	Default reply used by **select** and **read**.
SECONDS[=n]	Number of seconds since the shell was started, or, if n is given, number of seconds + n since the shell started.

Other Shell Variables

The variables below are not automatically set by the shell. They are typically used in your **.profile** file, where you can define them to suit your needs. Variables can be assigned values by issuing commands of the form:

$ *variable=value*

The list below includes the type of value expected when defining these variables. Those that are specific to the Korn shell are marked as (K).

CDPATH=*dirs*	Directories searched by **cd**; allows shortcuts in changing directories; unset by default.
COLUMNS=*n*	(K) Screen's column width; used in line edit modes and **select** lists.
EDITOR=*file*	(K) Pathname of line edit mode to turn on (can end in **emacs** or **vi**); used when VISUAL is not set.
ENV=*file*	(K) Name of script that gets executed at startup; useful for storing alias and function definitions. For example, **ENV=$HOME/.kshrc** (like C shell's **.cshrc**).
FCEDIT=*file*	(K) Editor used by **fc** command (default is **/bin/ed**).
FPATH=*dirs*	(K) Directories to search for function definitions; undefined functions are set via **typeset –fu**; FPATH is searched when these functions are first referenced.
HISTFILE=*file*	(K) File in which to store command history (must be set before **ksh** is started); default is **$HOME/.sh_history**.
HISTSIZE=*n*	(K) Number of history commands available (must be set before **ksh** is started); default is 128.
HOME=*dir*	Home directory; set by **login** (from **passwd** file).
IFS='*chars*'	Internal field separators; default is space, tab, and newline.
LANG=*dir*	Directory to use for certain language-dependent programs.
LINES=*n*	(K) Screen's line length; used for **select** lists.
MAIL=*file*	Default file in which to receive mail; set by **login**.
MAILCHECK=*n*	Number of seconds between mail checks; default is 10 minutes.
MAILPATH=*files*	One or more files, delimited by a colon, in which to receive mail. Each file is printed. The Korn shell prompt is **?** and the default message is *You have mail in $_*. The Bourne shell prompt is **%** and the default message is *You have mail*.
PATH=*dir*	One or more pathnames, delimited by a colon, in which to search for commands to execute; default is **/usr/bin**.
PS1=*string*	Primary prompt string; default is **$**.
PS2=*string*	Secondary prompt (used in multi-line commands); default is **>**.
PS3=*string*	(K) Prompt string in **select** loops; default is **#?**.
PS4=*string*	(K) Prompt string for execution trace (**ksh –x** or **set –x**); default is **+**.

SHACCT=_file_	"Shell account"; file in which to log executed shell scripts. Not in Korn shell.
SHELL=_file_	Name of shell environment (e.g., **/bin/sh**).
TERM=_string_	Terminal type.
TMOUT=_n_	(K) If no command is typed after _n_ seconds, exit the shell.
VISUAL=_path_	(K) Same as EDITOR, but VISUAL is checked first.

Arrays

The Korn shell supports one-dimensional arrays of up to 1024 elements. The first element is numbered 0. An array _name_ can be initialized as follows:

> **set –A** _name value0 value1_ ...

where the specified values become elements of _name_. Declaring arrays is not required, however. Any valid reference to a subscripted variable can create an array.

When referencing arrays, you can use the **${** ... **}** syntax. This isn't needed when referencing arrays inside **(( ))** (the form of **let** that does automatic quoting). Note that **[** and **]** are typed literally (i.e., they don't stand for optional syntax).

`${name[i]}`	Use element _i_ of array _name_. _i_ can be any arithmetic expression as described under **let**. The expression must return a value between 0 and 1023.
`${name[*]}`	Use all elements of array _name_.
`${name}`	Use element 0 of array _name_.
`${name[*]}`	Use all elements in array _name_.
`${#name[*]}`	Use the number of elements in array _name_.
`${#name[@]}`	Use the number of elements in array _name_.

Arithmetic Expressions

The Korn shell's **let** command performs integer arithmetic. The Korn shell provides a way to substitute integer values (for use as command arguments or in variables); base conversion is also possible:

`$(( expr ))`	Use the value of the enclosed arithmetic expression.
`B#n`	Interpret integer _n_ in numeric base _B_. For example, **8#100** specifies the octal equivalent of decimal 64.

Operators

The Korn shell uses arithmetic operators from the C programming language; they are listed below in decreasing order of precedence:

–	Unary minus.
! ~	Logical negation; binary inversion (one's complement).
* / %	Multiplication; division; modulus (remainder).
+ –	Addition; subtraction.
<< >>	Bitwise left shift; bitwise right shift.
<= >=	Less than or equal to; greater than or equal to.
< >	Less than; greater than.
== !=	Equality; inequality (both evaluated left to right).
&	Bitwise AND.
^	Bitwise exclusive OR.
|	Bitwise OR.
&&	Logical AND.
||	Logical OR.
*= /= %= = += -= <<= >>= &= ^= |=	Assignment.

Bourne and Korn

Examples

See the **let** command for more information and examples.

```
let "count=0" "i = i + 1"          Assign i and count.
let "num % 2"                      Test for an even number.
(( percent >= 0 && percent <= 100 ))   Test the range of a value.
```

Command History

The Korn shell lets you display or modify previous commands. This is similar to the C shell's history mechanism. Commands in the history list can be modified using:

- Line-edit mode

- The **fc** command

Line-edit Mode

Line-edit mode lets you emulate many features of the vi or emacs editor. The history list is treated like a file. When the editor is invoked, you type editing keystrokes to move to the command line you want to execute. You can also change the line before executing it. When you're ready to issue the command, press RETURN.

Line-edit mode can be started in several ways. For example, these are equivalent:

```
$ VISUAL=vi
$ EDITOR=vi
$ set -o vi          Overrides value of VISUAL or EDITOR
```

Note that vi starts in input mode; to type a vi command, press ESCAPE first.

Common Editing Keystrokes

vi	emacs	Result
k	CTRL-p	Get previous command.
j	CTRL-n	Get next command.
/string	CTRL-r string	Get previous command containing *string*.
h	CTRL-b	Move back one character.
l	CTRL-f	Move forward one character.
b	ESC-b	Move back one word.
w	ESC-f	Move forward one word.
X	DEL	Delete previous character.
x	CTRL-d	Delete one character.
dw	ESC-d	Delete word forward.
db	ESC-h	Delete word back.
xp	CTRL-t	Transpose two characters.

The fc Command

Use **fc –l** to list history commands and **fc –e** to edit them. See the entry under built-in commands for more information.

Examples

```
$ history              List the last 16 commands.
$ fc -l 20 30          List commands 20 through 30.
$ fc -l -5             List the last five commands.
$ fc -l cat            List the last command beginning with cat.
$ fc -ln 5 > doit      Save command 5 to file doit.

$ fc -e vi 5 20        Edit commands 5 through 20 using vi.
$ fc -e emacs          Edit previous command using emacs.
$ r                    Re-execute previous command.
$ r cat                Re-execute last cat command.
$ r doc=Doc            Substitute, then re-execute last command.
$ r chap=doc c         Re-execute last command that begins with c,
                       but change string chap to doc.
```

Built-in Commands (Bourne and Korn Shell)

Examples to be entered as a command line are shown with the **$** prompt. Otherwise, examples should be treated as code fragments that might be included in a shell script. For convenience, some of the reserved words used by multi-line commands are also included.

# #

Ignore all text that follows on the same line. **#** is used in shell scripts as the comment character and is not really a command. (Take care when commenting a Bourne shell script. A file that has **#** as its first character is sometimes interpreted as a C shell script.)

#!*shell*

Used as the first line of a script to invoke the named *shell* (with optional arguments). Not supported in all shells. For example:

```
#!/bin/sh -v
```

#!*shell*

:

Null command. Returns an exit status of 0. Sometimes used as the first character in a file to denote a Bourne shell script. See example below and under **case**. In the Korn shell, shell variables can be placed after the **:** to expand them to their values.

Example

Check whether someone is logged in:

```
if who | grep $1 > /dev/null
then :                  # do nothing
                        # if pattern is found
else echo "User $1 is not logged in"
fi
```

. *file* [*arguments*]

Read and execute lines in *file*. *file* does not have to be executable but must reside in a directory searched by PATH. The Korn shell supports *arguments* that are stored in the positional parameters.

[[*expression*]]

Korn shell only. Same as **test** *expression* or [*expression*], except that **[[ ]]** allows additional operators. Word splitting and filename expansion are disabled. Note that the brackets (**[ ]**) are typed literally.

Additional operators

&&	Logical AND of test expressions.
||	Logical OR of test expressions.
>	First string is lexically "greater than" the second.
<	First string is lexically "less than" the second.

name () { *commands*; }

Define *name* as a function. Syntax can be written on one line or across many. Since the Bourne shell has no aliasing capability, simple

→

name ←	functions can serve as aliases. The Korn shell provides the **function** command, an alternate form that works the same way. *Example* ```\n$ count () {\n> ls	wc -l\n> }\n``` When issued at the command line, **count** will now display the number of files in the current directory.

alias	**alias** [*options*] [*name*[=*'cmd'*]]
	
	Korn shell only. Assign a shorthand *name* as a synonym for *cmd*. If =*'cmd'* is omitted, print the alias for *name*; if *name* is also omitted, print all aliases. See also **unalias**. The aliases below are built into the Korn shell. Some use names of existing Bourne shell or C shell commands (which points out the similarities among the shells).
	
	```\nautoload='typeset -fu'\necho='print -'\nfalse='let 0'\nfunction='typeset -f'\nhash='alias -t'\nhistory='fc -l'\ninteger='typeset -i'\nnohup='nohup '\npwd='print -r - $PWD'\nr='fc -e -'\ntrue=':'\ntype='whence -v'\n```
	
	Options
	
	-t Create a tracked alias for a UNIX command *name*. The Korn shell remembers the full pathname of the command, allowing it to be found more quickly and to be issued from any directory. If no name is supplied, current tracked aliases are listed. Tracked aliases are the same as hashed commands in the Bourne shell.
	
	-x Export the alias; it can now be used in shell scripts and other subshells. If no name is supplied, current exported aliases are listed.
	
	Example
	
	```\nalias dir='basename `pwd`'\n```

autoload	**autoload** [*functions*] Load (define) the *functions* only when they are first used. Korn shell alias for **typeset -fu**.

bg [*jobIDs*]   **bg**

Put current job or *jobIDs* in the background. See "Job Control."

---

break [*n*]   **break**

Exit from the innermost (most deeply nested) **for**, **while** or **until**
loop, or from the *n* innermost levels of the loop. Also exits from a
select list.

---

case *value* **in**   **case**
   pattern1 **)** *cmds1***;;**
   pattern2 **)** *cmds2***;;**
   .
   .
   .
esac

Execute the first set of commands (*cmds1*) if *value* matches *pattern1*,
execute the second set of commands (*cmds2*) if *value* matches *pat-
tern2*, etc. Be sure the last command in each set ends with **;;** . *value*
is typically a positional parameter or other shell variable. *cmds* are
typically UNIX commands, shell programming commands, or variable
assignments. Patterns can use file generation metacharacters. Multi-
ple patterns (separated by |) can be specified on the same line; in this
case, the associated *cmds* are executed whenever *value* matches any
of these patterns. See below and under **eval** for examples. (Note:
the Korn shell allows *pattern* to be preceded by an optional open
parenthesis, as in **(***pattern***)**. It's useful for balancing parentheses
inside a **$( )** construct.)

Examples

   Read first command-line argument and take appropriate action:

```
case $1 in              #match the first arg
    no|yes)  response=1;;
    -[tT])   table=TRUE;;
    *)       echo "unknown option"; exit 1;;
esac
```

   Read user-supplied lines until user exits:

```
while :                 # Null command; always true
do
    echo "Type . to finish ==> \c"
    read line
    case "$line" in
        .) echo "Message done"
           break ;;
        *) echo "$line" >> $message ;;
    esac
done
```

---

cd	**cd** [*dir*] **cd** [−] **cd** [*old new*]

With no arguments, change to home directory of user. Otherwise, change working directory to *dir*. If *dir* is a relative pathname but is not in the current directory, then the CDPATH variable is searched. The last two command forms are specific to the Korn shell, where − stands for the previous directory. The third syntax modifies the current directory name by replacing string *old* with *new*, then switches to the resulting directory.

Example

```
$ pwd
/usr/spool/cron
$ cd cron uucp       # cd prints the new directory
/usr/spool/uucp
```

---

continue	**continue** [*n*]

Skip remaining commands in a **for**, **while**, or **until** loop, resuming with the next iteration of the loop (or skipping *n* loops).

---

do	**do**

Reserved word that precedes the command sequence in a **for**, **while**, **until**, or **select** statement.

---

done	**done**

Reserved word that ends a **for**, **while**, **until**, or **select** statement.

---

echo	**echo** [−**n**] [*string*]

Write *string* to standard output; if −**n** is specified, the output is not terminated by a newline. If no *string* is supplied, echo a newline. In the Korn shell, **echo** is just an alias for **print** −. (See also **echo** in Section 2.) **echo** understands special escape characters, which must be quoted (or escaped with a \) to prevent interpretation by the shell:

\b	Backspace.
\c	Suppress the terminating newline (same as −**n**).
\f	Formfeed.
\n	Newline.
\r	Carriage return.
\t	Tab character.
\\	Backslash.
\0*nnn*	ASCII character represented by octal number *nnn*, where *nnn* is 1, 2, or 3 digits and is preceded by a 0.

```
$ echo "testing printer" | lp
$ echo "Warning: ringing bell \007"
```

esac   esac

Reserved word that ends a **case** statement. Omitting **esac** is a common programming error.

eval *args*   eval

Typically, **eval** is used in shell scripts, and *args* is a line of code that contains shell variables. **eval** forces variable expansion to happen first and then runs the resulting command. This "double-scanning" is useful any time shell variables contain input/output redirection symbols, aliases, or other shell variables. (For example, redirection normally happens before variable expansion, so a variable containing redirection symbols must be expanded first using **eval**; otherwise, the redirection symbols remain uninterpreted.) See the C-shell **eval** (Section 5) for another example.

Example

This fragment of a Bourne shell script shows how **eval** constructs a command that is interpreted in the right order:

```
for option
do
    case "$option" in    #define where output goes
        save) out=' > $newfile' ;;
        show) out=' | more' ;;
    esac
done
...
eval sort $file $out
```

exec [*command*]   exec

Execute *command* in place of the current process (instead of creating a new process). **exec** is also useful for opening, closing, or copying file descriptors.

Examples

`trap 'exec 2>&-' 0`	*Close standard error when shell script exits (signal 0).*
`$ exec /bin/csh`	*Replace Bourne shell with C shell.*
`$ exec < infile`	*Reassign standard input to infile.*

exit [*n*]   exit

Exit a shell script with status *n* (e.g., **exit 1**). *n* can be 0 (success) or nonzero (failure). If *n* is not given, exit status will be that of the most

→

exit
←
	recent command. **exit** can be issued at the command line to close a window (log out).
	
	``
	if [$# -eq 0]; then
	    echo "Usage: $0 [-c] [-d] file(s)"
	    exit 1 # Error status
	fi
	``

export	**export** [*variables*] **export** [*name*=[*value*]]... Pass (export) the value of one or more shell *variables*, giving global meaning to the variables (which are local by default). For example, a variable defined in one shell script must be exported if its value will be used in other programs called by the script. If no *variables* are given, **export** lists the variables exported by the current shell. The second form is the Korn shell version, which is similar to the first form except that you can set a variable *name* to a *value* before exporting it. *Example* In the Bourne shell, you would type: ``` TERM=vt100 export TERM ``` In the Korn shell, you could type this instead: ``` export TERM=vt100 ```
false	**false** Korn shell alias for **let 0**.
fc	**fc** [*options*] [*first* [*last*]] **fc** −e − [*old*=*new*] [*command*] Korn shell only. Display or edit commands in the history list. (Use only one of −l or −e.) **fc** provides capabilities similar to the C shell's **history** and **!** syntax. *first* and *last* are numbers or strings specifying the range of commands to display or edit. If *last* is omitted, **fc** applies to a single command (specified by *first*). If both *first* and *last* are omitted, **fc** edits the previous command or lists the last 16. The second form of **fc** takes a history *command*, replaces *old* string with *new* string, and executes the modified command. If no strings are specified, *command* is just re-executed. If no *command* is given either, the previous command is re-executed. *command* is a number or string like *first*. See examples under "Command History." *Options* −e [*editor*] Invoke *editor* to edit the specified history commands. The default *editor* is set by shell variable FCEDIT.

–e –	Execute (or redo) a history command; refer to second syntax line above.	**fc**
–l	List the specified command or range of commands, or list the last 16.	
–n	Suppress command numbering from the **–l** listing.	
–r	Reverse the order of the **–l** listing.	

fg [*jobIDs*]   **fg**

Bring current job or *jobIDs* to the foreground. See "Job Control."

fi   **fi**

Reserved word that ends an **if** statement. (Don't forget to use it!)

for *x* [**in** *list*]   **for**
do
   commands
done

For variable *x* (in optional *list* of values) do *commands*. If *list* is omitted, "**$@**" (positional parameters) is assumed.

Examples

Paginate files specified on the command line; save each result:

```
for file do
        pr $file > $file.tmp
done
```

Search chapters for a list of words (like **fgrep –f**):

```
for item in `cat program_list`
do
        echo "Checking chapters for"
        echo "references to program $item..."
        grep -c "$item.[co]" chap*
done
```

Extract a one-word title from each file and use as new filename:

```
for file do
        name=`sed -n 's/NAME: //p' $file`
        mv $file $name
done
```

function *name* { *commands*; }   **function**

Korn shell alias for **typeset –f**. See *name* earlier in this listing.

getopts	**getopts** *string name* [*args*]
	Process command-line arguments (or *args*, if specified) and check for legal options. **getopts** is used in shell script loops and is intended to ensure standard syntax for command-line options. Standard syntax dictates that command-line options begin with a + or a –. Options can be stacked; i.e., consecutive letters can follow a single –. End processing of options by specifying –– on the command line. *string* contains the option letters to be recognized by **getopts** when running the shell script. Valid options are processed in turn and stored in the shell variable *name*. If an option is followed by a colon, the option must be followed by one or more arguments. **getopts** uses the shell variables OPTARG and OPTIND. **getopts** is available to non-Bourne shell users as **/usr/bin/getopts**.
hash	**hash**
	Korn shell alias for **alias –t**. Emulates Bourne shell's **hash**.
hash	**hash** [**–r**] [*commands*]
	Bourne shell version. Search for *commands* and remember the directory in which each command resides. Before a new shell program has been hashed, it can be executed only from the directory in which it was created. Hashing a command allows it to be run from any directory. (Hashing a command adds it to a list of commands "known" to the shell.) Commands must also be hashed if you change your PATH variable. – removes commands from the hash list, either all of them or just the specified *commands*. With no arguments, **hash** lists the current hashed commands. The display shows *hits* (the number of times the command is called by the shell) and *cost* (the level of work needed to find the command).
history	**history**
	Show the last 16 commands. Korn shell alias for **fc –l**.
if	**if** *condition1* **then** *commands1* [**elif** *condition2* **then** *commands2*] . . . [**else** *commands3*] **fi**
	If *condition1* is met, do *commands1*; otherwise, if *condition2* is met, do *commands2*; if neither is met, do *commands3*. Conditions are usually specified with the **test** command. See additional examples under **:** and **exit**.

Examples

Insert a 0 before numbers less than 10:

```
if [ $counter -lt 10 ]
then number=0$counter
else number=$counter
fi
```

Make a directory if it doesn't exist:

```
if [ ! -d $dir ]; then
    mkdir $dir
    chmod 775 $dir
fi
```

---

integer   **integer**

Specify integer variables. Korn shell alias for **typeset −i**.

---

jobs [*options*] [*jobIDs*]   **jobs**

List all running or stopped jobs, or list those specified by *jobIDs*. For
example, you can check whether a long compilation or text format is
still running. Also useful before logging out. See "Job Control."

Options

  −l   List job IDs and process group IDs.

  −n   List only jobs whose status changed since last notifica-
          tion. Korn shell only.

  −p   List process group IDs only.

  −x *cmd* Replace each job ID found in *cmd* with the associated
          process ID and then execute *cmd*. Not valid for Korn
          shell.

---

kill [*options*] *IDs*   **kill**

Terminate each specified process *ID* or job *ID*. You must own the
process or be a privileged user. This built-in is similar to **/bin/kill**
described in Section 2. See also "Job Control."

Options

  −l   List the signal names. (Used by itself.)

  −*signal* The signal number (from **ps −f**) or name (from **kill −l**).
          With a signal number of 9, the kill is absolute.

Signals

Signals are defined in **/usr/include/sys/signal.h** and are listed
here without the SIG prefix.

```
HUP     1       hangup
INT     2       interrupt
QUIT    3       quit
```

→

The Bourne Shell and Korn Shell

kill	ILL	4	illegal instruction
←	TRAP	5	trace trap
	IOT	6	IOT instruction
	EMT	7	EMT instruction
	FPE	8	floating point exception
	KILL	9	kill
	BUS	10	bus error
	SEGV	11	segmentation violation
	SYS	12	bad argument to system call
	PIPE	13	write to pipe, but no process to read it
	ALRM	14	alarm clock
	TERM	15	software termination (the default signal)
	USR1	16	user-defined signal 1
	USR2	17	user-defined signal 2
	CLD	18	child process died
	PWR	19	restart after power failure

---

let

let *expressions*

or

((*expressions***))**

Korn shell only. Perform arithmetic as specified by one or more integer *expressions. expressions* consist of numbers, operators, and shell variables (which don't need a preceding **$**). Expressions must be quoted if they contain spaces or other special characters. The **(( ))** form does the quoting for you. For more information and examples, see "Arithmetic Expressions" earlier in this section. See also **expr** in Section 2.

Examples

Each example below adds 1 to variable **i**.

```
i=`expr $i + 1`
let i=i+1
let "i = i + 1"
(( i = i + 1 ))
```

---

newgrp

newgrp [*group*]

Change your group ID to *group*, or return to your default group.

---

nohup

nohup

Don't terminate a command after log out. **nohup** is a Korn shell alias:

```
nohup='nohup '
```

The embedded space at the end lets **nohup** interpret the following command as an alias, if needed.

print [*options*] [*string*]

Korn shell only. Display *string* (on standard output by default).
print includes the functions of **echo** and can be used in its place on
most UNIX systems.

Options

−	Ignore all subsequent options.
− −	Same as **−**.
−n	Don't end output with a newline.
−p	Send *string* to the process created by **|&**, instead of to standard output.
−r	Ignore the escape sequences often used with **echo**.
−R	Same as **−r** and ignore subsequent options (except **−n**).
−s	Send *string* to the history file.
−u[*n*]	Send *string* to file descriptor *n* (default is 1).

print

---

pwd .

Print your present working directory on standard output. In the Korn
shell, this is really an alias for **print −r − $PWD**.

pwd

---

r

Re-execute previous command. Korn shell alias for **fc −e −**.

r

---

read *variable1* [*variable2* ...]

Read one line of standard input, and assign each word to the corresponding *variable*, with all leftover words assigned to last variable. If
only one variable is specified, the entire line will be assigned to that
variable. See example below and under **case**. The return status is 0
unless *EOF* is reached.

Example

```
$ read first last address
Sarah Caldwell 123 Main Street

$ echo "$last, $first\n$address"
Caldwell, Sarah
123 Main Street
```

read

---

read [*options*] [*variable1?string*] [*variable2* ...]

Korn shell only. Same as in the Bourne shell, except that the Korn
shell version supports the options below as well as the **?** syntax for
prompting. If a variable is followed by **?***string*, then *string* is
displayed as a user prompt. If no variables are given, input is stored
in the REPLY variable.

read

→

read	*Options*
←	**−p** Read from the output of a **|&** coprocess.
	−r Raw mode; ignore \ as a line continuation character.
	−s Save input as a command in the history file.
	−u[*n*] Read input from file descriptor *n* (default is 0).

Example

Prompt yourself to enter two temperatures:

```
$ read n1?"High low: " n2
High low: 65 33
```

---

readonly   **readonly** [*variable1 variable2* ...]

Prevent the specified shell variables from being assigned new values. Variables can be accessed (read) but not overwritten. In the Korn shell, the syntax *variable=value* can be used to assign a new value that cannot be changed.

---

return   **return** [*n*]

Used inside a function definition. Exit the function with status *n* or with the exit status of the previously executed command.

---

select   **select** *x* [**in** *list*]
do
    commands
done

Korn shell only. Display a list of menu items on standard error, numbered in the order they are specified in *list*. If no *list* is given, items are read from the command line (via "**$@**"). Following the menu is a prompt string (set by **PS3**). At the **PS3** prompt, users select a menu item by typing its line number, or they redisplay the menu by typing RETURN. (User input is stored in the environment variable REPLY.) If a valid line number is typed, *commands* are executed.

Example

```
PS3="Select the item number:"

select event in Format Page View Exit
do
    case "$event" in
      Format) nroff $file | lp;;
      Page)   pr $file | lp;;
      View)   cat $file
      Exit)   exit 0;;
      *   )   echo "Invalid selection";;
    esac
done
```

The output of this script would look like this:

```
1. Format
2. Page
3. View
4. Exit
Select the item number:
```

---

set [*options arg1 arg2 ...*]

With no arguments, **set** prints the values of all variables known to the current shell. Options can be enabled (*–option*) or disabled (*+option*). Options can also be set when the shell is invoked, via **ksh** or **sh**. (See "Invoking the Shell" at the end of this section.) Arguments are assigned in order to **$1**, **$2**, etc.

Options

+A *name*

> Assign remaining arguments as elements of array *name*. Korn shell only.

–A *name*

> Same as **+A**, but unset *name* before making assignments. Korn shell only.

–a

> From now on, automatically mark variables for export after defining or changing them.

–e

> Exit if a command yields a nonzero exit status. In the Korn shell, the ERR trap is issued before the command exits.

–f

> Ignore filename metacharacters (e.g., * ? [ ]).

–h

> Locate commands as they are defined. The Korn shell creates tracked aliases, whereas the Bourne shell hashes function names. See **hash**.

–k

> Assignment of environment variables (*var=value*) will take effect regardless of where they appear on the command line. Normally, assignments must follow the command name.

–m

> Enable job control; background jobs will execute in a separate process group. **–m** is usually set automatically. Korn shell only.

–n

> Read commands but don't execute; useful for checking errors.

–o [*m*]

> List Korn shell modes, or turn on mode *m*. Many modes can be set by other options. Modes are:

> | | |
> |---|---|
> | **allexport** | Same as **–a**. |
> | **bgnice** | Run background jobs at lower priority. |
> | **emacs** | Set command-line editor to **emacs**. |
> | **errexit** | Same as **–e**. |
> | **ignoreeof** | Don't process *EOF* signals. To exit the shell, type **exit**. |
> | **keyword** | Same as **–k**. |

→

---

set		**markdirs**	Append / to directory names.
←		**monitor**	Same as **−m**.
		noclobber	Prevent overwriting via > redirection; use >| to overwrite files.
		noexec	Same as **−n**.
		noglob	Same as **−f**.
		nolog	Omit function definitions from history file.
		nounset	Same as **−u**.
		privileged	Same as **−p**.
		trackall	Same as **−h**.
		verbose	Same as **−v**.
		vi	Set command-line editor to **vi**.
		viraw	Same as **vi**, but process each character when it's typed.
		xtrace	Same as **−x**.

−p   Start up as a privileged user (i.e., don't process **$HOME/.profile**).

−s   Sort the positional parameters. Korn shell only.

−t   Exit after one command is executed.

−u   In substitutions, treat unset variables as errors.

−v   Show each shell command line when read.

−x   Show commands and arguments when executed, preceded by a +. This provides step-by-step debugging of shell scripts. (Same as **−o xtrace**.)

−   Turn off **−v** and **−x**, and turn off option processing. Included in Korn shell for compatibility with older versions of Bourne shell.

−−   Used as the last option; −− turns off option processing so that arguments beginning with − are not misinterpreted as options. (For example, you can set **$1** to −1.) If no arguments are given after −−, unset the positional parameters.

Examples

```
set -- "$num" -20 -30    Set $1 to $num, $2 to -20, $3 to -30.
set -vx                  Read each command line; show it;
                         execute it; show it again (with arguments).
set +x                   Stop command tracing.
set -o noclobber         Prevent file overwriting.
set +o noclobber         Allow file overwriting again.
```

shift	**shift** [*n*]

·Shift positional arguments (e.g., **$2** becomes **$1**). If *n* is given, shift to the left *n* places. Used in **while** loops to iterate through command-line arguments. In the Korn shell, *n* can be an integer expression.

stop [*jobIDs*]

Suspend the background job specified by *jobIDs*; this is the complement of **CTRL-Z** or **suspend**. Not valid in the Korn shell. See "Job Control."

suspend

Same as **CTRL-Z**. Often used to stop an **su** command. Not valid in the Korn shell.

test *condition*
   or
[*condition*]

Evaluate a *condition* and, if its value is true, return a zero exit status; otherwise, return a non-zero exit status. An alternate form of the command uses [ ] rather than the word *test*. The Korn shell allows an additional form, [[ ]]. *condition* is constructed using the expressions below. Conditions are true if the description holds true. Features that are Korn-shell-specific are marked with a (K).

File conditions

−**a** *file*	*file* exists. (K)
−**b** *file*	*file* exists and is a block special file.
−**c** *file*	*file* exists and is a character special file.
−**d** *file*	*file* exists and is a directory.
−**f** *file*	*file* exists and is a regular file.
−**G** *file*	*file* exists and its group is the effective group ID. (K)
−**g** *file*	*file* exists and its set-group-id bit is set.
−**k** *file*	*file* exists and its sticky bit is set.
−**L** *file*	*file* exists and is a symbolic link. (K)
−**O** *file*	*file* exists and its owner is the effective user ID. (K)
−**o** *c*	Option *c* is on. (K)
−**p** *file*	*file* exists and is a named pipe (fifo).
−**r** *file*	*file* exists and is readable.
−**S** *file*	*file* exists and is a socket. (K)
−**s** *file*	*file* exists and has a size greater than zero.
−**t** [*n*]	The open file descriptor *n* is associated with a terminal device; default *n* is 1.
−**u** *file*	*file* exists and its set-user-id bit is set.
−**w** *file*	*file* exists and is writable.
−**x** *file*	*file* exists and is executable.
f1 −**ef** *f2*	Files *f1* and *f2* are linked (refer to same file). (K)

Bourne
and Korn

→

f1 **−nt** *f2*   File *f1* is newer than *f2*. (K)

f1 **−ot** *f2*   File *f1* is older than *f2*. (K)

String conditions

−n *s1*   String *s1* has non-zero length.

−z *s1*   String *s1* has zero length.

s1 = *s2*   Strings *s1* and *s2* are identical. In the Korn shell, *s2* can be a regular expression.

s1 != *s2*   Strings *s1* and *s2* are *not* identical. In the Korn shell, *s2* can be a regular expression.

s1 < *s2*   ASCII value of *s1* precedes that of *s2*. (Valid only within **[[ ]]** construct). (K)

s1 > *s2*   ASCII value of *s1* follows that of *s2*. (Valid only within **[[ ]]** construct). (K)

string   *string* is not null.

Integer comparisons

n1 **−eq** *n2*   *n1* equals *n2*.

n1 **−ge** *n2*   *n1* is greater than or equal to *n2*.

n1 **−gt** *n2*   *n1* is greater than *n2*.

n1 **−le** *n2*   *n1* is less than or equal to *n2*.

n1 **−lt** *n2*   *n1* is less than or equal to *n2*.

n1 **−ne** *n2*   *n1* does not equal *n2*.

Combined forms

(condition**)**   True if *condition* is true (used for grouping). The **( )**'s should be preceded by a ****.

! *condition*   True if *condition* is false.

condition1 **−a** *condition2*
        True if both conditions are true.

condition1 **&&** *condition2*
        True if both conditions are true. (Valid only within **[[ ]]** construct.) (K)

condition1 **−o** *condition2*
        True if either condition is true.

condition1 **||** *condition2*
        True if either condition is true. (Valid only within **[[ ]]** construct.) (K)

Examples

Each example below shows the first line of various statements that might use a test condition:

```
while test $# -gt 0        While there are arguments ...
while [ -n "$1" ]          While there are nonempty arguments ...
if [ $count -lt 10 ]       If $count is less than 10 ...
if [ -d RCS ]              If the RCS directory exists ...
if [ "$answer" != "y" ]    If the answer is not y ...
if [ ! -r "$1" -o ! -f "$1" ]   If the first argument is not a
                                readable file or a regular file ...
```

time *command*

Execute *command* and print the total elapsed time, user time, and
system time (in seconds). Same as the UNIX command **time** (see
Section 2), except that the built-in version can also time other built-in
commands as well as all commands in a pipeline.

---

times

Print accumulated process times for user and system.

---

trap [[*commands*] *signals*]

Execute *commands* if any of *signals* is received. Common signals
include 0, 1, 2, and 15. Multiple commands should be quoted as a
group and separated by semicolons internally. If *commands* is the
null string (i.e., **trap "" *signals***), then *signals* will be ignored by the
shell. If *commands* are omitted entirely, reset processing of specified
signals to the default action. If both *commands* and *signals* are omitted, list current trap assignments. See examples below and under
exec.

Signals

Signals are listed along with what triggers them.

0	Exit from shell (usually when shell script finishes).
1	Hangup (usually logout).
2	Interrupt (usually CTRL-C).
3	Quit.
4	Illegal instruction.
5	Trace trap.
6	IOT instruction.
7	EMT instruction.
8	Floating point exception.
10	Bus error.
12	Bad argument to a system call.
13	Write to a pipe without a process to read it.
14	Alarm timeout.
15	Software termination (usually via **kill**).
ERR	Nonzero exit status. Korn shell only.
DEBUG	Execution of any command. Korn shell only.

Examples

```
trap "" 2            Ignore signal 2 (interrupts).
trap 2               Obey interrupts again.
```

→

trap
←
	Remove a **$tmp** file when the shell program exits, or if the user logs out, presses CTRL-C, or does a **kill**:
	
	```trap "rm -f $tmp; exit" 0 1 2 15```
	
	Print a "clean up" message when the shell program receives signals 1, 2, or 15:
	
	```trap 'echo Interrupt! Cleaning up...' 1 2 15```

type	**type** *commands*
	
	Show whether each command name is a UNIX command, a built-in command, or a defined shell function. In the Korn shell, this is simply an alias for **whence –v**.
	
	Example
	
	```$ type mv read```
	```mv is /bin/mv```
	```read is a shell builtin```

typeset	**typeset** [*options*] [*variable*[*=value* ...]] Korn shell only. Assign a type to each variable (along with an optional initial *value*), or, if no variables are supplied, display all variables of a particular type (as determined by the options). When variables are specified, *–option* enables the type and *+option* disables it. With no variables given, *–option* prints variable names and values; *+option* prints only the names. *Options* –**f**[*c*] The named variable is a function; no assignment is allowed. If no variable is given, list current function names. Flag *c* can be **t**, **u**, or **x**. **t** turns on tracing (same as **set –x**). **u** marks the function as undefined, which causes autoloading of the function (i.e., a search of FPATH will locate the function when it's first used). **x** exports the function. Note the aliases **autoload** and **function**. –**H** On non-UNIX systems, map UNIX filenames to host filenames. –**i**[*n*] Define variables as integers of base *n*. **integer** is an alias for **typeset –i**. –**L**[*n*] Define variables as flush-left strings, *n* characters long (truncate or pad with blanks on the right as needed). Leading blanks are stripped; leading 0's are stripped if **–Z** is also specified. If no *n* is supplied, field width is that of the variable's first assigned value. –**l** Convert uppercase to lowercase.

−R[*n*]	Define variables as flush-right strings, *n* characters long (truncate or pad with blanks on the left as needed). Trailing blanks are stripped. If no *n* is supplied, field width is that of the variable's first assigned value.
−r	Mark variables as read-only. See also **readonly**.
−t	Mark variables with a user-definable tag.
−u	Convert lowercase to uppercase.
−x	Mark variables for automatic export.
−Z[*n*]	When used with **−L**, strip leading 0's. When used alone, it's similar to **−R** except that **−Z** pads numeric values with 0's and pads text values with blanks.

Examples

```
typeset              List name, value, and type of all set variables.
typeset -x           List names and values of exported variables.
typeset +r PWD       End read-only status of PWD.
typeset -i n1 n2 n3  Three variables are integers.
typeset -R5 zipcode  zipcode is flush right, 5 characters wide.
```

ulimit [*options*] [*n*]

Print the value of one or more resource limits, or, if *n* is specified, set a resource limit to *n*. Resource limits can be either hard (**−H**) or soft (**−S**). By default, **ulimit** sets both limits or prints the soft limit. The options determine which resource is acted on.

Options

−H	Hard limit. Anyone can lower a hard limit; only privileged users can raise it.
−S	Soft limit. Must be lower than the hard limit.
−a	Print all limits.
−c	Maximum block size of core files.
−d	Maximum kbytes of data segment or heap.
−f	Maximum block size of files (the default option).
−n	Maximum file descriptor plus 1.
−s	Maximum kbytes of stack segment.
−t	Maximum CPU seconds.
−v	Maximum kbytes of virtual memory.

umask [*nnn*]

Display file creation mask or set file creation mask to octal value *nnn*. The file creation mask determines which permission bits are turned off (e.g., **umask 002** produces **rw-rw-r--**). **umask** is also a UNIX command (see Section 2).

unalias	**unalias** *names*
	Korn shell only. Remove *names* from the alias list. See also **alias**.
unset	**unset** [**−f**] *names*
	Erase definitions of functions or variables listed in *names*. In the Korn shell, functions must be specified explicitly with the **−f** option.
until	**until** *condition* **do** *commands* **done**
	Until *condition* is met, do *commands*. *condition* is usually specified with the **test** command.
wait	**wait** [*ID*]
	Pause in execution until all background jobs complete (exit status 0 will be returned), or pause until the specified background process *ID* or job *ID* completes (exit status of *ID* is returned). Note that the shell variable $! contains the process ID of the most recent background process. If job control is not in effect, *ID* can be only a process ID number. See "Job Control."
	Example
	wait $! *Wait for last background process to finish.*
whence	**whence** [*options*] *commands*
	Korn shell only. Show whether each command name is a UNIX command, a built-in command, a defined shell function, or an alias.
	Options
	−p Search for the pathname of *commands*.
	−v Verbose output; same as **type**.
while	**while** *condition* **do** *commands* **done**
	While *condition* is met, do *commands*. *condition* is usually specified with the **test** command. See examples under **case** and **test**.
filename	*filename*
	Read and execute commands from executable file *filename*.

Job Control

Job control lets you place foreground jobs in the background, bring background jobs to the foreground, or suspend (temporarily stop) running jobs. Job control is enabled by any of the following commands:

```
jsh -i                  Bourne shell

ksh -m -i               Korn shell (same as next two)
set -m
set -o monitor
```

Many job control commands take *jobID* as an argument. This argument can be specified as follows:

%*n*	Job number *n*.
%*s*	Job whose command line starts with string *s*.
%?*s*	Job whose command line contains string *s*.
%%	Current job.
%+	Current job (same as above).
%–	Previous job.

The Bourne and Korn shells provide the following job control commands. For more information on these commands, see "Built-in Commands" earlier in this section.

bg	Put a job in the background.
fg	Put a job in the foreground.
jobs	List active jobs.
kill	Terminate a job.
stop	Suspend a background job.
stty tostop	Stop background jobs if they try to send output to the terminal.
suspend	Same as **CTRL-Z**.
wait	Wait for background jobs to finish.
CTRL–Z	Suspend a foreground job. Then use **bg** or **fg**. (Your terminal may use something other than **CTRL-Z** as the suspend character.)

Invoking the Shell

The command interpreter for the Bourne shell (**sh**) or the Korn shell (**ksh**) can be invoked as follows:

> **sh** [*options*] [*arguments*]
> **ksh** [*options*] [*arguments*]

ksh and **sh** can execute commands from a terminal (when **–i** is specified), from a file (when the first *argument* is an executable script), or from standard input (if no arguments remain or if **–s** is specified).

Arguments

Arguments are assigned in order to the positional parameters $1, $2, etc. If array assignment is in effect (**–A** or **+A**), arguments are assigned as array elements. If the first argument is an executable script, commands are read from it, and remaining arguments are assigned to $1, $2, etc.

Options

−c *str* Read commands from string *str*.

−i   Create an interactive shell (prompt for input).

−p   Start up as a privileged user (i.e., don't process **$HOME/.profile**).

−r   Create a restricted shell (same as **rksh** or **rsh**).

−s   Read commands from standard input; output from built-in commands goes to file descriptor 1; all other shell output goes to file descriptor 2.

The remaining options to **sh** and **ksh** are listed under the **set** built-in command.

Restricted Shells

Restricted shells can be invoked in any of the following ways:

```
rksh                    Korn shell
ksh -r
set -r

rsh                     Bourne Shell
set -r
```

Restricted shells can also be set up by supplying **rksh** and **rsh** in the shell field of **/etc/passwd** or by using them as the value for the SHELL variable.

Restricted shells act the same as their non-restricted counterparts, except that the following are prohibited:

- Changing directory (i.e., using **cd**).

- Setting the PATH variable. **rksh** also prohibits setting ENV and SHELL.

- Specifying a **/** for command names or pathnames.

- Redirecting output (i.e., using > and >>).

Shell scripts can still be run, since in that case the restricted shell will call **ksh** or **sh** to run the script.

The C Shell

This section describes the C shell, so named because many of its programming constructs and symbols resemble those of the C programming language. The following topics are presented:

- Overview of features
- Syntax
- Variables
- Expressions
- Command history
- Built-in commands
- Job control
- Invoking the shell

Overview of Features

Features of the C shell include:

- Input/output redirection
- Wildcard characters (metacharacters) for filename abbreviation
- Shell variables for customizing your environment
- Integer arithmetic
- Access to previous commands (command history)
- Command name abbreviation (aliasing)
- A built-in command set for writing shell programs
- Job control

Syntax

This subsection describes the many symbols peculiar to the C shell. The topics are arranged as follows:

- Special files
- Filename metacharacters
- Quoting
- Command forms
- Redirection forms

Special Files

`~/.cshrc`	Executed at each instance of shell.
`~/.history`	History list saved from previous login.
`~/.login`	Executed by login shell after **.cshrc** at login.
`~/.logout`	Executed by login shell at logout.
`/etc/passwd`	Source of home directories for ˜*name* abbreviations.

Filename Metacharacters

`*`	Match any string of zero or more characters.
`?`	Match any single character.
`[abc...]`	Match any one of the enclosed characters; a hyphen can be used to specify a range (e.g., a-z, A-Z, 0-9).
`{abc,xxx,...}`	Expand each comma-separated string inside braces.
`~`	Home directory for the current user.
`~name`	Home directory of user *name*.

```
% ls new*         Match new and new.1.
% cat ch?         Match ch9 but not ch10.
% vi [D-R]*       Match files that begin with uppercase D through R.
% ls {ch,app}?    Expand, then match ch1, ch2, app1, app2.
% cd ~tom         Change to tom's home directory.
```

Quoting

Quoting disables a character's special meaning and allows it to be used literally, as itself. The following characters have special meaning to the C shell:

;	Command separator.
&	Background execution.
( )	Command grouping.
|	Pipe.
* ? [ ] ~	Filename metacharacters.
{ }	String expansion characters. Usually don't require quoting.
> < & !	Redirection symbols.
! ^	History substitution, quick substitution.
" ' \	Used in quoting other characters.
`	Command substitution.
$	Variable substitution.
newline space tab	Word separators.

The characters below can be used for quoting:

" "   Everything between " and " is taken literally, except for the following characters that keep their special meaning:

$	Variable substitution will occur.
`	Command substitution will occur.
"	This marks the end of the double quote.
\	Escape next character.
!	The history character.
newline	The newline character.

' '   Everything between ' and ' is taken literally except for ! (history) and another ', and newline.

\   The character following a \ is taken literally. Use within " " to escape ", $, and `. Often used to escape itself, spaces, or newlines. Always needed to escape a history character (usually !).

Examples

```
% echo 'Single quotes "protect" double quotes'
Single quotes "protect" double quotes

% echo "Well, isn't that \"special\"?"
Well, isn't that "special"?
```

```
% echo "You have `ls|wc -l` files in `pwd`"
You have 43 files in /home/bob

% echo "The value of \$x is $x"
The value of $x is 100
```

Command Forms

cmd **&**	Execute *cmd* in background.
cmd1 **;** *cmd2*	Command sequence; execute multiple *cmd*s on the same line.
(*cmd1* **;** *cmd2*)	Subshell; treat *cmd1* and *cmd2* as a command group.
cmd1 **|** *cmd2*	Pipe; use output from *cmd1* as input to *cmd2*.
cmd1 **`***cmd2***`**	Command substitution; use *cmd2* output as arguments to *cmd1*.
cmd1 **&&** *cmd2*	AND; execute *cmd1* and then (if *cmd1* succeeds) *cmd2*.
cmd1 **||** *cmd2*	OR; execute either *cmd1* or (if *cmd1* fails) *cmd2*.

Examples

% **nroff file &**	*Format in the background.*
% **cd; ls**	*Execute sequentially.*
% **(date; who; pwd) > logfile**	*All output is redirected.*
% **sort file	pr -3	lp**	*Sort file, page output, then print.*
% **vi `grep -l ifdef *.c`**	*Edit files found by grep.*
% **egrep '(yes|no)' `cat list`**	*Specify a list of files to search.*
% **grep XX file && lp file**	*Print file if it contains the pattern,*
% **grep XX file || echo XX not found**	*otherwise, echo an error message.*

Redirection Forms

File Descriptor	Name	Common Abbreviation	Typical Default
0	Standard Input	stdin	Keyboard
1	Standard Output	stdout	Terminal
2	Standard Error	stderr	Terminal

The usual input source or output destination can be changed as follows:

Simple Redirection

cmd **>** *file*	Send output of *cmd* to *file* (overwrite).
cmd **>!** *file*	Same as above, even if **noclobber** is set.
cmd **>>** *file*	Send output of *cmd* to *file* (append).
cmd **>>!** *file*	Same as above, but create *file* even if **noclobber** is set.
cmd **<** *file*	Take input for *cmd* from *file*.

`cmd << text`	Read standard input up to a line identical to *text* (*text* can be stored in a shell variable). Input is usually typed on the screen or in the shell program. Commands that typically use this syntax include **cat**, **echo**, **ex**, and **sed**. If *text* is enclosed in quotes, standard input will not undergo variable substitution, command substitution, etc.

Multiple Redirection

`cmd >& file`	Send both standard output and standard error to *file*.
`cmd >&! file`	Same as above, even if **noclobber** is set.
`cmd >>& file`	Append standard output and standard error to end of *file*.
`cmd >>&! file`	Same as above, but create *file* even if **noclobber** is set.
`cmd1 |& cmd2`	Pipe standard error together with standard output.
`(cmd > f1) >& f2`	Send standard output to file *f1*; standard error to file *f2*.
`cmd ⏐ tee files`	Send output of *cmd* to standard output (usually the terminal) and to *files*. (See the example in Section 2 under **tee**.)

Examples

```
% cat part1 > book
% cat part2 part3 >> book
% mail tim < report
% cc calc.c >& error_out
% cc newcalc.c >&! error_out
% grep UNIX ch* |& pr
% (find / -print > filelist) >& no_access

% sed 's/^/XX /g' << "END_ARCHIVE"
This is often how a shell archive is "wrapped",
bundling text for distribution.  You would normally
run sed from a shell program, not from the command line.
"END_ARCHIVE"
XX This is often how a shell archive is "wrapped",
XX bundling text for distribution.  You would normally
XX run sed from a shell program, not from the command line.
```

Variables

This subsection describes the following:

* Variable substitution

* Variable modifiers

* Predefined shell variables

* Example **.cshrc** file

* Environment variables

Variable Substitution

In the following substitutions, braces ({ }) are optional, except when needed to separate a variable name from following characters that would otherwise be a part of it.

`${var}`	The value of variable *var*.
`${var[i]}`	Select word or words in position *i* of *var*. *i* can be a single number, a range *m–n*, a range *–n* (missing *m* implies 1), a range *m–* (missing *n* implies all remaining words), or * (select all words). *i* can also be a variable that expands to one of these values.
`${#var}`	The number of words in *var*.
`${#argv}`	The number of arguments.
`$0`	Name of the program.
`${#argv[n]}`	Individual arguments on command line (positional parameters). *n* = 1-9.
`${n}`	Same as **$(argv[*n*])**.
`${#argv[*]}`	All arguments on command line.
`$*`	Same as **$argv[*]**.
`$argv[$#argv]`	The last argument.
`${?var}`	Return 1 if *var* is set; 0 if *var* is not set.
`$$`	Process number of current shell; useful as part of a filename for creating temporary files with unique names.
`$?0`	Return 1 if input filename is known; 0 if not.
`$<`	Read a line from standard input.

Examples

Sort the third through last arguments (files) and save the output in a unique temporary file:

```
sort $argv[3-] > tmp.$$
```

Process **.cshrc** commands only if the shell is interactive (i.e., the **prompt** variable must be set).

```
if ($?prompt) then
    set commands,
    alias commands,
    etc.
endif
```

Variable Modifiers

Except for **$?***var*, **$$**, **$?0**, and **$<**, the variable substitutions above may be followed by one of these modifiers. When braces are used, the modifier goes inside them.

:r	Return the variable's root.
:e	Return the variable's extension.
:h	Return the variable's header.
:t	Return the variable's tail.
:gr	Return all roots.
:ge	Return all extensions.
:gh	Return all headers.
:gt	Return all tails.
:q	Quote a wordlist variable, keeping the items separate. Useful when the variable contains filename metacharacters that should not be expanded.
:x	Quote a pattern, expanding it into a wordlist.

Examples Using Pathname Modifiers

The table below shows the use of pathname modifiers on the following variable:

```
aa=(/progs/num.c /book/chap.ps)
```

Variable Portion	Specification	Output Result
Normal Variable	echo $aa	/progs/num.c /book/chap.ps
Second Root	echo $aa[2]:r	/book/chap
Second Header	echo $aa[2]:h	/book
Second Tail	echo $aa[2]:t	chap.ps
Second Extension	echo $aa[2]:e	ps
Root	echo $aa:r	/progs/num /book/chap.ps
Global Root	echo $aa:gr	/progs/num /book/chap
Header	echo $aa:h	/progs /book/chap.ps
Global Header	echo $aa:gh	/progs /book
Tail	echo $aa:t	num.c /book/chap.ps
Global Tail	echo $aa:gt	num.c chap.ps
Extension	echo $aa:e	c /book/chap.ps
Global Extension	echo $aa:ge	c ps

Examples Using Quoting Modifiers

```
% set a="[a-z]*" A="[A-Z]*"
% echo "$a" "$A"
[a-z]* [A-Z]*

% echo $a $A
at cc m4 Book Doc

% echo $a:x $A
[a-z]* Book Doc

% set d=($a:q $A:q)
% echo $d
at cc m4 Book Doc
```

```
% echo $d:q
[a-z]* [A-Z]*

% echo $d[1] +++ $d[2]
at cc m4 +++ Book Doc

% echo $d[1]:q
[a-z]*
```

Predefined Shell Variables

Variables can be set in one of two ways, by assigning a value:

```
set var=value
```

or by simply turning them on:

```
set var
```

In the table below, variables that accept values are shown with the equal sign followed by the type of value they accept; the value is then described. (Note, however, that variables such as **argv**, **cwd**, or **status** are never explicitly assigned.) For variables that are turned on or off, the table describes what they do when set. The C shell automatically sets the variables **argv**, **cwd**, **home**, **path**, **prompt**, **shell**, **status**, **term**, and **user**.

argv=(args)	List of arguments passed to current command; default is ( ).
cdpath=(dirs)	List of alternate directories to search when locating arguments for **cd**, **popd**, or **pushd**.
cwd=dir	Full pathname of current directory.
echo	Re-display each command line before execution; same as **csh –x** command.
fignore=(chars)	List of filename suffixes to ignore during filename completion (see **filec**).
filec	If set, a filename that is partially-typed on the command line can be expanded to its full name when ESC is pressed. If more than one filename would match, type *EOF* to list possible completions.
hardpaths	Tell **dirs** to display the actual pathname of any directory that is a symbolic link.
histchars=ab	A two-character string that sets the characters to use in history-substitution and quick-substitution (default is !^).
history=n	Number of commands to save in history list.
home=dir	Home directory of user, initialized from HOME. The ˜ character is shorthand for this value.
ignoreeof	Ignore an end-of-file (*EOF*) from terminals; prevents accidental logout.
mail=(n file)	One or more files checked for new mail every 5 minutes or (if *n* is supplied) every *n* seconds.
nobeep	Don't ring bell for ambiguous file completion (see **filec**).

noclobber	Don't redirect output to an existing file; prevents accidental destruction of files.
noglob	Turn off filename expansion; useful in shell scripts.
nonomatch	Treat filename metacharacters as literal characters; e.g., **vi ch*** creates new file **ch*** instead of printing ``No match.''
notify	Notify user of completed jobs right away, instead of waiting for the next prompt.
path=(*dirs*)	List of pathnames in which to search for commands to execute. Initialized from PATH; default is **(. /usr/ucb /usr/bin)**.
prompt='*str*'	String that prompts for interactive input; default is **%**.
savehist=*n*	Number of history commands to save in **~/.history** upon logout; they can be accessed at the next login.
shell=*file*	Pathname of the shell program currently in use; default is **/bin/csh**.
status=*n*	Exit status of last command. Built-in commands return 0 (success) or 1 (failure).
term=*ID*	Name of terminal type, initialized to **/etc/ttytype**; same as TERM.
time='*n* %*c*'	If command execution takes more than *n* CPU seconds, report user time, system time, elapsed time, and CPU percentage. Supply optional **%***c* flags to show other data.
user=*name*	Login name of user, initialized from USER.
verbose	Display a command after history substitution; same as the command **csh –v**.

Example .cshrc File

```
# PREDEFINED VARIABLES

set path=(~ ~/bin /usr/ucb /bin /usr/bin . )
set mail=(/usr/mail/tom)

if ($?prompt) then            # settings for interactive use
  set echo
  set filec
  set noclobber ignoreeof

  set cdpath=(/usr/lib /usr/spool/uucp)
# Now I can type cd macros
# instead of cd /usr/lib/macros

  set fignore=.o              # ignore object files for filec
  set history=100 savehist=25
  set prompt='tom \!% '       # includes history number
  set time=3
```

```
# MY VARIABLES

    set man1="/usr/man/man1"      # lets me do    cd $man1, ls $man1
    set a="[a-z]*"                # lets me do    vi $a
    set A="[A-Z]*"               # or            grep string $A

# ALIASES

    alias c "clear; dirs"         # use quotes to protect ; or |
    alias h "history|more"
    alias j jobs -l
    alias ls ls -sFC              # redefine ls command
    alias del 'mv \!* ~/tmp_dir'  # a safe alternative to rm
endif
```

Environment Variables

The C shell maintains a set of *environment variables*, which are distinct from shell variables and aren't really part of the C shell. Shell variables are meaningful only within the current shell, but environment variables are automatically exported, making them available globally. For example, C shell variables are accessible only to a particular script in which they're defined, whereas environment variables can be used by any shell scripts, mail utilities, or editors you might invoke.

Environment variables are assigned as follows:

```
setenv VAR value
```

By convention, environment variable names are all uppercase. You can create your own environment variables, or you can use the predefined environment variables below.

These environment variables have a corresponding C shell variable. When either one changes, the value is copied to the other:

HOME	Home directory; same as **home**.
PATH	Search path for commands; same as **path**.
TERM	Terminal type; same as **term**.
USER	User name; same as **user**.

Other environment variables include the following:

EXINIT	A string of ex commands similar to those found in the startup *.exrc* file (e.g., **set ai**). Used by vi and ex.
LOGNAME	Another name for the USER variable.
MAIL	The file that holds mail. Used by mail programs. This is not the same as the C shell **mail** variable, which only checks for new mail.
PWD	The current directory; the value is copied from **cwd**.
SHELL	Undefined by default; once initialized to **shell**, the two are identical.
TERMCAP	The file that holds the cursor-positioning codes for your terminal type. Default is **/etc/termcap**.

Expressions

Expressions are used in **@**, **if**, and **while** statements to perform arithmetic, string comparisons, file testing, etc. **exit** and **set** can also specify expressions. Expressions are formed by combining variables and constants with operators that resemble those in the C programming language. Operator precedence is the same as in C but can be remembered as follows:

1. `*  /  %`

2. `+  -`

Group all other expressions inside ( )'s. Parentheses are required if the expression contains <, >, &, or | .

Operators

Operators can be one of the following types:

Assignment Operators

`=`	Assign value.
`+=   -=`	Reassign after addition/subtraction.
`*=   /=   %=`	Reassign after multiplication/division/remainder.
`&=   ^=   |=`	Reassign after bitwise AND/XOR/OR.
`++`	Increment
`-`	Decrement.

Arithmetic Operators

`*   /   %`	Multiplication; integer division; modulus (remainder).
`+   -`	Addition; subtraction.

Bitwise and Logical Operators

`~`	Binary inversion (one's complement).
`!`	Logical negation.
`<<   >>`	Bitwise left shift; bitwise right shift.
`&`	Bitwise AND.
`^`	Bitwise exclusive OR.
`|`	Bitwise OR.
`&&`	Logical AND.
`||`	Logical OR.
`{ command }`	Return 1 if command is successful; 0 otherwise. Note that this is the opposite of *command*'s normal return code. The **$status** variable may be more practical.

Comparison Operators

`==` `!=`	Equality; inequality.
`<=` `>=`	Less than or equal to; greater than or equal to.
`<` `>`	Less than; greater than.
`=~`	String on left matches a filename pattern containing *, ?, or [...].
`!~`	String on left does not match a filename pattern containing *, ?, or [...].

File Inquiry Operators

Command substitution and filename expansion are performed on *file* before the test is performed.

-d *file*	The file is a directory.
-e *file*	The file exists.
-f *file*	The file is a plain file.
-o *file*	The user owns the file.
-r *file*	The user has read permission.
-w *file*	The user has write permission.
-x *file*	The user has execute permission.
-z *file*	The file has zero size.
!	Reverse the sense of any inquiry above.

Examples

The following examples show **@** commands and assume **n** = 4:

Expression	Value of $x
`@ x = ($n > 10 || $n < 5)`	1
`@ x = ($n >= 0 && $n < 3)`	0
`@ x = ($n << 2)`	16
`@ x = ($n >> 2)`	1
`@ x = $n % 2`	0
`@ x = $n % 3`	1

The following examples show the first line of **if** or **while** statements:

Expression	Meaning
`while ($#argv != 0)`	While there are arguments ...
`if ($today[1] == "Fri")`	If the first word is "Fri" ...
`if ($file !~ *.[zZ])`	If the file doesn't end with **.z** or **.Z** ...
`if ($argv[1] =~ chap?)`	If the first argument is **chap** followed by a single character ...
`if (-f $argv[1])`	If the first argument is a plain file ...
`if (! -d $tmpdir)`	If **tmpdir** is not a directory ...

Command History

Previously executed commands are stored in a history list. The C shell lets you access this list so you can verify commands, repeat them, or execute modified versions of them. The **history** built-in command displays the history list; the predefined variables **histchars**, **history**, and **savehist** also affect the history mechanism. Accessing the history list involves three things:

- Making command substitutions (using ! and ^).

- Making argument substitutions (specific words within a command).

- Using modifiers to extract or replace parts of a command or word.

Command Substitution

`!`	Begin a history substitution.
`!!`	Previous command.
`!N`	Command number *N* in history list.
`!-N`	*N*th command back from current command.
`!string`	Most recent command that starts with *string*.
`!?string?`	Most recent command that contains *string*.
`!?string?%`	Most recent command argument that contains *string*.
`!$`	Last argument of previous command.
`!!string`	Previous command, then append *string*.
`!N string`	Command *N*, then append *string*.
`!{s1}s2`	Most recent command starting with string *s1*, then append string *s2*.
`^old^new^`	Quick substitution; change string *old* to *new* in previous command; execute modified command.

Command Substitution Examples

The following command is assumed:

```
%3 vi cprogs/01.c ch002 ch03
```

Event Number	Command Typed	Command Executed
4	`^00^0`	`vi cprogs/01.c ch02 ch03`
5	`nroff !*`	`nroff cprogs/01.c ch02 ch03`
6	`nroff !$`	`nroff ch03`
7	`!vi`	`vi cprogs/01.c ch02 ch03`
8	`!6`	`nroff ch03`

Event Number	Command Typed	Command Executed
9	!?01	vi cprogs/01.c ch02 ch03
10	!{nr}.new	nroff ch03.new
11	!!|lp	nroff ch03.new | lp
12	more !?pr?%	more cprogs/01.c

Word Substitution

Colons may precede any word specifier. After an event number, colons are optional unless shown below:

:0	Command name.
:n	Argument number n.
^	First argument.
$	Last argument.
:n-m	Arguments n through m.
-m	Words 0 through m; same as :0–m.
:n-	Arguments n through next-to-last.
:n*	Arguments n through last; same as n–$.
*	All arguments; same as ^–$ or 1–$.
#	Current command line up to this point; fairly useless.

Word Substitution Examples

The following command is assumed:

%13 cat ch01 ch02 ch03 biblio back

Event Number	Command Typed	Command Executed
14	ls !13^	ls ch01
15	sort !13:*	sort ch01 ch02 ch03 biblio back
16	lp !cat:3*	more ch03 biblio back
17	!cat:0-3	cat ch01 ch02 ch03
18	vi !-5:4	vi biblio

History Modifiers

Command and word substitutions can be modified by one or more of the following:

Printing, Substitution, and Quoting

:p	Display command but don't execute.
:s/*old*/*new*	Substitute string *new* for *old*, first instance only.
:gs/*old*/*new*	Substitute string *new* for *old*, all instances.
:&	Repeat previous substitution (**:s** or ^ command), first instance only.
:g&	Repeat previous substitution, all instances.
:q	Quote a wordlist.
:x	Quote separate words.

Truncation

:r	Extract the first available pathname root.
:gr	Extract all pathname roots.
:e	Extract the first available pathname extension.
:ge	Extract all pathname extensions.
:h	Extract the first available pathname header.
:gh	Extract all pathname headers.
:t	Extract the first available pathname tail.
:gt	Extract all pathname tails.

History Modifier Examples

From above, command number 17 is:

```
%17 cat ch01 ch02 ch03
```

Event Number	Command Typed	Command Executed
19	!17:s/ch/CH/	cat CH01 ch02 ch03
20	!:g&	cat CH01 CH02 CH03
21	!more:p	more cprogs/01.c (displayed only)
22	cd !$:h	cd cprogs
23	vi !mo:$:t	vi 01.c
24	grep stdio !$	grep stdio 01.c
25	^stdio^include stdio^:q	grep "include stdio" 01.c
26	nroff !21:t:p	nroff 01.c (is that want I wanted?)
27	!!	nroff 01.c (execute it)

#	**#**
	Ignore all text that follows on the same line. **#** is used in shell scripts as the comment character and is not really a command. In addition, a script that uses **#** as its first character is interpreted as a C shell script.
#!*shell*	**#!***shell*
	Used as the first line of a script to invoke the named *shell* (with optional arguments). Not supported in all shells. For example:
	```#!/bin/csh -f```
:	**:**
	Null command. Returns an exit status of 0.
alias	**alias** [*name* [*command*]]
	Assign *name* as the shorthand name, or alias, for *command*. If *command* is omitted, print the alias for *name*; if *name* is also omitted, print all aliases. Aliases can be defined on the command line, but they are more often stored in **.cshrc** so that they take effect upon logging in. (See the sample **.cshrc** file earlier in this section.) Alias definitions can reference command-line arguments, much like the history list. Use \!* to refer to all command-line arguments, \!^ for the first argument, \!$ for the last, etc. An alias *name* can be any valid UNIX command; however, you lose the original command's meaning unless you type *name*. See also **unalias**.
	Examples
	Set the size for xterm windows under the X Window System:
	```alias R 'set noglob; eval `resize`; unset noglob'```
	Show aliases that contain the string *ls*:
	``alias	grep ls```
	Run nroff on all command-line arguments:
	```alias ms 'nroff -ms \!*'```
	Copy the file that is named as the first argument:
	```alias back 'cp \!^ \!^.old'```
	Use the regular **ls**, not its alias:
	```% \ls```

bg [*jobIDs*]   **bg**

Put the current job or the *jobIDs* in the background. See also "Job Control" at the end of this section.

Example

To place a time-consuming process in the background, you might begin with:

```
4% nroff -ms report
CTRL-Z
```

and then issue any one of the following:

```
5% bg
5% bg %          Current job
5% bg %1         Job number 1
5% bg %nr        Match initial string nroff
5% % &
```

---

break   **break**

Resume execution following the **end** command of the nearest enclosing **while** or **foreach**.

---

breaksw   **breaksw**

Break from a **switch**; continue execution after the **endsw**.

---

case *pattern* :   **case**

Identify a *pattern* in a **switch**.

---

cd [*dir*]   **cd**

Change working directory to *dir*; default is home directory of user. If *dir* is a relative pathname but is not in the current directory, the **cdpath** variable is searched. See the sample **.cshrc** file earlier in this section.

---

chdir [*dir*]   **chdir**

Same as **cd**. Useful if you are redefining **cd**.

---

continue   **continue**

Resume execution of nearest enclosing **while** or **foreach**.

---

default :   **default**

Label the default case (typically last) in a **switch**.

dirs	**dirs** [**−l**]

Print the directory stack, showing the current directory first; use **−l** to expand the home directory symbol (˜) to the actual directory name. See also **popd** and **pushd**. |
| **echo** | **echo** [**−n**] *string*

Write *string* to standard output; if **−n** is specified, the output is not terminated by a newline. Unlike the UNIX version (**/bin/echo**) and the Bourne shell version, the C shell's **echo** doesn't support escape characters. See also **echo** in Sections 2 and 4. |
| **end** | **end**

Reserved word that ends a **foreach** or **switch** statement. |
| **endif** | **endif**

Reserved word that ends an **if** statement. |
| **eval** | **eval** *args*

Typically, **eval** is used in shell scripts, and *args* is a line of code that contains shell variables. **eval** forces variable expansion to happen first and then runs the resulting command. This "double-scanning" is useful any time shell variables contain input/output redirection symbols, aliases, or other shell variables. (For example, redirection normally happens before variable expansion, so a variable containing redirection symbols must be expanded first using **eval**; otherwise, the redirection symbols remain uninterpreted.) A Bourne shell example can be found under **eval** in Section 4. Other uses of **eval** are shown below and under **alias**.

Examples

The following lines can be placed in the **.login** file to set up terminal characteristics:

```
set noglob
eval `tset -s xterm`
unset noglob
```

The following commands show the effect of **eval**:

```
% set b='$a'
% set a=hello

% echo $b                Read the command line once.
$a
% eval echo $b           Read the command line twice.
hello
``` |

exec *command*

Execute *command* in place of current shell. This terminates the current shell, rather than creating a new process under it.

---

exit [(*expr*)]

Exit a shell script with the status given by *expr*. A status of 0 means success; nonzero means failure. If *expr* is not specified, the exit value is that of the **status** variable. **exit** can be issued at the command line to close a window (log out).

---

fg [*jobIDs*]

Bring the current job or the *jobIDs* to the foreground. See also "Job Control" at the end of this section.

Example

If you suspend a vi editing session (by pressing **CTRL-Z**), you might resume vi using any of these commands:

```
8% %
8% fg
8% fg %
8% fg %vi        Match initial string
```

---

foreach *name* (*wordlist*)
    commands
end

Assign variable *name* to each value in *wordlist*, and execute *commands* between **foreach** and **end**. You can use **foreach** as a multi-line command issued at the C-shell prompt (first example below), or you can use it in a shell script (second example).

Examples

Rename all files that begin with a capital letter:

```
% foreach i ([A-Z]*)
? mv $i $i.new
? end
```

Check whether each command-line argument is an option or not:

```
foreach arg ($argv)
    # does it begin with - ?
    if ("$arg" =~ -*) then
        echo "Argument is an option"
    else
        echo "Argument is a filename"
    endif
end
```

glob	**glob** *wordlist*
	Do filename, variable, and history substitutions on *wordlist.* This expands it much like **echo**, except that no \ escapes are recognized, and words are delimited by null characters. **glob** is typically used in shell scripts to "hardcode" a value so that it remains the same for the rest of the script.
goto	**goto** *string*
	Skip to a line whose first non-blank character is *string* followed by a **:**, and continue execution below that line. On the **goto** line, *string* can be a variable or filename pattern, but the label branched to must be a literal, expanded value and must not occur within a **foreach** or **while**.
hashstat	**hashstat**
	Display statistics that show the hash table's level of success at locating commands via the **path** variable.
history	**history** [*options*]
	Display the list of history events. (History syntax is discussed earlier in "Command History.")

Options

    −h   Print history list without event numbers.

    −r   Print in reverse order; show oldest commands last.

    n   Display only the last **n** history commands, instead of the number set by the **history** shell variable.

Example

To save and execute the last five commands:

```
history -h 5 > do_it
source do_it
```

if	**if**
	Begin a conditional statement. The simple format is:

```
if (expr) cmd
```

There are three other possible formats, shown side-by-side:

```
if (expr) then      if (expr) then      if (expr) then
    cmds                cmds1               cmds1
endif               else                else if (expr) then
                        cmds2               cmds2
                    endif               else
                                            cmds3
                                        endif
```

In the simplest form, execute *cmd* if *expr* is true; otherwise do nothing (redirection still occurs; this is a bug). In the other forms, execute one or more commands. If *expr* is true, continue with the commands after **then**; if *expr* is false, branch to the commands after **else** (or after the **else if** and continue checking). For more examples, see "Expressions" earlier in this section, or **shift** or **while**.

Example

Take a default action if no command-line arguments are given:

```
if ($#argv == 0) then
    echo "No filename given.  Sending to Report."
    set outfile = Report
else
    set outfile = $argv[1]
endif
```

jobs [–l]

List all running or stopped jobs; **–l** includes process IDs. For example, you can check whether a long compilation or text format is still running. Also useful before logging out.

kill [*options*] *ID*

Terminate each specified process *ID* or job *ID*. You must own the process or be a privileged user. This built-in is similar to **/bin/kill** described in Section 2 but also allows symbolic job names. Stubborn processes can be killed using signal 9. See also "Job Control" at the end of this section.

Options

–l	List the signal names. (Used by itself.)
–signal	The signal number (from **ps –f**) or name (from **kill –l**).

Signals

Signals are defined in **/usr/include/sys/signal.h** and are listed here without the SIG prefix.

HUP	1	hangup
INT	2	interrupt
QUIT	3	quit
ILL	4	illegal instruction
TRAP	5	trace trap
IOT	6	IOT instruction
EMT	7	EMT instruction
FPE	8	floating point exception
KILL	9	kill
BUS	10	bus error
SEGV	11	segmentation violation
SYS	12	bad argument to system call
PIPE	13	write to pipe, but no process to read it
ALRM	14	alarm clock
TERM	15	software termination (the default signal)

C Shell

→

USR1	16	user-defined signal 1
USR2	17	user-defined signal 2
CLD	18	child process died
PWR	19	restart after power failure

Examples

If you've issued the following command:

```
44% nroff -ms report &
```

you can terminate it in any of the following ways:

45% **kill 19536**	*Process ID*
45% **kill %**	*Current job*
45% **kill %1**	*Job number 1*
45% **kill %nr**	*Initial string*
45% **kill %?report**	*Matching string*

---

limit

limit [**−h**] [*resource* [*limit*]]

Display limits or set a *limit* on resources used by the current process and by each process it creates. If no *limit* is given, the current limit is printed for *resource*. If *resource* is also omitted, all limits are printed. By default, the current limits are shown or set; with **−h**, hard limits are used. A hard limit imposes an absolute limit that can't be exceeded. Only a privileged user may raise it. See also **unlimit**.

Resource

cputime	Maximum number of seconds the CPU can spend; can be abbreviated as **cpu**.
filesize	Maximum size of any one file.
datasize	Maximum size of data (including stack).
stacksize	Maximum size of stack.
coredumpsize	Maximum size of a core dump file.

Limit

A number followed by an optional character (a unit specifier).

For **cputime**:	*n***h** (for *n* hours)
	*n***m** (for *n* minutes)
	*mm***:***ss* (minutes and seconds)
For others:	*n***k** (for *n* kilobytes, the default)
	*n***m** (for *n* megabytes)

---

login

login [*user* | **−p**]

Replace *user*'s login shell with **/bin/login**. **−p** is used to preserve environment variables.

---

logout

logout

Terminate the login shell.

nice [±*n*] *command*

Change the execution priority for *command*, or, if none is given, change priority for the current shell. (See also **nice** in Section 2.) The priority range is -20 to 20, with a default of 4. The range seems backwards: -20 gives the highest priority (fastest execution); 20 gives the lowest.

+*n*	Add *n* to the priority value (lower job priority).
−*n*	Subtract *n* from the priority value (raise job priority). Privileged users only.

---

nohup [*command*]

"No hangup signals." Do not terminate *command* after terminal line is closed (i.e., when you hang up from a phone or log out). Use without *command* in shell scripts to keep script from being terminated. (See also **nohup** in Section 2.)

---

notify [*jobID*]

Report immediately when a background job finishes (instead of waiting for you to exit a long editing session, for example). If no *jobID* is given, the current background job is assumed.

---

onintr *label*
onintr −
onintr

"On interrupt." Used in shell scripts to handle interrupt signals (similar to the Bourne shell's **trap 2** and **trap "" 2** commands). The first form is like a **goto** *label*. The script will branch to *label*: if it catches an interrupt signal (e.g., CTRL-C). The second form lets the script ignore interrupts. This is useful at the beginning of a script or before any code segment that needs to run unhindered (e.g., when moving files). The third form restores interrupt handling that was previously disabled with **onintr −**.

Example

```
onintr cleanup      # go to "cleanup" on interrupt
   .
   .                # shell script commands
   .
cleanup:            # label for interrupts
   onintr -         # ignore additional interrupts
   rm -f $tmpfiles  # remove any files created
   exit 2           # exit with an error status
```

popd	**popd** [+*n*] Remove the current entry from the directory stack, or remove the *n*th entry from the stack. The current entry has number 0 and appears on the left. See also **dirs** and **pushd**.

pushd	**pushd** *name*
	pushd [+*n*]
	pushd
	
	The first form changes the working directory to *name* and adds it to the directory stack. The second form rotates the *n*th entry to the beginning, making it the working directory. (Entry numbers begin at 0.) With no arguments, **pushd** switches the first two entries and changes to the new current directory. See also **dirs** and **popd**.
	
	Examples
	
	`%5 dirs`
	`/home/bob /usr`
	
	`%6 pushd /etc` *Add* /etc *to directory stack*
	`/etc /home/bob /usr`
	
	`%7 pushd +2` *Switch to third directory*
	`/usr /etc /home/bob`
	
	`%8 pushd` *Switch top two directories*
	`/etc /usr /home/bob`
	
	`%9 popd` *Discard current entry; go to next*
	`/usr /home/bob`

rehash	**rehash** Recompute the hash table for the **path** variable. Use **rehash** whenever a new command is created during the current session. This allows the **path** variable to locate and execute the command. (If the new command resides in a directory not listed in **path**, add this directory to **path** before rehashing.) See also **unhash**.
repeat	**repeat** *n command* Execute *n* instances of *command*. *Examples* Print three copies of **memo**: `% repeat 3 pr memo	lp`  Read 10 lines from the terminal and store in **item_list**:  `% repeat 10 line > item_list`

Append 50 boilerplate files to **report**: `% repeat 50 cat template >> report`	**repeat**

---

set *variable* **=** *value*
set *variable*[*n*] **=** *value*
set

Set *variable* to *value*, or if multiple values are specified, set the variable to the list of words in the value list. If an index *n* is specified, set the *n*th word in the variable to *value*. (The variable must already contain at least that number of words.) With no arguments, display the names and values of all set variables. See also "Predefined Shell Variables" earlier in this section.

Examples

```
% set list=(yes no mabye)      Assign a wordlist
% set list[3]=maybe            Assign an item in existing wordlist
% set quote="Make my day"      Assign a variable
% set x=5 y=10 history=100     Assign several variables
% set blank                    Assign a null value to blank
```

set (right margin)

---

setenv [*name* [*value*]]   **setenv**

Assign a *value* to an environment variable *name*. By convention, *name* must be uppercase. *value* can be a single word or a quoted string. If no *value* is given, the null value is assigned. With no arguments, display the names and values of all environment variables. **setenv** is not necessary for the USER, TERM, and PATH variables because they are automatically exported from **user**, **term**, and **path**. See also "Environment Variables" earlier in this section.

C Shell

---

shift [*variable*]   **shift**

If *variable* is given, shift the words in a wordlist variable; i.e., *name*[**2**] becomes *name*[**1**]. With no argument, shift the positional parameters (command-line arguments); i.e., **$2** becomes **$1**. **shift** is typically used in a **while** loop. See additional example under **while**.

Example

```
while ($#argv)        # while there are arguments
    if (-f $argv[1])
        wc -l $argv[1]
    else
        echo "$argv[1] is not a regular file"
    endif
    shift             # get the next argument
end
```

---

source	## source [−h] *script*
	Read and execute commands from a C shell script. With **−h**, the commands are added to the history list but aren't executed.
	### Example
| | ```
source ~/.cshrc
``` |
stop	## stop [*jobIDs*]
	Suspend the current background job or the background job specified by *jobIDs*; this is the complement of **CTRL-Z** or **suspend**.
suspend	## suspend
	Suspend the current foreground job; same as **CTRL-Z**. Often used to stop an **su** command.
switch	## switch
	Process commands depending on value of a variable. When you need to handle more than three choices, **switch** is a useful alternative to an **if-then-else** statement. If the *string* variable matches *pattern1*, the first set of *commands* are executed; if *string* matches *pattern2*, the second set of *commands* are executed; and so on. If no patterns match, execute commands under the **default** case. *string* can be specified using command substitution, variable substitution, or filename expansion. Patterns can be specified using pattern-matching symbols *****, **?**, and **[ ]**. **breaksw** is used to exit the **switch** after *commands* are executed. If **breaksw** is omitted (which is rarely done), the **switch** continues to execute another set of commands until it reaches a **breaksw** or **endsw**. Below is the general syntax of **switch**, side-by-side with an example that processes the first command-line argument.

```
switch (string)                switch ($argv[1])
    case pattern1:                 case -[nN]:
        commands                       nroff $file | lp
        breaksw                        breaksw
    case pattern2:                 case -[Pp]:
        commands                       pr $file | lp
        breaksw                        breaksw
    case pattern3:                 case -[Mm]:
        commands                       more $file
        breaksw                        breaksw
          .                        case -[Ss]:
          .                            sort $file
          .                            breaksw
    default:                       default:
        commands                       echo "Error--no such option"
                                       exit 1
        breaksw                        breaksw
endsw                          endsw
```
```

time [*command*]

Execute a *command* and show how much time it uses. With no argument, **time** can be used in a shell script to time it.

time

---

umask [*nnn*]

Display file creation mask or set file creation mask to octal *nnn*. The file creation mask determines which permission bits are turned off. **umask** is also a UNIX command. See the entry in Section 2 for examples.

umask

---

unalias *name*

Remove *name* from the alias list. See **alias** for more information.

unalias

---

unhash

Remove internal hash table. The C shell will stop using hashed values and will spend time searching the **path** directories to locate a command. See also **rehash**.

unhash

---

unlimit [*resource*]

Remove the allocation limits on *resource*. If *resource* is not specified, remove limits for all resources. See **limit** for more information.

unlimit

---

unset *variables*

Remove one or more *variables*. Variable names may be specified as a pattern, using filename metacharacters. See **set**.

unset

---

unsetenv *variable*

Remove an environment variable. Filename matching is *not* valid. See **setenv**.

unsetenv

---

wait

Pause in execution until all background jobs complete, or until an interrupt signal is received.

wait

---

while (*expression*)
    commands
end

As long as *expression* is true (evaluates to non-zero), evaluate *commands* between **while** and **end**. **break** and **continue** can be used to terminate or continue the loop. See also example under **shift**.

while

→

C Shell

while ←	*Example*

```
set user = (alice bob carol ted)
while ($argv[1] != $user[1])
   #Cycle through each user, checking for a match
   shift user
   #If we cycled through with no match...
   if ($#user == 0) then
     echo "$argv[1] is not on the list of users"
     exit 1
   endif
end
```

@	**@** *variable* = *expression* **@** *variable*[*n*] = *expression* **@**

Assign the value of the arithmetic *expression* to *variable*, or to the *n*th element of *variable* if the index *n* is specified. With no *variable* or *expression* specified, print the values of all shell variables (same as **set**). Expression operators as well as examples are listed under "Expressions," earlier in this section. Two special forms are also valid:

| **@** *variable*++ | Increment *variable* by one. |
| **@** *variable*– – | Decrement *variable* by one. |

Job Control

Job control lets you place foreground jobs in the background, bring background jobs to the foreground, or suspend (temporarily stop) running jobs. The C shell provides the following commands for job control. For more information on these commands, see "Built-in Commands" earlier in this section.

bg	Put a job in the background.
fg	Put a job in the foreground.
jobs	List active jobs.
kill	Terminate a job.
notify	Notify when a background job finishes.
stop	Suspend a background job.
CTRL–Z	Suspend a foreground job.

Many job control commands take *jobID* as an argument. This argument can be specified as follows:

%*n*	Job number *n*.
%*s*	Job whose command line starts with string *s*.
%?*s*	Job whose command line contains string *s*.

%%	Current job.
%	Current job (same as above).
%+	Current job (same as above).
%−	Previous job.

Invoking the Shell

The C-shell command interpreter can be invoked as follows:

csh [*options*] [*arguments*]

csh uses syntax resembling C and executes commands from a terminal or a file. Options **−n**, **−v**, and **−x** are useful when debugging scripts.

Options

−b	Allow the remaining command-line options to be interpreted as options to a specified command, rather than as options to **csh** itself.
−c	Execute commands located in first filename argument.
−e	Exit if a command produces errors.
−f	Fast start up; start **csh** without executing **.cshrc** or **.login**.
−i	Invoke interactive shell (prompt for input).
−n	Parse commands but do not execute.
−s	Read commands from the standard input.
−t	Exit after executing one command.
−v	Display commands before executing them; expand history substitutions but don't expand other substitutions (e.g., filename, variable, and command). Same as setting **verbose**.
−V	Same as **−v**, but also display **.cshrc**.
−x	Display commands before executing them, but expand all substitutions. Same as setting **echo**. **−x** is often combined with **−v**.
−X	Same as **−x**, but also display **.cshrc**.

C Shell

Part II

Text Editing

Part II summarizes the command set for the text editors and related utilities available in UNIX. The first section reviews pattern matching, an important aspect of text editing.

Section 6 - *Pattern Matching*

Section 7 - *The Emacs Editor*

Section 8 - *The Vi Editor*

Section 9 - *The Ex Editor*

Section 10 - *The Sed Editor*

Section 11 - *The Awk Scripting Language*

Pattern Matching

A number of UNIX text-editing utilities let you search for, and in some cases change, text patterns rather than fixed strings. These utilities include the editing programs ed, ex, vi, and sed, the awk scripting language, and the commands **grep** and **egrep**. Text patterns (also called regular expressions) contain normal characters mixed with special characters (also called metacharacters).

This section presents the following topics:

- Filenames versus patterns

- List of metacharacters available to each program

- Description of metacharacters

- Examples

Filenames Versus Patterns

Metacharacters used in pattern matching are different from metacharacters used for filename expansion (see Sections 4 and 5). When you issue a command on the command line, special characters are seen first by the shell, then by the program; therefore, unquoted metacharacters are interpreted by the shell for filename expansion. The command:

```
$ grep [A-Z]* chap[12]
```

could, for example, be interpreted by the shell as:

```
$ grep Array.c Bug.c Comp.c chap1 chap2
```

and would then try to find the pattern *Array.c* in files **Bug.c**, **Comp.c**, **chap1**, and **chap2**. To bypass the shell and pass the special characters to **grep**, use quotes:

```
$ grep "[A-Z]*" chap[12]
```

Double quotes suffice in most cases, but single quotes are the safest bet.

(Note also that in pattern matching, ? matches zero or one instance of a regular expression; in filename expansion, ? matches a single character.)

Metacharacters, Listed by UNIX Program

Some metacharacters are valid for one program but not for another. Those that are available to a UNIX program are marked by a bullet (•) in the table below. Full descriptions are provided after the table.

Symbol	ed	ex	vi	sed	awk	grep	egrep	Action
.	•	•	•	•	•	•	•	Match any character.
*	•	•	•	•	•	•	•	Match zero or more preceding.
^	•	•	•	•	•	•	•	Match beginning of line.
$	•	•	•	•	•	•	•	Match end of line.
\	•	•	•	•	•	•	•	Escape character following.
[ ]	•	•	•	•	•	•	•	Match one from a set.
\(\)	•	•	•					Store pattern for later replay.
\{ \}	•		•			•		Match a range of instances.
\< \>	•	•	•					Match word's beginning or end.
+					•		•	Match one or more preceding.
?					•		•	Match zero or one preceding.
|					•		•	Separate choices to match.
( )					•		•	Group expressions to match.

In ed, ex, and sed, note that you specify both a search pattern (on the left) and a replacement pattern (on the right). The metacharacters above are meaningful only in a search pattern.

UNIX in a Nutshell

In ed, ex, and sed, the following additional metacharacters are valid only in a replacement pattern:

Symbol	ex	sed	ed	Action
\	•	•	•	Escape character following.
n	•	•	•	Reuse pattern stored in \(\).
&	•	•		Reuse previous search pattern.
~	•			Reuse previous replacement pattern.
\u \U	•			Change character(s) to uppercase.
\l \L	•			Change character(s) to lowercase.
\E	•			Turn off previous \U or \L.
\e	•			Turn off previous \u or \l.

Metacharacters

The characters below have special meaning only in search patterns:

.   Match any *single* character except newline.

*   Match any number (or none) of the single character that immediately precedes it. The preceding character can also be a regular expression. E.g., since . (dot) means any character, .* means "match any number of any character."

^   Match the following regular expression at the beginning of the line.

$ Match the preceding regular expression at the end of the line.

[ ]   Match any *one* of the enclosed characters.

     A hyphen (–) indicates a range of consecutive characters. A circumflex (^) as the first character in the brackets reverses the sense: it matches any one character *not* in the list. A hyphen or close bracket (]) as the first character is treated as a member of the list. All other metacharacters are treated as members of the list.

\{*n*,*m*\}   Match a range of occurrences of the single character that immediately precedes it. The preceding character can also be a regular expression. \{*n*\} matches exactly *n* occurrences, \{*n*,\} matches at least *n* occurrences, and \{*n*,*m*\} matches any number of occurrences between *n* and *m*. *n* and *m* must be between 0 and 256, inclusive.

\   Turn off the special meaning of the character that follows.

\(\)   Save the pattern enclosed between \(and \) into a special holding space. Up to nine patterns can be saved on a single line. They can be ``replayed'' in substitutions by the escape sequences \1 to \9.

\< \>   Match characters at beginning (\<) or end (\>) of a word.

+   Match one or more instances of preceding regular expression.

?   Match zero or one instances of preceding regular expression.

| Match the regular expression specified before or after.

( )   Apply a match to the enclosed group of regular expressions.

The characters below have special meaning only in replacement patterns.

\	Turn off the special meaning of the character that follows.
\n	Restore the *n*th pattern previously saved by \(and \). *n* is a number from 1 to 9, with 1 starting on the left.
&	Reuse the search pattern as part of the replacement pattern.
~	Reuse the previous replacement pattern in the current replacement pattern.
\u	Convert first character of replacement pattern to uppercase.
\U	Convert replacement pattern to uppercase.
\l	Convert first character of replacement pattern to lowercase.
\L	Convert replacement pattern to lowercase.

Examples of Searching

When used with **grep** or **egrep**, regular expressions are surrounded by quotes. (If the pattern contains a $, you must use single quotes; e.g., *'pattern'*.) When used with ed, ex, sed, and awk, regular expressions are usually surrounded by / (although any delimiter works). Here are some example patterns:

Pattern	*What does it match?*
bag	The string *bag*.
^bag	*bag* at beginning of line.
bag$	*bag* at end of line.
^bag$	*bag* as the only word on line.
[Bb]ag	*Bag* or *bag*.
b[aeiou]g	Second letter is a vowel.
b[^aeiou]g	Second letter is a consonant (or uppercase or symbol).
b.g	Second letter is any character.
^...$	Any line containing exactly three characters.
^\.	Any line that begins with a dot.
^\.[a-z][a-z]	Same, followed by two lowercase letters (e.g., troff requests).
^\.[a-z]\{2\}	Same as previous, **grep** or sed only.
^[^.]	Any line that doesn't begin with a dot.
bugs*	*bug*, *bugs*, *bugss*, etc.
"word"	A word in quotes.
"*word"*	A word, with or without quotes.
[A-Z][A-Z]*	One or more uppercase letters.
[A-Z]+	Same, **egrep** or awk only.
[A-Z].*	An uppercase letter, followed by zero or more characters.
[A-Z]*	Zero or more uppercase letters.
[a-zA-Z]	Any letter.
[^0-9A-Za-z]	Any symbol (not a letter or a number).

egrep or awk pattern	What does it match?
[567]	One of the numbers 5, 6, or 7.
five|six|seven	One of the words *five*, *six*, or *seven*.
80[23]?86	*8086, 80286,* or *80386*
compan(y|ies)	*company* or *companies*

ex or vi pattern	What does it match?
\<the	Words like *theater* or *the*.
the\>	Words like *breathe* or *the*.
\<the\>	The word *the*.

sed or grep pattern	What does it match?
0\{5,\}	Five or more zeros in a row.
[0-9]\{3\}-[0-9]\{2\}-[0-9]\{4\}	Social security number (*nnn-nn-nnnn*).

Examples of Searching and Replacing

The following examples show the metacharacters available to sed or ex. Note that ex commands begin with a colon. A space is marked by a □; a tab is marked by *tab*.

Command	Result
s/.*/(&)/	Redo the entire line, but add parentheses.
s/.*/mv & &.old/	Change a wordlist (one word per line) into **mv** commands.
/^$/d	Delete blank lines.
:g/^$/d	Same as previous, in ex editor.
/^[□tab]*$/d	Delete blank lines, plus lines containing spaces or tabs.
:g/^[□tab]*$/d	Same as previous, in ex editor.
s/□□*/□/g	Turn one or more spaces into one space.
:%s/□□*/□/g	Same as previous, in ex editor.
:s/[0-9]/Item &:/	Turn a number into an item label (on the current line).
:s	Repeat the substitution on the first occurrence.
:&	Same as previous.
:sg	Same, but for all occurrences on the line.
:&g	Same as previous.
:%&g	Repeat the substitution globally.
:.,$s/Fortran/\U&/g	Change word to uppercase, on current line to last line.
:%s/.*/\L&/	Lowercase entire file.
:s/\<./\u&/g	Uppercase first letter of each word on current line. (Useful for titles.)
:%s/yes/No/g	Globally change a word to *No*.
:%s/Yes/~/g	Globally change a different word to *No* (previous replacement).

Pattern Matching

Finally, some sed examples for transposing words. A simple transposition of two words might look like this:

```
s/die or do/do or die/                    Transpose words.
```

The real trick is to use hold buffers to transpose variable patterns. For example:

```
s/\([Dd]ie\) or \([Dd]o\)/\2 or \1/       Transpose, using hold buffers.
```

The Emacs Editor

This section presents the following topics:

- Introduction

- Summary of emacs commands by group

- Summary of emacs commands by key

- Summary of emacs commands by name

Introduction

Although emacs is not part of SVR4 or Solaris 2.0, this text editor is found on many UNIX systems because it is a popular alternative to vi. Many versions are available. This book documents GNU emacs, which is available from the Free Software Foundation in Cambridge, Mass. For more information about emacs, see the Nutshell Handbook *Learning GNU Emacs*.

To start an emacs editing session, type:

emacs [*file*]

On some systems, GNU emacs is invoked by typing "gmacs" instead of "emacs."

Notes on the Tables

Emacs commands use the Control key and the Meta key (Meta is usually the ESCAPE key). In this section, the notation **C-** indicates that the Control key is pressed at the same time as the character that follows. Similarly, **M-** indicates the use of the Meta key. It's not necessary, however, to keep the Meta key pressed down while typing the next key.

In the command tables that follow, the first column lists the keystroke and the last column describes it. When there is a middle column, it lists the command name. This name is accessed by typing M-x followed by the command name. If you're unsure of the name, you can type a space or a carriage return, and emacs will list possible completions of what you've typed so far.

Because emacs is such a comprehensive editor, containing hundreds of commands, some commands must be omitted for the sake of preserving a "quick" reference. You can browse the command set by typing C-h (for help) or M-x (for command names).

Absolutely Essential Commands

If you're just getting started with emacs, here's a short list of the most important commands to know:

C-h	Enter the online help system.
C-x C-s	Save the file.
C-x C-c	Exit emacs.
C-x u	Undo last edit (can be repeated).
C-g	Get out of current command operation.
C-p C-n C-f C-b	Up/down/forward/back by line or character.
C-v M-v	Forward/backward by one screen.
C-s	Search for characters.
C-d	Delete a character.

Summary of Commands by Group

Reminder: Tables list keystrokes, command name, and description. C- indicates the Control key; M- indicates the Meta key.

File-handling Commands

C-x C-f	find-file	Find file and read it.
C-x C-v	find-alternate-file	Read another file; replace the one read with C-x C-f.
C-x i	insert-file	Insert file at cursor position.
C-x C-s	save-buffer	Save file (may hang terminal; use C-q to restart).
C-x C-w	write-file	Write buffer contents to file.
C-x C-c	save-buffers-kill-emacs	Exit emacs.
C-z	suspend-emacs	Suspend emacs (use exit or fg to restart).

Cursor Movement Commands

C-f	forward-char	Move *forward* one character (right).
C-b	backward-char	Move *backward* one character (left).
C-p	previous-line	Move to *previous* line (up).
C-n	next-line	Move to *next* line (down).
M-f	forward-word	Move one word *forward*.
M-b	backward-word	Move one word *backward*.
C-a	beginning-of-line	Move to beginning of line.
C-e	end-of-line	Move to *end* of line.
M-a	backward-sentence	Move backward one sentence.
M-e	forward-sentence	Move forward one sentence.
M-[	backward-paragraph	Move backward one paragraph.
M-]	forward-paragraph	Move forward one paragraph.
C-v	scroll-up	Move forward one screen.
M-v	scroll-down	Move backward one screen.
C-x [	backward-page	Move backward one page.
C-x]	forward-page	Move forward one page.
M->	end-of-buffer	Move to end of file.
M-<	beginning-of-buffer	Move to beginning of file.
(none)	goto-line	Go to line n of file.
(none)	goto-char	Go to character n of file.
C-l	recenter	Redraw screen with current line in the center.
M-n	digit-argument	Repeat the next command n times.
C-u n	universal-argument	Repeat the next command n times.

Deletion Commands

DEL	backward-delete-char	Delete previous character.
C-d	delete-char	Delete character under cursor.
M-DEL	backward-kill-word	Delete previous word.
M-d	kill-word	Delete the word the cursor is on.
C-k	kill-line	Delete from cursor to end of line.
M-k	kill-sentence	Delete sentence the cursor is on.
C-x DEL	backward-kill-sentence	Delete previous sentence.
C-y	yank	Restore what you've deleted.
C-w	kill-region	Delete a marked region (see next section).
(none)	backward-kill-paragraph	Delete previous paragraph.
(none)	kill-paragraph	Delete from the cursor to the end of the paragraph.

Paragraphs and Regions

C-@	set-mark-command	Mark the beginning (or end) of a region.
C-SPACE	(same as above)	
C-x C-p	mark-page	Mark page.
C-x C-x	exchange-point-and-mark	Exchange location of cursor and mark.
C-x h	mark-whole-buffer	Mark buffer.
M-q	fill-paragraph	Reformat paragraph.
M-g	fill-region	Reformat individual paragraphs within a region.
M-h	mark-paragraph	Mark paragraph.

Stopping and Undoing Commands

C-g	keyboard-quit	Abort current command.
C-x u	advertised-undo	Undo last edit (can be done repeatedly).
(none)	revert-buffer	Restore buffer to the state it was in when the file was last saved (or auto-saved).

Transposition Commands

C-t	transpose-chars	Transpose two letters.
M-t	transpose-words	Transpose two words.
C-x C-t	transpose-lines	Transpose two lines.
(none)	transpose-sentences	Transpose two sentences.
(none)	transpose-paragraphs	Transpose two paragraphs.

Capitalization Commands

M-c	capitalize-word	Capitalize first letter of word.
M-u	upcase-word	Uppercase word.
M-l	downcase-word	Lowercase word.
M- – M-c	negative-argument; capitalize-word	Capitalize previous word.
M- – M-u	negative-argument; upcase-word	Uppercase previous word.
M- – M-l	negative-argument; downcase-word	Lowercase previous word.
(none)	capitalize-region	Capitalize region.
C-x C-u	upcase-region	Uppercase region
C-x C-l	downcase-region	Lowercase region.

Incremental Search Commands

C-s	isearch-forward	Start incremental search forward.
C-r	isearch-backward	Start incremental search backward.
Meta	(none)	Exit a successful search.
C-g	keyboard-quit	Cancel incremental search; return to starting point.
DEL	(none)	Delete incorrect character of search string.

Word Abbreviation Commands

(none)	abbrev-mode	Enter (or exit) word abbreviation mode.
C-x -	inverse-add-global-abbrev	Type global abbreviation, then definition.
C-x C-h	inverse-add-local-abbrev	Type local abbreviation, then definition.
(none)	unexpand-abbrev	Undo the last word abbreviation.
(none)	write-abbrev-file	Write the word abbreviation file.
(none)	edit-abbrevs	Edit the word abbreviations.
(none)	list-abbrevs	View the word abbreviations.
(none)	kill-all-abbrevs	Kill abbreviations for this session.

Buffer Manipulation Commands

C-x b	switch-to-buffer	Move to specified buffer.
C-x C-b	list-buffers	Display buffer list.
C-x k	kill-buffer	Delete specified buffer.
(none)	kill-some-buffers	Ask about deleting each buffer.
(none)	rename-buffer	Change buffer name to specified name.
C-x s	save-some-buffers	Ask whether to save each modified buffer.

Emacs

Window Commands

C-x 2	split-window-horizontally	Divide the current window horizontally into two.
C-x 5	split-window-vertically	Divide the current window vertically into two.
C-x >	scroll-right	Scroll the window right.
C-x <	scroll-left	Scroll the window left.
C-x o	other-window	Move to the other window.
C-x 0	delete-window	Delete current window.
C-x 1	delete-other-windows	Delete all windows but this one.
(none)	delete-windows-on	Delete all windows on a given buffer.
C-x ^	enlarge-window	Make window taller.
(none)	shrink-window	Make window shorter.
C-x }	enlarge-window-horizontally	Make window wider.
C-x {	shrink-window-horizontally	Make window narrower.
M-C-v	scroll-other-window	Scroll other window.
C-x 4 f	find-file-other-window	Find a file in the other window.
C-x 4 b	switch-to-buffer-other-window	Select a buffer in the other window.
(none)	compare-windows	Compare two buffers; show first difference.

Special Shell Characters

C-c C-c	interrupt-shell-subjob	Terminate the current job.
C-c C-d	shell-send-eof	End of file character.
C-c C-u	kill-shell-input	Erase current line.
C-c C-w	backward-kill-word	Erase the previous word.
C-c C-z	stop-shell-subjob	Suspend the current job.

Indentation Commands

C-x	set-fill-prefix	Prepend each line in paragraph with characters from beginning of line up to cursor column; cancel prefix by typing this command in column 1.
(none)	indented-text-mode	Major mode: each tab defines a new indent for subsequent lines.
(none)	text-mode	Exit indented text mode; return to text mode.
M-C-\	indent-region	Indent a region to match first line in region.
M-m	back-to-indentation	Move cursor to first character on line.
M-C-o	split-line	Split line at cursor; indent to column of cursor.
(none)	fill-individual-paragraphs	Reformat indented paragraphs, keeping indentation.

Centering Commands

M-s	center-line	Center line that cursor is on.
(none)	center-paragraph	Center paragraph that cursor is on.
(none)	center-region	Center currently defined region.

Macro Commands

C-x (	start-kbd-macro	Start macro definition.
C-x)	end-kbd-macro	End macro definition.
C-x e	call-last-kbd-macro	Execute last macro defined.
M-*n* C-x e	digit-argument and call-last-kbd-macro	Execute last macro defined, *n* times.
C-u C-x (	start-kbd-macro	Execute last macro defined, then add keystrokes.
(none)	name-last-kbd-macro	Name last macro you created (before saving it).
(none)	insert-last-keyboard-macro	Insert the macro you named into a file.
(none)	load-file	Load macro files you've saved.
(none)	*macroname*	Execute a keyboard macro you've saved.
C-x q	kbd-macro-query	Insert a query in a macro definition.
C-u C-x q	(none)	Insert a recursive edit in a macro definition.
M-C-c	exit-recursive-edit	Exit a recursive edit.

Basic Indentation Commands

M-C-\	indent-region	Indent a region to match first line in region.
M-m	back-to-indentation	Move to first non-blank character on line.
M-^	delete-indentation	Join this line to the previous one.

Detail Information Help Commands

C-h a	command-apropos	What commands involve this concept?
(none)	apropos	What functions and variables involve this concept?
C-h c	describe-key-briefly	What command does this keystroke sequence run?
C-h b	describe-bindings	What are all the key bindings for this buffer?
C-h k	describe-key	What command does this keystroke sequence run, and what does it do?
C-h l	view-lossage	What are the last 100 characters I typed?
C-h w	where-is	What is the key binding for this command?
C-h f	describe-function	What does this function do?
C-h v	describe-variable	What does this variable mean, and what is its value?
C-h m	describe-mode	Tell me about the mode the current buffer is in.
C-h s	describe-syntax	What is the syntax table for this buffer?

Emacs

Help Commands

C-h t	help-with-tutorial	Run the emacs tutorial.
C-h i	info	Start the info documentation reader.
C-h n	view-emacs-news	View news about updates to emacs.
C-h C-c	describe-copying	View the emacs General Public License.
C-h C-d	describe-distribution	View information on ordering emacs from FSF.
C-h C-w	describe-no-warranty	View the (non-)warranty for emacs.

Summary of Commands by Key

Emacs commands are presented below in two alphabetical lists. Reminder: Tables list keystrokes, command name, and description. C- indicates the Control key; M- indicates the Meta key.

Control-key Sequences

C-@	set-mark-command	Mark the beginning (or end) of a region.
C-SPACE	(same as previous)	
C-]	(none)	Exit recursive edit and exit query-replace.
C-a	beginning-of-line	Move to beginning of line.
C-b	backward-char	Move *backward* one character (left).
C-c C-c	interrupt-shell-subjob	Terminate the current job.
C-c C-d	shell-send-eof	End of file character.
C-c C-u	kill-shell-input	Erase current line.
C-c C-w	backward-kill-word	Erase the previous word.
C-c C-z	stop-shell-subjob	Suspend the current job.
C-d	delete-char	Delete character under cursor.
C-e	end-of-line	Move to *end* of line.
C-f	forward-char	Move *forward* one character (right).
C-g	keyboard-quit	Abort current command.
C-h	help-command	Enter the online help system.
C-h a	command-apropos	What commands involve this concept?
C-h b	describe-bindings	What are all the key bindings for this buffer?
C-h C-c	describe-copying	View the emacs General Public License.
C-h C-d	describe-distribution	View information on ordering emacs from FSF.
C-h C-w	describe-no-warranty	View the (non-)warranty for emacs.
C-h c	describe-key-briefly	What command does this keystroke sequence run?
C-h f	describe-function	What does this function do?
C-h i	info	Start the info documentation reader.
C-h k	describe-key	What command does this keystroke sequence run, and what does it do?
C-h l	view-lossage	What are the last 100 characters I typed?
C-h m	describe-mode	Tell me about the mode the current buffer is in.
C-h n	view-emacs-news	View news about updates to emacs.
C-h s	describe-syntax	What is the syntax table for this buffer?
C-h t	help-with-tutorial	Run the emacs tutorial.

Key	Command	Description
C-h v	describe-variable	What does this variable mean, and what is its value?
C-h w	where-is	What is the key binding for this command?
C-k	kill-line	Delete from cursor to end of line.
C-l	recenter	Redraw screen with current line in the center.
C-n	next-line	Move to *next* line (down).
C-p	previous-line	Move to *previous* line (up).
C-r Meta	(none)	Start nonincremental search backwards.
C-r	(none)	Repeat nonincremental search backward.
C-r	(none)	Enter recursive edit (during query replace).
C-r	isearch-backward	Start incremental search backward.
C-s Meta	(none)	Start nonincremental search forward.
C-s	(none)	Repeat nonincremental search forward.
C-s	isearch-forward	Start incremental search forward.
C-t	transpose-chars	Transpose two letters.
C-u *n*	universal-argument	Repeat the next command *n* times.
C-u C-x (	start-kbd-macro	Execute last macro defined, then add keystrokes.
C-u C-x q	(none)	Insert recursive edit in a macro definition.
C-v	scroll-up	Move forward one screen.
C-w	kill-region	Delete a marked region.
C-x (	start-kbd-macro	Start macro definition.
C-x)	end-kbd-macro	End macro definition.
C-x [	backward-page	Move backward one page.
C-x]	forward-page	Move forward one page.
C-x ^	enlarge-window	Make window taller.
C-x {	shrink-window-horizontally	Make window narrower.
C-x }	enlarge-window-horizontally	Make window wider.
C-x <	scroll-left	Scroll the window left.
C-x >	scroll-right	Scroll the window right.
C-x -	inverse-add-global-abbrev	Type global abbreviation, then definition.
C-x .	set-fill-prefix	Prepend each line in paragraph with characters from beginning of line up to cursor column; cancel prefix by typing this command in column 1.
C-x 0	delete-window	Delete current window.
C-x 1	delete-other-windows	Delete all windows but this one.
C-x 2	split-window-horizontally	Divide current window horizontally into two.
C-x 4 b	switch-to-buffer-other-window	Select a buffer in the other window.
C-x 4 f	find-file-other-window	Find a file in the other window.
C-x 5	split-window-vertically	Divide current window vertically into two.
C-x b	switch-to-buffer	Move to the buffer specified.
C-x C-b	list-buffers	Display the buffer list.
C-x C-c	save-buffers-kill-emacs	Exit emacs.
C-x C-f	find-file	Find file and read it.
C-x C-h	inverse-add-local-abbrev	Type local abbreviation, then definition.
C-x C-l	downcase-region	Lowercase region.
C-x C-p	mark-page	Mark page.
C-x C-q	(none)	Toggle read-only status of buffer.

Emacs

C-x C-s	save-buffer	Save file (may hang terminal; use C-q to restart).
C-x C-t	transpose-lines	Transpose two lines.
C-x C-u	upcase-region	Uppercase region
C-x C-v	find-alternate-file	Read an alternate file, replacing the one read with C-x C-f.
C-x C-w	write-file	Write buffer contents to file.
C-x C-x	exchange-point-and-mark	Exchange location of cursor and mark.
C-x DEL	backward-kill-sentence	Delete previous sentence.
C-x e	call-last-kbd-macro	Execute last macro defined.
C-x h	mark-whole-buffer	Mark buffer.
C-x i	insert-file	Insert file at cursor position.
C-x k	kill-buffer	Delete the buffer specified.
C-x o	other-window	Move to the other window.
C-x q	kbd-macro-query	Inserts a query in a macro definition.
C-x s	save-some-buffers	Ask whether to save each modified buffer.
C-x u	advertised-undo	Undo last edit (can be done repeatedly).
C-y	yank	Restore what you've deleted.
C-z	suspend-emacs	Suspend emacs (use exit or fg to restart).

Meta-key Sequences

Meta	(none)	Exit a query-replace or successful search.
M- – M-c	negative-argument; capitalize-word	Capitalize previous word.
M- – M-l	negative-argument; downcase-word	Lowercase previous word.
M- – M-u	negative-argument; upcase-word	Uppercase previous word.
M-$	spell-word	Check spelling of word after cursor.
M-<	beginning-of-buffer	Move to beginning of file.
M->	end-of-buffer	Move to end of file.
M-[	backward-paragraph	Move backward one paragraph.
M-]	forward-paragraph	Move forward one paragraph.
M-^	delete-indentation	Join this line to the previous one.
M-n	digit-argument	Repeat the next command n times.
M-n C-x e	digit-argument and call-last-kbd-macro	Execute the last defined macro, n times.
M-a	backward-sentence	Move backward one sentence.
M-b	backward-word	Move one word *backward*.
M-C-\	indent-region	Indent a region to match first line in region.
M-C-c	exit-recursive-edit	Exit a recursive edit.
M-C-o	split-line	Split line at cursor; indent to column of cursor.
M-C-v	scroll-other-window	Scroll other window.
M-c	capitalize-word	Capitalize first letter of word.
M-d	kill-word	Delete word that cursor is on.
M-DEL	backward-kill-word	Delete previous word.
M-e	forward-sentence	Move forward one sentence.
M-f	forward-word	Move one word *forward*.

M-g	fill-region	Reformat individual paragraphs within a region.
M-h	mark-paragraph	Mark paragraph.
M-k	kill-sentence	Delete sentence the cursor is on.
M-l	downcase-word	Lowercase word.
M-m	back-to-indentation	Move cursor to first non-blank character on line.
M-q	fill-paragraph	Reformat paragraph.
M-s	center-line	Center line that cursor is on.
M-t	transpose-words	Transpose two words.
M-u	upcase-word	Uppercase word.
M-v	scroll-down	Move backward one screen.
M-x	(none)	Access text name of command keystrokes.

Summary of Commands by Name

The emacs commands below are presented alphabetically by command name. Use M-x to access the command name. Reminder: Tables list command name, keystroke, and description. C- indicates the Control key; M- indicates the Meta key.

macroname	(none)	Execute a keyboard macro you've saved.
abbrev-mode	(none)	Enter (or exit) word abbreviation mode.
advertised-undo	C-x u	Undo last edit (can be done repeatedly).
apropos	(none)	What functions and variables involve this concept?
back-to-indentation	M-m	Move cursor to first non-blank character on line.
backward-char	C-b	Move backward one character (left).
backward-delete-char	DEL	Delete previous character.
backward-kill-paragraph	(none)	Delete previous paragraph.
backward-kill-sentence	C-x DEL	Delete previous sentence.
backward-kill-word	C-c C-w	Erase previous word.
backward-kill-word	M-DEL	Delete previous word.
backward-page	C-x [	Move backward one page.
backward-paragraph	M-[	Move backward one paragraph.
backward-sentence	M-a	Move backward one sentence.
backward-word	M-b	Move backward one word.
beginning-of-buffer	M-<	Move to beginning of file.
beginning-of-line	C-a	Move to beginning of line.
call-last-kbd-macro	C-x e	Execute last macro defined.
capitalize-region	(none)	Capitalize region.
capitalize-word	M-c	Capitalize first letter of word.
center-line	M-s	Center line that cursor is on.
center-paragraph	(none)	Center paragraph that cursor is on.
center-region	(none)	Center currently defined region.
command-apropos	C-h a	What commands involve this concept?
compare-windows	(none)	Compare two buffers; show first difference.
delete-char	C-d	Delete character under cursor.
delete-indentation	M-^	Join this line to previous one.
delete-other-windows	C-x 1	Delete all windows but this one.
delete-window	C-x 0	Delete current window.
delete-windows-on	(none)	Delete all windows on a given buffer.
describe-bindings	C-h b	What are all the key bindings for in this buffer?

Emacs

describe-copying	C-h C-c	View the emacs General Public License.
describe-distribution	C-h C-d	View information on ordering emacs from FSF.
describe-function	C-h f	What does this function do?
describe-key	C-h k	What command does this keystroke sequence run, and what does it do?
describe-key-briefly	C-h c	What command does this keystroke sequence run?
describe-mode	C-h m	Tell me about the mode the current buffer is in.
describe-no-warranty	C-h C-w	View the (non-)warranty for emacs.
describe-syntax	C-h s	What is the syntax table for this buffer?
describe-variable	C-h v	What does this variable mean, and what is its value?
digit-argument and call-last-kbd-macro	M-n C-x e	Execute the last defined macro, n times.
digit-argument	M-n	Repeat next command, n times.
downcase-region	C-x C-l	Lowercase region.
downcase-word	M-l	Lowercase word.
edit-abbrevs	(none)	Edit word abbreviations.
end-kbd-macro	C-x)	End macro definition.
end-of-buffer	M->	Move to end of file.
end-of-line	C-e	Move to end of line.
enlarge-window	C-x ^	Make window taller.
enlarge-window-horizontally	C-x }	Make window wider.
exchange-point-and-mark	C-x C-x	Exchange location of cursor and mark.
exit-recursive-edit	M-C-c	Exit a recursive edit.
fill-individual-paragraphs	(none)	Reformat indented paragraphs, keeping indentation.
fill-paragraph	M-q	Reformat paragraph.
fill-region	M-g	Reformat individual paragraphs within a region.
find-alternate-file	C-x C-v	Read an alternate file, replacing the one read with C-x C-f.
find-file	C-x C-f	Find file and read it.
find-file-other-window	C-x 4 f	Find a file in the other window.
forward-char	C-f	Move forward one character (right).
forward-page	C-x]	Move forward one page.
forward-paragraph	M-]	Move forward one paragraph.
forward-sentence	M-e	Move forward one sentence.
forward-word	M-f	Move forward one word.
goto-char	(none)	Go to character n of file.
goto-line	(none)	Go to line n of file.
help-command	C-h	Enter the online help system.
help-with-tutorial	C-h t	Run the emacs tutorial.
indent-region	M-C-\	Indent a region to match first line in region.
indented-text-mode	(none)	Major mode: each tab defines a new indent for subsequent lines.
info	C-h i	Start the info documentation reader.
insert-file	C-x i	Insert file at cursor position.
insert-last-keyboard-macro	(none)	Insert the macro you named into a file.
interrupt-shell-subjob	C-c C-c	Terminate the current job.
inverse-add-global-abbrev	C-x -	Type global abbreviation, then definition.
inverse-add-local-abbrev	C-x C-h	Type local abbreviation, then definition.
isearch-backward	C-r	Start incremental search backward.

isearch-backward-regexp	C-r	Same, but search for regular expression.
isearch-forward	C-s	Start incremental search forward.
isearch-forward-regexp	C-r	Same, but search for regular expression.
kbd-macro-query	C-x q	Insert a query in a macro definition.
keyboard-quit	C-g	Abort current command.
kill-all-abbrevs	(none)	Kill abbreviations for this session.
kill-buffer	C-x k	Delete the buffer specified.
kill-line	C-k	Delete from cursor to end of line.
kill-paragraph	(none)	Delete from cursor to end of paragraph.
kill-region	C-w	Delete a marked region.
kill-sentence	M-k	Delete sentence the cursor is on.
kill-shell-input	C-c C-u	Erase current line.
kill-some-buffers	(none)	Ask about deleting each buffer.
kill-word	M-d	Delete word the cursor is on.
list-abbrevs	(none)	View word abbreviations.
list-buffers	C-x C-b	Display buffer list.
load-file	(none)	Load macro files you've saved.
mark-page	C-x C-p	Mark page.
mark-paragraph	M-h	Mark paragraph.
mark-whole-buffer	C-x h	Mark buffer.
name-last-kbd-macro	(none)	Name last macro you created (before saving it).
negative-argument; capitalize-word	M- - M-c	Capitalize previous word.
negative-argument; downcase-word	M- - M-l	Lowercase previous word.
negative-argument; upcase-word	M- - M-u	Uppercase previous word.
next-line	C-n	Move to next line (down).
other-window	C-x o	Move to the other window.
previous-line	C-p	Move to previous line (up).
query-replace-regexp	(none)	Query-replace a regular expression.
recenter	C-l	Redraw screen, with current line in center.
rename-buffer	(none)	Change buffer name to specified name.
replace-regexp	(none)	Replace a regular expression unconditionally.
re-search-backward	(none)	Simple regular expression search backward.
re-search-forward	(none)	Simple regular expression search forward.
revert-buffer	(none)	Restore buffer to the state it was in when the file was last saved (or auto-saved).
save-buffer	C-x C-s	Save file (may hang terminal; use C-q to restart).
save-buffers-kill-emacs	C-x C-c	Exit emacs.
save-some-buffers	C-x s	Ask whether to save each modified buffer.
scroll-down	M-v	Move backward one screen.
scroll-left	C-x <	Scroll the window left.
scroll-other-window	M-C-v	Scroll other window.
scroll-right	C-x >	Scroll the window right.
scroll-up	C-v	Move forward one screen.
set-fill-prefix	C-x .	Prepend each line in paragraph with characters from beginning of line up to cursor column; cancel prefix by typing this command in column 1.
set-mark-command	C-@ or C-SPACE	Mark the beginning (or end) of a region.
shell-send-eof	C-c C-d	End of file character.
shrink-window	(none)	Make window shorter.

Emacs

shrink-window-horizontally	C-x {	Make window narrower.
spell-buffer	(none)	Check spelling of current buffer.
spell-region	(none)	Check spelling of current region.
spell-string	(none)	Check spelling of string typed in minibuffer.
spell-word	M-$	Check spelling of word after cursor.
split-line	M-C-o	Split line at cursor; indent to column of cursor.
split-window-horizontally	C-x 2	Divide current window horizontally into two.
split-window-vertically	C-x 5	Divide current window vertically into two.
start-kbd-macro	C-u C-x (	Execute last macro defined, then add keystrokes to it.
start-kbd-macro	C-x (	Start macro definition.
stop-shell-subjob	C-c C-z	Suspend current job.
suspend-emacs	C-z	Suspend emacs (use exit or fg to restart).
switch-to-buffer	C-x b	Move to the buffer specified.
switch-to-buffer-other-window	C-x 4 b	Select a buffer in the other window.
text-mode	(none)	Exit indented text mode; return to text mode.
transpose-chars	C-t	Transpose two letters.
transpose-lines	C-x C-t	Transpose two lines.
transpose-paragraphs	(none)	Transpose two paragraphs.
transpose-sentences	(none)	Transpose two sentences.
transpose-words	M-t	Transpose two words.
unexpand-abbrev	(none)	Undo the last word abbreviation.
universal-argument	C-u *n*	Repeat the next command *n* times.
upcase-region	C-x C-u	Uppercase region.
upcase-word	M-u	Uppercase word.
view-emacs-news	C-h n	View news about updates to emacs.
view-lossage	C-h l	What are the last 100 characters I typed?
where-is	C-h w	What is the key binding for this command?
write-abbrev-file	(none)	Write the word abbreviation file.
write-file	C-x C-w	Write buffer contents to file.
yank	C-y	Restore what you've deleted.

The Vi Editor

This section presents the following topics:

- Review of vi operations
- Movement commands
- Edit commands
- Saving and exiting
- Accessing multiple files
- Interacting with UNIX
- Macros
- Miscellaneous commands
- Alphabetical list of keys
- Setting up vi

Review of Vi Operations

This subsection provides a review of the following:

- Command-line syntax
- Vi modes
- Syntax of vi commands
- Status-line commands

For more information on *vi*, refer to the Nutshell Handbook *Learning the vi Editor*.

Command-line Syntax

The three most common ways of starting a vi session are:

vi *file*
vi +*n* *file*
vi +/*pattern* *file*

You can open *file* for editing, optionally at line *n* or at the first line matching *pattern*. If no *file* is specified, vi opens with an empty buffer. See Section 2 for more information on command-line options for vi.

Command Mode

Once the file is opened, you are in command mode. From command mode, you can:

- Invoke insert mode
- Issue editing commands
- Move the cursor to a different position in the file
- Invoke ex commands
- Invoke a UNIX shell
- Save or exit the current version of the file

Insert Mode

In insert mode, you can enter new text in the file. Press the ESCAPE key to exit insert mode and return to command mode. The following commands invoke insert mode:

a	Append after cursor.
A	Append at end of line.
c	Begin change operation.

C	Change to end of line.
i	Insert before cursor.
I	Insert at beginning of line.
o	Open a line below current line.
O	Open a line above current line.
R	Begin overwriting text.
s	Substitute a character.
S	Substitute entire line.

Syntax of Vi Commands

In vi, commands have the following general form:

[*n*] *operator* [*m*] *object*

The basic editing *operators* are:

c	Begin a change.
d	Begin a deletion.
y	Begin a yank (or copy).

If the current line is the object of the operation, then the operator is the same as the object: **cc**, **dd**, **yy**. Otherwise, the editing operators act on objects specified by cursor-movement commands or pattern-matching commands. *n* and *m* are the number of times the operation is performed, or the number of objects the operation is performed on. If both *n* and *m* are specified, the effect is *n* × *m*.

An object can represent any of the following text blocks:

word	Includes characters up to a space or punctuation mark. A capitalized object is a variant form that recognizes only blank spaces.
sentence	Is up to ., !, ? followed by two spaces.
paragraph	Is up to next blank line or paragraph macro defined by **para=** option.
section	Is up to next section heading defined by **sect=** option.

Examples

2cw	Change the next two words.
d}	Delete up to next paragraph.
d^	Delete back to beginning of line.
5yy	Copy the next five lines.
y]]	Copy up to the next section.

Status-line Commands

Most commands are not echoed on the screen as you input them. However, the status line at the bottom of the screen is used to echo input for the following commands:

/	Search forward for a pattern.
?	Search backward for a pattern.
:	Invoke an ex command.
!	Invoke a UNIX command that takes as its input an object in the buffer and replaces it with output from the command.

Commands that are input on the status line must be entered by pressing the RETURN key. In addition, error messages and output from the **CTRL-G** command are displayed on the status line.

Movement Commands

A number preceding a command repeats the movement. Movement commands are also objects for change, delete, and yank operations.

Character

h, j, k, l	Left, down, up, right ($\leftarrow$, $\downarrow$, $\uparrow$, $\rightarrow$).
SPACEBAR	Right.

Text

w, W, b, B	Forward, backward by word.
e, E	End of word.
), (	Beginning of next, current sentence.
}, {	Beginning of next, current paragraph.
]], [[	Beginning of next, current section.

Lines

0, $	First, last position of current line.
^	First nonblank character of current line.
+, -	First character of next, previous line.
RETURN	First character of next line.
n		Column n of current line.
H	Top line of screen.
M	Middle line of screen.
L	Last line of screen.
nH	n lines after top line.
nL	n lines before last line.

Screens

CTRL-F, CTRL-B	Scroll forward, backward one screen.
CTRL-D, CTRL-U	Scroll down, up one-half screen.
CTRL-E, CTRL-Y	Show one more line at bottom, top of window.
z RETURN	Reposition line with cursor: to top of screen.
z .	Reposition line with cursor: to middle of screen.
z –	Reposition line with cursor: to bottom of screen.
CTRL-L, CTRL-R	Redraw screen (without scrolling).

Searches

/ *text*	Search forward for *text*.
n	Repeat previous search.
N	Repeat search in opposite direction.
/	Repeat forward search.
?	Repeat previous search backward.
? *text*	Search backward for *text*.
/ *text* **/+n**	Go to line *n* after *text*.
? *text* **?-n**	Go to line *n* before *text*.
%	Find match of current parenthesis, brace, or bracket.
f *x*	Move search forward to *x* on current line.
F *x*	Move search backward to *x* on current line.
t *x*	Search forward before *x* in current line.
T *x*	Search back after *x* in current line.
,	Reverse search direction of last **f**, **F**, **t**, or **T**.
;	Repeat last character search (**f**, **F**, **t**, or **T**).

Line Numbering

CTRL-G	Display current line number.
*n***G**	Move to line number *n*.
G	Move to last line in file.
: *n*	Move to line number *n*.

Marking Position

m *x*	Mark current position with character *x*.
**` ** *x*	Move cursor to mark *x*.
´ *x*	Move to start of line containing *x*.
` `	Return to previous mark (or to location prior to a search).
´ ´	Like above, but return to start of line.

Edit Commands

Recall that **c**, **d**, and **y** are the basic editing operators.

Inserting New Text

a	Append after cursor.
A	Append to end of line.
i	Insert before cursor.
I	Insert at beginning of line.
o	Open a line below cursor.
O	Open a line above cursor.
ESC	Terminate insert mode.
CTRL-J	Move down one line.
RETURN	Move down one line.
CTRL-I	Insert a tab.
CTRL-T	Move to next tab setting.
BACKSPACE	Move back one character.
CTRL-H	Move back one character.
CTRL-U	Delete current line.
CTRL-V	Quote next character.
CTRL-W	Move back one word.

The last four control characters are set by **stty**. Your terminal settings may differ.

Changing and Deleting Text

cw	Change word.
cc	Change line.
C	Change text from current position to end of line.
dd	Delete current line.
ndd	Delete *n* lines.
D	Delete remainder of line.
dw	Delete a word.
d}	Delete up to next paragraph.
d^	Delete back to beginning of line.
d/pat	Delete up to first occurrence of pattern.
dn	Delete up to next occurrence of pattern.
dfa	Delete up to and including *a* on current line.
dta	Delete up to (not including) *a* on current line.
dL	Delete up to last line on screen.
dG	Delete to end of file.
p	Insert last deleted text after cursor.
P	Insert last deleted text before cursor.
rx	Replace character with *x*.
Rtext	Replace *text* beginning at cursor.
s	Substitute character.
4s	Substitute four characters.
S	Substitute entire line.
u	Undo last change.
U	Restore current line.
x	Delete current cursor position.
X	Delete back one character.

`5X`	Delete previous five characters.
`.`	Repeat last change.
`~`	Reverse case.

Copying and Moving

`Y`	Copy current line to new buffer.
`yy`	Copy current line.
`"xyy`	Yank current line to buffer *x*.
`"xd`	Delete into buffer *x*.
`"Xd`	Delete and append into buffer *x*.
`"xp`	Put contents of buffer *x*.
`y]]`	Copy up to next section heading.
`ye`	Copy to end of word.

Saving and Exiting

Writing a file means saving the edits and updating the file's modification time.

`ZZ`	Quit vi, writing the file only if changes were made.
`:x`	Same as **ZZ**.
`:wq`	Write and quit file.
`:w`	Write file.
`:w file`	Save copy to *file*.
`:n1,n2w file`	Write lines *n1* to *n2* to new *file*.
`:n1,n2w >> file`	Append lines *n1* to *n2* to existing *file*.
`:w!`	Write file (overriding protection).
`:w! file`	Overwrite *file* with current buffer.
`:w %.new`	Write current buffer named *file* as *file.new*.
`:q`	Quit file.
`:q!`	Quit file (discarding edits).
`Q`	Quit vi and invoke ex.
`:vi`	Return to vi after **Q** command.
`:e file2`	Edit *file2* without leaving vi.
`:n`	Edit next file.
`:e!`	Return to version of current file at time of last write.
`:e#`	Edit alternate file.
`%`	Current filename.
`#`	Alternate filename.

Accessing Multiple Files

`:e file`	Edit another *file*; current file becomes alternate.
`:e!`	Restore last saved version of current file.
`:e + file`	Begin editing at end of *file*.
`:e +n file`	Open *file* at line *n*.
`:e #`	Open to previous position in alternate file.
`:ta tag`	Edit file at location *tag*.
`:n`	Edit next file.
`:n!`	Forces next file.
`:n files`	Specify new list of *files*.

CTRL-G	Show current file and line number.
:args	Display multiple files to be edited.
:rew	Rewind list of multiple files to top.

Interacting with UNIX

:r file	Read in contents of *file* after cursor.
:r !command	Read in output from *command* after current line.
:nr !command	Like above, but place after line *n* (0 for top of file).
:!command	Run *command*, then return.
!object command	Send buffer *object* to UNIX *command*; replace with output.
:n1,n2! command	Send lines *n1 – n2* to *command*; replace with output.
n!!command	Send *n* lines to UNIX *command*; replace with output.
!!	Repeat last system command.
:sh	Create subshell; return to file with *EOF*.
CTRL-Z	Suspend editor, resume with **fg** (not in all versions).
:so file	Read and execute commands from *file*.

Macros

:ab in out	Use *in* as abbreviation for *out*.
:unab in	Remove abbreviation for *in*.
:ab	List abbreviations.
:map c sequence	Map character *c* as *sequence* of commands.
:unmap c	Disable map for character *c*.
:map	List characters that are mapped.
:map! c sequence	Map character *c* to input mode *sequence*.
:unmap! c	Disable input mode map (you may need to quote the character with CTRL-V).
:map!	List characters that are mapped to input mode.

The following characters are unused in command mode and can be mapped as user-defined commands.

Letters:	g K q V v
Control keys:	^A ^K ^O ^T ^W ^X
Symbols:	_ * \ =

(Note: The = is used by vi if Lisp mode is set.)

Miscellaneous Commands

J	Join two lines.
:j!	Join two lines, preserving blank spaces.
<<	Shift this line left one shift width (default is 8 spaces).
>>	Shift this line right one shift width (default is 8 spaces).
>}	Shift right to end of paragraph.
<%	Shift left until matching parenthesis, brace, bracket, etc. (Cursor must be on the matching symbol.)

Alphabetical List of Keys

For brevity, control characters are marked by ^.

a	Append text after cursor.
A	Append text at end of line.
^A	Unused.
b	Back up to beginning of word in current line.
B	Back up to word, ignoring punctuation.
^B	Scroll backward one window.
c	Change operator.
C	Change to end of current line.
^C	Unused in command mode; ends insert mode.
d	Delete operator.
D	Delete to end of current line.
^D	Scroll down half-window.
e	Move to end of word.
E	Move to end of word, ignoring punctuation.
^E	Show one more line at bottom of window.
f	Find next character typed forward on current line.
F	Find next character typed backward on current line.
^F	Scroll forward one window.
g	Unused.
G	Go to specified line or end of file.
^G	Print information about file on status line.
h	Left arrow cursor key.
H	Move cursor to Home position.
^H	Left arrow cursor key; Backspace key in insert mode.
i	Insert text before cursor.
I	Insert text before first nonblank character on line.
^I	Unused in command mode; in insert mode, same as TAB key.
j	Down arrow cursor key.
J	Join two lines.
^J	Down arrow cursor key; in insert mode, move down a line.
k	Up arrow cursor key.
K	Unused.
^K	Unused.
l	Right arrow cursor key.
L	Move cursor to Last position in window.
^L	Redraw screen.
m	Mark the current cursor position in register (a-z).
M	Move cursor to Middle position in window.
^M	Carriage return.
n	Repeat the last search command.
N	Repeat the last search command in reverse direction.
^N	Down arrow cursor key.

o	Open line below current line.
O	Open line above current line.
^O	Unused.
p	Put yanked or deleted text after or below cursor.
P	Put yanked or deleted text before or above cursor.
^P	Up arrow cursor key.
q	Unused.
Q	Quit vi and invoke ex.
^Q	Unused (on some terminals, resume data flow).
r	Replace character at cursor with the next character you type.
R	Replace characters.
^R	Redraw the screen.
s	Change the character under the cursor to typed characters.
S	Change entire line.
^S	Unused (on some terminals, stop data flow).
t	Move cursor forward to character before next character typed.
T	Move cursor backward to character after next character typed.
^T	Unused in command mode; in insert mode, use if **autoindent** is set.
u	Undo the last change made.
U	Restore current line, discarding changes.
^U	Scroll the screen upward half-window.
v	Unused.
V	Unused.
^V	Unused in command mode; in insert mode, quote next character.
w	Move to beginning of next word.
W	Move to beginning of next word, ignoring punctuation.
^W	Unused in command mode; in insert mode, back up to beginning of word.
x	Delete character under cursor.
X	Delete character before cursor.
^X	Unused.
y	Yank or copy operator.
Y	Make copy of current line.
^Y	Show one more line at top of window.
z	Reposition line containing cursor. **z** must be followed either by: RETURN (reposition line to top of screen), . (reposition line to middle of screen), or − (reposition line to bottom of screen).
ZZ	Exit the editor, saving changes.
^Z	Suspend vi (only on systems that have job control).

Setting Up Vi

This subsection describes the following:

- The **:set** command

- Options available with **:set**

- Example **.exrc** file

The :set Command

The **:set** command allows you to specify options that change characteristics of your editing environment. Options may be put in the **.exrc** file or set during a vi session.

The colon should not be typed if the command is put in **.exrc**.

`:set x`	Enable option *x*.
`:set nox`	Disable option *x*.
`:set x=val`	Give *value* to option *x*.
`:set`	Show changed options.
`:set all`	Show all options.
`:set x?`	Show value of option *x*.

Options Used by :set

The following table describes the options to **:set**. The first column includes the optional abbreviation, if there is one, and uses an equal sign to show that the option takes a value. The second column gives the default, and the third column describes the behavior of the enabled option.

Option	Default	Description
autoindent (ai)	noai	In insert mode, indent each line to the same level as the line above or below. Use with **shiftwidth** option.
autoprint (ap)	ap	Display changes after each editor command. (For global replacement, display last replacement.)
autowrite (aw)	noaw	Automatically write (save) file if changed before opening another file with **:n** or before giving UNIX command with **:!**.
beautify (bf)	nobf	Ignore all control characters during input (except tab, newline, or formfeed).
directory= (dir)	/tmp	Name the directory in which ex stores buffer files. (Directory must be writable.)

Option	Default	Description
edcompatible	noed-compatible	Use ed-like features on substitute commands.
errorbells (eb)	errorbells	Sound bell when an error occurs.
exrc (ex)	noexrc	Allow the execution of **.exrc** files that reside outside the user's home directory.
hardtabs= (ht)	8	Define boundaries for terminal hardware tabs.
ignorecase (ic)	noic	Disregard case during a search.
lisp	nolisp	Insert indents in appropriate lisp format. ( ), { }, [[, and]] are modified to have meaning for lisp.
list	nolist	Print tabs as ^I; mark ends of lines with $. (Use **list** to tell if end character is a tab or a space.)
magic	magic	Wildcard characters **.** (dot), ***** (asterisk), and [ ] (brackets) have special meaning in patterns.
mesg	mesg	Permit system messages to display on terminal while editing in vi.
number (nu)	nonu	Display line numbers on left of screen during editing session.
open optimize (opt)	open noopt	Allow entry to open mode from ex. Abolish carriage returns at the end of lines when printing multiple lines, speeds output on dumb terminals when printing lines with leading white space (blanks or tabs).
paragraphs= (para)	IPLPPPQP LIpplpipbp	Define paragraph delimiters for movement by { or }. The pairs of characters in the value are the names of nroff/troff macros that begin paragraphs.
prompt	prompt	Display the ex prompt (:) when vi's **Q** command is given.
readonly (ro)	noro	Any writes (saves) of a file will fail unless you use **!** after the write (works with **w**, **ZZ**, or **autowrite**).
redraw (re)	noredraw	Terminal redraws screen whenever edits are made (in other words, insert mode pushes over existing characters, and deleted lines immediately close up). Default depends on line speed and terminal type. **noredraw** is useful at slow speeds on a dumb terminal: deleted lines show up as @, and inserted text appears to overwrite existing text until you press ESC.

Option	Default	Description
remap	remap	Allow nested map sequences.
report=	5	Display a message on the prompt line whenever you make an edit that affects at least a certain number of lines. For example, **6dd** reports the message "6 lines deleted."
scroll=	<1/2 window>	Amount of screen to scroll.
sections= (sect)	SHNHH HU	Define section delimiters for [[ ]] movement. The pairs of characters in the value are the names of nroff/troff macros that begin sections.
shell= (sh)	/bin/sh	Pathname of shell used for shell escape (**:!**) and shell command (**:sh**). Default value is derived from SHELL variable, which varies on different systems.
shiftwidth= (sw)	8	Define number of spaces in backward (**^D**) tabs when using the **autoindent** option.
showmatch (sm)	nosm	In vi, when) or } is entered, cursor moves briefly to matching (or {. (If match is not on the screen, rings the error message bell.) Very useful for programming.
showmode	noshowmode	In insert mode, displays a message on the prompt line indicating the type of insert you are making. For example, "Open Mode," or "Append Mode."
slowopen (slow)		Hold off display during insert. Default depends on line speed and terminal type.
tabstop= (ts)	8	Define number of spaces that a TAB indents during editing session. (Printer still uses system tab of 8.)
taglength= (tl)	0	Define number of characters that are significant for tags. Default (zero) means that all characters are significant.
tags=	tags /usr/lib/tags	Define pathname of files containing tags (see the UNIX **ctags** command.) By default, the system looks for files **tags** (in the current directory) and **/usr/lib/tags**.
term=		Set terminal type.
terse	noterse	Display shorter error messages.
timeout (to)	timeout	Keyboard maps "time out" after 1 second.
ttytype=		Set terminal type.

Option	Default	Description
warn	warn	Display the message, "No write since last change."
window= (w)		Show a certain number of lines of the file on the screen. Default depends on line speed and terminal type.
wrapmargin= (wm)	0	Define right margin. If greater than zero, automatically inserts carriage returns to break lines.
wrapscan (ws)	ws	Searches wrap around either end of file.
writeany (wa)	nowa	Allow saving to any file.

Example .exrc File

```
set nowrapscan wrapmargin=7
set sections=SeAhBhChDh nomesg
map q :w^M:n^M
map v dwElp
ab ORA O'Reilly & Associates, Inc.
```

The Ex Editor

Ex is a line editor that serves as the foundation for the screen editor vi. Ex commands work on the current line or on a range of lines in a file. Most often, you use ex from within vi. In vi, ex commands are preceded by a colon and entered by pressing RETURN.

But you can invoke ex on its own—from the command line—just as you would invoke vi. (You could execute an ex script this way.) You can also use the vi command **Q** to quit the vi editor and enter ex.

This section presents the following topics:

- Syntax of ex commands

- Alphabetical summary of commands

For more information, see the Nutshell Handbook *Learning the vi Editor*.

Ex

Syntax of Ex Commands

To enter an ex command from vi, type:

:[*address*] *command* [*options*]

An initial **:** indicates an ex command. As you type the command, it is echoed on the status line. Enter the command by pressing RETURN. *address* is the line number or range of lines that are the object of *command*. *options* and *addresses* are described below. Ex commands are described in the alphabetical summary.

You can exit ex in several ways:

:x	Exit (save changes and quit).
:q!	Quit without saving changes.
:vi	Quit and enter the vi editor.

Options

!	Indicates a variant command form, overriding the normal behavior.
count	The number of times the command is to be repeated. Unlike in vi commands, *count* cannot precede the command, because a number preceding an ex command is treated as a line address. For example, **d3** deletes three lines beginning with the current line; **3d** deletes line 3.
file	The name of a file that is affected by the command. **%** stands for current file; **#** stands for previous file.

Addresses

If no address is given, the current line is the object of the command. If the address specifies a range of lines, the format is:

x,*y*

where *x* and *y* are the first and last addressed lines (*x* must precede *y* in the buffer). *x* and *y* may be a line number or a symbol. Using **;** instead of **,** sets the current line to *x* before interpreting *y*. The notation **1,$** addresses all lines in the file, as does **%**.

Address Symbols

1,$	All lines in the file.
%	All lines; same as **1,$**.
x,*y*	Lines *x* through *y*.
x;*y*	Lines *x* through *y*, with current line reset to *x*.
0	Top of file.
.	Current line.
n	Absolute line number *n*.
$	Last line.
x-*n*	*n* lines before *x*.

x+n	*n* lines after *x*.
–[*n*]	One or *n* lines previous.
+[*n*]	One or *n* lines ahead.
´*x*	Line marked with *x*.
´´	Previous mark.
/pattern/	Forward to line matching *pattern*.
?pattern?	Backward to line matching *pattern*.

See Section 6 for more information on using patterns.

Alphabetical Summary of Ex Commands

Ex commands can be entered by specifying any unique abbreviation. In this listing, the full name appears in the margin, and the shortest possible abbreviation is used in the syntax line. Examples are assumed to be typed from vi, so they include the : prompt.

---

ab [*string text*]   **abbrev**

Define *string* when typed to be translated into *text*. If *string* and *text* are not specified, list all current abbreviations.

Examples

Note: ^M appears when you type ^V followed by RETURN.

```
:ab ora O'Reilly & Associates, Inc.
:ab id Name:^MRank:^MPhone:
```

[*address*] **a**[**!**]   **append**
text
.

Append *text* at specified *address*, or at present address if none is specified. Add a **!** to switch the **autoindent** setting that will be used during input. E.g., if **autoindent** was enabled, **!** disables it.

---

ar   **args**

Print filename arguments (the list of files to edit). The current argument is shown in brackets ([]).

[*address*] **c**[**!**]   **change**
text
.

Replace the specified lines with *text*. Add a **!** to switch the **autoindent** setting during input of *text*.

copy	[*address*] **co** *destination*
	Copy the lines included in *address* to the specified *destination* address. The command **t** is a synonym for **copy**.
	Example
| | ```
:1,10 co 50
``` |
delete	[*address*] **d** [*buffer*]
	Delete the lines included in *address*. If *buffer* is specified, save or append the text to the named buffer.
	Examples
| | ```
:/Part I/,/Part II/-1d    Delete to line above "Part II"
:/main/+d                 Delete line below "main"
:.,$/d                    Delete from this line to last line
``` |
edit	**e**[**!**] [**+***n*] [*file*]
	Begin editing *file*. Add a **!** to discard any changes to the current file. If no *file* is given, edit another copy of the current file. With the **+***n* argument, begin editing on line *n*.
	Examples
| | ```
:e file
:e#
:e!
``` |
file	**f** [*filename*]
	Change the name of the current file to *filename*, which is considered "not edited." If no *filename* is specified, print the current status of the file.
	Example
| | ```
:f %.new
``` |
global	[*address*] **g**[**!**]/*pattern*/[*commands*]
	Execute *commands* on all lines that contain *pattern* or, if *address* is specified, on all lines within that range. If *commands* are not specified, print all such lines. If **!** is used, execute *commands* on all lines that *don't* contain *pattern*. See **v**.
	Examples
| | ```
:g/Unix/p
:g/Name:/s/tom/Tom/
``` |
```

[*address*] **i**[**!**] *text* . Insert *text* at line before the specified address, or at present address if none is specified. Add a **!** to switch the **autoindent** setting during input of *text*.	**insert**
[*address*] **j**[**!**] [*count*] Place the text in the specified range on one line, with white space adjusted to provide two blank characters after a period (.), no blank characters after a), and one blank character otherwise. Add a **!** to prevent white space adjustment. *Example* :1,5j! *Join first five lines, preserving white space*	**join**
[*address*] **k** *char* Mark the given *address* with *char*. Return later to the line with '**x**.	**k**
[*address*] **l** [*count*] Print the specified lines so that tabs display as **^I** and the ends of lines display as **$**. **l** is a temporary version of **:set list**.	**list**

map[**!**] [*char commands*]
 	
Define a keyboard macro named *char* as the specified sequence of commands. *char* is usually a single character, or the sequence #*n*, representing a function key on the keyboard. Use a **!** to create a macro for input mode. With no arguments, list the currently defined macros.
 	
Examples
 	
  :map K dwwP   *Transpose two words*
  :map q :w^M:n^M   *Write current file; go to next*
  :map! + ^[bi(^[ea) *Enclose previous word in parentheses*
	map

[*address*] **ma** *char* Mark the specified line with *char*, a single lowercase letter. Return later to the line with '**x**. Same as **k**.	**mark**

Ex

move	*[address]* **m** *destination*
	Move the lines specified by *address* to the *destination* address.
	Example
	`:.,/Note/m /END/` *Move text block after line containing "END"*
next	**n**[**!**] [[**+***command*] *filelist*]
	Edit the next file from the command-line argument list. Use **args** to list these files. If *filelist* is provided, replace the current argument list with *filelist* and begin editing on the first file; if *command* is given (containing no spaces), execute *command* after editing the first such file.
	Example
	`:n chap*` *Start editing all "chapter" files*
number	*[address]* **nu** *[count]*
	Print each line specified by *address*, preceded by its buffer line number. Use **#** as an alternate abbreviation for **number**. *count* specifies the number of lines to show, starting with *address*.
open	*[address]* **o** *[/pattern/]*
	Enter vi's open mode at the lines specified by *address*, or at the lines matching *pattern*. Enter and exit open mode with **Q**. Open mode lets you use the regular vi commands, but only one line at a time. May be useful on slow dialup lines.
preserve	**pre**
	Save the current editor buffer as though the system had crashed.
print	*[address]* **p** *[count]*
	Print the lines specified by *address*. *count* specifies the number of lines to print, starting with *address*. **P** is another abbreviation.
	Example
	`:100;+5p` *Show line 100 and the next five lines*
put	*[address]* **pu** *[char]*
	Restore the lines that were previously deleted or yanked from named buffer *char*, and put them after the line specified by *address*. If *char* is not specified, restore the last deleted or yanked text.

q[!]	**quit**

Terminate current editing session. Use **!** to discard changes made since the last save. If the editing session includes additional files in the argument list that were never accessed, quit by typing **q!** or by typing **q** twice.

[*address*] **r** *file*	**read**

Copy in the text from *file* on the line below the specified *address*. If *file* is not specified, the current filename is used.

Example

```
:0r $HOME/data          Read file in at top of current file
```

[*address*] **r** *!command*	**read**

Read the output of UNIX *command* into the text after the line specified by *address*.

Example

```
:$r !cal                Place a calendar at end of file
```

rec [*file*]	**recover**

Recover *file* from system save area.

rew[!]	**rewind**

Rewind argument list and begin editing the first file in the list. The **!** flag rewinds, discarding any changes to the current file that haven't been saved.

se *parameter1 parameter2* ...	**set**

Set a value to an option with each *parameter*, or if no *parameter* is supplied, print all options that have been changed from their defaults. For Boolean-valued options, each *parameter* can be phrased as *option* or **no***option*; other options can be assigned with the syntax *option=value*. Specify **all** to list current settings.

Examples

```
:set nows wm=10
:set all
```

sh	**shell**

Create a new shell. Resume editing when the shell is terminated.

source	**so** *file* Read and execute ex commands from *file*. *Examples* `:so $HOME/.exrc`

substitute	[*address*] **s** [*/pattern/replacement/*] [*options*] [*count*]
	
	Replace each instance of *pattern* on the specified lines with *replacement*. If *pattern* and *replacement* are omitted, repeat last substitution. *count* specifies the number of lines on which to substitute, starting with *address*. See additional examples in Section 6.
	
	Options
	
	  c Prompt for confirmation before each change.
	  g Substitute all instances of *pattern* on each line.
	  p Print the last line on which a substitution was made.
	
	Examples
	
	`:1,10s/yes/no/g` *Substitute on first 10 lines*
	`:%s/[Hh]ello/Hi/gc` *Confirm global substitutions*
	`:s/Fortran/\U&/ 3` *Uppercase "Fortran" on next three lines*

t	[*address*] **t** *destination* Copy the lines included in *address* to the specified *destination* address. **t** is an alias for **copy**. *Example* `:%t$` *Copy the file and add it to the end*

tag	[*address*] **ta** *tag*
	
	Switch the editing session to the file containing *tag*.
	
	Example
	Run **ctags**, then switch to the file containing *myfunction*:
	
	`:!ctags *.c`
	`:tag myfunction`

unabbreviate	**una** *word* Remove *word* from the list of abbreviations.
undo	**u** Reverse the changes made by the last editing command.

unm[!] char	**unmap**
Remove *char* from the list of keyboard macros. Use **!** to remove a macro for input mode.	
[*address*] **v**/*pattern*/[*commands*]	**v**
Execute *commands* on all lines *not* containing *pattern*. If *commands* are not specified, print all such lines. **v** is equivalent to **g!**.	
Example	
`:v/#include/d` *Delete all lines except "#include" lines*	
ve	**version**
Print the editor's current version number and date of last change.	
[*address*] **vi** [*type*] [*count*]	**visual**
Enter visual mode (vi) at the line specified by *address*. Exit with **Q**. *type* can be one of −, ^, or **.** (See the **z** command). *count* specifies an initial window size.	
vi [+*n*] file	**visual**
Begin editing *file* in visual mode (vi), optionally at line *n*.	
[*address*] **w**[!] [[>>] *file*]	**write**
Write lines specified by *address* to *file*, or write full contents of buffer if *address* is not specified. If *file* is also omitted, save the contents of the buffer to the current filename. If **>>** *file* is used, write contents to the end of an existing *file*. The **!** flag forces the editor to write over any current contents of *file*.	
[*address*] **w** !*command*	**write**
Write lines specified by *address* to *command*.	
Examples	
`:1,10w name_list` *Copy first 10 lines to* `name_list` `:50w >> name_list` *Now append line 50*	
wq[!]	**wq**
Write and quit the file in one movement. The **!** flag forces the editor to write over any current contents of *file*.	

Ex

xit	**x** Write the file if it was changed since the last write; then quit.
yank	[*address*] **ya** [*char*] [*count*] Place lines specified by *address* in named buffer *char*. If no *char* is given, place lines in general buffer. *count* specifies the number of lines to yank, starting with *address*. ***Example*** `:101,200 ya a`
z	[*address*] **z** [*type*] [*count*] Print a window of text, with the line specified by *address* at the top. *count* specifies the number of lines to be displayed. ***Type*** <table><tr><td>+</td><td>Place specified line at top of window (the default).</td></tr><tr><td>—</td><td>Place specified line at bottom of window.</td></tr><tr><td>.</td><td>Place specified line in center of window.</td></tr><tr><td>^</td><td>Print the previous window.</td></tr><tr><td>=</td><td>Place specified line in center of window, and leave this line as the current line.</td></tr></table>
!	[*address*] **!***command* Execute UNIX *command* in a shell. If *address* is specified, apply the lines contained in *address* as standard input to *command*, and replace the lines with the output. ***Examples*** `:!ls` *List files in the current directory* `:11,20!sort -f` *Sort lines 11-20 of current file*
=	[*address*] **=** Print the line number of the next line matching *address*. If no address is given, print the number of the last line.
< >	[*address*] **<** [*count*] or [*address*] **>** [*count*] Shift lines specified by *address* either left (<) or right (>). Only blanks and tabs are shifted in a left shift. *count* specifies the number of lines to shift, starting with *address*.

address	*address*
Print the line specified in *address*.	

RETURN	RETURN
Print the next line in the file.	

[*address*] **&** [*options*] [*count*]   **&**

Repeat the previous substitution (**s**) command. *count* specifies the number of lines on which to substitute, starting with *address*.

Examples

```
:s/Overdue/Paid/    Substitute once on current line
:g/Status/&         Redo substitution on all "Status" lines
```

[*address*] **~** [*count*]   **~**

Replace the previous regular expression with the previous replacement pattern from a substitute (**s**) command.

Ex

The Sed Editor

This section presents the following topics:

- Command-line syntax
- Conceptual overview of sed
- Syntax of sed commands
- Group summary of sed commands
- Alphabetical summary of sed commands

For more information, see the Nutshell Handbook *sed & awk.*

Command-line Syntax

The syntax for invoking sed has two forms:

> **sed** [*options*] '*command*' *file(s)*
> **sed** [*options*] **-f** *scriptfile file(s)*

The first form allows you to specify an editing command on the command line, surrounded by single quotes. The second form allows you to specify a *scriptfile*, a file containing sed commands. If no files are specified, sed reads from standard input.

The following *options* are recognized:

-n   Suppress the default output; sed displays only those lines specified with the **p** command, or with the **p** flag of the **s** command.

-e *cmd* Next argument is an editing command; not needed unless specifying two or more editing commands.

-f *file* Next argument is a file containing editing commands.

Conceptual Overview

Sed is a non-interactive, or **s**tream-oriented, **ed**itor. It interprets a script and performs the actions in the script. Sed is stream-oriented because, like many UNIX programs, input flows through the program and is directed to standard output. For example, **sort** is stream-oriented; vi is not. Sed's input typically comes from a file but can be directed from the keyboard. Output goes to the screen by default but can be captured in a file instead.

Typical Uses of Sed Include:

* Editing one or more files automatically.

* Simplifying repetitive edits to multiple files.

* Writing conversion programs.

Sed Operates as Follows:

* Each line of input is copied into a pattern space.

* All editing commands in a sed script are applied in order to each line of input.

* Editing commands are applied to all lines (globally) unless line addressing restricts the lines affected.

* If a command changes the input, subsequent command-addresses will be applied to the current line in the pattern space, not the original input line.

* The original input file is unchanged because the editing commands modify a copy of the original input line. The copy is sent to standard output (but can be redirected to a file).

Syntax of Sed Commands

Sed commands have the general form:

[*address*][, *address*][!]*command* [*arguments*]

Sed commands consist of *addresses* and editing *commands*. *commands* consist of a single letter or symbol; they are described later, alphabetically and by group. *arguments* include the label supplied to **b** or **t**, the filename supplied to **r** or **w**, and the substitution flags for **s**. *addresses* are described below.

Pattern Addressing

A sed command can specify zero, one, or two addresses. An address can be a line number, the symbol **$** (for last line), or a regular expression enclosed in slashes (*/pattern/*). Regular expressions are described in Section 6. Additionally, \n can be used to match any newline in the pattern space (resulting from the **N** command), but not the newline at the end of the pattern space.

If the command specifies:	Then the command is applied to:
No address	Each input line
One address	Any line matching the address. Some commands accept only one address: **a**, **i**, **r**, **q**, and **=**.
Two comma-separated addresses	First matching line and all succeeding lines up to and including a line matching the second address.
An address followed by **!**	All lines that do *not* match the address.

Examples

s/xx/yy/g	Substitute on all lines (all occurrences).
/BSD/d	Delete lines containing BSD.
/^BEGIN/,/^END/p	Print between BEGIN and END, inclusive.
/SAVE/!d	Delete any line that doesn't contain SAVE.
/BEGIN/,/END/!s/xx/yy/g	Substitute on all lines, except between BEGIN and END.

Braces ({}) are used in sed to nest one address inside another or to apply multiple commands at the same address.

    [/pattern/][,/pattern/]{
    command1
    command2
    }

The opening curly brace must end a line, and the closing curly brace must be on a line by itself. Be sure there are no blank spaces after the braces.

Group Summary of Sed Commands

In the lists below, the sed commands are grouped by function and are described tersely. Full descriptions, including syntax and examples, can be found afterward in the alphabetical summary.

Basic Editing

a	Append text after a line.
c	Replace text (usually a text block).
i	Insert text after a line.
d	Delete lines.
s	Make substitutions.
y	Translate characters (like a UNIX **tr**).

Line Information

=	Display line number of a line.
l	Display control characters in ASCII.
p	Display the line.

Input/Output Processing

n	Skip current line and go to line below.
r	Read another file's contents into the input.
w	Write input lines to another file.
q	Quit the sed script (no further output).

Yanking and Putting

h	Copy into hold space; wipe out what's there.
H	Copy into hold space; append to what's there.
g	Get the hold space back; wipe out the destination line.
G	Get the hold space back; append on line below.
x	Exchange contents of hold space and pattern space.

Branching Commands

b	Branch to *label* or to end of script.
t	Same as **b**, but branch only after substitution.
:*label*	Label branched to by **t** or **b**.

Multi-line Input Processing

N	Read another line of input (creates embedded newline).
D	Delete up to the embedded newline.
P	Print up to the embedded newline.

Alphabetical Summary of Sed Commands

Sed

#

Begin a comment in a sed script. Valid only as the first character of the first line.

#

:*label*

Label a line in the script for the transfer of control by **b** or **t**. *label* may contain up to seven characters.

:

[/*pattern***/]=**

Write to standard output the line number of each line addressed by *pattern*.

=

[*address***]a**
text

Append *text* following each line matched by *address*. If *text* goes over more than one line, newlines must be "hidden" by preceding them with a backslash. The *text* will be terminated by the first newline that is not hidden in this way. The *text* is not available in the pattern space, and subsequent commands cannot be applied to it. The results of this command are sent to standard output when the list of editing commands is finished, regardless of what happens to the current line in the pattern space.

a

Example

```
$a\
This goes after the last line in the file\
(marked by $).  This text is escaped at the\
end of each line, except for the last one.
```

[*address1***][,***address2***]b[***label***]**

Transfer control unconditionally to **:***label* elsewhere in script. That is, the command following the *label* is the next command applied to the current line. If no *label* is specified, control falls through to the end of the script, so no more commands are applied to the current line.

b

Example

```
# Ignore tbl tables; resume script after TE:
/^\.TS/,/^\.TE/b
```

[*address1***][,***address2***]c**
text

Replace the lines selected by the address with *text*. When a range of lines is specified, all lines as a group are replaced by a single copy of *text*. The newline following each line of *text* must be escaped by a backslash, except the

c

$\rightarrow$

---

c ←	last line. The contents of the pattern space are, in effect, deleted and no sub-sequent editing commands can be applied to it (or *text*). ***Example*** ``` # Replace first 100 lines in a file: 1,100c\ \ <First 100 names to be supplied> ```
d	[*address1*][,*address2*]**d** Delete the addressed line (or lines) from the pattern space. Thus, the line is not passed to standard output. A new line of input is read, and editing resumes with the first command in the script. ***Example*** ``` # delete all blank lines: /^$/d ```

D	[*address1*][,*address2*]**D**
	
	Delete first part (up to embedded newline) of multi-line pattern space created by **N** command and resume editing with first command in script. If this command empties the pattern space, then a new line of input is read, as if the **d** had been executed.
	
	Example
	
	``
	# Strip multiple blank lines, leaving only one:
	/^$/{
	N
	/^\n$/D
	}
	``

g	[*address1*][,*address2*]**g** Paste the contents of the hold space (see **h** or **H** command) back into the pattern space, wiping out the previous contents of the pattern space. The example shows a simple way to copy lines. ***Example*** This script collects all lines containing the word *Item:* and copies them to a place marker later in the file. The place marker is overwritten. ``` /Item:/H /<Replace this line with the item list>/g ```
G	[*address1*][,*address2*]**G** Same as **g**, except that the hold space is pasted below the address instead of overwriting it. The example shows a simple way to "cut and paste" lines.

Example

This script collects all lines containing the word *Item:* and moves them after a place marker later in the file. The original *Item:* lines are deleted.

```
/Item:/{
H
d
}
/Summary of items:/G
```

[*address1*][,*address2*]**h**

Copy the pattern space into the hold space, a special temporary buffer. The previous contents of the hold space are obliterated. You can use **h** to save a line before editing it.

Example

```
# Edit a line; print the change; replay the original
/UNIX/{
h
s/.* UNIX \(.*\) .*/\1:/
p
x
}
```

Sample input:

```
This describes the UNIX ls command.
This describes the UNIX cp command.
```

Sample output:

```
ls:
This describes the UNIX ls command.
cp:
This describes the UNIX cp command.
```

[*address1*][,*address2*]**H**

Append the contents of the pattern space (preceded by a newline) to the contents of the hold space. Even if the hold space is empty, **H** still appends a newline. **H** is like an incremental copy. See examples under **g** and **G**.

[*address1*]**i**\
text

Insert *text* before each line matched by *address*. (See **a** for details on *text*.)

Example

```
/Item 1/i\
The five items are listed below:
```

l	**[**address1**][,**address2**]l**
	List the contents of the pattern space, showing nonprinting characters as ASCII codes. Long lines are wrapped.

n	**[**address1**][,**address2**]n**
	Read next line of input into pattern space. The current line is sent to standard output, and the next line becomes the current line. Control passes to the command following **n** instead of resuming at the top of the script.

Example

> In the ms macros, a section header occurs on the line below an **.NH** macro. To print all lines of header text, invoke this script with **sed −n**:

```
/^\.NH/{
n
p
}
```

N	**[**address1**][,**address2**]N**
	Append next input line to contents of pattern space; the two lines are separated by an embedded newline. (This command is designed to allow pattern matches across two lines.) Using \n to match the embedded newline, you can match patterns across multiple lines. See example under **D**.

Examples

> Like previous example, but print **.NH** line as well as header title:

```
/^\.NH/{
N
p
}
```

> Join two lines (replace newline with space):

```
/^\.NH/{
N
s/\n/ /
p
}
```

p	**[**address1**][,**address2**]p** *Sed -n 'line#, line# p' filename >* —
	'extract specific line #'s
	Print the addressed line(s). Unless the **-n** command-line option is used, this command will cause duplicate lines to be output. Also, it is typically used before commands that change flow control (**d**, **N**, **b**) and that might prevent the current line from being output. See examples under **h**, **n**, and **N**.

P	**[**address1**][,**address2**]P**
	Print first part (up to embedded newline) of multi-line pattern created by **N** command. Same as **p** if **N** has not been applied to a line.

Example

Suppose you have function references in two formats:

```
function(a,b,c)
function(a,
         b,
         c)
```

The following script changes argument **c**, regardless of whether it appears on the same line as the function name:

```
s/function(a,b,c)/function(a,b,XX)/
/function(/{
N
s/c/XX/
P
D
}
```

[*address*]q

q

Quit when *address* is encountered. The addressed line is first written to output (if default output is not suppressed), along with any text appended to it by previous **a** or **r** commands.

Example

Delete everything after the addressed line:

```
/Garbled text follows:/q
```

Print only the first 50 lines of a file:

```
50q
```

[*address*]**r** *file*

r

Read contents of *file* and append after the contents of the pattern space. Exactly one space must be put between the **r** and the filename.

Example

```
/The list of items follow:/r item_file
```

[*address1*][,*address2*]**s**/*pattern*/*replacement*/[*flags*]

s

Substitute *replacement* for *pattern* on each addressed line. If pattern addresses are used, the pattern // represents the last pattern address specified. The following flags can be specified:

n	Replace *n*th instance of /*pattern*/ on each addressed line. *n* is any number in the range 1 to 512; the default is 1.
g	Replace all instances of /*pattern*/ on each addressed line, not just the first instance.

$\rightarrow$

p   Print the line if a successful substitution is done. If several successful substitutions are done, multiple copies of the line will be printed.

w *file*   Write the line to a *file* if a replacement was done. A maximum of 10 different *files* can be opened.

Examples

Here are some short, commented scripts:

```
# Change third and fourth quote to ( and ):
/function/{
s/"/(/3
s/"/)/4
}

# Remove all quotes on a given line:
/Title/s/"//g

# Remove first colon or all quotes; print resulting lines:
s/://p
s/"//gp

# Change first "if" but leave "ifdef" alone:
/ifdef/!s/if/   if/
```

---

t

[*address1*][,*address2*]**t** [*label*]

Test if any substitutions have been made on addressed lines, and if so, branch to line marked by **:***label*. (See **b** and **:**.) If *label* is not specified, control falls through to bottom of script. The **t** command is like a case statement in the C programming language or the shell programming languages. You test each case: when it's true, you exit the construct.

Example

Suppose you want to fill empty fields of a database. You have this:

```
ID: 1    Name: greg    Rate: 45
ID: 2    Name: dale
ID: 3
```

You want this:

```
ID: 1    Name: greg    Rate: 45    Phone: ??
ID: 2    Name: dale    Rate: ??    Phone: ??
ID: 3    Name: ????    Rate: ??    Phone: ??
```

You need to test the number of fields already there. Here's the script (fields are tab-separated):

```
/ID/{
s/ID: .* Name: .* Rate: .*/&    Phone: ??/p
t
s/ID: .* Name: .*/&    Rate: ??    Phone: ??/p
t
s/ID: .*/&    Name: ??    Rate: ??    Phone: ??/p
}
```

[*address1*][,*address2*]**w** *file*

Append contents of pattern space to *file*. This action occurs when the command is encountered rather than when the pattern space is output. Exactly one space must separate the **w** and the filename. A maximum of ten different files can be opened in a script. This command will create the file if it does not exist; if the file exists, its contents will be overwritten each time the script is executed. Multiple write commands that direct output to the same file append to the end of the file.

Example

```
# Store tbl and eqn blocks in a file:
/^\.TS/,/^\.TE/w troff_stuff
/^\.EQ/,/^\.EN/w troff_stuff
```

[*address1*][,*address2*]**x**

Exchange contents of the pattern space with the contents of the hold space. See **h** for an example.

[*address1*][,*address2*]**y**/*abc*/*xyz*/

Translate characters. Change every instance of *a* to *x*, *b* to *y*, *c* to *z*, etc.

Example

```
# Change item 1, 2, 3 to Item A, B, C ...
/^item [1-9]/y/i123456789/IABCDEFGHI/
```

The Awk Scripting Language

This section presents the following topics:

- Command-line syntax
- Conceptual overview
- Patterns and procedures
- System variables
- Operators
- Variable and array assignment
- Group listing of commands
- Alphabetical summary of commands

For more information, see the Nutshell Handbook *sed & awk*.

Command-line Syntax

The syntax for invoking awk has two forms:

> **awk** [*options*] *'script' var=value file(s)*
> **awk** [*options*] **-f** *scriptfile var=value file(s)*

You can specify a *script* directly on the command line, or you can store a script in a *scriptfile* and specify it with **-f**. Variables can be assigned a value on the command line. The value can be a literal, a shell variable (**$**name), or a command substitution (`cmd`), but the value is available only after a line of input is read (i.e., after the **BEGIN** statement). Awk operates on one or more *files*. If none are specified (or if −is specified), awk reads from the standard input.

The recognized *options* are:

-Fc   Set the field separator to character *c*. This is the same as setting the system variable **FS**. Nawk allows *c* to be a regular expression. Each input line, or record, is divided into fields by white space (blanks or tabs) or by some other user-definable record separator. Fields are referred to by the variables **$1**, **$2**, ... , **$**n. **$0** refers to the entire record.

-v *var=value*   Assign a *value* to variable *var*. This allows assignment before the script begins execution. (Available in nawk only.)

For example, to print the first three (colon-separated) fields on a separate line:

```
awk -F: '{print $1; print $2; print $3}' /etc/passwd
```

Numerous examples are shown later in this section under "Patterns and Procedures."

Conceptual Overview

Awk is a pattern-matching program for processing files, especially when they are databases. The new version of awk, called nawk, provides additional capabilities and is now the standard in SVR4. Awk is still available under the same name (it is really just a link to the command **oawk**). In the next major release of System V, nawk will become the default. (The Free Software Foundation has a version of awk called gawk. All features in nawk are available in gawk.)

With original awk, you can:

- Think of a text file as made up of records and fields in a textual database.

- Use variables to change the database.

- Perform arithmetic and string operations.

- Use programming constructs such as loops and conditionals.

- Produce formatted reports.

With nawk, you can also:

- Define your own functions.

- Execute UNIX commands from a script.

- Process the result of UNIX commands.

- Process command-line arguments more gracefully.

- Work more easily with multiple input streams.

Patterns and Procedures

Awk scripts consist of patterns and procedures:

> *pattern* {*procedure*}

Both are optional. If *pattern* is missing, {*procedure*} is applied to all lines. If {*procedure*} is missing, the matched line is printed.

Patterns

A pattern can be any of the following:

> / *regular expression* /
> *relational expression*
> *pattern-matching expression*
> **BEGIN**
> **END**

- Expressions can be composed of quoted strings, numbers, operators, functions, defined variables, or any of the predefined variables described later under "Awk System Variables".

- Regular expressions use the extended set of metacharacters and are described in Section 6.

- In addition, ^ and $ can be used to refer to the beginning and end of a field, respectively, rather than the beginning and end of a line.

- Relational expressions use the relational operators listed under "Operators" later in this section. Comparisons can be either string or numeric. For example, **$2 > $1** selects lines for which the second field is greater than the first.

- Pattern-matching expressions use the operators ~ (match) and !~ (don't match). See "Operators" later in this section.

- The **BEGIN** pattern lets you specify procedures that will take place *before* the first input line is processed. (Generally, you set global variables here.)

- The **END** pattern lets you specify procedures that will take place *after* the last input record is read.

Except for **BEGIN** and **END**, patterns can be combined with the Boolean operators | | (or), **&&** (and), and **!** (not). A range of lines can also be specified using comma-separated patterns:

> *pattern, pattern*

Procedures

Procedures consist of one or more commands, functions, or variable assignments, separated by newlines or semicolons, and contained within curly braces. Commands fall into four groups:

- Variable or array assignments

- Printing commands

- Built-in functions

- Control-flow commands

Simple Pattern-Procedure Examples

1. Print first field of each line:

   ```
   { print $1 }
   ```

2. Print all lines that contain *pattern*:

   ```
   /pattern/
   ```

3. Print first field of lines that contain *pattern*:

   ```
   /pattern/{ print $1 }
   ```

4. Select records containing more than two fields:

   ```
   NF > 2
   ```

5. Interpret input records as a group of lines up to a blank line:

   ```
   BEGIN { FS = "\n"; RS = "" }
   ```

6. Print fields 2 and 3 in switched order, but only on lines whose first field matches the string "URGENT":

   ```
   $1 ~ /URGENT/ { print $3, $2 }
   ```

7. Count and print the number of *pattern* found:

   ```
   /pattern/ { ++x }
   END { print x }
   ```

8. Add numbers in second column and print total:

```
{total += $2 };
END { print "column total is", total}
```

9. Print lines that contain less than 20 characters:

```
length < 20
```

10. Print each line that begins with *Name:* and that contains exactly seven fields:

```
NF == 7 && /^Name:/
```

11. Reverse the order of fields:

```
{ for (i = NF; i >= 1; i--) print $i }
```

Awk

Awk System Variables

Version	Variable	Description
awk	FILENAME	Current filename.
	FS	Field separator (default is a blank).
	NF	Number of fields in current record.
	NR	Number of the current record.
	OFS	Output field separator (default is a blank).
	ORS	Output record separator (default is a newline).
	RS	Record separator (default is a newline).
	$0	Entire input record.
	$*n*	*n*th field in current record; fields are separated by **FS**.
nawk	ARGC	Number of arguments on command line.
	ARGV	An array containing the command-line arguments.
	FNR	Like NR, but relative to the current file.
	OFMT	Output format for numbers (default is %.6g).
	RSTART	First position in the string matched by **match** function.
	RLENGTH	Length of the string matched by **match** function.
	SUBSEP	Separator character for array subscripts (default is \034).
gawk	ENVIRON	An associative array of environment variables.
	IGNORECASE	An associative array of environment variables.

Operators

The table below lists the operators, in order of increasing precedence, that are available in awk.

Symbol	Meaning
= =+ -= *= /= %= ^=	Assignment.
? :	C conditional expression (nawk and gawk).
| |	Logical OR.
&&	Logical AND.
~ !~	Match regular expression and negation.
< <= > >= != ==	Relational operators.

Symbol	Meaning
(blank)	Concatenation.
+ -	Addition, subtraction.
* / %	Multiplication, division, and modulus.
+ - !	Unary plus and minus, and logical negation.
^	Exponentiation.
++ --	Increment and decrement, either prefix or postfix.
$	Field reference.

Variables and Array Assignments

Variables can be assigned a value with an = sign. For example:

```
FS = ","
```

Expressions using the operators **+**, **−**, **/**, and **%** (modulo) can be assigned to variables.

Arrays can be created with the **split** function (see below), or they can simply be named in an assignment statement.   **++**, **+=**, and **−=** are used to increment or decrement an array, as in the C language. Array elements can be subscripted with numbers (*array*[**1**], ..., *array*[*n*]) or with names. For example, to count the number of occurrences of a pattern, you could use the following script:

```
/pattern/ { array["/pattern/"]++ }
END { print array["/pattern/"] }
```

Group Listing of Awk Commands

Awk commands may be classified as follows:

Arithmetic Functions	String Functions	Control Flow Statements	Input/Output Processing	Miscellaneous
atan2*	gsub*	break	close*	delete*
cos	index	continue	getline*	function*
exp	length	do/while*	next*	system*
int	match*	exit	print	
log	split	for	printf	
rand*	sub*	if	sprintf	
sin	substr	return*		
sqrt	tolower†	while		
srand*	toupper†			

* Available in nawk
† Available in gawk

Alphabetical Summary of Commands

The following alphabetical list of statements and functions includes all that are available in awk, nawk, or gawk. Nawk includes all old awk commands, plus some additional commands (marked as {N}). Gawk includes all nawk commands, plus some additional commands (marked as {G}). Commands that aren't marked with a symbol are available in all versions.

atan2(*y,x* **)** Return the arctangent of *y/x* in radians. {N}	**atan2**
break Exit from a **while** or **for** loop.	**break**
close(*filename–expr* **)** **close(** *command-expr* **)** In most implementations of awk, you can only have ten files open simultaneously and one pipe. Therefore, nawk provides a **close** statement that allows you to close a file or a pipe. It takes as an argument the same expression that opened the pipe or file. {N}	**close**
continue Begin next iteration of **while** or **for** loop without reaching the bottom.	**continue**
cos(*x* **)** Return the cosine of *x*, an angle in radians.	**cos**
delete(*array*[*element*]**)** Delete element of array. {N}	**delete**
do *body* **while (** *expr* **)** Looping statement. Execute statements in *body*, then evaluate *expr*. If **expr** is true, execute *body* again. {N}	**do**
exit Do not execute remaining instruction and read no new input. END procedures will be executed.	**exit**

exp	**exp(** *arg* **)**
	Return the natural exponent of *arg* (the inverse of **log**).
for	**for (** *i=lower* ; *i<=upper* ; *i++* **)** *command*
	While the value of variable *i* is in the range between *lower* and *upper*, do *command*. A series of commands must be put within braces. <= or any relational operator can be used; ++ or – – can be used to increment or decrement the variable.
for	**for (** *item* **in** *array* **)** *command*
	For each *item* in an associative *array*, do *command*. More than one command must be put inside braces. Refer to each element of the array as *array*[*item*].

function	**function** *name* (*parameter–list*) {
	    statements
	 }

	Create *name* as a user-defined function consisting of awk *statements* that apply to the specified list of parameters.
getline	**getline** [*var*] [*<file*] or *command* **|** **getline** [*var*]
	Read next line of input. Original awk does not support the syntax to open multiple input streams. The first form reads input from *file* and the second form reads the output of *command*. Both forms read one line at a time, and each time the statement is executed it gets the next line of input. The line of input is assigned to $0 and it is parsed into fields, setting **NF**, **NR** and **FNR**. If *var* is specified, the result is assigned to *var* and the $0 is not changed. Thus, if the result is assigned to a variable, the current line does not change. It is actually a function and it returns 1 if it reads a record successfully, 0 if end-of-line is encountered, and –1 if for some reason it is otherwise unsuccessful. {**N**}
gsub	**gsub(** *r, s, t* **)**
	Globally substitute *s* for each match of the regular expression *r* in the string *t*. Return the number of substitutions. If *t* is not supplied, defaults to $0. {**N**}

if *(condition)*
  command
[**else**]
  [*command*]

If *condition* is true, do *command(s)*, otherwise do *command* in **else** clause. Condition can be an expression using any of the relational operators <, <=, ==, !=, >=, or >, as well as the pattern-matching operator ~ (e.g., "**if $1** ~ **/[Aa].*/**"). A series of commands must be put within braces.

---

index(*substr*,*str*)

Return the position of substring in string.

---

int(*arg*)

Return the integer value of *arg*.

---

length(*arg*)

Return the length of *arg*. If *arg* is not supplied, **$0** is assumed. Therefore, **length** can be used as a predefined variable that contains the length of the current record.

---

log(*arg*)

Return the natural logarithm of *arg* (the inverse of **exp**).

---

match(*s*,*r*)

Function that matches the pattern, specified by the regular expression *r*, in the string *s* and returns either the position in *s* where the match begins, or 0 if no occurrences are found. Sets the value of **RSTART** and **RLENGTH**. {**N**}

---

next

Read next input line and start new cycle through pattern/procedures statements.

---

print [*args*] [*destination*]

Print *args* on output. *Args* is usually one or more fields, but may also be one or more of the predefined variables. Literal strings must be quoted. Fields are printed in the order they are listed. If separated by commas in the argument list, they are separated in the output by the character specified by **OFS**. If separated by spaces, they are concatenated in the output. *destination* is a UNIX redirection or pipe expression (e.g., > *file*) that redirects the default output.

printf	**printf** [*format* [, *expression(s)*]]
	Formatted print statement. Fields or variables can be formatted according to instructions in the *format* argument. The number of arguments must correspond to the number specified in the format sections.
	format follows the conventions of the C-language *printf* statement. Here are a few of the most common formats:

%s	A string.
%d	A decimal number.
%*n.m*f	A floating point number; *n* = total number of digits. *m* = number of digits after decimal point.
%[–]*nc*	*n* specifies minimum field length for format type *c*, while – justifies value in field; otherwise value is right justified.

format can also contain embedded escape sequences: **\n** (newline) or **\t** (tab) being the most common.

Spaces and literal text can be placed in the *format* argument by quoting the entire argument. If there are multiple expressions to be printed, there should be multiple formats specified.

Example

Using the script:

```
{printf ("The sum on line %s is %d \n", NR, $1+$2)}
```

The following input line:

```
5    5
```

produces this output, followed by a newline:

```
The sum on line 1 is 10.
```

---

rand **rand()**

Generate a random number between 0 and 1. This function returns the same number each time the script is executed, unless the random number generator is seeded using the **srand()** function. {**N**}

---

return **return** [*expr*]

Used at end of user-defined functions to exit function, returning value of expression. {**N**}

---

sin **sin**(*x*)

Return the sine of *x*, an angle in radians.

split(*string*,*array*[,*sep*])

Split *string* into elements of array *array*[**1**], . . . ,*array*[*n*]. The string is split at each occurrence of separator *sep*. If *sep* is not specified, **FS** is used. The number of array elements created is returned.

split

---

sprintf [*format* [, *expression(s)*]]

Return the value of one or more *expressions*, using the specified *format* (see **printf**). Data is formatted but not printed. {**N**}

sprintf

---

sqrt(*arg*)

Return square root of *arg*.

sqrt

---

srand(*expr*)

Use *expr* to set a new seed for random number generator. Default is time of day. {**N**}

srand

---

sub(*r*,*s*,*t*)

Substitute *s* for first match of the regular expression *r* in the string *t*. Return 1 if successful; 0 otherwise. If *t* is not supplied, defaults to $0. {**N**}

sub

---

substr(*string*,*m*,[*n*])

Return substring of *string* beginning at character position *m* and consisting of the next *n* characters. If *n* is omitted, include all characters to the end of string.

substr

---

system(*command*)

Function that executes the specified *command* and returns its status. The status of the command that is executed typically indicates its success (1), completion (0) or unexpected error (–1). The output of the command is not available for processing within the awk script. Use "*command* | **getline**" to read the output of the command into the script. {**N**}

system

---

tolower(*str*)

Translate all uppercase characters in *str* to lowercase and return the new string. {**G**}

tolower

---

toupper(*str*)

Translate all lowercase characters in *str* to uppercase and returns the new string. {**G**}

toupper

---

while (*condition*)
command

Do *command* while *condition* is true (see **if** for a description of allow-
able conditions). A series of commands must be put within braces.

Part III

Text Formatting

Part III describes the UNIX tools for document formatting. These tools are no longer part of standard SVR4 but are provided in the (BSD or BSD/SunOS) compatibility packages that come with SVR4 or Solaris 2.0. (Actually, because the *mm* macros were never part of BSD, they aren't in the compatibility packages either.)

Many UNIX vendors supply an enhanced set of formatting tools—in some cases, as an extra-cost option.

Section 12 - *Nroff and Troff*

Section 13 - *mm Macros*

Section 14 - *ms Macros*

Section 15 - *me Macros*

Section 16 - *Preprocessors*

12

Nroff and Troff

This section presents the following topics:

- Introduction
- Command-line invocation
- Using the requests: an overview
- Default operation of requests
- Group summary of requests
- Alphabetical summary of requests
- Escape sequences
- Predefined number registers
- Special characters

Introduction

Nroff and troff are UNIX programs for formatting text files. Nroff is designed to format output for line printers and letter-quality printers; you can also display the output on your screen. Troff is designed for typesetting. Except for some functions that are specific to typesetting, the same commands work for both programs.

Nroff and troff are not part of standard SVR4 but are included in the compatibility packages. It is this version that is documented here. Note, however, that some UNIX distributors include a vendor-specific version of nroff/troff. Various enhanced packages are also available, such as sqtroff from SoftQuad or groff from the Free Software Foundation. These packages might include additional requests or escape sequences. For completely accurate information, we recommend that you consult the text processing manuals that come with your specific UNIX implementation.

In addition, we make references to ditroff, or device-independent troff, which is a later version of troff. For the most part, ditroff works the same as troff; where there are distinctions, the original troff is referred to as *otroff*.

Command-line Invocation

Nroff and troff are invoked from the command line as follows:

> **/usr/ucb/nroff** [*options*] [*files*]
> **/usr/ucb/troff** [*options*] [*files*]

Many of the options are the same for both formatters.

Nroff/troff options

−F*dir*	Search for font tables in directory *dir*.
−i	Read standard input after *files* are processed.
−m*name*	Prepend a macro file to input *files*. Troff prepends **/usr/lib/tmac/tmac.***name*. Nroff prepends **/usr/share/lib/tmac/tmac.***name*.
−n*N*	First output page has page number *N*.
−o*list*	Print pages contained only in the comma-separated *list*. Page ranges can be specified as *n-m*, *-m* (first page through *m*), or *n-* (*n* through end of file).
−r*aN*	Set register *a* to *N*.
−s*N*	Stop every *n* pages. This allows changing of a paper cassette. Resume by pressing RETURN (in nroff) or by pressing the start button on the typesetter (in troff).
−T*name*	Prepare output designed for printer or typesetter *name*. For device names, see your specific documentation or a local expert.
−u*N*	The font in position 3 is overstruck *N* times. Typically used to adjust the weight of the bold font.
−z	Discard output except messages generated by **.tm** request.

Nroff-only options

−e	When justifying output lines, space words equally (using terminal resolution instead of full space increments).

−h	Hasten output by replacing 8 horizontal spaces with a tab.
−q	Invoke simultaneous input/output of **.rd** requests.

Troff-only options

−a	Format a printable ASCII approximation. Useful for finding page counts without producing printed output.
−f	Don't stop typesetter when formatting is done.

Examples

Run **chap1** through the tbl preprocessor, then format the result using the *mm* macros, with register **N** set to 5 (sets the page-numbering style), etc.:

```
tbl chap1 | troff -mm -rN5 | spooler &
```

Format **chap2** using the *ms* macros; the first page is 7, but print only pages 8-10, 15, and 18 through the end of the file:

```
nroff -ms -n7 -o8-10,15,18- chap2 &
```

Using the Requests: An Overview

Formatting is specified by embedding brief codes into the text source file. These codes act as directives to nroff and troff when they are invoked. For example, to center a line of text, type the following code in a file:

```
.ce
This text should be centered.
```

When formatted, the output appears centered:

```
                This text should be centered.
```

There are two types of formatting codes:

- *Requests*, which provide the most elementary instructions, and

- *Macros*, which are predefined combinations of requests.

Requests, also known as *primitives*, allow direct control of almost any feature of page layout and formatting. Macros combine requests to create a total effect. In a sense, requests are like atoms, and macros are like molecules.

See Sections 13, 14, and 15 for more information on macros.

Common Requests

The most commonly used requests are:

```
.ad    .ds    .ll    .nr    .sp
.br    .fi    .na    .po    .ta
.bp    .ft    .ne    .ps    .ti
.ce    .in    .nf    .so    .vs
.de    .ls
```

For example, a simple macro could be written as follows:

```
                       \" Ps macro -- show literal text display
.de Ps                 \" Define a macro named "Ps"
.sp .5                 \" Space down half a line
.in 1i                 \" Indent one inch
.ta 10n +10n           \" Set new tabstops
.ps 8                  \" Use 8-point type
.vs 10                 \" Use 10-point vertical spacing
.ft CW                 \" Use constant width font
.br                    \" Break line (.ne begins count on next line)
.ne 3                  \" Keep 3 lines together
.nf                    \" No-fill mode (output lines as is)
..                     \" End macro definition
```

Specifying Measurements

With some requests, the numeric argument can be followed by a scale indicator that specifies a unit of measurement. The valid indicators and their meanings are listed below. Note that all measurements are internally converted to basic units (this conversion is shown in the last column). A basic unit is the smallest possible size on the printer device. The device resolution (e.g., 300 dots per inch), determines the size of a basic unit. In the following table, T specifies the current point size and R specifies the device resolution.

Scale Indicator	Meaning	Equivalent Unit	Number of Basic Units
c	Centimeter	2.54 inches	$R / 2.54$
i	Inch	6 picas or 72 points	R
m	Em	T points	$R \times T / 72$
n	En	0.5 em	$R \times T / 144$
p	Point	1/72 inch	$R / 72$
P	Pica	1/6 inch	$R / 6$
u	Basic unit		1
v	Vertical line space		(Current value in basic units)
None	Default		

You can specify a scale indicator for any of the requests below, except for **.ps**, which always uses points. If no unit is given, the default unit is used. (The second column lists the scale indicators as described in the previous table.) For horizontally oriented requests, the default unit is ems. For vertically oriented requests, the default is usually vertical lines.

Request	Default Scale	Request	Default Scale
.ch	v	.pl	v
.dt	v	.po	v
.ie	u	.ps	p
.if	u	.rt	v
.in	m	.sp	v
.ll	m	.sv	v
.lt	m	.ta	m
.mc	m	.ti	m
.ne	v	.vs	p
.nr	u	.wh	v

Requests That Cause a Line Break

Most requests can be interspersed with text without causing a line break in the output. The following requests cause a break:

```
.bp    .ce    .fi    .in    .sp
.br    .cf    .fl    .nf    .ti
```

If you need to prevent these requests from causing a break, begin them with the "no break" character (normally ') instead of a dot (.). For example, **.sp** takes effect right away, but **'sp** waits until the output line is completely filled. Only then does it add a line space.

Default Operation of Requests

Nroff/troff initializes the formatting environment. For example, unless you reset the line length, nroff/troff uses 6.5 inches. Most requests can change the default environment, and those that can are listed in the table below. The second column lists the initial or default value in effect before the request is used. If no initial value applies, a hyphen (-) is used. The third column shows the effect if a request's optional argument is not used. Here, a hyphen is used if the request doesn't accept an argument or if the argument is required.

Request	Initial Value	If No Argument	Description
`.ad`	Justify	Previous adjust	Adjust margins.
`.af`	Lowercase arabic	–	Assign a format to a register.
`.am`	–	End call with . .	Append to a macro.
`.bd`	Off	–	Embolden font.
`.c2`	;	;	Set no-break control character.
`.cc`	.	.	Set control character.
`.ce`	Off	Center one line	Center lines.
`.ch`	–	Turn off trap	Change trap position.
`.cs`	Off	–	Set constant-width spacing.
`.cu`	0	1 line	Continuous underline/italicize.
`.da`	–	End the diversion	Divert text and append to a macro.
`.de`	–	End macro with . .	Define a macro.
`.di`	–	End the diversion	Divert text to a macro.
`.dt`	–	Turn off trap	Set a diversion trap.
`.ec`	\	\	Set escape character.
`.eo`	On	–	Turn off escape character.
`.ev`	0	Prev. environment	Change environment.
`.fc`	Off	Off	Set field delimiter and pad character.
`.fi`	Fill	–	Fill lines.
`.fp`	1 = R 2 = I 3 = B 4 = S	–	Mount font (on positions 1-4).
`.ft`	Roman	Previous font	Set font.
`.hc`	\%	\%	Set hyphenation character.
`.hy`	Mode 1	Previous mode	Set hyphenation mode.
`.ig`	–	End with . .	Suppress (ignore) text in output.
`.in`	0	Previous indent	Indent.
`.it`	–	Turn off trap	Set a trap for input line counting.
`.lc`	.	None	Set leader character.
`.lg`	On	On	Ligature mode.
`.ll`	6.5"	Prev. line length	Set line length.
`.ls`	Single-space	Previous mode	Set line spacing.
`.lt`	6.5"	Prev. title length	Set length of title.
`.mc`	–	Turn off	Set the margin character.
`.mk`	–	Internal	Mark vertical position.
`.na`	Adjust	–	Don't adjust margins.
`.ne`	–	One vertical line	Keep lines on same page if there's room.
`.nf`	Fill	–	Don't fill lines.
`.nh`	On	–	Turn of hyphenation.
`.nm`	Off	Off	Line-numbering mode.
`.nn`	–	Number one line	Don't number lines.
`.ns`	Space mode	–	Enable no-space mode.

Request	Initial Value	If No Argument	Description
.nx	–	End of file	Go to a file.
.pc	%	Off	Set page character.
.pl	11"	11"	Set page length.
.pn	Page 1	–	Set page number.
.po	0 (nroff) 26/27" (troff)	Previous offset	Change page offset.
.ps	10	Prev. point size	Set point size.
.rd	–	Ring bell	Read from the terminal.
.rt	–	Internal	Return to marked vertical place.
.sp	–	One vertical line	Output blank spacing.
.ss	12/36 em	–	Set character spacing.
.sv	–	One vertical line	Save (store) spacing.
.ta	.5" (troff) 8 em (nroff)	–	Define tab settings.
.ti	0	–	Indent next line.
.tm	–	Newline	Print a message, then continue.
.uf	Italic	Italic	Set font for underlining.
.ul	0	1 line	Underline/italicize.
.vs	1/6" (nroff) 12 pts (troff)	Previous value	Set vertical spacing for lines.

Group Summary of Requests

As an aid to finding the right request for a particular task, the 84 nroff/troff requests are listed below by subject:

Character Output

.cu	Continuous underline/italicize.
.lg	Ligature mode.
.tr	Translate characters.
.uf	Set font for underlining.
.ul	Underline/italicize.

Conditional Processing

.el	*Else* portion of *if-else*.
.ie	*If* portion of *if-else*.
.if	*If* statement.

Customizing Troff/Nroff Requests

.c2	Set no-break control character.
.cc	Set control character.
.ec	Set escape character.
.eo	Turn off escape character.
.hc	Set hyphenation character.
.pc	Set page character.

Diagnostic Output

.ab	Print a message, then abort.
.fl	Flush output buffer.
.ig	Suppress (ignore) text in output.
.mc	Set the margin character.
.pm	Print name and size of macros.
.tm	Print a message, then continue.

Font and Character Size

.bd	Embolden font.
.cs	Set constant-width spacing.
.fp	Mount font (on positions 1-4).
.ft	Set font.
.ps	Set point size.
.ss	Set character spacing.

Horizontal Positioning

.in	Indent.
.ll	Set line length.
.lt	Set length of title.
.po	Change page offset.
.ti	Indent next line.
.tl	Specify three-part title.

Hyphenation

.hw	Set hard-coded hyphenation.
.hy	Set hyphenation mode.
.nh	Turn of hyphenation.

Input/Output Switching

.cf	Copy raw file to output.
.ex	Exit from nroff/troff.
.nx	Go to a file.
.pi	Pipe output to a UNIX command.
.rd	Read from the terminal.
.so	Go to a file, then return.
.sy	Execute a UNIX command.

Line Numbering

.nm	Line-numbering mode.
.nn	Don't number lines.

Macro and String Processing

.am	Append to a macro.
.as	Append to a string.
.ch	Change trap position.
.da	Divert text; append to a macro.
.de	Define a macro.
.di	Divert text to a macro.
.ds	Define a string.
.dt	Set a diversion trap.
.em	Set the ending macro.
.ev	Change environment.

.it	Set trap for input line counting.
.rm	Remove macro, request, or string.
.rn	Rename macro, request, or string.
.wh	Set a page trap.

Number Registers

.af	Assign a format to a register.
.nr	Define a number register.
.rr	Remove a number register.

Pagination

.bp	Begin a new page.
.mk	Mark vertical position.
.ne	Keep lines on same page if there's ro
.pl	Set page length.
.pn	Set page number.
.rt	Return to marked vertical place.

Tabs

.fc	Set a field delimiter and a pad charac
.lc	Set leader character.
.ta	Define tab settings.
.tc	Set tab character.

Text Adjustments

.ad	Adjust margins.
.br	Break the output line.
.ce	Center lines.
.fi	Fill lines.
.na	Don't adjust margins.
.nf	Don't fill lines.

Vertical Spacing

.ls	Line spacing (e.g., single-spaced).
.ns	Enable no-space mode.
.os	Output vertical space from .sv.
.rs	Restore spacing mode.
.sp	Output blank spacing.
.sv	Save (store) spacing.
.vs	Set vertical spacing for lines.

.ab [*text*] .ab

Abort and print *text* as message. If *text* is not specified, the message *User Abort* is printed.

.ad [*c*] .ad

Adjust output lines according to format *c*. Fill mode must be on (see **.fi**). With no argument, return to previous adjustment. The current adjustment mode is stored in register **.j**, with the following values: 0=l, 1=b, 3=c, 5=r (see **.na**).

Values for c

b	Lines are justified.
n	Lines are justified.
c	Lines are centered.
l	Lines are flush left.
r	Lines are flush right.

.af *r c* .af

Assign format *c* to register *r*.

Values for c

1	0, 1, 2, etc.
001	000, 001, 002, etc.
i	Lowercase roman numerals.
I	Uppercase roman numerals.
a	Lowercase alphabetic.
A	Uppercase alphabetic.

Example

Paginate front matter using the *ms* macros:

```
.af PN i      \" Set page number register PN to i
```

.am *xx* [*yy*] .am

Take the requests (etc.) that follow and append them to the definition of macro *xx*; end the append at call of *.yy* (or **..**, if *yy* is omitted).

.as *xx string* .as

Append *string* to string register *xx*. *string* may contain spaces, and is terminated by a newline. An initial quote (") is ignored.

Nroff / Troff

.bd	**.bd** [**s**] *f n*
	Overstrike characters in font *f n* times. If **s** is specified, overstrike characters in special font *n* times when font *f* is in effect.
.bp	**.bp** [*n*]
	Begin new page. Number next page *n*.
.br	**.br**
	Break to a newline (output partial line).
.c2	**.c2** *c*
	Use *c* (instead of ') as the no-break control character.
.cc	**.cc** *c*
	Use *c* (instead of **.**) as the control character to introduce requests and macros.
.ce	**.ce** [*n*]
	Center next *n* lines (default is 1); if *n* is 0, stop centering. *n* applies only to lines containing output text. Blank lines don't count.
.cf	**.cf** *file*
	Copy contents of *file* into output, and don't interpret (ditroff only).
.ch	**.ch** *xx* [*n*]
	Change trap position for macro *xx* to *n*. If *n* is absent, remove the trap.
.cs	**.cs** *f n m*
	Use constant spacing for font *f*. Constant character width will be *n*/36 ems. If *m* is given, the em is taken to be *m* points.
	Example
| | ```
.cs CW 18   \" squeeze spacing of constant width font
``` |
| **.cu** | **.cu** [*n*] |
| | Continuous underline (including inter-word spaces) on next *n* lines. If *n* is 0, stop underlining. Use **.ul** to underline visible characters only. Underline font can be switched in troff with **.uf** request. In troff, **.cu** and **.ul** produce italics (you must use a macro to underline). |
```

.da [*xx*]

Divert following text and append it to macro *xx*. If no argument, end the diversion.

.de *xx* [*yy*]

Define macro *xx*. End definition at call of **.***yy* (or **..**, if *yy* is omitted).

.di [*xx*]

Divert following text into a newly defined macro *xx*. If no argument, end the diversion.

.ds *xx string*

Define *xx* to contain *string*.

.dt *n xx*

Install diversion trap at position *n*, within diversion, to invoke macro *xx*.

.ec [*c*]

Set escape character to *c*. Default is \.

.el

Else portion of **if-else** (see **.ie** below).

.em *xx*

Set end macro to be *xx*. *xx* will automatically be executed when all other output has been completed.

.eo

Turn escape character mechanism off. All escape characters will be printed literally.

.ev [*n*]

Change environment to *n*. For example, many requests that affect horizontal position, hyphenation, or text adjustment are stored in the current environment. If *n* is omitted, restore previous environment. The initial value of *n* is 0, and $0 \leq n \leq 2$. You must return to the previous environment by using **.ev** with no argument, or you will get a stack overflow.

.ex	**.ex** Exit from formatter and perform no further text processing. Typically used with **.nx** for form-letter generation.
.fc	**.fc** *a b* Set field delimiter to *a* and pad character to *b*.
.fi	**.fi** Turn on fill mode, the inverse of **.nf**. Default is on.
.fl	**.fl** Flush output buffer. Useful for interactive debugging.

.fp	**.fp** *n f*
	
	Assign font *f* to position *n*. *n* ranges from 1 to 4 (in otroff) and from 1 to 9 (in ditroff).
	
	Examples
	
	`.fp 7 CW    \" position 7 is constant width`
	`.fp 8 CI    \" position 8 is constant italic`
	`.fp 9 CB    \" position 9 is constant bold`

.ft	**.ft** *f* Change font to *f*, where *f* is a one- or two-character font name, or a font position assigned with **.fp**. Similar to escape sequence **\f**.
.hc	**.hc** [*c*] Change input hyphenation-indication character to *c*. Default is **\%**.
.hw	**.hw** *words* Specify hyphenation points for *words* (e.g., **.hw spe-ci-fy**).
.hy	**.hy** *n* Turn hyphenation on (*n*≥1) or off (*n*=0). See also **.nh**. ***Values for n*** **1** Hyphenate whenever necessary. **2** Don't hyphenate last word on page.

4	Don't split off first two characters.	**.hy**
8	Don't split off last two characters.	
14	Use all three restrictions.	

.ie [**!**] *condition anything*   **.ie**
.el *anything*

If portion of *if-else*. If *condition* is true, do *anything*. Otherwise do *any-thing* following **.el** request. **.ie/.el** pairs can be nested. Syntax for *condition* is described under **.if**.

Example

If first argument isn't 2, columns are 1.8 inches wide; otherwise, columns are 2.5 inches wide:

```
.ie !'\\$1'2'  .MC 1.8i 0.2i
.el .MC 2.5i 0.25i
```

.if [**!**] *condition anything*   **.if**

If *condition* is true, do *anything*. The presence of an **!** negates the condition. If *anything* runs over more than one line, it can be delimited by **\{** and **\}**.

Conditions

o	True if the page number is odd.
e	True if the page number is even.
n	True if the processor is nroff.
t	True if the processor is troff.
" *str1* **"** *str2* **"**	True if *str1* is identical to *str2*. Often used to test the value of arguments passed to a macro.
expr	True if the value of expression *expr* is greater than zero.

Expressions

Expressions typically contain number register interpolations, and can use any of the following operators:

+ −	Addition, subtraction.
/ *	Multiplication, division.
%	Modulo.
> <	Greater than, less than.
>= =	Greater than or equal, less than or equal.
= ==	Equal.
&	Logical AND.
:	Logical OR.

→

.if ←	*Examples* ``` .if t .nr PD 0.5v \" Set spacing between ms paragraphs ``` ``` .if !"\\$2"" \{\ \" If 2nd arg is nonnull .sp \f3\\$2\fP\} \" Use font 3 for 2nd argument ```
.ig	**.ig** [*yy*] Ignore following text, up to line beginning with *.yy* (default is **..**, as with **.de**). Useful for commenting out large blocks of text or macro definitions.
.in	**.in** [±][*n*] Set indent to *n* or increment indent by ±*n*. If no argument, restore previous indent. Current indent is stored in register **.i**. Default scale is ems.
.it	**.it** *n xx* Set trap for input-line count, so as to invoke macro *xx* after *n* lines of input text have been read.
.lc	**.lc** *c* Set leader repetition character to *c* instead of **.** (dot). Similar to **\a**.
.lg	**.lg** *n* Turn ligature mode on if *n* is absent or non-zero.
.ll	**.ll** [±][*n*] Set line length to *n* or increment line length by ±*n*. If no argument, restore previous line length. Current line length is stored in register **.l**. Default value is 6.5 inches; default scale is ems.
.ls	**.ls** [*n*] Set line spacing to *n*. If no argument, restore previous line spacing. Initial value is 1. *Example* ``` .ls 2 \" Produce double-spaced output ```
.lt	**.lt** [*n*] Set title length to *n* (default scale is ems). If no argument, restore previous value.

.mc [*c*] [*n*]

Set margin character to *c*, and place it *n* spaces to the right of margin. If *c* is missing, turn margin character off. If *n* is missing, use previous value. Initial value for *n* is .2 inches in nroff and 1 em in troff.

.mc

.mk [*r*]

Mark current vertical place in register *r*. Return to mark with **.rt** or **.sp** l \ n *r*.

.mk

.na

Do not adjust margins. Current adjustment mode is stored in register **.j**. See also **.ad**.

.na

.ne *n*

If *n* lines do not remain on this page, start a new page.

.ne

.nf

Do not fill or adjust output lines. See also **.ad** and **.fi**.

.nf

.nh

Turn hyphenation off. See also **.hy**.

.nh

.nm [*n m s i*]

Number output lines (if *n*≥0), or turn numbering off (if *n*=0). ±*n* sets initial line number; *m* sets numbering interval; *s* sets separation of numbers and text; *i* sets indent of text. Useful for code segments, poetry, etc. See also **.nn**.

.nm

.nn *n*

Do not number next *n* lines, but keep track of numbering sequence, which can be resumed with **.nm +0**. See **.nm**.

.nn

.nr *r n* [*m*]

Assign value *n* to number register *r*, and optionally set auto-increment to *m*.

Examples

Set the "box width" register to line length minus indent:

```
.nr BW \n(.l-\n(.i
```

.nr

→

.nr
←
	Set page layout values for ms macros:
	
	`.nr LL 6i                 \" line length`
	`.nr PO ((8.25i-\n(LLu)/2u)  \" page offset`
	`.nr VS \n(PS+2             \" vertical spacing`
	
	In sqtroff, auto-increment a footnote-counter register:
	
	`.nr footcount 0 1     \" Reset to zero on each page`
	
	Note: inside a macro definition, **\n** should be **\\n**.

.ns	**.ns** Turn on no-space mode. See also **.rs**.
.nx	**.nx** *file* Switch to *file* and do not return to current file. See also **.so**.
.os	**.os** Output saved space specified in previous **.sv** request.
.pc	**.pc** *c* Use *c* (instead of **%**) as the page number character within nroff/troff coding.
.pi	**.pi** *command* Pipe the formatter output through a UNIX *command*, instead of placing it on standard output (ditroff and nroff only). Request must occur before any output. ***Example*** `.pi /bin/sort        \" Sort the output (which follows)`
.pl	**.pl** [±][*n*] Set page length to *n* or increment page length by ±*n*. If no argument, restore default. Current page length is stored in register **.p**. Default is 11 inches.
.pm	**.pm** Print names and sizes of all defined macros.
.pn	**.pn** [±][*n*] Set next page number to *n*, or increment page number by ±*n*. Current page number is stored in register **%**.

.po [±][*n*]

Offset text a distance of *n* from left edge of page, or else increment the current offset by ±*n*. If no argument, return to previous offset. Current page offset is stored in register **.o**.

.ps *n*

Set point size to *n* (troff only). Current point size is stored in register **.s**. Default is 10 points.

.rd [*prompt*]

Read input from terminal, after printing optional *prompt*.

.rm *xx*

Remove macro or string *xx*.

.rn *xx yy*

Rename request, macro, or string *xx* to *yy*.

.rr *r*

Remove register *r*. See also **.nr**.

.rs

Restore spacing (disable no-space mode). See **.ns**.

.rt [±*n*]

Return (upward only) to marked vertical place, or to ±*n* from top of page or diversion. See also **.mk**.

.so *file*

Switch out to *file*, then return to current file. That is, read the contents of another *file* into the current file. See also **.nx**.

.sp *n*

Leave *n* blank lines. Default is 1.

.ss *n*

Set space-character size to *n*/36 em (no effect in nroff).

.sv	**.sv** *n*
	Save *n* lines of space; output saved space with **.os**.

.sy	**.sy** *command* [*args*]
	Execute UNIX *command* with optional arguments (ditroff only).

Example

Search for the first argument; accumulate in a temp file:

```
.sy sed -n 's/\\$1/Note: \1/p' list >> /tmp/notesfile
```

.ta	**.ta** *n*[*t*] [+] *m*[*t*] ...
	Set tab stops at positions *n*, *m*, etc. If *t* is not given, tab is left-adjusting. Use a + to move relative to the previous tab stop. The **\t** escape is similar.

Values for t

L	Left adjust.
R	Right adjust.
C	Center.

.tc	**.tc** *c*
	Define tab repetition character as *c* (instead of white space). For example, **.tc .** draws a series of dots up to the next tab position.

.ti	**.ti** [±][*n*]
	Temporary indent. Indent the next output line by *n*, or increment the current indent by ±*n* for the next output line. Default scale is ems.

Example

```
.in 10
.ti -5
The first line of this paragraph sticks out by 5 ems ...
.in -10
```

.tl	**.tl** '*l*'*c*'*r*'
	Specify **l**eft, **c**entered, or **r**ight title. Title length is specified by **.lt**, not **.ll**.

.tm	**.tm** *text*
	Terminal message. Print *text* on standard error. Useful for debugging.

.tr	**.tr** *ab*
	Translate character *a* (first of a pair) to *b* (second of pair).

Example	**.tr**
Produce uppercase, and later restore. Useful for title macros:	

```
.tr aAbBcCdDeEfFgGhHiIjJkKlLmM        Et cetera

.tr aabbccddeeffgghhiijjkkllmm        Et cetera
```

.uf *f*

Set underline font to *f* (to be switched to by **.ul** or **.cu**). Default is *italics.*

.ul [*n*]

Underline (italicize in troff) next *n* input lines. Do not underline inter-word spaces. Use **.cu** for continuous underline. Underline font can be switched in troff with **.uf** request. However, you must use a macro to underline in troff.

.vs [*n*]

Set vertical line spacing to *n*. If no argument, restore previous spacing. Current vertical spacing is stored in register **.v**. Default is 1/6 inch in nroff, 12 points in troff.

.wh *n* [*xx*]

The "when" request. When position *n* is reached, execute macro *xx*; negative values are with respect to page bottom. If *xx* is not supplied, remove any trap(s) at that location. (A trap is the position on the page where a given macro is executed.) Two traps can be at the same location if one is moved over the other with **.ch**. They cannot be placed at the same location with **.wh**.

Escape Sequences

Sequence	Effect
\\	Prevent or delay the interpretation of \ .
\e	Printable version of the current \ escape character.
\'	´ (acute accent); equivalent to **\(aa**.
\`	` (grave accent); equivalent to **\(ga**.
\-	– Minus sign in the current font.
\.	Period (dot).
\(space)	Unpaddable space-size space character.
\(newline)	Concealed (ignored) newline.
\0	Digit width space.

Sequence	Effect
\\|	1/6-em narrow space character (zero width in nroff).
\\^	1/12-em half-narrow space character (zero width in nroff).
\\&	Non-printing, zero width character.
\\!	Transparent line indicator.
\\"	Beginning of comment.
\\$n	Interpolate argument 1≤n≤9.
\\%	Default optional hyphenation character.
\\(xx	Character named xx.
*x or *(xx	Interpolate string x or xx.
\\a	Noninterpreted leader character.
\\b´abc...´	Bracket building function.
\\c	Make next line continuous with current.
\\d	Forward (down) 1/2-em vertical motion (1/2 line in nroff).
\\D´l x,y´	Draw a line from current position to coordinates x,y (ditroff only).
\\D´c d´	Draw circle of diameter d with left edge at current position (ditroff only).
\\D´e d1 d2´	Draw ellipse with horizontal diameter d1 and vertical diameter d2, with left edge at current position (ditroff only).
\\D´a x1 y1 x2 y2´	Draw arc counterclockwise from current position, with center at x1,y1 and endpoint at x1+x2,y1+y2 (ditroff only).
\\D´~ x1 y1 x2 y2...´	Draw spline from current position through the specified coordinates (ditroff only).
\\fx or \\f(xx or \\fn	Change to font named x or xx or to position n.
\\h´n´	Local horizontal motion; move right n or if n is negative move left.
\\H´n´	Set character height to n points, without changing width (ditroff only).
\\kx	Mark horizontal *input* place in register x.
\\l´nc´	Draw horizontal line of length n (optionally with c).
\\L´nc´	Draw vertical line of length n (optionally with c).
\\nx, \\n(xx	Interpolate number register x or xx.
\\o´abc...´	Overstrike characters a, b, c...
\\p	Break and spread output line.
\\r	Reverse 1-em vertical motion (reverse line in nroff).
\\sn, \\s±n	Change point-size to n or increment by n. For example, \\s0 returns to previous point size.
\\S´n´	Slant output n degrees to the right. Negative values slant to the left. A value of zero turns off slanting (ditroff only).
\\t	Non-interpreted horizontal tab.

Sequence	Effect
\u	Reverse (up) 1/2-em vertical motion (1/2 line in nroff).
\v´n´	Local vertical motion; move down *n* or if *n* is negative move up.
\w´string´	Interpolate width of *string*.
\x´n´	Extra line-space function (*n* negative provides space before, *n* positive provides after).
\zc	Print *c* with zero width (without spacing).
\{	Begin multi-line conditional input.
\}	End multi-line conditional input.
\x	*x*, any character *not* listed above.

Predefined Number Registers

There are two types of predefined registers: read-only and read-write.

Read-only Registers

.$	Number of arguments available at the current macro level.
.$$	Process id of troff process (ditroff only).
.A	Set to 1 in troff, if **−a** option used; always 1 in nroff.
.H	Available horizontal resolution in basic units.
.T	Set to 1 in nroff, if **−T** option used; always 0 in troff; in ditroff, the string *(.T contains the value of **−T**.
.V	Available vertical resolution in basic units.
.a	Post-line extra line-space most recently utilized using \x´n´.
.c	Number of lines read from current input file.
.d	Current vertical place in current diversion; equal to register **nl** when there is no diversion.
.f	Current font as physical quadrant (1 to 4 in otroff; 1 to 9 in ditroff).
.h	Text baseline high-water mark on current page or diversion.
.i	Current indent.
.j	Current adjustment mode.
.l	Current line length.
.n	Length of text portion on previous output line.
.o	Current page offset.
.p	Current page length.
.s	Current point size.
.t	Distance to the next trap.
.u	Equal to 1 in fill mode and 0 in no-fill mode.
.v	Current vertical line spacing.
.w	Width of previous character.
.x	Reserved version-dependent register.
.y	Reserved version-dependent register.
.z	Name of current diversion.

Read-write Registers

%	Current page number.
ct	Character type (set by *width* function).
dl	Width (maximum) of last completed diversion.
dn	Height (vertical size) of last completed diversion.
dw	Current day of the week (1 to 7).
dy	Current day of the month (1 to 31).
hp	Current horizontal place on *input* line.
ln	Output line number.
mo	Current month (1 to 12).
nl	Vertical position of last printed text baseline.
sb	Depth of string below baseline (generated by *width* function).
st	Height of string above base line (generated by *width* function).
yr	Last two digits of current year.

Special Characters

This subsection lists the following special characters:

- Characters that reside on the standard fonts

- Miscellaneous characters

- Bracket building symbols

- Mathematics symbols

- Greek characters

The characters in the first table below are available on the standard fonts. The characters in the remaining tables are available only on the special font.

On the Standard Fonts

Char	Input	Character Name
'	'	Close quote
`	`	Open quote
—	\ (em	3/4 em dash
-	–	Hyphen or
-	\ (hy	Hyphen
—	\ –	Minus in current font
•	\ (bu	Bullet
□	\ (sq	Square
_	\ (ru	Rule
$1/4$	\ (14	1/4
$1/2$	\ (12	1/2
$3/4$	\ (34	3/4
fi	\ (fi	fi ligature
fl	\ (fl	fl ligature

On the Standard Fonts (continued)

Char	Input	Character Name
ff	\ (ff	ff ligature
ffi	\ (Fi	ffi ligature
ffl	\ (Fl	ffl ligature
°	\ (de	Degree
†	\ (dg	Dagger
′	\ (fm	Foot mark
¢	\ (ct	Cent sign
®	\ (rg	Registered
©	\ (co	Copyright

Miscellaneous Characters

Char	Input	Character Name
§	\ (sc	Section
´	\ (aa	Acute accent
`	\ (ga	Grave accent
_	\ (ul	Underrule
→	\ (->	Right arrow
←	\ (<-	Left arrow
↑	\ (ua	Up arrow
↓	\ (da	Down arrow
|	\ (br	Box rule
‡	\ (dd	Double dagger
☞	\ (rh	Right hand
☜	\ (lh	Left hand
○	\(ci	Circle
⊕	\ (vs	Visible space indicator (ditroff only)

Bracket Building Symbols

Char	Input	Character Name
⎧	\ (lt	Left top of big curly bracket
⎨	\ (lk	Left center of big curly bracket
⎩	\ (lb	Left bottom of big curly bracket
⎫	\ (rt	Right top of big curly bracket
⎬	\ (rk	Right center of big curly bracket
⎭	\ (rb	Right bottom of big curly bracket
⌈	\ (lc	Left ceiling (left top) of big square bracket
|	\ (bv	Bold vertical
⌊	\ (lf	Left floor left bottom of big square bracket
⌉	\ (rc	Right ceiling (right top) of big square bracket
⌋	\ (rf	Right floor (right bottom) of big square bracket

Mathematics Symbols

Char	Input	Character Name
+	\ (pl	Math plus
−	\ (mi	Math minus
=	\ (eq	Math equals
*	\ (**	Math star
/	\ (sl	Slash (matching backslash)
√	\ (sr	Square root
	\ (rn	Root en extender
≥	\ (>=	Greater than or equal to
≤	\ (<=	Less than or equal to
≡	\ (==	Identically equal
≈	\ (~~	Approx equal
~	\ (ap	Approximates
≠	\ (!=	Not equal
×	\ (mu	Multiply
÷	\ (di	Divide
±	\ (+−	Plus-minus
∪	\ (cu	Cup (union)
∩	\ (ca	Cap (intersection)
⊂	\ (sb	Subset of
⊃	\ (sp	Superset of
⊆	\ (ib	Improper subset
⊇	\ (ip	Improper superset
∞	\ (if	Infinity
∂	\ (pd	Partial derivative
∇	\ (gr	Gradient
¬	\ (no	Not
∫	\ (is	Integral sign
∝	\ (pt	Proportional to
∅	\ (es	Empty set
∈	\ (mo	Member of
|	\ (or	Or

Greek Characters

Characters that have equivalents as uppercase English letters are available on the standard fonts; otherwise, the characters below exist only on the special font.

Char	Input	Char Name	Char	Input	Char Name
α	\ (*a	alpha	A	\ (*A	ALPHA
β	\ (*b	beta	B	\ (*B	BETA
γ	\ (*g	gamma	Γ	\ (*G	GAMMA
δ	\ (*d	delta	Δ	\ (*D	DELTA
ε	\ (*e	epsilon	E	\ (*E	EPSILON
ζ	\ (*z	zeta	Z	\ (*Z	ZETA
η	\ (*y	eta	H	\ (*Y	ETA
θ	\ (*h	theta	Θ	\ (*H	THETA
ι	\ (*i	iota	I	\ (*I	IOTA
κ	\ (*k	kappa	K	\ (*K	KAPPA
λ	\ (*l	lambda	Λ	\ (*L	LAMBDA
μ	\ (*m	mu	M	\ (*M	MU
ν	\ (*n	nu	N	\ (*N	NU
ξ	\ (*c	xi	Ξ	\ (*C	XI
ο	\ (*o	omicron	O	\ (*O	OMICRON
π	\ (*p	pi	Π	\ (*P	PI
ρ	\ (*r	rho	P	\ (*R	RHO
σ	\ (*s	sigma	Σ	\ (*S	SIGMA
ς	\ (ts	terminal sigma			
τ	\ (*t	tau	T	\ (*T	TAU
υ	\ (*u	upsilon	Y	\ (*U	UPSILON
φ	\ (*f	phi	Φ	\ (*F	PHI
χ	\ (*x	chi	X	\ (*X	CHI
ψ	\ (*q	psi	Ψ	\ (*Q	PSI
ω	\ (*w	omega	Ω	\ (*W	OMEGA

mm Macros

This section presents the following topics:

- Alphabetical summary of *mm* macros

- Predefined string names

- Number registers

- Other reserved names

Alphabetical Summary of mm Macros

.1C	**.1C** Return to single-column format.
.2C	**.2C** Start two-column format.
.AE	**.AE** End abstract (see **.AS**).
.AF	**.AF** [*company name*] Alternate format for first page. Change first-page "Subject/Date/From" format. If argument is given, other headings are not affected. No argument suppresses company name and headings.
.AL	**.AL** [*type*] [*indent*] [**1**] Initialize numbered or alphabetized list. Specify *list*, *type*, and *indent* of text. If 3rd argument is 1, spacing between items is suppressed. Mark each item in list with **.LI**; end list with **.LE**. Default is numbered listing. Default text indent is specified in register **Li**. *Type* <table><tr><td>**1**</td><td>Arabic numbers.</td></tr><tr><td>**A**</td><td>Uppercase letters.</td></tr><tr><td>**a**</td><td>Lowercase letters.</td></tr><tr><td>**I**</td><td>Roman numerals, uppercase.</td></tr><tr><td>**i**</td><td>Roman numerals, lowercase.</td></tr></table>
.AS	**.AS** [*type*][*n*] Start abstract of specified *type*, indenting *n* spaces. Used only with **.TM** and **.RP** only. End with **.AE**. *Type* <table><tr><td>**1**</td><td>Abstract on cover sheet and first page.</td></tr><tr><td>**2**</td><td>Abstract only on cover sheet.</td></tr><tr><td>**3**</td><td>Abstract only on Memorandum for File cover sheet.</td></tr></table>
.AT	**.AT** *title* Author's *title* appears after author's name in formal memoranda.

.AU *name*

Author's *name* and other information (up to nine arguments) supplied at beginning of formal memoranda.

.AV *name*

Approval signature line for *name*. Closing macro in formal memoranda.

.B [*barg*] [*parg*] ...

Set *barg* in bold (underline in nroff) and *parg* in previous font; up to 6 arguments.

.BE

End bottom block and print after footnotes (if any), but before footer. See **.BS**.

.BI [*barg*] [*iarg*]

Set *barg* in bold (underline in nroff) and *iarg* in italics; up to 6 arguments.

.BL [*indent*] [**1**]

Initialize bullet list. Specify indent of text. Default indent is 3 and is specified in register **Pi**. If second argument is 1, suppress blank line between items.

.BR [*barg*] [*rarg*]

Set *barg* in bold (underline in nroff) and *rarg* in roman; up to 6 arguments.

.BS

Begin block of text to be printed at bottom of page, after footnotes (if any), but before footer. End with **.BE**.

.CS [*pgs*] [*other*] [*tot*] [*figs*] [*tbls*] [*ref*]

Cover sheet information supplied for formal memoranda.

.DE

End static display started with **.DS** or floating display started with **.DF**.

.DF [*type*] [*mode*] [*rindent*]

Start floating display. That is, if the amount of space required to output text exceeds the space remaining on the current page, the display is saved for the next page, while text following the display is used to fill the current

→

mm Macros

.DF
←
	page. (See also registers **De** and **Df**.) Default *type* is no indent; default *mode* is no-fill. *rindent* is the amount by which to shorten the line length in order to bring text in from the right margin. End display with **.DE**.
	
	Type
	
	    L or **0** No indent (default).
	    I or **1** Indent standard amount.
	    C or **2** Center each line individually.
	    CB or **3** Center as a block.
	
	Mode
	
	    N or **0** No-fill mode (default).
	    F or **0** Fill mode.

.DL	**.DL** [*indent*] [**1**] Initialize dashed list. Specify indent of text. Default indent is 3 and is specified in register **Pi**. If second argument is 1, suppress blank line between items.
.DS	**.DS** [*type*] [*mode*] [*rindent*] Start static display. That is, if the display doesn't fit in the remaining space on the page, a page break occurs, placing the display at the top of the next page. See **.DF** about *type*, *mode*, and *rindent*. End display with **.DE**.

.EC	**.EC** [*caption*] [*n*] [*flag*]
	
	Equation *caption*. Arguments optionally override default numbering, where *flag* determines use of number *n*. See **.EQ**.
	
	Flag
	
	    0 *n* is a prefix to number (the default).
	    1 *n* is a suffix.
	    2 *n* replaces number.

.EF	**.EF** [*'left' center' right'*] Print three-part string as even page footer; parts are left-justified, centered, and right-justified at bottom of every even page.
.EH	**.EH** [*'left' center' right'*] Print three-part string as even page header; parts are left-justified, centered, and right-justified at top of every even page.
.EN	**.EN** End equation display. See **.EQ**.

.EQ [*text*]   .EQ

Start equation display to be processed by eqn, using *text* as label (see **.EC**).
End with **.EN**. See Section 16 for more information on eqn.

.EX [*caption*] [*n*] [*flag*]   .EX

Exhibit *caption*. Arguments optionally override default numbering, where
flag determines use of number *n*.

Flag

0	*n* is a prefix to number (the default).
1	*n* is a suffix.
2	*n* replaces number.

.FC [*text*]   .FC

Use *text* for formal closing.

.FD [*n*]   .FD

Set default footnote format to *n*, an integer from 0 to 11.

FE   FE

End footnote. See **.FS**.

.FG [*title*]   .FG

Figure *title* follows.

.FS [*c*]   .FS

Start footnote using *c* as indicator. Default is numbered footnote. End with
.FE.

.H *n* [*heading*]   .H

Print a numbered *heading* at level *n*, where *n* is from 1 to 7. See any of the
following for more information:

Number registers

Ej	Page eject.
Hb	Break after heading.
Hc	Centered heading.
Hi	Type of first paragraph after heading.
Hs	Space after heading.
Hu	Unnumbered headings.

→

.H
←
	Strings
	    HF Font control.
	    HP Point size.
	
	Macros
	    .HM Heading mark.
	    .HU Unnumbered headings.
	    .HX, .HY, .HZ
	            User-supplied macros invoked during output of header.

.HC	**.HC** [*c*] Use character *c* as hyphenation indicator.
.HM	**.HM** [*mark*] Heading *mark* style is arabic (**1** or **001**), roman (**i** or **I**), or alpha (**a** or **A**).
.HU	**.HU** *heading* Unnumbered *heading* follows. Same as **.H** except that no heading mark is printed (see number register **Hu**).
.HX	**.HX** User-supplied exit macro executed before printing heading.
.HY	**.HY** User-supplied exit macro executed in middle of printing heading.
.HZ	**.HZ** User-supplied macro executed after heading.
.I	**.I** [*iarg*] [*parg*] Set *iarg* in italics (underline in nroff) and *parg* in previous font. Up to 6 arguments.
.IA	**.IA** Start inside (recipient's) address for business letter. End with **.IE**.
.IB	**.IB** [*iarg*] [*barg*] Set *iarg* in italics (underline in nroff) and *barg* in bold. Up to 6 arguments.

.IE

End inside (recipient's) address for business letter (see **.IA**).

.IR [*iarg*] [*rarg*]

Set *iarg* in italics (underline in nroff) and *rarg* in roman. Up to 6 arguments.

.LB *n m pad type* [*mark*] [*LI–space*] [*LB–space*]

List beginning. Allows complete control over list format. Begin each list item list with **.LI**; end list with **.LE**.

n	Text indent.
m	Mark indent.
pad	Padding associated with mark.
type	If 0, use the specified *mark*. If non-zero, and *mark* is 1, A, a, I, i, list is automatically numbered or alphabetically sequenced. In this case, *type* controls how *mark* is displayed. For example, if *mark* is currently 1, *type* will have the following results:

Type	*Result*
1	1.
2	1)
3	(1)
4	[1]
5	<1>
6	{1}

mark	Symbol or text to label each list entry. *mark* can be null (creates hanging indent), a text string, or **1**, **A**, **a**, **I**, or **i** to create an automatically numbered or lettered list. See **.AL**.
LI–space	Number of blank lines to output between each following **.LI** macro. Default is 1.
LB–space	Number of blank lines to output by **.LB** macro itself. Default is 0.

.LC [*n*]

Clear list level up to *n*.

.LE [**1**]

End item list started by **.AL**, **.BL**, **.DL**, **.LB**, **.ML**, or **.VL**. An argument of 1 produces a line of white space (.5v) after the list.

mm Macros

.LI	**.LI** [*mark*] [**1**] *text* Item in list. List must be initialized (see **.AL**, **.BL**, **.DL**, **.LB**, **.ML**, and **.VL**) and then closed using **.LE**. If *mark* is specified, it replaces mark set by list-initialization macro. If *mark* is specified along with second argument of 1, then mark is prefixed to current mark.

.LO	**.LO** *type* [*notation*]
	
	Specify *type* and the string to appear as *notation* in a business letter.
	
	Type
	   AT Attention
	   CN Confidential
	   RN Reference
	   SA Salutation
	   SJ Subject

.LT	**.LT** [*type*]
	
	Business letter type.
	
	Type
	   BL Blocked (the default)
	   SB Semi-blocked
	   FB Full-blocked
	   SP Simplified

.ML	**.ML** *mark* [*indent*] [**1**] Initialize list with specified *mark*, which can be one or more characters. Specify *indent* of text (default is one space wider than *mark*). If third argument is 1, omit space between items in list.

.MT	**.MT** [*type*] [*title*]
	
	Specify memorandum *type* and *title*. Controls format of formal memoranda and must be specified after other elements, such as **.TL**, **.AF**, **.AU**, **.AS**, and **.AE**. User-supplied *title* is prefixed to page number.
	
	Type
	   0 No type
	   1 Memorandum for file {default}
	   2 Programmer's notes
	   3 Engineer's notes
	   4 Released paper
	   5 External letter
	  string *string* is printed

.ND *date*

New date. Change date that appears in formal memoranda.

.NE

Notation end. See **.NS**.

.nP

Numbered paragraphs with double-line indent at start of paragraph. See also **.P**.

.NS [*type*]

Notation start. Used with **.MT 1** and **.AS 2/.AE** (memorandum for file) to specify note for cover sheet. Otherwise used at end of formal memoranda. Specify notation *type*.

Type

0	Copy to (the default)
1	Copy (with attention) to
2	Copy (without att.) to
3	Att
4	Atts
5	Enc
6	Encs
7	Under Separate Cover
8	Letter to
9	Memorandum to
10	Copy (with atts.) to
11	Copy (without atts.) to
12	Abstract Only to
13	Complete Memorandum to
string	Copy *string* to

.OF ['*left*'*center*'*right*']

Print three-part string as odd page footer; parts are left-justified, centered, and right-justified at bottom of every odd page.

.OH ['*left*'*center*'*right*']

Print three-part string as odd page header; parts are left-justified, centered, and right-justified at bottom of every odd page.

.OK	**.OK** [*topic*]
	Other keywords. Specify *topic* to appear on cover sheet of formal memoranda. Up to 9 arguments.
.OP	**.OP**
	Force an odd page.
.P	**.P** [*type*]
	Start new paragraph. A paragraph *type* can be specified, overriding default. Various registers can be set to control default formats:

Pt   Paragraph type for document (default is 0).

Pi   Amount of indent (default is 3v).

Ps   Spacing between paragraphs (default is one line of white space).

Np   Set this to 1 to produce numbered paragraphs.

Type

0   Left-justified (the default)

1   Indented

2   Indented except after displays (**.DE**), lists (**.LE**), and headings (**.H**).

.PF	**.PF** [*'left' center' right'*]
	Print three-part string as footer; parts are left-justified, centered, and right-justified at bottom of every page. Use \\\\nP in string to obtain page number. See also **.EF** and **.OF**.
.PH	**.PH** [*'left' center' right'*]
	Print three-part string as header; parts are left-justified, centered, and right-justified at top of every page. Use \\\\nP in string to obtain page number. See also **.EH** and **.OH**.
.PM	**.PM** [*type*]
	Proprietary marking on each page.

Type

P   Private

N   Notice

.PX	**.PX**
	Page-heading user exit. Invoked after restoration of default environment. See **.TP**.

.R   .R

Return to roman font (end underlining in nroff).

.RB [*rarg*] [*barg*]   .RB

Set *rarg* in roman and *barg* in bold. Up to 6 arguments.

.RD [*prompt*]   .RD

Read input from terminal, supplying optional *prompt*.

.RF   .RF

End of reference text. See also **.RS**.

.RI [*rarg*] [*barg*]   .RI

Set *rarg* in roman and *barg* in italics. Up to 6 arguments.

.RL [*indent*] [**1**]   .RL

Initialize reference list, essentially a numbered list with number set within
brackets ([]). Specify *indent* of text; the default (6) is set through register **Li**.
If second argument is 1, omit space between list items.

.RP   .RP

Produce reference page.

.RS [*n*]   .RS

Start automatically numbered reference, optionally at *n*. End with **.RF**.

.S [±] [*n*] [±] [*m*]   .S

Set point size to *n* and vertical spacing to *m* (troff only). Alternatively, either
argument can be specified by incrementing or decrementing current value
(**C**), default value (**D**), or previous value (**P**). Defaults point size is 10;
default vertical spacing is 12.

.SA [*n*]   .SA

Set right margin justification to *n*. Defaults are no justification for nroff, justification for troff.

Values for n

0   No justification.
1   Justification.

mm Macros

.SG	**.SG** [*name*] Use *name* for signature line.
.SK	**.SK** *n* Skip *n* pages. Similar to a **.bp** request.
.SM	**.SM** *x* [*y z*] Reduce string *x* by one point. If strings *y* and *z* are also specified, *y* is reduced by one point.
.SP	**.SP** [*n*] Output *n* blank vertical spaces. The spacing requests of two consecutive **.SP** macros do not accumulate.
.TB	**.TB** [*title*][*n*][*flag*] Supply table *title*. Arguments optionally override default numbering, where *flag* determines use of number *n*. **Flag** **0** *n* is a prefix to number (default). **1** *n* is a suffix. **2** *n* replaces number.
.TC	**.TC** [*slevel*] [*spacing*] [*tlevel*] [*tab*] [*head1*] ... Generate table of contents in format specified by arguments. The levels of headings that are saved for table of contents is determined by setting the **Cl** register. *slevel* sets the levels of headings that will have spacing before them. *spacing* sets the amount of spacing. Default is 1; first-level headings have a blank line before them. *tlevel* and *tab* affect location of page number. Heading levels less than or equal to *tlevel* are output with page numbers at right margin; otherwise, heading and page number are separated by two spaces. If page numbers are at right margin, and if *tab* is 0, a leader will be output using dots; otherwise, spaces are used.
.TE	**.TE** End table. See **.TS**.

.TH [**N**]

End table header. Must be used with a preceding **.TS H**. Use **N** to suppress table headers until a new page.

.TH

.TL *title*

Supply *title* for formal memoranda.

.TL

.TM [*n*]

Supply number *n* for formal memoranda.

.TM

.TP

Page top macro, invoked automatically at the beginning of a new page. Executed in environment in which heading is output. See also **.PH**.

.TP

.TS [**H**]

Start table to be processed by tbl. Use **H** to put a table header on all pages (end table header with **.TH**). End table with **.TE**. See Section 16 for more information on tbl.

.TS

.TX

User-supplied macro executed before table-of-contents titles.

.TX

.TY

User-supplied macro executed before table-of-contents header.

.TY

.VL *n* [*m*] [**1**]

Initialize variable item list. Used to produce indented or labeled paragraphs. Indent text *n* spaces and indent mark *m* spaces. If third argument is 1, omit space between list items. Begin each item with **.LI**, specifying a label for each item; end list with **.LE**.

.VL

.VM [*n*] [*m*]

Add *n* lines to top margin and *m* lines to bottom.

.VM

.WA

Start of writer's address in business letter. End with **.WE**.

.WA

.WE

End of writer's address in business letter. Start with **.WA**.

.WE

mm Macros

.WC	.WC [x]

Change column or footnote width to *x*.

Values for x

FF	All footnotes same as first.
−FF	Turn off FF mode.
N	Normal default mode.
WD	Wide displays.
−WD	Use default column mode.
WF	Wide footnotes.
−WF	Turn off WF mode.

Predefined String Names

BU	Bullet; same as \ (bu.
Ci	List of indents for table of contents levels.
DT	Current date, unless overridden. Month, day, year (e.g., July 28, 1986).
EM	Em dash string (em dash in troff and a double hyphen in nroff).
F	Footnote number generator.
HF	Fonts used for each level of heading (1 = roman, 2 = italic, 3 = bold).
HP	Point size used for each level of heading.
Le	Title set for ``List Of Equations.''
Lf	Title set for ``List Of Figures.''
Lt	Title set for ``List Of Tables.''
Lx	Title set for ``List Of Exhibits.''
RE	SCCS release and level of *mm*.
Rf	Reference number generator.
Rp	Title for ``References.''
TM	Trademark string. Places the letters ``TM'' one-half line above the text that it follows.

Number Registers Used in mm

A dagger (†) next to a register name indicates that the register can be set *only* from the command line or before the *mm* macro definitions are read by the formatter. Any register having a single-character name can be set from the command line with the **−r** option.

A†	If set to 1, omit technical memorandum headings and provide spaces appropriate for letterhead (see **.AF** macro).
Au	Omit author information on first page (see **.AU** macro).
C†	Flag indicating type of copy (original, draft, etc.).
Cl	Level of headings saved for table of contents (see **.TC** macro). Default is 2.
Cp	If set to 1 (default), list of figures and tables appear on same page as table of contents. Otherwise, they start on a new page.

D†	If set to 1, use debug mode (*mm* continues even after encountering normally fatal errors). Default is 0.
De	If set to 1, eject page after each floating display. Default is 0.
Df	Set format of floating displays (see **.DF** macro).
Ds	Set space used before and after static displays.
E†	Font for Subject/Date/From. 0 (bold, the default) or 1 (roman).
Ec	Equation counter, incremented for each **.EC** macro.
Ej	Heading level for page eject before headings. Default is 0 and no eject.
Eq	If set to 1, place equation label at left margin. Default is 0.
Ex	Exhibit counter, incremented for each **.EX** macro.
Fg	Figure counter, incremented for each **.FG** macro.
Fs	Vertical spacing between footnotes.
H*n*	Heading counter for level *n* (1 to 7), incremented by **.H** macro of corresponding level or by **.HU** macro if at level given by register **Hu**. Registers **H2** to **H7** are reset to 0 by any **.H** (or **.HU**) macro at a lower-numbered level.
Hb	Level of heading for which break occurs before output of body text. Default is 2.
Hc	Level of heading for which centering occurs. Default is 0.
Hi	Type of indent after heading. Values are 0 (left-justified), 1 (indented, the default), 2 (indented except after **.H**, **.LC**, **.DE**).
Hs	Level of heading for which space after heading occurs. Default is 2.
Ht	Numbering type of heading: 1 (single) or 0 (concatenated, the default).
Hu	Set level of heading at which unnumbered headings occur. Default is 2.
Hy	If set to 1, enable hyphenation. Default is 0.
L†	Set length of page. Default is 66v.
Le	Flag to print list of equations after table of contents: 0 (don't print, the default) or 1 (print).
Lf	Like **Le**, but for list of figures.
Li	Default indent of lists. Default is 5.
Ls	Set spacing between items in nested lists. Default is 6 (spacing between all levels of list).
Lt	Like **Le**, but for list of tables.
Lx	Like **Le**, but for list of exhibits.
N†	Set page numbering style: 0 All pages get header (the default) 1 Header printed as footer on page 1 2 No header on page 1 3 Section-page as footer 4 No header unless **.PH** has been invoked 5 Section-page and section-figure as footer
Np	Set numbering style for paragraphs: 0 (unnumbered) or 1 (numbered).
O	Offset of page. For nroff, value is unscaled number representing character positions; default is 9 (7.5i). For troff, value is scaled; default is .5i.
Oc	Set numbering style for pages in table of contents: 0 (lowercase roman, the default) or 1 (arabic).

Of	Set separator for figure number in captions. 0 (use period, the default); 1 (use hyphen).
P	Current page number.
Pi	Amount of indent for paragraph. Default is 5 for nroff and 3 for troff.
Ps	Amount of spacing between paragraphs. Default is 3v.
Pt	Paragraph type. Values are 0 (left-justified, the default), 1 (indented), 2 (indented except after **.H**, **.LC**, **.DE**).
Pv	Suppress ``PRIVATE'' header.
Rf	Reference counter, incremented for each **.RS**.
S†	Default point size for troff. Default is 10. Vertical spacing is \nS+2.
Si	Standard indent for displays. Default is 5 for nroff and 3 for troff.
T†	Type of nroff output device. Sets registers for specific devices.
Tb	Table counter, incremented for each **.TB**.
U†	Style of nroff underlining for **.H** and **.HU**. If not set, use continuous underline; if set, don't underline punctuation and white space. Default is 0.
W†	Width of page (line and title length). Default is 6i.

Other Reserved Macro and String Names

In *mm*, the only macro and string names you can safely use are names consisting of a single lowercase letter, or two character names whose first character is a lowercase letter and whose second character is *anything but* a lowercase letter. Of these, only **c2** and **nP** are already used.

14

ms Macros

This section presents the following topics:

- Alphabetical summary of *ms* macros

- Number registers for page layout

- Reserved macro and string names

- Reserved number register names

Alphabetical Summary of ms Macros

.1C	**.1C** Return to single-column format after **.2C** or **.MC**. The **.1C** macro necessarily causes a page break.
.2C	**.2C** Start two-column format. Return to single-column with **.1C**.
.AB	**.AB** Begin abstract in cover sheet. End abstract with **.AE**.
.AE	**.AE** End abstract begun with **.AB**.
.AI	**.AI** *name* Print name of author's institution. Generally follows **.AU** in a cover sheet sequence; may be repeated up to nine times for multiple author/institution pairs.
.AU	**.AU** *name* Print author's name. Generally follows **.TL** and precedes **.AI** in a cover sheet sequence; may be repeated up to nine times for multiple authors.
.B	**.B** [*text*] Print *text* in boldface. If *text* is missing, equivalent to **.ft 3**.
.B1	**.B1** Enclose following text in a box. End box with **.B2**.
.B2	**.B2** End boxed text (started with **.B1**).
.BD	**.BD** Start block display. Text is output exactly as it appears in the source file, centered around the longest line. Same as **.DS B**. End with **.DE**.
.BR	**.BR** Start bibliographic format (used to precede bibliographic record).

.BX *word*

Surround *word* in a box. Usually doesn't work for more than one word at a time, due to problems with filling. To box more than one word, separate each with an unpaddable space (\ ).

.CD

Start centered display. Each line in the display is individually centered. Same as **.DS C**. End with **.DE**.

.DA

Print today's date as the center footer of each page.

.DE

End displayed text started with **.DS**.

.DS [*type*]

Start displayed text. End with **.DE**.

Type

B	Left-justified block, centered; see **.BD**.
C	Centered display; see **.CD**.
I	Indented display (the default); see **.ID**.
L	Left-centered display; see **.LD**.

.EN

End equation display started with **.EQ**.

.EQ

Start equation display to be processed by eqn. End with **.EN**. See Section 16 for more information on eqn.

.FS

Start footnote. Text of footnote follows on succeeding lines. End with **.FE**.

.FE

End footnote started with **.FS**.

.GO

Start processing text (run various package-startup procedures). For cover sheet to appear on a separate page, cover sheet macros should precede **.GO**.

ms Macros

.I	**.I** [*text*] Print *text* in italics. If *text* is missing, equivalent to **.ft 2**.
.ID	**.ID** Start indented display. Text is output exactly as it is in the source file, but indented 8 ens. Same as **.DS I**. End with **.DE**.
.IP	**.IP** *label n* Indent paragraph *n* spaces with hanging *label*. **.RS** and **.RE** can be used for nested indents.
.KE	**.KE** End static keep started with **.KS** or floating keep started with **.KF**.
.KF	**.KF** Begin floating keep. End with **.KE**. Enclosed text stays on same page. If enclosed text doesn't fit on current page, it is output on the next page, and succeeding text "floats" before it to fill the current page.
.KS	**.KS** Start keep. End with **.KE**. Enclosed text stays on same page. If text won't fit on current page, a page break occurs.
.LD	**.LD** Start left-justified display. Block is centered, but individual lines are left justified in the block. Same as **.DS L**. End with **.DE**.
.LG	**.LG** Increase type size by two points (troff only). Restore normal type with **.NL**.
.LP	**.LP** Start block paragraph. Inter-paragraph spacing is determined by register **PD**. Default is .5v in troff and 1 line in nroff.
.MC	**.MC** *cw gw* Start multi-column mode, with column-width *cw* and gutter width *gw*. The macro generates as many columns as can fit in the current line length. Return to single-column mode with **.1C**.

.ND

Suppress printing of date. See **.DA**.

.NH *n*
heading text

Numbered section heading; level *n* of the section number is automatically incremented.

.NL

Restore default type size (troff only). Used after **.LG** or **.SM**.

.PP

Start standard indented paragraph. Size of paragraph indent is stored in register **PI** (default is 5 ens).

.QE

End quoted paragraph started by **.QS**.

.QP

Begin quoted paragraph: indented on both sides, with blank lines above and below, and (in troff) with the type size reduced by 1 point.

.QS

Begin quoted paragraph, retaining current point size and vertical spacing. End with **.QE**.

.R [*text*]

Print *text* in roman. If *text* is missing, equivalent to **.ft R**.

.RE

End one level of relative indent started with **.RS**.

.RP

Initiate title page for a "released paper."

.RS

Right shift. Increase relative indent one level. End with **.RE**. Often used with **.IP**.

ms Macros

.SB	**.SB** *word chars* Use *chars* as a subscript for *word*. See also **.SU**.
.SG	**.SG** Print a signature line.
.SH	**.SH** *heading text* Unnumbered section heading. See also **.NH**.
.SM	**.SM** Change to smaller type size (troff only). Restore normal type with **.NL**.
.SU	**.SU** *word chars* Use *chars* as a superscript for *word*. See also **.SB**.
.TE	**.TE** End table to be processed by tbl. See **.TS**.
.TH	**.TH** End of table header. Must be used with a preceding **.TS H**.
.TL	**.TL** *multi-line title* Title line(s) for cover sheet. A multi-line title can be specified, ended by the next macro (usually **.AU** in the cover sheet sequence).
.TS	**.TS [H]** Start table to be processed by tbl. Use **H** to put a table header on all pages (end table header with **.TH**). End table with **.TE**. See Section 16 for more information on tbl.
.UL	**.UL** Underline following text, even in troff.

Number Registers for Page Layout

Name	Meaning	Default
BI	Bibliographical indent	3 ens
CW	Column width	7/15 of line length
FL	Footnote length	11/12 of line length
FM	Bottom margin	1 inch
GW	Intercolumn gap	1/15 of line length
HM	Top margin	1 inch
LL	Line length	6 inches
LT	Title length	6 inches
PD	Paragraph spacing	.3v
PI	Paragraph indent	5 ens
PO	Page offset	26/27 inches
PS	Point size	10 point
QI	Quotation indent	5 ens
VS	Vertical line spacing	12 point

Reserved Macro and String Names

The following macro and string names are used by the *ms* package. Avoid using these names for compatibility with the existing macros. An italicized *n* means that the name contains a numeral (generally the interpolated value of a number register).

,	.]	:	[.	[c	[o	^	`	~
1C	2C	AB	AE	AI	A*n*	AT	AU	AX
B	B1	B2	BB	BG	BT	BX	C	C1
C2	CA	CC	CF	CH	CM	CT	DA	DW
DY	EE	EG	EL	EM	EN	E*n*	EQ	EZ
FA	FE	FF	FG	FJ	FK	FL	FN	FO
FS	FV	FX	FY	HO	I	IE	IH	IM
I*n*	IP	IZ	KD	KF	KJ	KS	LB	LG
LP	LT	MC	ME	MF	MH	MN	MO	MR
ND	NH	NL	NP	OD	OK	PP	PT	PY
QE	QF	QP	QS	R	R3	RA	RC	RE
R*n*	RP	RS	RT	S0	S2	S3	SG	SH
SM	SN	SY	TA	TC	TD	TE	TH	TL
TM	TQ	TR	TS	TT	TX	UL	US	UX
WB	WH	WT	XF	XK	XP			

Reserved Number Register Names

The following number register names are used by the *ms* package. An italicized *n* means that the name contains a numeral (generally the interpolated value of another number register).

*n*T	AJ	AV	BC	BD	BE	BH	BI	BQ
BW	CW	EF	FC	FL	FM	FP	GA	GW
H1	H2	H3	H4	H5	HM	HT	I0	IF
IK	IM	IP	IR	IS	IT	IX	I*n*	J*n*
KG	KI	KM	L1	LE	LL	LT	MC	MF
MG	ML	MM	MN	NA	NC	ND	NQ	NS
NX	OJ	PD	PE	PF	PI	PN	PO	PQ
PS	PX	QI	QP	RO	SJ	ST	T.	TB
TC	TD	TK	TN	TQ	TV	TY	TZ	VS
WF	XX	YE	YY	ZN				

When you're writing your own macros, the safest bet is to use mixed case letters for macro names. (Using uppercase letters could conflict with reserved *ms* names, and using lowercase letters could conflict with troff requests.)

me Macros

This section presents the following topics:

- Alphabetical summary of *me* macros
- Predefined strings

Alphabetical Summary of me Macros

.1c	**.1c** Return to single-column format. See **.2c**.
.2c	**.2c** Enter two-column format. Force a new column with **.bc**; end two-column mode with **.1c**.
.ar	**.ar** Set page number in arabic.
.b	**.b** *w x* Set *w* in bold and *x* in previous font.

.(b	**.(b** *type*
	Begin block keep. End with **.)b**.
	
	Type
	    C Centered block keep
	    F Filled block keep
	    L Left-justified block keep

.)b	**.)b** End block keep started with **.(b**.
.ba	**.ba** *n* Set the base indent to *n*.
.bc	**.bc** Begin column; used after **.2c**.
.bi	**.bi** *w x* Set *w* in bold italics and *x* in previous font.
.bl	**.bl** *n* Leave *n* lines of white space. Equivalent to **.sp** *n* inside a block.

.bu

Begin paragraph marked by a bullet.

.bx *w x*

Set *w* in a box and *x* immediately outside the box.

.+c *title*

Begin chapter with *title*.

.$c *title*

Begin numbered chapter with *title*.

.$C *keyword n title*

User-definable macro. Called by **.$c**, supplying *keyword* (e.g., "Chapter" or "Appendix"), chapter or appendix number (*n*), and *title*.

.(c

Begin centered block. End with **.)c**.

.)c

End centered block started with **.(c**.

.(d

Begin delayed text. End with **.)d**.

.)d

End delayed text. Print text with **.pd**.

.ef '*l*'*c*'*r*'

Print three-part footer on all *even* pages. Parts are left-justified, centered, and right-justified at bottom of every even page.

.eh '*l*'*c*'*r*'

Print three-part heading on all *even* pages. Parts are left-justified, centered, and right-justified at top of every even page.

.EN

End equation display started with **.EQ**.

me Macros

.ep	**.ep** End this page and print footnotes.

.EQ	**.EQ** *format title*
	Start equation display to be processed by eqn, using output *format* and having *title* printed on the right margin next to the equation. End with **.EN**. See Section 16 for more information on eqn.
	
	Format
	    C Centered
	    I Indented
	    L Left justified

.$f	**.$f** Call to print footer.
.(f	**.(f** Begin text for footnote. End with **.)f**.
.)f	**.)f** End footnote text started with **.(f**.
.fo	**.fo** '*l*'*c*'*r*' Print three-part footer on *all* pages. Parts are left-justified, centered, and right-justified at bottom of every page.
.$H	**.$H** Normally undefined macro, called immediately before printing text on a page. Can be used for column headings, etc.
.$h	**.$h** Call to print header.
.he	**.he** '*l*'*c*'*r*' Print three-part heading on *all* pages. Parts are left-justified, centered, and right-justified at top of every page.
.hl	**.hl** Draw a horizontal line equal to the width of page.

.hx

Don't print headings and footers on next page.

.i *w x*

Set *w* in italics (underline in nroff) and *x* in previous font.

.ip *label n*

Indent paragraph *n* spaces with hanging *label*.

.ix [±*n*]

Indent but don't break the line. Equivalent to **'in** *n*.

.(l *type*

Begin list. End with **.)l**.

Type

C	Centered list
F	Filled list
L	Left-justified list

.)l

End list started with **.(l**.

.ll +*n*

Set line length to +*n* (all environments).

.lo

Load a locally defined set of macros (usually **/usr/lib/me/local.me**).

.lp

Begin block paragraph (left-justified).

.m1 *n*

Set *n* spaces between top of page and heading.

.m2 *n*

Set *n* spaces between heading and first line of text.

me Macros

.m3	**.m3** *n* Set *n* spaces between footer and text.
.m4	**.m4** *n* Set *n* spaces between footer and bottom of page.
.n1	**.n1** Number lines in margin beginning with 1.
.n2	**.n2** *n* Number lines in margin beginning with *n*; stop numbering if *n* is 0.
.np	**.np** Begin a numbered paragraph. Current number is accessed via **\n($p**.
.of	**.of** ’*l*’*c*’*r*’ Print three-part footer on *all* odd pages. Parts are left-justified, centered, and right-justified at bottom of every odd page.
.oh	**.oh** ’*l*’*c*’*r*’ Print three-part heading on *all* odd pages. Parts are left-justified, centered, and right-justified at top of every odd page.
.$p	**.$p** *title n d* Print section heading with specified *title*, section number *n*, and depth of section *d*.
.$0	**.$0** *title n d* Called automatically after every call to **.$p**. Normally undefined, but may be used to automatically put every section title into table of contents, or for some similar function.
.$<em>n</em>	**.$**n These are traps called just before printing section of depth *n* (*n* is 1-6). Called from **.$p**.
.pa	**.pa** [±*n*] Equivalent to **.bp**.

.pd

Print delayed text, indicated by **.(d** and **.)d**.

.pp

Begin indented paragraph.

.q *w x*

Surround *w* with double quotes and *x* immediately outside quotes.

.(q

Begin major quote. End with **.)q**.

.)q

End major quote started with **.(q**.

.r *w x*

Set *w* in roman font and *x* in previous font.

.rb *w x*

Set *w* in bold and *x* in previous font.

.re

Reset tabs to every 0.5 inches (in troff) or to every 0.8 inch (in nroff).

.ro

Set page number in roman numerals.

.$s

Separate footnotes with a 1.5-inch horizontal line.

.sh

Begin numbered section heading.

.sk

Leave next page blank. Like the troff **.bp** request.

me Macros

.sx	**.sx +** *n* Begin a paragraph at level *n*.
.sz	**.sz** *n* Set character point size to *n*, with line spacing set proportionally.
.TE	**.TE** End table. See **.TS**.
.TH	**.TH** End table header. Must be used with a preceding **.TS H**.
.th	**.th** Initialize for a thesis.
.tp	**.tp** Initialize for a title page.
.TS	**.TS [H]** Start table to be processed by tbl. Use **H** to put a table header on all pages (end table header with **.TH**). End table with **.TE**. See Section 16 for more information on tbl.
.u	**.u** *w x* Underline *w* and set *x* in previous font.
.uh	**.uh** *title* Begin unnumbered section heading using *title*.
.(x	**.(x** Begin index entry. End with **.)x**.
.)x	**.)x** End index entry started with **.(x**. Print index with **.xp**.
.)x_	**.)x_** Omit page number for index.

.x1 *n*   .x1

Set the line length to *n* (current environment only).

.xp   .xp

Print index. See also **.(x**.

.(z   .(z

Begin floating keep.

.)z   .)z

End floating keep.

.++ *type header*   .++

Define the section of the paper being entered. Specify a *type* with a *header*
title string.

Type

A	Appendix
AB	Abstract
B	Bibliography
C	Chapter
P	Preliminary section (table of contents, etc.)
RA	Appendix, with page numbers reset to 1
RC	Chapter, with page numbers reset to 1

Predefined Strings

*	Footnote number, incremented by **.)f** macro
#	Delayed text number
[	Superscript; move up and shrink type size
]	Undo superscript
<	Subscript; move down and shrink type size
>	Undo subscript
−	3/4 em dash
dw	Day of week, as a word
mo	Month, as a word
td	Today's date
lq	Left quote mark
rq	Right quote mark

Preprocessors

This section is divided into the following three subsections, each covering a different preprocessor of the nroff/troff formatting system:

- The tbl preprocessor

- The eqn preprocessor

- The pic graphics language

Each of these preprocessors translates code into nroff/troff requests and escape sequences, which run independently of the formatter. Usually, one or more of these preprocessors are invoked as part of a command pipeline to format a file:

```
% pic file | tbl | eqn | troff | spooler
```

On multi-user systems, it is typical to have a general-purpose shell script for formatting. You would then select various command-line options to specify which (if any) preprocessors to include in your particular format command. But you can also invoke the preprocessors individually. This is useful for confirming that syntax is correct or for determining where it fails. For example, the command:

```
% tbl file
```

takes input between each .TS/.TE macro pair and converts it into tbl code. All other input is passed to output unchanged.

Tbl

Tbl is a preprocessor for formatting tables in nroff/troff. When used in a command pipeline, tbl should precede eqn. This makes output processing more efficient. Tbl has the following command-line syntax:

/usr/ucb/tbl [*options*] [*files*]

Options

—me   Prepend the *me* macros to the front of *files*.

—mm   Prepend the *mm* macros to the front of *files*.

—ms   Prepend the *ms* macros to the front of *files*.

—TX   Produce output using only full vertical line motions. This is useful when formatting with nroff or when printing to a device that does not support fractional line motion.

General Coding Scheme

In a text file, coding for tbl might look like this:

```
.TS H
options;
format1
format2.
Column Titles
.TH
Item1      Item2      Item3
Item1      Item2      Item3 ...
.TE
```

Successful processing of a table by tbl depends largely on the header lines, which consist of one line listing the options and one or more format lines. Each field of the table input must be separated by a tab or designated tab symbol, with each row typed entirely on a single line unless a field is enclosed by the text block symbols **T{** and **T}**.

Tbl Macros

.TS   Start table.

.TE   End table.

.TS H   Used when the table will continue onto more than one page. Used with **.TH** to define a header that will print on every page.

.TH   With **.TS H**, ends the header portion of the table.

.T&   Continue table after changing format line.

Options

Options affect the entire table. Options can be separated by commas or spaces, but the line must end with a semicolon.

center   Center with *current* margins.
expand   Flush with current right *and* left margins.
\<blank\>   Flush with current left margin (the default).

box   Enclose table in a box.
doublebox   Enclose table in two boxes.
allbox   Enclose each table entry in a box.

tab (x)   Define the tab symbol to be x instead of a tab.

linesize n Set type size of lines or rules (e.g., from box) to n points.

delim xy Recognize x and y as the eqn delimiters.

Format

The format line affects the layout of individual columns and rows of the table. Each line contains a key letter for each column of the table. The column entries should be separated by spaces, and the format section must end with a period. Each line of format corresponds to one line of the table, except for the last, which corresponds to all following lines up to the next **.T&**, if any.

Key Letters

c   Center.
l   Flush left.
r   Flush right.

n   Align numerical entries.
a   Align alphabetic subcolumns.

s   Horizontally span previous column entry across this column.
^   Vertically span (center) entry from previous row down through this row.

Key Modifiers

These must follow a key letter.

b   Boldface.
i   Italics.
fx Font x.

pn Point size.
vn Vertical line spacing, in points. Applies *only* to text blocks.

Tbl, Eqn, and Pic

t	Begin any corresponding vertically-spanned table entry (i.e., from ^) at the top line of its range.
e	Equal width columns.
w(n**)**	Minimum column width. Also used with text blocks. n can be given in any acceptable troff units.
n	Amount of separation (in ens) between columns (default is 3).
|	Separate columns with a single vertical line. Typed between key letters.
| |	Separate columns with a double vertical line. Typed between key letters.
_	Separate rows with a single horizontal line. Used in place of a key letter.
=	Separate rows with a double horizontal line. Used in place of a key letter.

Data

The data portion includes both the heading and text of the table. Each table entry must be separated by a tab symbol.

.xx	Troff requests may be used (such as **.sp** n, **.na**, etc.).
\	As last character in a line, combine following line with current line (hide newline).
\^	Span table entry that is above this row, bringing it down to be verticall centered.
_ or =	As the only character in a line, extend a single or double horizontal lin the full width of the table.
\$_ or \$=	Extend a single or double horizontal line the full width of the column.
_	Extend a single horizontal line the width of the column's contents.
\R*x*	Print *x*'s as wide as the column's contents.
... [*tab*]**T{**	Start text block as a table entry. Must end a line. Necessary when a line c text is input over more than one line, or will span more than one line c output.
... **T}**[*tab*]	End text block. Must begin a line.

A Tbl Example

Input:

```
.TS
center box linesize(6) tab(@);
cb s s.
Horizontal Local Motions
_
.T&
ci | ci s
ci | ci s
ci | ci | ci
c | l s.
Function@Effect in
\^@_
\^@troff@nroff
_
\eh'n'@Move distance N
\e(space)@Unpaddable space-size space
\e0@Digit-size space
_
.T&
c | l | l.
\e|@1/6 em space@ignored
\e^@1/12 em space@ignored
.TE
```

Result:

Horizontal Local Motions		
Function	*Effect in*	
	troff	*nroff*
\h'n'	Move distance N	
\(space)	Unpaddable space-size space	
\0	Digit-size space	
|	1/6 em space	ignored
\^	1/12 em space	ignored

Tbl, Eqn, and Pic

Eqn

Eqn is a preprocessor designed to facilitate the typesetting of mathematical equations. Use neqn with nroff. Eqn has the following command-line syntax:

/usr/ucb/eqn [*options*] [*files*]

Options

−d*xy*   Use *x* and *y* as start and stop delimiters; same as specifying the eqn directive **delim***xy*.

−f*n*   Change to font *n*; same as the **gfont** directive.

−p*n*   Reduce size of superscripts and subscripts by *n* points. If **−p** is not specified, the default reduction is 3 points.

−s*n*   Reduce the point size by *n* points; same as the **gsize** directive.

−T*dev*   Format output to device *dev*. The default value comes from the TYPESETTER environment variable. Not available with neqn.

Eqn Macros

.EQ   Start typesetting mathematics.

.EN   End typesetting mathematics.

Use the **checkeq** command to check for unmatched macro pairs.

Mathematical Characters

The character sequences below are recognized and translated as shown:

Character	Translation	Character	Translation
>=	$\geq$	approx	$\approx$
<=	$\leq$	nothing	
==	$\equiv$	cdot	$\cdot$
!=	$\neq$	times	$\times$
+-	$\pm$	del	∇
->	$\rightarrow$	grad	∇
<-	$\leftarrow$	. . .	. . .
<<	$\ll$	, . . . ,	, . . . ,
>>	$\gg$	sum	$\sum$
inf	∞	int	$\int$
partial	∂	prod	$\prod$
half	$1/2$	union	$\cup$
prime	$\prime$	inter	$\cap$

Mathematical Text

Digits, parentheses, brackets, punctuation marks, and the following mathematical words are printed out in Roman font:

```
sin    cos    tan    arc
sinh   cosh   tanh
and    if     for    det
max    min    lim
log    ln     exp
Re     Im
```

Greek Characters

Greek letters can be printed in uppercase or lowercase. To obtain Greek letters, simply spell them out. Some uppercase Greek letters are not supported because they can be specified by an Arabic equivalent (e.g, A for alpha, B for beta).

Character	Translation	Character	Translation
alpha	α	tau	τ
beta	β	upsilon	υ
gamma	γ	phi	φ
delta	δ	chi	χ
epsilon	ε	psi	ψ
zeta	ζ	omega	ω
eta	η	GAMMA	Γ
theta	θ	DELTA	Δ
iota	ι	THETA	Θ
kappa	κ	LAMBDA	Λ
lambda	λ	XI	Ξ
mu	μ	PI	Π
nu	ν	SIGMA	Σ
xi	ξ	UPSILON	Y
omicron	o	PHI	Φ
pi	π	PSI	Ψ
rho	ρ	OMEGA	Ω
sigma	σ		

Diacritical Marks

Several keywords are available to mark the tops of characters. Eqn centers a mark at the correct height. **bar** and **under** will span the necessary length.

Character	Translation
x dot	$\dot{x}$
x dotdot	$\ddot{x}$
x hat	$\hat{x}$
x tilde	$\tilde{x}$
x vec	$\vec{x}$
x dyad	$\overleftrightarrow{x}$
x bar	$\bar{x}$
x under	$\underline{x}$

Keywords Recognized by Eqn

In addition to character names and diacritical marks, eqn recognizes the following keywords:

above   Separate the pieces of a pile or matrix column.

back *n*   Move backwards horizontally *n* 1/100's of an m.

bold   Change to bold font.

ccol   Center align a column of a matrix.

cpile   Make a centered pile (same as pile).

define   Create a name for a frequently used string.

delim *xy*   Define two characters to mark the left and right ends of an eqn equation to be printed in line. Use **delim off** to turn of delimiters.

down *n*   Move down *n* 1/100's of an m.

fat   Widen the current font by overstriking it.

font *x*   Change to font *x*, where *x* is the one-character name or the number of a font.

from   Used in summations, integrals, and similar constructions to signify the lower limit.

fwd *n*   Move forward horizontally *n* 1/100's of an em.

gfont *x*   Set a global font *x* for all equations.

gsize *n*   Set a global size for all equations.

italic   Change to italic font.

lcol   Left justify a column of a matrix.

left   Create big brackets, big braces, big bars, etc.

lineup   Line up marks in equations on different lines.

lpile   Left justify the elements of a pile.

mark	Remember the horizontal position in an equation. Used with lineup.
matrix	Create a matrix.
ndefine	Create a definition which takes effect only when neqn is running.
over	Make a fraction.
pile	Make a vertical pile with elements centered above one another.
rcol	Right adjust a column of a matrix.
right	Create big brackets, big braces, big bars, etc.
roman	Change to roman font.
rpile	Right justify the elements of a pile.
size n	Change the size of the font to n.
sqrt	Draw a square root sign.
sub	Start a subscript.
sup	Start a superscript.
tdefine	Make a definition which will apply only for eqn.
to	Used in summations, integrals, and similar constructions to signify the upper limit.
up n	Move up n 1/100's of an em.
~	Force extra space into the output.
^	Force a space one half the size of the space forced by ~
{ }	Force eqn to treat an element as a unit.
'...'	A string within quotes is not subject to alterations by eqn.

Precedence

If you don't use braces, eqn will do operations in the order shown in this list, reading from left to right.

```
dyad    vec     under   bar
tilde   hat     dot     dotdot
fwd     back    down    up
fat     roman   italic  bold
size    sub     sup     sqrt
over    from    to
```

These operations group to the left:

```
over    sqrt    left    right
```

All others group to the right.

Eqn Examples

Input:

```
.EQ
delim %%
.EN
%sum from i=0 to inf c sup i~=~lim from {m -> inf}
sum from i=0 to m c sup i%
.EQ
delim off
.EN
```

Result:

$$\sum_{i=0}^{\infty} c^i = \lim_{m \to \infty} \sum_{i=0}^{m} c^i$$

Input:

```
.EQ
delim %%
.EN
%x ~=~ left [ { -b ~+-~ sqrt {b sup 2 - ~4ac} }
over 2a right ]%
.EQ
delim off
.EN
```

Result:

$$x = \left[\frac{-b \pm \sqrt{b^2 - 4ac}}{2a} \right]$$

Pic

Pic is a graphics language program that facilitates the drawing of simple flowcharts and diagrams. Pic offers dozens of ways to draw a picture, not only because of the many abbreviations it allows, but because pic tries to combine the language of geometry with English. For example, you can specify a line by its direction, magnitude, and starting point, yet you can often achieve the same effect by simply stating, "from *there* to *there*."

Pic has the following command-line syntax:

/usr/ucb/pic [*files*]

Full descriptions of primitive objects in pic can be ended by starting another line, or by the semicolon character (;). A single primitive description can be continued on the next line, however, by ending the first with a backslash character (\). Comments may be placed on lines beginning with the pound sign (#).

Pic Macros

.PS [*h* [*w*]]   Start pic description. *h* and *w*, if specified, are the desired height and width of the picture; the full picture will be made to expand or contract to fill this space.

.PS < *file*   Read contents of *file* in place of current line.

.PE   End pic description.

.PF   End pic description and return to vertical position before matching **PS**.

.*xx*   Troff request (or macro) *xx*.

Declarations

At the beginning of a pic description, you may declare a new scale, and declare any number of variables. Pic assumes you want a 1-to-1 scale, where units are inches by default. You can declare a different scale, say 1 = one-*n*th of an inch, by declaring:

```
scale = n
```

Pic takes variable substitutions for numbers used in the description. Instead of:

```
line right n
```

you may use a lowercase character as a variable, for example **a**, by declaring at the top of the description:

```
a = n
```

You may then write:

```
line right a
```

Primitives

Pic recognizes several basic graphical objects, or primitives. These primitives are specified by the following keywords:

```
arc        circle     move
arrow      ellipse    spline
box        line       "text"
```

Syntax

Primitives may be followed by relevant options. Options are discussed later in this section.

arc [**cw**] [*options*] [*"text"*]   A fraction of a circle (default is 1/4 of a circle). The **cw** option specifies a clockwise arc; default is counter-clockwise.

arrow [*options*] [*"text"*]   Draw an arrow. Essentially the same as **line** –>.

box [*options*] [" *text* "]	Draw a box.
circle [*options*] [" *text* "]	Draw a circle.
ellipse [*options*] [" *text* "]	Draw an ellipse.
line [*options*] [" *text* "]	Draw a line.
move [*options*] [" *text* "]	A move of position in the drawing. Essentially, an invisible line.
spline [*options*] [" *text* "]	A line, with the feature that a **then** option results in a gradual (sloped) change in direction.
" *text* "	Text centered at current point.

Options

The options below are grouped by function. Note that **at**, **with**, and **from** specify points. Points may be expressed as Cartesian coordinates or with respect to previous objects.

right [*n*] **left** [*n*] **up** [*n*] **down** [*n*]	The direction of the primitive; default is the direction in which the previous description had been heading. Create diagonal motion by using two directions on the option line. Each direction can be followed by a specified length *n*.
rad *n* **diam** *n*	Create the primitive using radius or diameter *n*.
ht *n* **wid** *n*	Create the primitive using height or width *n*. For an arrow, line, or spline, height and width refer to arrowhead size.
same	Create the primitive using the same dimensions specified for the most recent matching primitive.
at *point*	Center the primitive at *point*.
with .*position* **at** *point*	Designate the *position* of the primitive to be at *point*.
from *point1* **to** *point2*	Draw the primitive from *point1* to *point2*.
–>	Direct the arrowhead forward.
<–	Direct the arrowhead backward.
<–>	Direct the arrowhead both ways.
chop *n m*	Chop off *n* from beginning of primitive, and *m* from end. With only one argument, the same value will be chopped from both ends.
dotted **dashed** **invis**	Draw the primitive using lines that are dotted, dashed, or invisible. (An invisible object still occupies space in the output.) Default is solid line.
then ...	Continue primitive in a new direction. Relevant only to lines, splines, moves, and arrows. Can be placed before or after any text.

Text

Text must be placed within quotes. To break the line, break into two (or more) sets of quotes. Text always appears centered within the object, unless given one of the following arguments:

ljust   Text appears flush left, vertically centered.
rjust   Text appears flush right, vertically centered.
above   Text appears above the center.
below   Text appears below the center.

Object Blocks

Several primitives can be combined to make a complex object (for example, an octagon). This complex object can be treated as a single object by declaring it as a block:

```
Object: [
      description
         .
         .
         .
]
```

Brackets are used as delimiters. Note that the object is declared as a proper noun, hence should begin with a capital letter.

Macros

The same sequence of commands can be repeated by using macros. The syntax is:

```
define sequence %
      description
         .
         .
         .
      %
```

Here we used the percent sign (%) as the delimiter, but you can use any character that isn't in the description.

Macros can take variables, expressed in the definition as **$1** through **$9**. Invoke the macro with the syntax:

```
sequence(value1,value2,...)
```

Positioning

In a pic description, the first action begins at (0,0) unless otherwise specified with coordinates. Thus, as objects are placed above and left of the first object, the point (0,0) moves down and right on the drawing.

All points are ultimately translated by the formatter into x- and y-coordinates. You may therefore refer to a specific point in the picture by incrementing or decrementing the coordinates. For example:

```
2nd ellipse - (3,1)
```

You may refer to the x- and y-coordinates of an object by placing **.x** or **.y** at the end. For example:

```
last box.x
```

refers to the x-coordinate of the most recent box drawn. You can refer to some of the object's physical attributes in a similar way:

.x	x-coordinate of object's center.
.y	y-coordinate of object's center.
.ht	Height of object.
.wid	Width of object.
.rad	Radius of object.

Unless otherwise positioned, each object begins at the point where the last object left off. However, if a command (or sequence of commands) is set off by curly braces ({ }), pic then returns to the position before the first brace.

Positioning Between Objects

To refer to a previous object, use proper names. This can be done two ways:

1. By referring to it by order. For example:

```
1st box
3rd box
last box
2nd last box
```

2. By declaring it with a name, in initial caps, on its declaration line. For example:

```
Line1: line 1.5 right from last box.sw
```

To refer to a point between two objects, or between two points on the same object, you may write:

fraction **of the way between** *first.position* **and** *second.position*

or (abbreviated):

fraction< first.position, second.position>

Corners

When you refer to a previous object, pic assumes you mean the object's center unless you specify a corner. To specify a corner, use either of these forms:

```
.corner of object
object.corner
```

For example:

```
.sw of last box
last box.sw
```

Valid corners can be specified as any of the following:

n	North
s	South
e	East
w	West
ne	Northeast
nw	Northwest
se	Southeast
sw	Southwest
t	Top (same as **n**)
b	Bottom (same as **s**)
r	Right (same as **e**)
l	Left (same as **w**)
start	Point where drawing of object began
end	Point where drawing of object ended

You may also refer to the following parts of an object:

```
upper right        lower right
upper left         lower left
```

Arithmetic Operators

Pic recognizes the operators below:

+	Addition.
−	Subtraction.
*	Multiplication.
/	Division
%	Modulus (remainder after division).

Default Values

The default dimensions of objects are controlled by various system variables. You can change these defaults by typing a description line of the form:

```
variable = value
```

Variable	Default	Variable	Default
arcrad	0.25	ellipsewid	0.75
arrowwid	0.05	linewid	0.5
arrowht	0.1	lineht	0.5
boxwid	0.75	movewid	0.5
boxht	0.5	moveht	0.5
circlerad	0.25	scale	1
dashwid	0.05	textht	0
ellipseht	0.5	textwid	0

A Pic Example

Input:

```
.PS
define smile %
a = $1
circle radius a at 0,0
arc cw radius a*.75 from a*.5,-a*.25 to -a*.5,-a*.25
"\(bu" at a*.33,a*.25
"\(bu" at a*-.33,a*.25
%
smile(.5)
.PE
```

Result:

Part IV

Software Development

The UNIX operating system earned its reputation by providing an unexcelled environment for software development. SCCS, RCS, and **make** are major contributors to the efficiency of this environment. SCCS and RCS allow multiple versions of a source file to be stored in a single archival file. **make** automatically updates a group of interrelated programs. Part IV also summarizes the debugging utilities sdb and dbx.

Section 17 - *The SCCS Utility*

Section 18 - *The RCS Utility*

Section 19 - *The make Utility*

Section 20 - *Program Debugging*

17

The SCCS Utility

This section presents the following topics:

- Overview of commands

- Basic operation

- Identification keywords

- Data keywords

- Alphabetical summary of commands

- **sccs** and pseudo-commands

Note: SCCS users who are more familiar with RCS may benefit from the "Conversion Guide for SCCS Users" in Section 18. This lists SCCS commands and their RCS equivalents.

The Source Code Control System (SCCS) lets you keep track of each revision of a document, avoiding the confusion that often arises from having several versions of one file on line. SCCS is particularly useful when programs are enhanced but the original version is still needed.

All changes to a file are stored in a file named **s.**_file_, which is called an SCCS file. Each time a file is "entered" into SCCS, SCCS notes which lines have been changed or deleted since the most recent version. From that information, SCCS can regenerate the file on demand. Each set of changes depends on all previous sets of changes.

Each set of changes is called a _delta_ and is assigned an **S**CCS **id**entification string (_sid_). The _sid_ consists of either two components, release and level numbers (in the form _a.b_), or of four components: the release, level, branch, and sequence numbers (in the form _a.b.c.d_). The branches and sequences are for situations when two on-running versions of the same file are recorded in SCCS. For example, _delta 3.2.1.1_ refers to release 3, level 2, branch 1, sequence 1.

Overview of Commands

SCCS commands fall into several categories:

Basic Set Up and Editing

admin	Create new SCCS files and change their parameters.
get	Retrieve versions of SCCS files.
delta	Create a new version of an SCCS file (i.e., append a new _delta_).
unget	Cancel a **get** operation; don't create a new delta.

Fixing Deltas

cdc	Change the comment associated with a delta.
comb	Combine consecutive deltas into a single delta.
rmdel	Remove an accidental delta from an SCCS file.

Information

help	Print a command synopsis or clarify diagnostic messages.
prs	Print portions of SCCS files in a specified format.
sact	Show editing activity on SCCS files.
what	Search for all occurrences of the pattern **get** substitutes for **%Z%**, and print out the following text.

Comparing Files

sccsdiff	Show the differences between any two SCCS files.
val	Validate an SCCS file.

Basic Operation

This subsection outlines the steps to follow when using SCCS:

- Creating an SCCS file

- Retrieving a file

- Creating new releases and branches

- Recording changes

Creating an SCCS File

The **admin** command with the **-i** option creates and initializes SCCS files. For example:

```
admin -ich01 s.ch01
```

creates a new SCCS file and initializes it with the contents of **ch01**, which will become *delta 1.1*. The message, "No id keywords (cm7)" appears if you do not specify any keywords. In general, "id keywords" refer to variables in the files that are replaced with appropriate values by **get**, identifying the date and time of creation, the version retrieved, etc. A listing of identification keywords occurs later in this section.

Once the **s.ch01** file is created, the original file **ch01** can be removed, since it can be easily regenerated with the **get** command.

Retrieving a File

The **get** command can retrieve any version of a file from SCCS. Using the example above, you can retrieve **ch01** by entering:

```
get -e s.ch01
```

and the messages:

```
1.1
new delta 1.2
272 lines
```

may appear. This indicates that you are "getting" *delta 1.1*, and the resulting file has 272 lines of text. When the file is reentered into the SCCS file **s.ch01** with the **delta** command, its changes are *delta 1.2*.

The **-e** option indicates to SCCS that you intend to make more changes to the file and then reenter it into SCCS. Without this option, you will receive the file with read-only permissions. The **-e** option, besides releasing the file with read-write permissions, also creates a file **p.ch01**, which records information that will be used by SCCS when the file is returned.

Creating New Releases and Branches

The **−r** option to **get** tells SCCS what release and level number you want, but if no level is specified it defaults to the highest level available. With the command:

```
get -r3.2 ch01
```

delta 3.2 will be the release. However, the command:

```
get -r3 ch01
```

returns the highest-numbered level in release 3, for example **3.8**. With the **−r** option omitted, **get** defaults to the highest release, highest level — in other words, the latest version.

When major changes are in store for a file, you may want to begin a new release of the file. You can do that by "getting" the file with the next highest release number. For example, if the latest release of a file is 3.2, and you want to start release 4, enter:

```
get -e -r4 ch01
```

You will receive the message:

```
3.2
new delta 4.1
53 lines
```

If you want to make a change to an older version of the same file, you can enter:

```
get -e -r2.2 ch01
```

and receive the message:

```
2.2
new delta 2.2.1.1
121 lines
```

You have now created a new branch from the trunk, stemming from version 2.2. Changes in this delta will not affect those in the trunk deltas, i.e., 2.3, 3.1, etc.

Recording Changes

Once changes have been made to the SCCS file, return it to SCCS with the command:

```
delta s.ch01
```

You are prompted for comments on the changes. The **delta** command then does its own **get** and uses **diff** to compare the new version of the file with the most recent version. It then prints messages giving the new release number and the number of lines that were inserted, deleted, and unchanged.

Identification Keywords

The keywords below may be used in an SCCS file. A **get** command will expand these keywords to the value described.

%A%	Shorthand for providing **what** strings for program files; **%A% = %Z%%Y% %M% %I%%Z%**
%B%	Branch number.
%C%	Current line number, intended for identifying where error occurred.
%D%	Current date (YY/MM/DD).
%E%	Date newest applied delta was created (YY/MM/DD).
%F%	SCCS file name.
%G%	Date newest applied delta was created (MM/DD/YY).
%H%	Current date (MM/DD/YY).
%I%	*sid* of the retrieved text (**%R%.%L%.%B%.%S%**).
%L%	Level number.
%M%	Module name (filename without **.s** prefix).
%P%	Fully qualified SCCS file name.
%Q%	Value of *string*, as defined by **admin −fq***string*.
%R%	Release number.
%S%	Sequence number.
%T%	Current time (HH:MM:SS).
%U%	Time newest applied delta was created (HH:MM:SS).
%W%	Another shorthand like **%A%**; **%W% = %Z% %M%** *tab* **%I%**
%Y%	Module type, as defined by **admin −ft***type*.
%Z%	String recognized by **what**; that is, **@(#)**.

Data Keywords

Data keywords specify which parts of an SCCS file are to be retrieved and output using the **−d** option of the **prs** command.

:A:	Form of **what** string.
:B:	Branch number.
:BD:	Body.
:BF:	Branch flag.
:C:	Comments for delta.
:CB:	Ceiling boundary.
:D:	Date delta created (**:Dy:/:Dm:/:Dd:**).
:Dd:	Day delta created.
:Dg:	Deltas ignored (sequence number).
:DI:	Sequence number of deltas (**:Dn:/:Dx:/:Dg:**).
:DL:	Delta line statistics (**:Li:/:Ld:/:Lu:**).
:Dm:	Month delta created.
:Dn:	Deltas included (sequence number).

SCCS

`:DP:`	Predecessor delta sequence number.
`:Ds:`	Default sid.
`:DS:`	Delta sequence number.
`:Dt:`	Delta information.
`:DT:`	Delta type.
`:Dx:`	Deltas excluded (sequence number).
`:Dy:`	Year delta created.
`:F:`	SCCS file name.
`:FB:`	Floor boundary.
`:FD:`	File descriptive text.
`:FL:`	Flag list.
`:GB:`	Gotten body.
`:I:`	SCCS ID string (sid) (**:R:.:L:.:B:.:S:**).
`:J:`	Joint edit flag.
`:KF:`	Keyword error/warning flag.
`:KV:`	Keyword validation string.
`:L:`	Level number.
`:Ld:`	Lines deleted by delta.
`:Li:`	Lines inserted by delta.
`:LK:`	Locked releases.
`:Lu:`	Lines unchanged by delta.
`:M:`	Module name.
`:MF:`	Modification validation flag.
`:MP:`	Modification validation program name.
`:MR:`	Modification numbers for delta.
`:ND:`	Null delta flag.
`:P:`	Username of programmer who created delta.
`:PN:`	SCCS file pathname.
`:Q:`	User-defined keyword.
`:R:`	Release number.
`:S:`	Sequence number.
`:T:`	Time delta created (**:Th:::Tm:::Ts:.**).
`:Th:`	Hour delta created.
`:Tm:`	Minutes delta created.
`:Ts:`	Seconds delta created.
`:UN:`	User names.
`:W:`	Form of **what** string.
`:Y:`	Module type flag.
`:Z:`	**what** string delimiter.

Alphabetical Summary of SCCS Commands

File arguments to SCCS commands can be either filenames or directory names. Naming a directory will cause all the files in that directory to be processed, with nonapplicable and nonreadable files ignored. If in place of a file argument a dash (–) is entered, the command will read from standard input for the names of files to be processed, one on each line.

---

admin [*options*] *files*   **admin**

Add *files* to SCCS or change *options* of SCCS *files*.

Options

   –a[*user* | *groupid*]

      Assign *user* or *groupid* permission to make deltas; a !
      before *user* or *groupid* denies permission. If no list is
      given, anyone has permission.

  –d*flag*   Delete *flag* previously set with **–f**. Applicable *flags* are:

b	Enable the **–b** option in a **get** command; this allows branch deltas.
c*n*	Set highest release to *n* (default is 9999).
d*n*	Set **get** default delta number to *n*.
f*n*	Set lowest release to *n* (default is 1).
i[*string*]	Treat "No id keywords (ge6)" as a fatal error. *string*, if present, forces a fatal error if keywords do not exactly match *string*.
j	Allow multiple concurrent **get**s.
l*list*	Releases in *list* cannot accept changes; use the letter **a** to specify all releases.
m*name*	Substitute **%M%** keyword with module *name*.
n	Create a null delta from which to branch.
q*string*	Substitute **%Q%** keyword with *string*.
t*type*	Substitute **%Y%** keyword with module *type*.
v[*prog*]	Force **delta** command to prompt for modification request numbers as the reason for creating a delta. Run program file *prog* to check for valid numbers.

  –e[*user* | *groupid*]

      Permission to make deltas is denied to each *user* or
      groupid.

  –f*flag*   Set *flag* (see **–d** above).

  –h   Check an existing SCCS file for possible corruption.

  –i[*file*]   Create a new SCCS file using the contents of *file* as the initial delta. If *file* is omitted, use standard input.

  –m[*list*] Insert *list* of modification request numbers as the reason for creating the file.

→

---

admin ←	**−n**	Create a new SCCS file that is empty.
	−r *n.n*	Set initial delta to release number *n.n*. Default is 1.1. Must be used with **−i**.
	−t[*file*]	Replace SCCS file description with contents of *file*. If *file* is missing, the existing description is deleted.
	−y[*text*]	Insert *text* as comment for initial delta (valid only with **−i** or **−n**).
	−z	Recompute the SCCS file checksum and store in first line.

cdc	**cdc −r***sid* [*options*] *files*

Change the delta comments of the specified *sid* (SCCS ID) of one or more SCCS *files*.

Options

−m[*list*]   Add the *list* of modification request numbers (use a ! before any number to delete it). **−m** is useful only when **admin** has set the **v** flag for *file*. If **−m** is omitted, the terminal displays **MRs?** as an input prompt.

−y[*string*]   Add *string* to the comments for the specified delta. If **−y** is omitted, the terminal displays **comments?** as an input prompt.

Example

For delta 1.3 of file **s.prog.c**, add modification numbers x01-5 and x02-8 and then add comments:

```
cdc -r1.3 s.prog.c
MRs? x01-5 x02-8
comments? this went out to review
```

comb	**comb** [*options*] *files*

Reduce the size of the specified SCCS *files*. This is done by pruning selected deltas and combining those that remain, thereby reconstructing the SCCS file. The default behavior prunes all but the most recent delta in a particular branch and keeps only those ancestors needed to preserve the tree structure. **comb** produces a shell script on standard output. Actual reconstruction of the SCCS files is done by running the script.

Options

−c*list*   Preserve only those deltas whose SCCS IDs are specified in the comma-separated *list*. Use a hyphen (−) to supply a range; e.g., 1.3,2.1-2.5.

−o   Access the reconstructed *file* at the release number of the delta that is created, instead of at the most recent ancestor. This option may change the tree structure.

−p*sid*   In reconstructing *file*, discard all deltas whose SCCS identification string is older than *sid*.

−s	Generate a shell script that calculates how much the file has been reduced in size. **−s** is useful as a preview of what **comb** will do when actually run.	**comb**

delta [*options*] *files*   **delta**

Incorporate changes (add a delta) to one or more SCCS *files*. **delta** is used to store changes made to a text file that was retrieved by **get −e** and then edited. **delta** normally removes the text file.

Options

−g*list*	Ignore deltas whose SCCS IDs (version numbers) are specified in the comma-separated *list*. Use – to supply a range; e.g., 1.3,2.1-2.5.
−m[*list*]	Supply a *list* of modification request numbers as reasons for creating new deltas. **−m** is useful only when **admin** has set the **v** flag for *file*. If **−m** is omitted, the terminal displays **MRs?** as an input prompt.
−n	Do not remove the edited file (extracted by **get −e**) after execution of **delta**.
−p	Print a **diff**-style listing of delta changes to *file*.
−r*SID*	Delta version number that identifies *file*. **−r** is needed only when more than one version of an SCCS file is being edited simultaneously.
−s	Suppress printing of new SID and other delta information.
−y[*string*]	Insert *string* as a comment describing why the delta was made. If **−y** is omitted, the terminal displays **comments?** as an input prompt.

get [*options*] *files*   **get**

Retrieve a text version of an SCCS *file*. The retrieved text file (also called the g-file) has the same name as the SCCS file but drops the **s.** prefix. For each SCCS *file*, **get** prints its version number and the number of lines retrieved. See "Identification Keywords" for a list of keywords that can be placed in text files.

Options

−a*n*	Retrieve delta sequence number *n*; not very useful (used by **comb**).
−b	Create new branch (use with **−e**).
−c*date*	Retrieve a version that includes only those changes made before *date*. *date* is a series of two-digit numbers indicating the year, followed by an optional month, day, hour, minute, and second. Symbolic characters can be used as field separators.
−e	Retrieve a text file for editing; this is the most commonly used option.

SCCS

→

–g   Suppress the text and just retrieve the SCCS ID (version number), typically to check it.

–G*name*
Save retrieved text in file *name* (default is to drop **s.** prefix). (Solaris 2.0 only.)

–i*list*   Incorporate into the retrieved text file any deltas whose SCCS IDs (version numbers) are specified in the comma-separated *list*. Use a hyphen (–) to supply a range (e.g., 1.3,2.1-2.5).

–k   Do not expand ID keywords to their values; use in place of **–e** to regenerate (overwrite) a text file that was ruined during editing.

–l[p]   Create a delta summary (saved to a file or, with **–lp**, displayed on standard output).

–m   Precede each text line with the SCCS ID of the delta it relates to.

–n   Precede each text line with the **%M%** keyword (typically the name of the text file).

–p   Write retrieved text to standard output instead of to a file.

–r*sid*   Retrieve SCCS ID (version number) *sid*.

–s   Suppress normal output (show error messages only).

–t   Retrieve the top (most recent) version of a release.

–w*string*
Replace the **%W%** keyword with *string*; **%W%** is the header label used by **what**.

–x*list*   Exclude the *list* of deltas from the retrieved text file; the inverse of **–i**.

Examples

Retrieve file **prog.c** for editing; a subsequent **delta** creates a branch at version 1.3:

```
get -e -b -r1.3 s.prog.c
```

Retrieve file **prog.c**; contents will exclude changes made after 2:30 p.m. on June 1, 1990 (except for deltas 2.6 and 2.7, which are included):

```
get -c'90/06/01 14:30:00' -i'2.6,2.7' s.prog.c
```

Display the contents of **s.text.c** (all revisions except 1.1 - 1.7):

```
get -p -x1.1-1.7 s.text.c
```

---

help

help [*commands* | *error_codes*]

Online help facility to explain SCCS commands or error messages. With no arguments, **help** prompts for a command name or an error code. To display a brief syntax, supply the SCCS command name. To display an explanation of an error message, supply the code that appears after an SCCS error message. The **help** files usually reside in **/usr/ccs/lib**.

Error messages produced by aborted SCCS commands are of the form:

```
ERROR filename: message (code)
```

The *code* is useful for finding out the nature of your error. To do this, type:

```
help code
```

Example

When everything else fails, try this:

```
help stuck
```

---

prs [*options*] *files*

Print formatted information for one or more SCCS *files*.

Options

−a	Include information for removed deltas.
−c*date*	Cutoff *date* used with **−e** or **−l** (see **get** for format of *date*).
−d[*format*]	Specify output *format* by supplying text and/or SCCS keywords. See "Data Keywords" for a list of valid keywords.
−e	With **−r**, list data for deltas earlier than or including *sid*; with **−c**, list data for deltas not newer than *date*.
−l	Like **−e**, but later than or including *sid* or *date*.
−r[*sid*]	Specify SCCS ID *sid*; default is the most recent delta.

Example

The following command:

```
prs -d"program :M: version :I: by :P:" -r s.yes.c
```

might produce this output:

```
program yes.c version 2.4.6 by daniel
```

---

rmdel −r*sid files*

Remove a delta from one or more SCCS *files*, where *sid* is the SCCS ID. The delta must be the most recent in its branch.

---

sact *files*

For the specified SCCS *files*, report which deltas are about to change (i.e., which files are currently being edited via **get −e** but haven't yet been updated via **delta**). **sact** lists output in five fields: SCCS ID of the current delta being edited, SCCS ID of the new delta to create, user who issued the **get −e**, date and time it was issued.

sccsdiff	**sccsdiff** −r*sid1* −r*sid2* [*options*] *files*
	Report differences between two versions of an SCCS *file*. *sid1* and *sid2* identify the deltas to be compared. This command invokes **bdiff** (which in turn calls **diff**).
	Options
	−p Pipe output through **pr**.
	−s*n* Use file segment size *n* (*n* is passed to **bdiff**).
unget	**unget** [*options*] *files*
	Cancel a previous **get** −e for one or more SCCS *files*. If a file is being edited via **get** −e, issuing **delta** will process the edits (creating a new delta), whereas **unget** will delete the edited version (preventing a new delta from being made).
	Options
	−n Do not remove file retrieved with **get** −e.
	−r*sid* The SCCS ID of the delta to cancel; needed only if **get** −e was issued more than once for the same SCCS file.
	−s Suppress display of the intended delta's *sid*.
val	**val** [*options*] *files*
	Validate that the SCCS *files* meet the characteristics specified in the options. **val** produces messages on the standard output for each file and returns an 8-bit code upon exit.
	Options
	− Read standard input and interpret each line as a **val** command line argument. Exit with an *EOF*. This option is used by itself.
	−m*name*
	Compare *name* with **%M%** keyword in *file*.
	−r*sid* Check whether the SCCS ID is ambiguous or invalid.
	−s Silence any error message.
	−y*type* Compare *type* with **%Y%** keyword in *file*.
what	**what** [*option*] *files*
	Search *files* for the pattern **@(#)** and print the text that follows it. Actually, the pattern searched for is the value of **%Z%**, but the **get** command expands this keyword to **@(#)**. The main purpose of **what** is to print identification strings.
	Option
	−s Quit after finding the first occurrence of a pattern.

sccs and Pseudo-commands

The compatibility packages include **sccs**, a front end to the SCCS utility. This command provides a user-friendly interface to SCCS and has the following command-line syntax:

/usr/ucb/sccs [*options*] *command* [*SCCS_flags*] [*files*]

In addition to providing all of the regular SCCS commands, **sccs** offers pseudo-commands. These are easy-to-use, prebuilt combinations of the regular SCCS commands. *options* apply only to the **sccs** interface. *command* is the SCCS command or pseudo-command to run, and *SCCS_flags* are specific options passed to the SCCS command being run.

sccs makes it easier to specify files because it automatically prepends **SCCS/s.** to any filename arguments. For example:

```
sccs get -e file.c
```

would be interpreted as:

```
get -e SCCS/s.file.c
```

Options

−d*prepath*   Locate files in *prepath* rather than in current directory. For example:

```
sccs -d/home get file.c
```

is interpreted as:

```
get /home/SCCS/s.file.c
```

−p*endpath*   Access files from directory *endpath* instead of SCCS. For example:

```
sccs -pVERSIONS get file.c
```

is interpreted as:

```
get VERSIONS/s.file.c
```

−r   Invoke **sccs** as the real user instead of as the effective user.

Pseudo-commands

Equivalent SCCS actions are indicated in parentheses.

check   Like **info**, but return nonzero exit codes instead of filenames.

clean   Remove from current directory any files that aren't being edited under SCCS (via **get −e**, for example).

create   Create SCCS files (**admin −i** followed by **get**).

deledit   Same as **delta** followed by **get −e**.

delget   Same as **delta** followed by **get**.

diffs   Compare file's current version and SCCS version (like **sccsdiff**).

edit	Get a file to edit (**get** **−e**).
enter	Like **create** but without the subsequent **get** (**admin** **−i**).
fix	Same as **rmdel** (must be followed by **−r**).
info	List files being edited (similar to **sact**).
print	Print information (like **prs** **−e** followed by **get** **−p** **−m**)
tell	Like **info**, but list one filename per line.
unedit	Same as **unget**.

The RCS Utility

This section presents the following topics:

- Overview of commands

- Basic operation

- General RCS specifications

- Conversion guide for SCCS users

- Alphabetical summary of commands

As with SCCS in the preceding section, the Revision Control System (RCS) is designed to keep track of multiple file revisions, thereby reducing the amount of storage space needed. With RCS you can automatically store and retrieve revisions, merge or compare revisions, keep a complete history (or log) of changes, and identify revisions using symbolic keywords. RCS is believed to be more efficient than SCCS. RCS is not part of standard SVR4 but can be obtained from the Free Software Foundation in Cambridge, Mass. This section describes Version 5.6, although we note important differences in versions 4 and 5.

RCS

Overview of Commands

The three most important RCS commands are:

ci   Check in revisions (put a file under RCS control).

co   Check out revisions.

rcs   Set up or change attributes of RCS files.

Two commands provide information about RCS files:

ident   Extract keyword values from an RCS file.

rlog   Display a summary (log) about the revisions in an RCS file.

You can compare RCS files with these commands:

merge   Incorporate changes from two files into a third file.

rcsdiff   Report differences between revisions.

rcsmerge Incorporate changes from two RCS files into a third RCS file.

The following commands help with configuration management. However, they are considered optional, so they are not always installed.

rcsclean Remove working files that have not been changed.

rcsfreeze Label the files that make up a configuration.

Basic Operation

Normally, you maintain RCS files in a subdirectory called **RCS**, so the first step in using RCS should be:

```
mkdir RCS
```

Next, you place an existing file (or files) under RCS control by running the check-in command:

```
ci file
```

This creates a file called *file*,**v** in directory **RCS**. *file*,**v** is called an RCS file, and it will store all future revisions of *file*. When you run **ci** on a file for the first time, you are prompted to describe the contents. **ci** then deposits *file* into the RCS file as revision 1.1.

To edit a new revision, check out a copy:

```
co -l file
```

This causes RCS to extract a copy of *file* from the RCS file. You must lock the file with –l to make it writable by you. This copy is called a working file. When you're done editing, you can record the changes by checking the working file back in again:

```
ci file
```

This time, you are prompted to enter a log of the changes made, and the file is deposited as revision 1.2. Note that a check in normally removes the working file. To retrieve a read-only copy, do a check out without a lock:

```
co file
```

This is useful when you need to keep a copy on hand for compiling or searching. As a shortcut to the previous **ci/co**, you could type:

```
ci -u file
```

This checks in the file but immediately checks out a read-only copy. To compare changes between a working file and its latest revision, you can type:

```
rcsdiff file
```

Another useful command is **rlog**, which shows a summary of log messages. System administrators can use the **rcs** command to set up default behavior of RCS.

General RCS Specifications

This subsection discusses:

- Keyword substitution

- Revision numbering

- Specifying the date

- Specifying states

- Standard options and environment variables

Keyword Substitution

RCS lets you place keyword variables in your working files. These variables are later expanded into revision notes. You can then use the notes either as embedded comments in the input file, or as text strings that appear when the output is printed. To create revision notes via keyword substitution, follow this procedure:

1. In your working file, type any of the keywords listed below.

2. Check the file in.

3. Check the file out again. Upon checkout, the **co** command expands each keyword to include its value. That is, **co** replaces instances of:

    ```
    $keyword$
    ```

    with:

    ```
    $keyword:value$.
    ```

4. Subsequent check in and check out of a file will update any existing keyword values. Unless otherwise noted below, existing values are replaced by new values.

Note: In RCS Version 5, many commands have a **−k** option that provides more flexibility during keyword substitution.

Keywords

$Author$	Username of person who checked in revision.
$Date$	Date and time of check in.
$Header$	A title that includes RCS file's full pathname, revision number, date, author, state, and (if locked) the person who locked the file.
Id	Same as **$Header$**, but exclude the full pathname of the RCS file.
$Locker$	Username of person who locked the revision. If the file isn't locked, this value is empty.
Log	The message that was typed during check in to describe the file, preceded by the RCS filename, revision number, author, and date. Log messages accumulate rather than being overwritten.
$RCSfile$	The RCS filename, without its pathname.
$Revision$	The assigned revision number.
$Source$	The RCS filename, including its pathname.
$State$	The state assigned by the **−s** option of **ci** or **rcs**.

Example Values

Let's assume that the file **/projects/new/chapter3** has been checked in and out by a user named **daniel**. Here's what keyword substitution would produce for each keyword, for the second revision of the file:

```
$Author: daniel $

$Date: 92/03/18 17:51:36 $

$Header: /projects/new/chapter3,v 1.2 92/03/18 17:51:36 daniel \
    Exp Locker: daniel $

$Id: chapter3,v 1.2 92/03/18 17:51:36 daniel Exp Locker: daniel $

$Locker: daniel $

$Log:     chapter3,v $
# Revision 1.2  92/03/18  17:51:36  daniel
# Added section on error-handling
#
# Revision 1.1  92/03/18  16:49:59  daniel
# Initial revision
#

$RCSfile: chapter3,v $

$Revision: 1.2 $

$Source: /projects/new/chapter3,v $

$State: Exp $
```

Revision Numbering

Unless told otherwise, RCS commands typically operate on the latest revision. Some commands have a **−r** option that is used to specify a revision number. In addition, many options accept a revision number as an optional argument. (In the command summary, this argument is shown as [R].) Revision numbers consist of up to four fields: release, level, branch, and sequence, but most revisions consist of only the release and level. For example, you can check out revision 1.4 as follows:

```
co -l -r1.4 ch01
```

When you check it in again, the new revision will be marked as 1.5. But suppose the edited copy needs to be checked in as the next release. You would type:

```
ci -r2 ch01
```

This creates revision 2.1. You can also create a branch from an earlier revision. The following command creates revision 1.4.1.1:

```
ci -r1.4.1 ch01
```

Numbers are not the only way to specify revisions, though. You can assign a text label as a revision name, using the **−n** option of **ci** or **rcs**. You can also specify this name in any option that accepts a revision number for an argument. For example, you could check in each of your C programs, using the same label regardless of the current revision number:

```
ci -u -nPrototype *.c
```

In addition, RCS version 5.6 lets you specify a $, which means the revision number extracted from the keywords of a working file. For example:

```
rcsdiff -r$ ch01
```

compares **ch01** to the revision that is checked in. You can also combine names and symbols. The command:

```
rcs -nDraft:$ ch*
```

assigns a name to the revision numbers associated with several chapter files.

Specifying the Date

Revisions are timestamped by time and date of check in. Several keyword strings include the date in their values. Dates can be supplied in options to **ci**, **co**, and **rlog**. RCS uses the following date format as its default:

```
1995/10/16 02:00:00    (year/month/day  time)
```

The default timezone is Greenwich Mean Time (GMT), which is also referred to as Coordinated Universal Time (UTC). Dates can be supplied in free format. This lets you specify many different styles. Here are some of the more common ones, which show the same time as in the example above:

```
6:00 pm lt                    (assuming today is Oct. 16, 1995)
2:00 AM, Oct. 16, 1995
Mon Oct 16 18:00:00 1995 LT
Mon Oct 16 18:00:00 PST 1995
```

The uppercase or lowercase "lt" indicates local time (here, Pacific Standard Time). The third line shows **ctime** format (plus the "LT"); the fourth line is the **date** command format.

Specifying States

In some situations, particularly programming environments, you want to know the status of a set of revisions. RCS files are marked by a text string that describes their *state*. The default state is **Exp** (experimental). Other common choices include **Stab** (stable) or **Rel** (released). These words are user-defined and have no special internal meaning. Several keyword strings include the state in their values. In addition, states can be supplied in options to **ci**, **co**, **rcs**, and **rlog**.

Standard Options

RCS Version 5.6 defines an environment variable RCSINIT, which is used to set up default options for RCS commands. If you set RCSINIT to a space-separated list of options, they will be prepended to the command-line options you supply to any RCS command. Three options are useful to include in RCSINIT: **−q**, **−V**, and **−x**. They can be thought of as standard options because most RCS commands accept them. Note that **−V** is new in RCS Version 5 and that **−x** is new in Version 5.6.

−q[*R*]   Quiet mode; don't show diagnostic output. *R* specifies a file revision.

−V*n*   Emulate version *n* of RCS; useful when trading files between systems that run different versions. *n* can be 3, 4, or 5.

−x*suffixes*   Specify an alternate list of *suffixes* for RCS files. Each suffix is separated by a /. On UNIX systems, RCS files normally end with the characters **,v**. The **−x** option provides a workaround for systems that don't allow a **,** character in filenames.

For example, when depositing a working file into an RCS file, the command:

```
ci -x,v/ ch01            (second suffix is blank)
```

searches in order for the RCS filenames:

```
RCS/ch01,v
ch01,v
RCS/ch01
```

Conversion Guide for SCCS Users

SCCS commands have functional equivalents to RCS commands. The following table provides a very general guide for SCCS users:

SCCS	RCS
admin	rcs
admin –i	ci
cdc	rcs –m
delta	ci
get	co
prs	ident or rlog
rmdel	rcs –o
sact	rlog
sccsdiff	rcsdiff
unget	co (with overwrite), or ci with rcs –o
what	ident

Alphabetical Summary of Commands

For details on the syntax of keywords, revision numbers, dates, states, and standard options, refer to the previous discussions.

---

ci [*options*] *files*   **ci**

Check in revisions. **ci** stores the contents of the specified working *files* into their corresponding RCS files. Normally, **ci** deletes the working file after storing it. If no RCS file exists, then the working file is an initial revision. In this case, the RCS file is created and you are prompted to enter a description of the file. If an RCS file exists, **ci** increments the revision number and prompts you to enter a message that logs the changes made. In RCS Version 5.6, if a working file is checked in without changes, the file reverts to the previous revision. In older RCS versions, you may end up having to check in a new revision that contains no changes.

The mutually exclusive options **–u**, **–l**, and **–r**, are the most common. Use **–u** to keep a read-only copy of the working file (for example, so that the file can be compiled or searched). Use **–l** to update a revision and then immediately check it out again with a lock. This allows you to save intermediate changes but continue editing (for example, during a long editing session). Use **–r** to check in a file with a different release number. **ci** accepts the standard options **–q**, **–V**, and **–x**.

→

RCS

ci

←

Options

−d[*date*] Check the file in with a timestamp of *date* or, if no date is specified, with the time of last modification.

−f[*R*] Force a check in even if there are no differences.

−I[*R*] Interactive mode; prompt user even when standard input is not a terminal (e.g., when **ci** is part of a command pipeline). **−I** is new in RCS Version 5.

−k[*R*] Assign a revision number, creation date, state, and author from keyword values that were placed in the working file, instead of computing the revision information from the local environment. **−k** is useful for software distribution: the preset keywords serve as a timestamp shared by all distribution sites.

−l[*R*] Do a **co −l** after checking in. This leaves a locked copy of the next revision.

−m*msg* Use the *msg* string as the log message for all files checked in. When checking in multiple files, **ci** normally prompts whether to reuse the log message of the previous file. **−m** bypasses this prompting.

−M[*R*] Set the working file's modification time to that of the retrieved version. Use of **−M** can confuse **make** and should be used with care. (New in RCS Version 5.6.)

−n*name* Associate a text *name* with the new revision number.

−N*name* Same as **−n**, but override a previous *name*.

−r[*R*] Check the file in as revision *R*.

−s*state* Set the *state* of the checked-in revision.

−t*file* Replace RCS file description with contents of *file*. As of Version 5, this works only for initial check in.

−t−*string* Replace RCS file description with *string*. As of Version 5, this works only for initial check in.

−u[*R*] Do a **co −u** after checking in. This leaves a read-only copy.

−w*user* Set the author field to *user* in the checked-in revision.

Examples

Check in chapter files using the same log message:

```
ci -m'First round edits' chap*
```

Check in edits to **prog.c**, leaving a read-only copy:

```
ci -u prog.c
```

Start revision level 2; refer to revision 2.1 as "Prototype":

```
ci -r2 -nPrototype prog.c
```

co [*options*] *files*

Retrieve a previously checked-in revision, and place it in the corresponding working file (or print to standard output if **−p** is specified). If you intend to edit the working file and check it in again, specify **−l** to lock the file. **co** accepts the standard options **−q**, **−V**, and **−x**.

Options

−d*date*	Retrieve latest revision whose check-in timestamp is on or before *date*.
−f[*R*]	Force the working file to be overwritten.
−I[*R*]	Interactive mode; prompt user even when standard input is not a terminal. (New in RCS Version 5.)
−j*R2:R3*	This works like **rcsmerge**. *R2* and *R3* specify two revisions whose changes are merged into a third file: either the corresponding working file, or a third revision (any *R* specified by other **co** options).
−k*c*	Expand keyword symbols according to flag *c*. *c* can be:

kv	Expand symbols to keyword and value (the default). Insert the locker's name only during a **ci −l** or **co −l**.
kvl	Like **kv**, but always insert the locker's name.
k	Expand symbols to keywords only (no values). This is useful for ignoring trivial differences during file comparison.
o	Expand symbols to keyword and value present in previous revision. This is useful for binary files that don't allow substring changes.
v	Expand symbols to values only (no keywords). This prevents further keyword substitution and is not recommended.

−l[*R*]	Same as **−r**, but also lock the retrieved revision.
−M[*R*]	Set the working file's modification time to that of the retrieved version. Use of **−M** can confuse **make** and should be used with care. (New in RCS Version 5.6.)
−p[*R*]	Send retrieved revision to standard output instead of to a working file. Useful for output redirection or filtering.
−r[*R*]	Retrieve the latest revision or, if *R* is given, retrieve the latest revision that is equal to or lower than *R*.
−s*state*	Retrieve the latest revision having the given *state*.
−u[*R*]	Same as **−r**, but also unlock the retrieved revision if you locked it previously.
−w[*user*]	Retrieve the latest revision that was checked in either by the invoking user or by the specified *user*.

→

co
←

Examples

Sort the latest stored version of *file*:

```
co -p file | sort
```

Check out (and lock) all uppercase filenames for editing:

```
co -l [A-Z]*
```

Note that filename expansion fails unless a working copy resides in the current directory. Therefore, this example works only if the files were previously checked in via **ci −u**.

Finally, here are some different ways to extract the working files for a set of RCS files (in the current directory):

```
co -r3 *,v                Latest revisions of release 3
co -r3 -wjim *,v          Same, but only if checked in by jim
co -d'May 5, 2 pm LT' *,v Latest revisions that were
                          modified on or before the date
co -rPrototype *,v        Latest revisions named Prototype
```

---

ident

ident [*option*] [*files*]

Extract keyword/value symbols from *files*. *files* can be text files, object files, or dumps.

Option

  −q   Suppress warning message when no keyword patterns are found.

Examples

If file **prog.c** is compiled, and it contains this line of code:

```
char rcsID[] = "$Author: george $
```

then the following output is produced:

```
% ident prog.c prog.o
prog.c:
     $Author: george $
prog.o:
     $Author: george $
```

Show keywords for all RCS files (suppress warnings):

```
co -p RCS/*,v | ident -q
```

---

merge

merge [*options*] *file1 file2 file3*

Perform a three-way merge of files (via **diff3**) and place changes in *file1*. *file2* is the original file. *file1* is the "good" modification of *file2*. *file3* is another, conflicting modification of *file2*. **merge** finds the differences between *file2* and *file3*, and then incorporates those changes into *file1*. If both *file1* and *file3* have changes to common lines, **merge**

---

warns about overlapping lines and inserts both choices in *file1*. The   **merge**
insertion appears as follows:

```
<<<<<<< file1
lines from file1
========
lines from file3
>>>>>>> file3
```

You'll need to edit *file1* by deleting one of the choices. **merge** exits
with a status of 0 (no overlaps), 1 (some overlaps), or 2 (unknown
problem). See also **rcsmerge**.

Options

−**L** *text1*   In overlapping lines, replace the label "<<<<<<< *file1*"
with the label "<<<<<<< *text1*".

−**L** *text3*   In overlapping lines, replace the label "<<<<<<< *file1*"
with the label "<<<<<<< *text1*". Valid only with −**L**
text1.

−**p**   Send merged version to standard output instead of to
file1.

−**q**   Produce overlap insertions but don't warn about them.

---

rcs [*options*] *files*   **rcs**

An administrative command for setting up or changing the default attributes of RCS files. Among other things, **rcs** lets you set strict locking
(−**L**), delete revisions (−**o**), and override locks set by **co** (−**l** and −**u**).
RCS files have an access list (created via −**a**); anyone whose username
is on the list can run **rcs**. The access list is often empty, meaning that
rcs is available to everyone. In addition, you can always invoke **rcs** if
you own the file, if you're a privileged user, or if you run **rcs** with −**i**.
rcs accepts the standard options −**q**, −**V**, and −**x**.

Options

−**a***users*   Append the comma-separated list of *users* to the access
list.

−**A***otherfile*
Append *otherfile*'s access list to the access list of *files*.

−**b**[*R*]   Set the default branch to *R* or, if *R* is omitted, to the
highest branch on the trunk.

−**c**'*s*'   The comment character for **$Log** keywords is set to
string *s*. By default, **co** expands embedded **$Log** key-
words into comments preceded by **#**. You could, for
example, set *s* to **.\"** for troff files or set *s* to ***** for C
programs. (You would need to manually insert an
enclosing **/*** and ***/** before and after **$Log**.)

−**e**[*users*]   Erase everyone (or only the specified *users*) from the
access list.

RCS

−i		Create (initialize) an RCS file but don't deposit a revision.
−I		Interactive mode; prompt user even when standard input is not a terminal. (New in RCS Version 5.)
−k_c_		Use _c_ as the default style for keyword substitution. (See **co** for values of _c._) **−kkv** restores the default substitution style; all other styles create incompatibilities with RCS Version 4 or earlier.
−l[_R_]		Lock revision **R** or the latest revision. **−l** "retroactively locks" a file and is useful if you checked out a file incorrectly by typing **co** instead of **co −l**.
−L		Turn on strict locking (the default). This means that everyone, including the owner of the RCS file, must use **co −l** to edit files. Strict locking is recommended when files are to be shared. (See **−U**.)
−m_R:msg_		Use the _msg_ string to replace the log message of revision _R._ (New in RCS Version 5.6.)
−n_flags_		Add or delete an association between a revision and a name. _flags_ can be:
	name:R	Associate _name_ with revision _R._
	name:	Associate _name_ with latest revision.
	name	Remove association of _name._
−N_flags_		Same as **−n** but overwrite existing _names._
−o_R_list_		Delete (outdate) revisions listed in _R_list._ _R_list_ can be specified as: _R1, R1-R2, R1-,_ or _-R2._ When a branch is given, **−o** deletes only the latest revision on it. RCS Version 5.6 has changed the range separator character to **:**, although **−** is still valid.
−s_state_[_:R_]		
		Set the state of revision _R_ (or the latest revision) to the word _state._
−t[_file_]		Replace RCS file description with contents of _file_ or, if no file is given, with standard output.
−t−_string_		Replace RCS file description with _string._
−u[_R_]		The complement of **−l**: unlock a revision that was previously checked out via **co −l**. If someone else did the check out, you are prompted to state the reason for breaking the lock. This message is mailed to the original locker.
−U		Turn on non-strict locking. Everyone except the file owner must use **co −l** to edit files. (See **−L**.)

Examples

Associate the label **To_customer** with the latest revision of all RCS files:

```
rcs -nTo_customer: RCS/*
```

Add three users to the access list of file **beatle_deals**:

```
rcs -ageorge,paul,ringo beatle_deals
```

Delete revisions 1.2 through 1.5:

```
rcs -o1.2-1.5 doc
```

Replace an RCS file description with the contents of a variable:

```
echo "$description" | rcs -t file
```

---

rcsclean [*options*] [*files*]

Although included with RCS, this command is optional and might not be installed on your system. **rcsclean** compares checked-out files against the corresponding latest revision or revision *R* (as given by the options). If no differences are found, the working file is removed. (Use **rcsdiff** to find differences.) **rcsclean** is useful in makefiles. For example, you could specify a "clean up" target to update your directories. **rcsclean** is also useful prior to running **rcsfreeze**. **rcsclean** accepts the standard options **–q**, **–V**, and **–x**.

Options

–k*c* When comparing revisions, expand keywords using style *c*. (See **co** for values of *c*.)

–n[*R*] Show what would happen but don't actually execute.

–r[*R*] Compare against revision *R*. *R* can be supplied as arguments to other options, so **–r** is redundant.

–u[*R*] Unlock the revision if it's the same as the working file.

Examples

Remove unchanged copies of program and header files:

```
rcsclean *.c *.h
```

---

rcsdiff [*options*] [*diff_options*] *files*

Compare revisions via **diff**. Specify revisions using **–r** as follows:

Number of Revisions specified:	Comparison made:
None	Working file against latest revision
One	Working file against specified revision
Two	One revision against the other

rcsdiff accepts the standard options **–q**, **–V**, and **–x**, as well as *diff_options*, which can be any valid **diff** option. **rcsdiff** exits with a

→

RCS

rcsdiff ←	status of 0 (no differences), 1 (some differences), or 2 (unknown problem).

Options

−k*c* When comparing revisions, expand keywords using style *c*. (See **co** for values of *c*.)

−r*R1* Use revision *R1* in the comparison.

−r*R2* Use revision *R2* in the comparison. (**−r***R1* must also be specified.)

---

rcsfreeze	**rcsfreeze** [*name*]

Although included with RCS, this shell script is optional and might not be installed on your system. **rcsfreeze** assigns a name to an entire set of RCS files, which must already be checked in. This is useful for marking a group of files as a single configuration. The default *name* is C_*n*, where *n* is incremented each time you run **rcsfreeze**.

---

rcsmerge	**rcsmerge** [*options*] *file*

Perform a three-way merge of file revisions, taking two differing versions and incorporating the changes into the working *file*. You must provide either one or two revisions to merge (typically with **−r**). Overlaps are handled the same as with **merge**, by placing warnings in the resulting file. **rcsmerge** accepts the standard options **−q**, **−V**, and **−x**. **rcsmerge** exits with a status of 0 (no overlaps), 1 (some overlaps), or 2 (unknown problem).

Options

−k*c* When comparing revisions, expand keywords using style *c*. (See **co** for values of *c*.)

−p[*R*] Send merged version to standard output instead of overwriting *file*.

−r[*R*] Merge revision *R* or, if no *R* is given, merge the latest revision.

Examples

Suppose you need to add updates to an old revision (1.3) of **prog.c**, but the current file is already at revision 1.6. To incorporate the changes:

```
co -l prog.c
```
(edit latest revision by adding revision 1.3 updates, then:)
```
rcsmerge -p -r1.3 -r1.6 prog.c > prog.updated.c
```

Undo changes between revisions 3.5 and 3.2, and overwrite the working file:

```
rcsmerge -r3.5 -r3.2 chap08
```

Display identification information for RCS *files*, including the log message associated with each revision, the number of lines added or removed, date of last check in, etc. With no options, **rlog** displays all information. Use options to display specific items. **rlog** accepts the standard options **−V** and **−x**.

Options

−b   Prune the display; print only about the default branch.

−d*dates*   Display information for revisions whose check-in timestamp falls in the range of *dates* (a list separated by semicolons). Be sure to use quotes. Each date can be specified as:

      d1 < d2   Select revisions between date *d1* and *d2*, inclusive.

      d1 <   Select revisions made on or after *date1*.

      d1 >   Select revisions made on or before *date1*.

−h   Display the beginning of the normal **rlog** listing.

−l[*users*]   Display information only about locked revisions or, if *lockers* is specified, only about revisions locked by the list of *users*.

−L   Skip files that aren't locked.

−r[*list*]   Display information for revisions in the comma-separated *list* of revision numbers. If no *list* is given, the latest revision is used. Items can be specified as:

      R1   Select revision *R1*. If *R1* is a branch, select all revisions on it.

      R1.   If *R1* is a branch, select its latest revision.

      R1-R2   Select revisions *R1* through *R2*.

      -R1   Select revisions from beginning of branch through *R1*.

      R1-   Select revisions from *R1* through end of branch.

      RCS Version 5.6 has changed the range separator character to **:**, although **−** is still valid.

−R   Display only the name of the RCS file.

−s*states*   Display information for revisions whose state matches one from the comma-separated list of *states*.

−t   Same as **−h**, but also display the file's description.

−w[*users*] Display information for revisions checked in by anyone in the comma-separated list of *users*. If no *users* are supplied, assume the name of the invoking user.

rlog
←

Examples

Display a file's revision history:

```
rlog RCS/*,v | more
```

Display names of RCS files that are locked by user **daniel**.

```
rlog -R -L -ldaniel RCS/*
```

Display the "title" portion (no revision history) of a working file:

```
rlog -t calc.c
```

19

The make Utility

This section presents the following topics:

- Command-line syntax

- Description file lines

- Macros

- Special target names

- Sample default macros, suffixes, and rules

For a detailed description of **make**, refer to the Nutshell Handbook, *Managing Projects with make*.

The **make** program generates a sequence of commands for execution by the UNIX shell. It uses a table of file dependencies input by the programmer, and with this information, can perform updating tasks automatically for the user. It can keep track of the sequence of commands that create certain files, and the list of files that require other files to be current before they can operate efficiently. When a program is changed, **make** can create the proper files with a minimum of effort.

Command-line Syntax

> **make** [*options*] [*targets*] [*macro definitions*]

Options, targets, and macro definitions can appear in any order. Macros definitions are typed as:

```
name=string
```

Options

−e	Environment variables will override any macros defined in description files.
−f *file*	Use *file* as the description file; a filename of − denotes standard input. **−f** can be used more than once to concatenate multiple description files. Default file is **makefile** or **Makefile**.
−i	Ignore error codes from commands (same as **.IGNORE**).
−k	Abandon the current entry when it fails, but keep working with unrelated entries.
−n	Print commands but don't execute (used for testing). **−n** prints lines even if they begin with @ in the description file.
−p	Print macro definitions, suffixes, and target descriptions.
−q	Query; return 0 if file is up-to-date; nonzero otherwise.
−r	Do not use the default rules.
−s	Do not display command lines (same as **.SILENT**).
−t	Touch the target files, causing them to be updated.

Description File Lines

Instructions in the description file are interpreted as single lines. If an instruction must span more than one input line, use a backslash (\ ) at the end of the line so that the next line is considered as a continuation. The description file may contain any of the following types of lines:

blank lines	Blank lines are ignored.
comment lines	A pound sign (#) can be used at the beginning of a line or anywhere in the middle. **make** ignores everything after the #.
dependency lines	Depending on one or more targets, certain commands that follow will be executed. Possible formats include:

```
targets : prerequisites
targets :: prerequisites
```

In the first form, subsequent commands are executed if the prerequisites are met. The second form is a variant that lets you specify the same targets on more than one dependency line. In both forms, if no prerequisites are supplied, then subsequent commands are *always* executed (whenever any of the targets are specified). No tab should precede any *targets*. (At the end of a dependency line, you can specify a command, preceded by a semicolon; however, commands are typically entered on their own lines, preceded by a tab.)

suffix rules
These specify that files ending with the first suffix can be prerequisites for files ending with the second suffix (assuming the root filenames are the same). Either of these formats can be used:

```
.suffix.suffix:
.suffix:
```

The second form means that the root filename depends on the filename with the corresponding suffix.

commands
Commands are grouped below the dependency line and are typed on lines that begin with a tab. If a command is preceded by a hyphen (–), **make** ignores any error returned. If a command is preceded by an at-sign (@), the command line won't echo on the display (unless **make** is called with **–n**).

macro definitions
These have the following form:

```
name = string
```

Blank space is optional around the =.

include statements
Similar to the C include directive, these have the form:

```
include file
```

Macros

This subsection summarizes internal macros, modifiers, string substitution, and special macros.

Internal Macros

$?   The list of prerequisites that have been changed more recently than the current target. Can be used only in normal description file entries—not suffix rules.

$@   The name of the current target, except in description file entries for making libraries, where it becomes the library name. Can be used both in normal description file entries and in suffix rules.

$$@   The name of the current target. Can be used only to the right of the colon in dependency lines.

$<   The name of the current prerequisite that has been modified more recently than the current target. Can be used only in suffix rules and in the **.DEFAULT:** entry.

$*   The name—without the suffix—of the current prerequisite that has been modified more recently than the current target. Can be used only in suffix rules.

$%   The name of the corresponding **.o** file when the current target is a library module. Can be used both in normal description file entries and in suffix rules.

Macro Modifiers

Macro modifiers are not available in all variants of **make**.

D   The directory portion of any internal macro name except **$?**. Valid uses are:

```
$(*D)    $$(@D)
$(<D)    ${%D)
$(@D)
```

F   The file portion of any internal macro name except **$?**. Valid uses are:

```
$(*F)    $$(@F)
$(<F)    ${%F}
$(@F)
```

Macro String Substitution

String substitution is not available in all variants of **make**.

${*macro:s1=s2}*

Evaluates to the current definition of **${*macro}***, after substituting the string *s1* for every occurrence of *s2* that occurs either immediately before a blank or tab, or at the end of the macro definition.

Macros with Special Handling

SHELL   Sets the shell that interprets commands. If this macro isn't defined in the description file, the value depends on your system. Some UNIX implementations use the shell from the user's environment (as with other macros). Other implementations (including SVR4) set the default SHELL to **/bin/sh**.

VPATH   (Not available in all variants of **make**.) Specifies a list of directories to search for prerequisites when they aren't found in the current directory.

Special Target Names

.DEFAULT: Commands associated with this target are executed if **make** can't find any description file entries or suffix rules with which to build a requested target.

.IGNORE: Ignore error codes. Same as the **–i** option.

.PRECIOUS: Files you specify for this target are not removed when you send a signal (such as interrupt) that aborts **make**, or when a command line in your description file returns an error.

.SILENT: Execute commands but do not echo them. Same as the **–s** option.

.SUFFIXES: Suffixes associated with this target are meaningful in suffixes rules. If no suffixes are listed, the existing list of suffix rules are effectively "turned off."

Sample Default Macros, Suffixes, and Rules

```
EDITOR = /usr/bin/vi
TERM = tvi950ns
SHELL = /bin/sh
PATH = .:/bin:/usr/bin:/usr/fred:/usr/local
LOGNAME = fred
HOME = /usr/fred
GFLAGS =
GET = get
ASFLAGS =
AS = as
FFLAGS =
FC = f77
CFLAGS = -O
CC = cc
LDFLAGS =
LD = ld
LFLAGS =
LEX = lex
YFLAGS =
YACC = yacc
MAKE = make
$ = $
MAKEFLAGS = b

.h~.h:
      $(GET) $(GFLAGS) -p $< > $*.h

.s~.a:
      $(GET) $(GFLAGS) -p $< > $*.s
      $(AS) $(ASFLAGS) -o $*.o $*.s
      ar rv $@ $*.o
      -rm -f $*.[so]

.r~.a:
      $(GET) $(GFLAGS) -p $< > $*.r
      $(FC) -c $(FFLAGS) $*.r
      ar rv $@ $*.o
      rm -f $*.[ro]
```

```
.e~.a:
     $(GET) $(GFLAGS) -p $< > $*.e
     $(FC) -c $(FFLAGS) $*.e
     ar rv $@ $*.o
     rm -f $*.[eo]

.f~.a:
     $(GET) $(GFLAGS) -p $< > $*.f
     $(FC) -c $(FFLAGS) $*.f
     ar rv $@ $*.o
     rm -f $*.[fo]

.r.a:
     $(FC) -c $(FFLAGS) $<
     ar rv $@ $*.o
     rm -f $*.o

.e.a:
     $(FC) -c $(FFLAGS) $<
     ar rv $@ $*.o
     rm -f $*.o

.f.a:
     $(FC) -c $(FFLAGS) $<
     ar rv $@ $*.o
     rm -f $*.o

.c~.a:
     $(GET) $(GFLAGS) -p $< > $*.c
     $(CC) -c $(CFLAGS) $*.c
     ar rv $@ $*.o
     rm -f $*.[co]

.c.a:
     $(CC) -c $(CFLAGS) $<
     ar rv $@ $*.o
     rm -f $*.o

.l.c:
     $(LEX) $<
     mv lex.yy.c $@

.y~.c:
     $(GET) $(GFLAGS) -p $< > $*.y
     $(YACC) $(YFLAGS) $*.y
     mv y.tab.c $*.c
     -rm -f $*.y

.y.c:
     $(YACC) $(YFLAGS) $<
     mv y.tab.c $@

.l~.o:
     $(GET) $(GFLAGS) -p $< > $*.l
     $(LEX) $(LFLAGS) $*.l
     $(CC) $(CFLAGS) -c lex.yy.c
     rm -f lex.yy.c $*.l
     mv lex.yy.o $*.o
```

```
.l.o:
     $(LEX) $(LFLAGS) $<
     $(CC) $(CFLAGS) -c lex.yy.c
     rm lex.yy.c
     mv lex.yy.o $@
.y~.o:
     $(GET) $(GFLAGS) -p $< > $*.y
     $(YACC) $(YFLAGS) $*.y
     $(CC) $(CFLAGS) -c y.tab.c
     rm -f y.tab.c $*.y
     mv y.tab.o $*.o
.y.o:
     $(YACC) $(YFLAGS) $<
     $(CC) $(CFLAGS) -c y.tab.c
     rm y.tab.c
     mv y.tab.o $@
.s~.o:
     $(GET) $(GFLAGS) -p $< > $*.s
     $(AS) $(ASFLAGS) -o $*.o $*.s
     -rm -f $*.s
.s.o:
     $(AS) $(ASFLAGS) -o $@ $<
.r~.o:
     $(GET) $(GFLAGS) -p $< > $*.r
     $(FC) $(FFLAGS) -c $*.r
     -rm -f $*.r
.e~.e:
     $(GET) $(GFLAGS) -p $< > $*.e
.e~.o:
     $(GET) $(GFLAGS) -p $< > $*.e
     $(FC) $(FFLAGS) -c $*.e
     -rm -f $*.e
.f~.f:
     $(GET) $(GFLAGS) -p $< > $*.f
.f~.o:
     $(GET) $(GFLAGS) -p $< > $*.f
     $(FC) $(FFLAGS) -c $*.f
     -rm -f $*.f
.r.o:
     $(FC) $(FFLAGS) -c $<
.e.o:
     $(FC) $(FFLAGS) -c $<
.f.o:
     $(FC) $(FFLAGS) -c $<
.c~.c:
     $(GET) $(GFLAGS) -p $< > $*.c
.c~.o:
     $(GET) $(GFLAGS) -p $< > $*.c
     $(CC) $(CFLAGS) -c $*.c
     -rm -f $*.c
```

```
.c.o:
     $(CC) $(CFLAGS) -c $<
.sh~:
     $(GET) $(GFLAGS) -p $< > $*.sh
     cp $*.sh $*
     -rm -f $*.sh

.sh:
     cp $< $@
.r~:
     $(GET) $(GFLAGS) -p $< > $*.r
     $(FC) -n $(FFLAGS) $*.r -o $*
     -rm -f $*.r

.r:
     $(FC) $(FFLAGS) $(LDFLAGS) $< -o $@
.e~:
     $(GET) $(GFLAGS) -p $< > $*.e
     $(FC) -n $(FFLAGS) $*.e -o $*
     -rm -f $*.e

.e:
     $(FC) $(FFLAGS) $(LDFLAGS) $< -o $@
.f~:
     $(GET) $(GFLAGS) -p $< > $*.f
     $(FC) -n $(FFLAGS) $*.f -o $*
     -rm -f $*.f

.f:
     $(FC) $(FFLAGS) $(LDFLAGS) $< -o $@
.c~:
     $(GET) $(GFLAGS) -p $< > $*.c
     $(CC) -n $(CFLAGS) $*.c -o $*
     -rm -f $*.c

.c:
     $(CC) $(CFLAGS) $(LDFLAGS) $< -o $@
.SUFFIXES:
     .o  .c  .c~  .f  .f~  .e  .e~  .r  .r~
     .y  .y~  .l  .l~  .s  .s~  .sh  .sh~  .h  .h~
```

Program Debugging

This section presents the debugging utilities for the UNIX environment:

- Sdb (available in SVR4 but not Solaris 2.0)

- Dbx (Solaris 2.0 only)

These debuggers take an executable object file and its corefile—the core image file produced when *objfile* is executed. The debuggers then provide a controlled environment for the execution of the program.

If *objfile* and *corefile* are not specified, **a.out** is taken as the default object file and **core** as the default core image file.

Each debugging utility is listed among the UNIX commands in Section 2 of this guide.

The Sdb Debugger

Sdb, the symbolic debugger, is used for checking assembly programs, executable C and FORTRAN programs, and core files resulting from aborted programs. It has the following command-line syntax:

sdb [*options*] [*objfile* [*corefile* [*dir*]]]

A – in place of *corefile* will force sdb to ignore any core image file.

Options

–e	Ignore symbolic data; treat addresses as file offsets.
–s *n*	Don't stop processes that receive signal number *n*. See the **signal** system call for values of *n*. **–s** may be used more than once.
–V	Print version information (and exit if no *objfile* is given).
–w	Make *objfile* and *corefile* writable.
–W	Suppress warning messages about older files.

Command Specifiers

In the "Commands" section below, commands use the specifiers *m*, *l*, and *n*. *m* is the display format of an address. (Addresses are specified by a variable or a line number.) *l* is the address length. *n* stands for the line number.

Values for m

a	Characters starting at variable's address.
c	Character.
d	Decimal.
f	32-bit floating.
g	64-bit double precision floating.
i	Disassemble machine-language instructions; print address using numbers and symbols.
I	Same as **i**, but print address using numbers only.
o	Octal.
p	Pointer to procedure.
s	Print character(s) at address pointed to by (string pointer) variable.
u	Unsigned decimal.
x	Hexadecimal.

Values for l

Length specifiers are meaningful only with *m* values of **c**, **d**, **o**, **u**, or **x**.

b	One byte.
h	Two bytes (half word).
l	Four bytes (long word).

Commands

Refer to the previous specifiers when reviewing the sdb commands, which are grouped below:

Formatted Printing

t	Print a stack trace.
T	Print the top line of the stack trace.
`variable/clm`	Print variable according to length l and format m. Number c specifies how much memory (in units of l) to display.
`n?lm` `variable:?lm`	Print from **a.out** and procedure *variable* according to length l and format m. Default lm is **i**.

`variable=lm`
`n=lm`
`number=lm`
	Print the address of *variable* or line number n, in the format specified by l and m. Use the last form to convert *number* to the format specified by l and m. Default lm is **lx**.

`variable!value`	Assign *value* to *variable*.
x	Display the machine registers and the machine instructions.
X	Display the machine instructions.

Examining the Source

e	Print name of current file.
e`proc`	Set current file to file containing procedure *proc*.
e`file`	Set current file to *file*.
e`dir/`	Append directory *dir* to directory list.
p	Print current line.
w	Print ten lines surrounding the current line.
z	Print ten lines (starting at current); reset current line to last line.
`/regexp/`	Search ahead for regular expression *regexp*.
`?regexp?`	Search back for regular expression *regexp*.
n	Set current line to n and print it.
`count+`	Advance *count* lines; print new current line.
`count-`	Go back *count* lines; print new current line.

Executing the Source

n **a**	Set a breakpoint at line number n and inform the user.
[*n*] **b** `commands`	Set breakpoint at line number n and optionally execute sdb *commands* (separated by ;) at breakpoint.

[*n*] **c** *count*	Continue after a breakpoint or, if *count* is given, stop after *count* breakpoints. If *n* is specified, set a temporary breakpoint at line number *n*.
[*n*] **C** *count*	Same as **c**, but reactivate any signal that stopped program.
n **g** *count*	Continue at line number *n* after a breakpoint. If *count* is given, ignore *count* breakpoints.
[*count*] **r** *args*	Run the program with the specified arguments. Ignore *count* breakpoints.
[*count*] **r**	Rerun the program with the previously specified arguments. Ignore *count* breakpoints.
[*count*] **R**	Run the program with the no arguments. Ignore *count* breakpoints.
[*level*] [**v**]	This command is used when single-stepping via **s**, **S**, or **m**. **v** turns off verbose mode; omit **v** to turn on verbose mode. If *level* is omitted, print only source file or function name when either changes; otherwise, set *level* to 1 (print C source lines before execution) or 2 or higher (print C source lines and assembler statements).
proc(*a1,a2,...*)	Execute procedure *proc* with arguments *a1*, *a2*, etc. Arguments can be constants, local variable names, or register names. Append **/m** in order to print the returned value in format *m* (default is **d**).

Breakpoint and Program Control

B	Print active breakpoints.
[*n*] **d**	Delete breakpoint at line number *n*.
D	Remove all breakpoints.
i *count*	Single-step *count* machine-language instructions.
I *count*	Same as **i**, but reactivate any signal that stopped program.
k	Kill the program you're debugging.
l	Print the previous line executed.
M	Print the address maps.
var$**m** *count* *addr*:**m** *count*	Single-step *count* lines until the specified variable or address is modified. Omitting *count* specifies an infinite count.
q	Exit sdb.
s [*count*]	Single-step *count* lines.
S [*count*]	Same as **s**, but skip called functions.

Miscellaneous Commands

`#text`	Supply a text comment ignored by sdb.
`!cmd`	Execute *cmd* with **sh**.
newline	Display the next line or memory location, or disassemble the next instruction.
EOF	Scroll the display ten lines.
`< file`	Execute commands contained in *file*.
`string`	Print a quoted *string*. C escape characters are recognized.
v	Print the sdb version number.

The Dbx Debugger

Dbx can be used to debug programs written in C, C++, FORTRAN, and Pascal. Dbx commands can be stored in a start-up **.dbxinit** file that resides in the current directory or in the user's home directory. These commands are executed just before reading the symbol table. The command-line syntax for dbx is as follows:

> **dbx** [*options*] [*objfile* [*corefile*]]

Options

–c *cmd*	Run dbx *cmd* after initialization.
–C	Collect profile data for debugged program.
–e	Echo input commands on standard output.
–i	Act as if standard input is a terminal.
–I *dir*	Add *dir* to the directory search path. The dbx command **use** resets the search path.
–kbd	Debug a program that puts the keyboard in up-down translation mode.
–P *file_des*	Pipe output to the **debugger** command via file descriptor *file_des*. **debugger** passes this option automatically.
–q	Suppress messages during loading (useful during auto-traceback).
–r	Execute *objfile* right away, then wait for user response from the keyboard.
–s *file*	Read initialization commands from start-up *file*.
–sr *tmp*	Like **–s**, but then delete start-up file (*tmp*).
– *pid*	Debug a currently running program whose process ID is *pid* (used mainly for auto-traceback).

Alphabetical Summary of Commands

Within dbx, the most useful commands are **run**, **where**, **print**, and **stop**. Use **help** to summarize the available commands. In the listing below, the term *func* is used to represent either a procedure or a function.

alias	**alias** *name command* **alias** *name*(*parameters*) *command string* Define *name* to be an alias for *command*. For example: `alias s(n) "stop at n"` means that the command **s(20)** expands to **stop at 20**. See also **unalias**.
assign	**assign** *var = expr* Assign the value of *expr* to variable *var*.
call	**call** *func* (*parameters*) Execute object code associated with *func*.
catch	**catch** [*signals*] Start trapping signals before they are sent to the program. Specify one or more *signals* by number or by name. Omit signal to display the currently caught signal. See also **ignore**.
cd	**cd** [*directory*] Change the working directory for dbx.
clear	**clear** [*n*] Clear breakpoints at source line *n* or at current stopping point.
cont	**cont** [at *n*] [**sig** *signal*] Continue execution from the point at which it was stopped. Resume from source line *n* or, if a *signal* name or number is specified, resume process as if it had received the signal.
CTRL –C	**CTRL –C** Interrupt program being debugged; return to dbx.
dbxenv	**dbxenv** [*args*] Display dbx attributes, or change attribute *args*. Type **help** for details.
debug	**debug** [*objfile* [*corefile*]] Restart dbx on the specified files or, with no arguments, print the current program name.

delete *n*   **delete**

Remove traces, stops, and whens corresponding to each command
number *n*, given by **status**. If *n* is **all**, remove all.

detach   **detach**

Separate the current program (or process) from dbx.

display [*expressions*]   **display**

Show the value of one or more *expressions* each time execution stops.
With no arguments, list expressions currently being shown. See also
undisplay.

down [*n*]   **down**

Move current function down *n* levels on stack. Default is 1. See also
up.

dump [*func*] [> *file*]   **dump**

Print names and values of variables in *func* (or in current procedure).
Optionally store output in *file*. If *func* is **.**, dump all active variables.

edit [*file*]   **edit**
edit *func*

Invoke editor either on *file*, on current source file (if no *file* is given),
or on file containing *func*. The EDITOR environment variable determines which editor is used.

file [*file*]   **file**

Change name of current source file to *file* or, if no *file* is given, print
name of current source file.

func [*func*]   **func**

Change current function to *func* or, if no *func* is given, print current
function.

help [*command*]   **help**

Print a synopsis of all dbx commands or of the given *command*.

history [*n*]   **history**

List the last *n* dbx commands issued (default is 15). Same as C shell's
history command. History substitutions are supported for reissuing
commands.

Program Debugging

ignore	**ignore** [*signals*]
	Stop trapping signals before they are sent to the program. Specify one or more *signals* by number or by name. Omit signal to display the currently ignored signal. See also **catch**.
kill	**kill**
	Stop execution or debugging of current program.
language	**language** [*name*]
	Set the programming language to *name*, which can be one of **c**, **c++**, **fortran**, or **pascal**. With no *name*, show the language currently in use.
list	**list** [*n1* [,*n2*]] **list** *func*
	List the source text between lines *n1* and *n2*, or on lines surrounding the first statement of *func*. With no arguments, list the next ten lines.
make	**make**
	Run **make** on the program being debugged.
modules	**modules**
	List object files for which debugging data is available.
next	**next** [*n*]
	Execute next *n* source lines. Default is 1. **next** doesn't go into functions.
nexti	**nexti**
	Same as **next**, but do a single instruction instead of a source line.
print	**print** *expressions*
	Print the values of one or more comma-separated *expressions*.
pwd	**pwd**
	Print the working directory for dbx.
quit	**quit**
	Exit dbx.

replay [*−n*]   **replay**

A save-restore combination. The default action (*n* is 1) works like an undo.

---

rerun [*arguments*]   **rerun**

Without *arguments*, redo the previous **run** command (and its arguments). Otherwise, this command is the same as **run**.

---

restore [*file*]   **restore**

Redo dbx commands stored via **save** in *file* or in special buffer.

---

return [*procedure*]   **return**

Continue until a return to *procedure* (or current procedure) is called.

---

run [*arguments*]   **run**

Begin executing the object file, passing optional command-line *arguments*. The arguments can include input or output redirection to a named file.

---

save [*−n*] [*file*]   **save**

Store dbx commands entered since last **run**, **rerun**, or **debug**. Or save all but the last *n*. Save either to *file* or to a buffer accessed by **restore**.

---

set *var* [= *expr*]   **set**

Define value *expr* for variable *var*. See also **unset**. Built-in variables include:

$frame	If set to an address, use the stack frame it points to. (Useful for kernel debugging.)
$hex*item*	When set, print hexadecimal values for specified *item*. *item* can be **chars**, **ints**, **offsets**, or **strings**.
$listwindow	Default number of lines to show using **list** command (default is 10).
$mapaddrs	When set, start mapping addresses; when unset, stop. (Useful for kernel debugging.)
$unsafecall	When set, turn off type checking of parameters in **call** statements. Use with care.
$unsafeassign	When set, turn off type checking in **assign** statements. Use with care.

setenv	**setenv** *VAR string*
	Set environment variable *VAR* to *string*.
sh	**sh** *command*
	Pass *command* to the shell for execution.
source	**source** *file*
	Read commands for dbx from *file*. E.g., *file* might be created by a previous **status** command.
status	**status** [> *file*]
	Show active **trace**, **stop**, and **when** commands; store output in *file*.
step	**step** [*n*]
	Execute *n* source lines. Default is 1. **step** goes into functions. See also **next**.
step	**step up**
	Take program up and out from current function; resume with the line after the function call.
stepi	**stepi**
	Same as **step**, but do a single instruction instead of a source line.
stop	**stop** *restriction* [**if** *cond*]
	Stop execution if specified *restriction* is true. See **trace** about *cond*.

Restriction

at *n*	Source line *n* is reached.
if *cond*	Condition *cond* is true.
in *func*	Procedure or function *func* is called.
inclass *class*	Each method of C++ class is called.
infunction *func*	Top-level function in a C++ module is called.
inmethod *member*	Named *member* of any C++ class is called.
var	Variable *var* has changed.

stopi	**stopi** *restriction* [**if** *cond*]
	Similar to **stop**, but set a stop using machine instruction addresses. See **trace** about *cond*.

Restriction	**stopi**

    at *address*   Stop execution at *address*

    var   Stop execution if value of variable *var* changes.

trace [*restriction*] [**if** *cond*]   **trace**

Report tracing information as program is executed, according to the *restriction*. With no arguments, all source lines are printed before being executed. *cond* is a Boolean expression; if it evaluates to false, then the tracing information is not printed.

Restriction

in *func*	Report while executing *func*.
inclass *class*	Print name of function that called any member of *class*.
infunction *func*	Print name of function that called any top-level C++ *func*.
inmethod *member*	Print name of function that called *member* of any class.
expr **at** *n*	Print value of *expr* each time line *n* is reached.
func	Print name of function that called *func*.
n	Show source line *n* before executing it.
var	Print value of *var* each time it changes.
var [**in** *func*]	Same as above, but print information only while executing from within the specified procedure or function.

tracei [*restriction*] [**if** *cond*]   **tracei**

Similar to **trace**, but trace using machine instruction addresses.

Restriction

addr	Start tracing at address *addr*.
var [**at** *addr*]	Start tracing variable *var* at address *addr*.

unalias *name*   **unalias**

Remove the alias *name*. See also **alias**.

undisplay [*expressions*]   **undisplay**

Stop displaying *expressions* (see **display**). *expression* can be a number, in which case it refers to the item-number in a **display** list.

unset *var*   **unset**

Remove the debugger variable *var*. See also **set**.

up	**up** [*n*]
	Move current function up *n* levels on stack. Default is 1. See also **down**.
use	**use** [*directories*]
	Define one or more *directories* to search when looking for source files. With no argument, print the current search directories.
whatis	**whatis** [**−r**] *name*
	Print the declaration of the identifier, class, or type *name*. **−r** recursively prints the declarations of inherited classes.
when	**when** *restriction commands*
	Execute one or more dbx *commands* (separated by semi-colons) when *restriction* is true. See **stop** for list of restrictions.
where	**where** [*n*]
	List all active functions on the stack, or only the top *n*.
whereis	**whereis** *identifier*
	Print the fully-qualified name of symbols that match *identifier*.
which	**which** *identifier*
	Print the fully-qualified name of *identifier*.
search	*search*
	Specify a *search* pattern of the form */regexp/* (to search forward for a regular expression) or *?regexp?* (to search backward). The matched line becomes the current line.
addr1/	*addr1/*
	Print contents of memory starting at the address *addr1*. Stop printing when a second address is reached or when *n* items have been printed, as shown by the syntax lines below:
	addr1, addr2/[*mode*] *addr1/*[*n*] [*mode*]
	mode specifies the output format. Default is **X**. Addresses may be **.** (next address), **&***addr* (symbolic address), and **$r***n* (register *n*). Addresses may include the symbols +, −, and * (indirection).

Mode		_addr1/_
b	Print a byte in octal.	
c	Print a byte as a character.	
d	Print a short word in decimal.	
D	Print a long word in decimal.	
f	Print a single-precision real number.	
F	Print a double-precision real number.	
i	Print a machine instruction.	
o	Print a short word in octal.	
O	Print a long word in octal.	
s	Print a string as characters terminated by a null byte.	
x	Print a short word in hexadecimal.	
X	Print a long word in hexadecimal.	

address = [_mode_]	_address_
Display the value of _address._	

Part V

Loose Ends

Part V contains a table of ASCII characters and an index to the commands presented in this guide.

ASCII Character Set

This section presents the set of ASCII characters, along with their equivalent values in decimal, octal, and hexadecimal. The first table shows nonprinting characters. This table would be useful when you need to represent nonprinting characters in some printed form, such as octal. For example, the **echo** and **tr** commands let you specify characters using octal values of the form \ *nnn*. Also, the **od** command can be used to display nonprinting characters in a variety of forms.

The second table shows printing characters. This table would be useful when using the commands mentioned above, but also when specifying a range of characters in a pattern-matching construct.

Nonprinting Characters

Decimal	Octal	Hex	Character	Remark
0	000	00	CTRL-@	NUL (Null prompt)
1	001	01	CTRL-A	SOH (Start of heading)
2	002	02	CTRL-B	STX (Start of text)
3	003	03	CTRL-C	ETX (End of text)
4	004	04	CTRL-D	EOT (End of transmission)
5	005	05	CTRL-E	ENQ (Enquiry)
6	006	06	CTRL-F	ACK (Acknowledge)
7	007	07	CTRL-G	BEL (Bell)
8	010	08	CTRL-H	BS (Backspace)
9	011	09	CTRL-I	HT (Horizontal tab)
10	012	0A	CTRL-J	LF (Linefeed)
11	013	0B	CTRL-K	VT (Vertical tab)
12	014	0C	CTRL-L	NP (New page) or FF (Formfeed)
13	015	0D	CTRL-M	CR (Carriage return)
14	016	0E	CTRL-N	SO (Shift out)
15	017	0F	CTRL-O	SI (Shift in)
16	020	10	CTRL-P	DLE (Data link escape)
17	021	11	CTRL-Q	DC1 (X-ON)
18	022	12	CTRL-R	DC2
19	023	13	CTRL-S	DC3 (X-OFF)
20	024	14	CTRL-T	DC4
21	025	15	CTRL-U	NAK (No acknowledge)
22	026	16	CTRL-V	SYN (Synchronous idle)
23	027	17	CTRL-W	ETB (End transmission blocks)
24	030	18	CTRL-X	CAN (Cancel)
25	031	19	CTRL-Y	EM (End of medium)
26	032	1A	CTRL-Z	SUB (Substitute)
27	033	1B	CTRL-[	ESC (Escape)
28	034	1C	CTRL-	FS (File separator)
29	035	1D	CTRL-]	GS (Group separator)
30	036	1E	CTRL-^	RS (Record separator)
31	037	1F	CTRL-_	US (Unit separator)
127	177	7F		DEL (Delete or rubout)

Printing Characters

Decimal	Octal	Hex	Character	Remark
32	040	20		Space
33	041	21	!	Exclamation Point
34	042	22	"	Double quote
35	043	23	#	Sharp Sign
36	044	24	$	Dollar Sign
37	045	25	%	Percent Sign
38	046	26	&	Ampersand
39	047	27	'	Apostrophe
40	050	28	(	Left Parenthesis
41	051	29	)	Right Parenthesis
42	052	2A	*	Asterisk
43	053	2B	+	Plus Sign
44	054	2C	,	Comma
45	055	2D	–	Hyphen
46	056	2E	.	Period
47	057	2F	/	Slash (Virgule)
48	060	30	0	
49	061	31	1	
50	062	32	2	
51	063	33	3	
52	064	34	4	
53	065	35	5	
54	066	36	6	
55	067	37	7	
56	070	38	8	
57	071	39	9	
58	072	3A	:	Colon
59	073	3B	;	Semicolon
60	074	3C	<	Left Angle Bracket
61	075	3D	=	Equal Sign
62	076	3E	>	Right Angle Bracket
63	077	3F	?	Question Mark
64	100	40	@	"At" Sign
65	101	41	A	
66	102	42	B	
67	103	43	C	
68	104	44	D	
69	105	45	E	
70	106	46	F	
71	107	47	G	
72	110	48	H	
73	111	49	I	
74	112	4A	J	

ASCII
Set

Decimal	Octal	Hex	Character	Remark
75	113	4B	K	
76	114	4C	L	
77	115	4D	M	
78	116	4E	N	
79	117	4F	O	
80	120	50	P	
81	121	51	Q	
82	122	52	R	
83	123	53	S	
84	124	54	T	
85	125	55	U	
86	126	56	V	
87	127	57	W	
88	130	58	X	
89	131	59	Y	
90	132	5A	Z	
91	133	5B	[	Left Square Bracket
92	134	5C	\	Backslash
93	135	5D	]	Right Square Bracket
94	136	5E	^	Caret
95	137	5F	_	Underscore
96	140	60	`	Back Quote
97	141	61	a	
98	142	62	b	
99	143	63	c	
100	144	64	d	
101	145	65	e	
102	146	66	f	
103	147	67	g	
104	150	68	h	
105	151	69	i	
106	152	6A	j	
107	153	6B	k	
108	154	6C	l	
109	155	6D	m	
110	156	6E	n	
111	157	6F	o	
112	160	70	p	
113	161	71	q	
114	162	72	r	
115	163	73	s	
116	164	74	t	
117	165	75	u	

Printing Characters (continued)

Decimal	Octal	Hex	Character	Remark
118	166	76	v	
119	167	77	w	
120	170	78	x	
121	171	79	y	
122	172	7A	z	
123	173	7B	{	Left Curly Brace
124	174	7C	|	Vertical Bar
125	175	7D	}	Right Curly Brace
126	176	7E	~	Tilde

22

Command Index

This section points you to the UNIX commands, shell built-in commands, RCS and SCCS commands, etc. that are presented in this quick reference. The page references are to the first page on which any significant discussion occurs.

Symbols

#!, 4-13, 5-16
@, 5-28
[[ ]], 4-13

A

admin, 17-7
alias, 4-14, 5-16
apropos, 2-2
ar, 2-2
as, 2-3
at, 2-3
atq, 2-4
atrm, 2-5
autoload, 4-14
awk, 2-5, 11-2

B

banner, 2-5
basename, 2-5
batch, 2-6
bc, 2-6
bdiff, 2-9
bfs, 2-9
bg, 4-15, 5-17
break, 4-15, 5-17
breaksw, 5-17

C

cal, 2-10
calendar, 2-10
cancel, 2-10
case, 4-15, 5-17
cat, 2-10
cb, 2-11
cc, 2-11
cd, 4-16, 5-17
cdc, 17-8
cflow, 2-14
chdir, 5-17
chgrp, 2-14
chkey, 2-15
chmod, 2-15

chown, 2-16
ci, 18-7
clear, 2-17
cmp, 2-17
co, 18-9
cof2elf, 2-17
col, 2-17
comb, 17-8
comm, 2-18
compress, 2-18
continue, 4-16, 5-17
cp, 2-19
cpio, 2-19
crontab, 2-21
crypt, 2-22
cscope, 2-22
csh, 5-29
csplit, 2-23
ctags, 2-24
ctrace, 2-25
cu, 2-25
cut, 2-27
cxref, 2-28

D

date, 2-28
dbx, 2-30, 20-5
dc, 2-31
dd, 2-31
default, 5-17
delta, 17-9
deroff, 2-33
df, 2-33
diff, 2-34
diff3, 2-35
diffmk, 2-35
dircmp, 2-36
dirname, 2-36
dirs, 5-18
dis, 2-36
do, 4-16
done, 4-16
download, 2-37
dpost, 2-37
du, 2-38

Command Index

Books That Help People Get More Out of Computers

Please send me the following:

❑ A free catalog of titles.

❑ A list of Bookstores in my area that carry your books (U.S. and Canada only).

❑ A list of book distributors outside the U.S. and Canada.

❑ Information about consulting services for documentation or programming.

❑ Information about bundling books with my product.

❑ On-line descriptions of your books.

Name _____

Address _____

_____

City _____

State, ZIP _____

Country _____

Phone _____

Email Address _____
(Internet or Uunet)

Books That Help People Get More Out of Computers

Please send me the following:

❑ A free catalog of titles.

❑ A list of Bookstores in my area that carry your books (U.S. and Canada only).

❑ A list of book distributors outside the U.S. and Canada.

❑ Information about consulting services for documentation or programming.

❑ Information about bundling books with my product.

❑ On-line descriptions of your books.

Name _____

Address _____

_____

City _____

State, ZIP _____

Country _____

Phone _____

Email Address _____
(Internet or Uunet)

NAME_____

COMPANY_____

ADDRESS_____

CITY _____ STATE _____ ZIP _____

BUSINESS REPLY MAIL

FIRST CLASS MAIL PERMIT NO. 80 SEBASTOPOL, CA

POSTAGE WILL BE PAID BY ADDRESSEE

O'REILLY & ASSOCIATES, INC.

103 Morris Street Suite A
Sebastopol CA 95472-9902

Iɪɪlɪɪɪlɪlɪɪlɪɪllɪɪɪlɪɪlɪllɪlɪɪlɪlɪɪllɪɪɪɪɪlɪlɪɪllɪl

NAME_____

COMPANY_____

ADDRESS_____

CITY _____ STATE _____ ZIP _____

BUSINESS REPLY MAIL

FIRST CLASS MAIL PERMIT NO. 80 SEBASTOPOL, CA

POSTAGE WILL BE PAID BY ADDRESSEE

O'REILLY & ASSOCIATES, INC.

103 Morris Street Suite A
Sebastopol CA 95472-9902

Iɪɪlɪɪɪlɪlɪɪlɪɪllɪɪɪlɪɪlɪllɪlɪɪlɪlɪɪllɪɪɪɪɪlɪlɪɪllɪl

OTHER TITLES

System Performance Tuning

By Mike Loukides

System Performance Tuning answers one of the most fundamental questions you can ask about your computer: "How can I get it to do more work without buying more hardware?" Anyone who has ever used a computer has wished that the system was faster, particularly at times when it was under heavy load.

If your system gets sluggish when you start a big job, if it feels as if you spend hours waiting for remote file access to complete, if your system stops dead when several users are active at the same time, you need to read this book. Some performance problems do require you to buy a bigger or faster computer, but many can be solved simply by making better use of the resources you already have.

336 pages, ISBN 0-937175-60-9

Essential System Administration

By Æleen Frisch

Like any other multi-user system, UNIX requires some care and feeding. *Essential System Administration* tells you how. This book strips away the myth and confusion surrounding this important topic and provides a compact, manageable introduction to the tasks faced by anyone responsible for a UNIX system.

If you use a stand-alone UNIX system, whether it's a PC or a workstation, you know how much you need this book: on these systems the fine line between a user and an administrator has vanished. Either you're both or you're in trouble. If you routinely provide administrative support for a larger shared system or a network of workstations, you will find this book indispensable. Even if you aren't directly responsible for system administration, you will find that understanding basic administrative functions greatly increases your ability to use UNIX effectively.

466 pages
ISBN 0-937175-80-3

Practical UNIX Security

By Simson Garfinkel & Gene Spafford

If you are a UNIX system administrator or user who needs to deal with security, you need this book.

Practical UNIX Security describes the issues, approaches, and methods for implementing security measures—spelling out what the varying approaches cost and require in the way of equipment. After presenting UNIX security basics and network security, this guide goes on to suggest how to keep intruders out, how to tell if they've gotten in, how to clean up after them, and even how to prosecute them. Filled with practical scripts, tricks and warnings, *Practical UNIX Security* tells you what you need to know to make your UNIX system as secure as it can be.

"Worried about who's in your Unix system? Losing sleep because someone might be messing with your computer? Having headaches from obscure computer manuals? Then *Practical Unix Security* is for you. This handy book tells you where the holes are and how to cork'em up.

"Moreover, you'll learn about how Unix security really works. Spafford and Garfinkel show you how to tighten up your Unix system without pain. No secrets here—just solid computing advice.

"Buy this book and save on aspirin."—Cliff Stoll
512 pages, ISBN 0-937175-72-2

Computer Security Basics

By Deborah Russell & G.T. Gangemi Sr.

There's a lot more consciousness of security today, but not a lot of understanding of what it means and how far it should go. This handbook describes complicated concepts like trusted systems, encryption and mandatory access control in simple terms.

For example, most U.S. government equipment acquisitions now require "Orange Book" (Trusted Computer System Evaluation Criteria) certification. A lot of people have a vague feeling that they ought to know about the Orange Book, but few make the effort to track it down and read it. *Computer Security Basics* contains a more readable introduction to the Orange Book—why it exists, what it contains, and what the different security levels are all about—than any other book or government publication.
464 pages, ISBN 0-937175-71-4

COMPUTER
SECURITY
BASICS

Deborah Russell and G. T. Gangemi Sr.
O'Reilly & Associates, Inc.

Managing UUCP and Usenet

10th Edition
By Tim O'Reilly & Grace Todino

For all its widespread use, UUCP is one of the most difficult UNIX utilities to master. Poor documentation, cryptic messages, and differences between various implementations make setting up UUCP links a nightmare for many a system administrator.

This handbook is meant for system administrators who want to install and manage the UUCP and Usenet software. It covers HoneyDanBer UUCP as well as standard Version 2 UUCP, with special notes on Xenix. As one reader noted over the Net, "Don't even TRY to install UUCP without it!"

The Tenth Edition of this classic work has been revised and expanded to include descriptions of:

- How to use NNTP (Network News Transfer Protocol) to transfer Usenet news over TCP/IP and other high-speed networks
- How to get DOS versions of UUCP
- How to set up DOS-based laptop computers as travelling UUCP nodes
- How the UUCP 'g' protocol works

368 pages, ISBN 0-937175-93-5

termcap & terminfo

3rd Edition
By John Strang, Linda Mui, & Tim O'Reilly

The *termcap* and *terminfo* databases are UNIX's solution to the difficulty of supporting many terminals without writing special drivers for each terminal. *termcap* (BSD) and *terminfo* (System V) describe the features of hundreds of terminals, together with a library of routines that allow programs to use those capabilities. This book documents hundreds of capabilities and syntax for each, writing and debugging terminal descriptions, and terminal initialization.

"*termcap & terminfo* has been invaluable at explaining what all those strange characters mean in /etc/termcap. The real value of this one would come if I decided to build my own terminal type. I haven't done that, but the book has surely won back its purchase price by helping me add some flashy screen handling to simple shell scripts."
—UNIX Today

270 pages, ISBN 0-937175-22-6

Using UUCP and Usenet

By Grace Todino & Dale Dougherty

Using UUCP shows how to communicate with both UNIX and non-UNIX systems using UUCP and *cu* or *tip*. It also shows how to read news and post your own articles and mail to other Usenet members. This handbook assumes that UUCP and Usenet links to other computer systems have already been established by your system administrator.

While clear enough for a novice, this book is packed with information that even experienced users will find indispensable. Take the mystery out of questions such as why files sent via UUCP don't always end up where you want them, how to find out the status of your file transfer requests, and how to execute programs remotely with *uux*.

210 pages, ISBN 0-937175-10-2

!%@:: A Directory of Electronic Mail Addressing & Networks

2nd Edition
By Donnalyn Frey & Rick Adams

This book is designed to answer the problem of addressing mail to people you've never met, on networks you've never heard of. It includes a general introduction to the concept of e-mail addressing, followed by a detailed reference section, which provides information for over 130 different networks around the world.

For each network, the book shows: general description, address structure and format, architecture, connections to other networks or sites, facilities available to users, contact name and address, cross references to other networks, future plans and the date of update. Appendixes include indexes to second-level domains, network names, country names, country codes, and a description of how Internet addresses are handled by UUCP sites.

If you routinely send e-mail and want concise, up-to-date information on many of the world's networks, this book is for you.

438 pages
ISBN 0-937175-15-3

Learning GNU Emacs

By Deb Cameron & Bill Rosenblatt

GNU Emacs is the most popular and widespread of the Emacs family of editors. It is also the most powerful and flexible. (Unlike all other text editors, GNU Emacs is a complete working environment—you can stay within Emacs all day without leaving.) This book tells you how to get started with the GNU Emacs editor. It will also "grow" with you: as you become more proficient, this book will help you learn how to use Emacs more effectively. It will take you from basic Emacs usage (simple text editing) to moderately complicated customization and programming.

The book is aimed at new Emacs users, whether or not they are programmers. Also useful for readers switching from other Emacs implementations to GNU Emacs.

442 pages, ISBN 0-937175-84-6

Learning the vi Editor

5th Edition
By Linda Lamb

For many users, working in the UNIX environment means using *vi*, a full-screen text editor available on most UNIX systems. Even those who know *vi* often make use of only a small number of its features. This is the complete guide to text editing with *vi*. Early chapters cover the basics; later chapters explain more advanced editing tools, such as *ex* commands and global search and replacement.

192 pages, ISBN 0-937175-67-6

Learning the UNIX Operating System

2nd Edition
By Grace Todino & John Strang

If you are new to UNIX, this concise introduction will tell you just what you need to get started, and no more. Why wade through a 600-page book when you can begin working productively in a matter of minutes?

Topics covered include:

- Logging in and logging out
- Managing UNIX files and directories
- Sending and receiving mail
- Redirecting input/output
- Pipes and filters
- Background processing
- Customizing your account

"If you have someone on your site who has never worked on a UNIX system and who needs a quick how-to, Nutshell has the right booklet. *Learning the UNIX Operating System* can get a newcomer rolling in a single session."—;login

84 pages, ISBN 0-937175-16-1

MH & xmh: E-mail for Users & Programmers

By Jerry Peek

Customizing your e-mail environment can save you time and make communicating more enjoyable. *MH & xmh: E-mail for Users and Programmers* explains how to use, customize, and program with the MH electronic mail commands, available on virtually any UNIX system. The handbook also covers *xmh*, an X Window System client that runs MH programs.

The basics are easy. But MH lets you do much more than what most people expect an e-mail system to be able to do. This handbook is packed with explanations and useful examples of MH features, some of which the standard MH documentation only hints at.

598 pages, ISBN 0-937175-63-3

Guide to OSF/1: A Technical Synopsis

By O'Reilly & Associates Staff

OSF/1, Mach, POSIX, SVID, SVR4, X/Open, 4.4BSD, XPG, B-1 security, parallelization, threads, virtual file systems, shared libraries, streams, extensible loader, internationalization.... Need help sorting it all out? If so, then this technically competent introduction to the mysteries of the OSF/1 operating system is a book for you. In addition to its exposition of OSF/1, it offers a list of differences between OSF/1 and System V, Release 4 and a look ahead at what is coming in DCE.

This is not the usual O'Reilly how-to book. It will not lead you through detailed programming examples under OSF/1. Instead, it asks the prior question, What is the nature of the beast? It helps you figure out how to approach the programming task by giving you a comprehensive technical overview of the operating system's features and services, and by showing how they work together.

304 pages, ISBN 0-937175-78-1

POSIX Programmer's Guide

By Donald Lewine

Most UNIX systems today are POSIX-compliant because the Federal government requires it. Even OSF and UI agree on support for POSIX. However, given the manufacturer's documentation, it can be difficult to distinguish system-specific features from those features defined by POSIX.

The *POSIX Programmer's Guide*, intended as an explanation of the POSIX standard and as a reference for the POSIX.1 programming library, will help you write more portable programs. This guide is especially helpful if you are writing programs that must run on multiple UNIX platforms. This guide will also help you convert existing UNIX programs for POSIX-compliance.

640 pages, ISBN 0-937175-73-0

Managing NFS and NIS

By Hal Stern

A modern computer system that is not part of a network is an anomaly. But managing a network and getting it to perform well can be a problem. This book describes two tools that are absolutely essential to distributed computing environments: the Network Filesystem (NFS) and the Network Information System (formerly called the "yellow pages" or YP).

As popular as NFS is, it is a black box for most users and administrators. This book provides a comprehensive discussion of how to plan, set up, and debug an NFS network. It is the only book we're aware of that discusses NFS and network performance tuning. This book also covers the NFS automounter, network security issues, diskless workstations, and PC/NFS. It also tells you how to use NIS to manage your own database applications, ranging from a simple telephone list to controlling access to network services. If you are managing a network of UNIX systems, or are thinking of setting up a UNIX network, you can't afford to overlook this book.

436 pages, ISBN 0-937175-75-7

Power Programming with RPC

By John Bloomer

A distributed application is designed to access resources across a network. In a broad sense, these resources could be user input, a central database, configuration files, etc., that are distributed on various computers across the network rather than found on a single computer. RPC, or remote procedure calling, is the ability to distribute the execution of functions on remote computers outside of the application's current address space. This allows you to break large or complex programming problems into routines that can be executed independently of one another to take advantage of multiple computers. Thus, RPC makes it possible to attack a problem using a form of parallel or multi-processing.

Written from a programmer's perspective, this book shows what you can do with RPC and presents a framework for learning it.

494 pages, ISBN 0-937175-77-3

Practical C Programming

By Steve Oualline

There are lots of introductory C books, but this is the first one that has the no-nonsense, practical approach that has made Nutshell Handbooks famous. C programming is more than just getting the syntax right. Style and debugging also play a tremendous part in creating well-running programs.

Practical C Programming teaches you how to create programs that are easy to read, maintain and debug. Practical rules are stressed. For example, there are 15 precedence rules in C (&& comes before || comes before ?:). The practical programmer simplifies these down to two: 1) Multiply and divide come before addition and subtraction and 2) Put parentheses around everything else. Electronic Archaeology, the art of going through someone else's code, is also described.

Topics covered include:

- Good programming style
- C syntax: what to use and what not to use
- The programming environment, including *make*
- The total programming process
- Floating point limitations
- Tricks and surprises

Covers Turbo C (DOS) as well as the UNIX C compiler.

420 pages, ISBN 0-937175-65-X

Using C on the UNIX System

By Dave Curry

Using C on the UNIX System provides a thorough introduction to the UNIX system call libraries. It is aimed at programmers who already know C but who want to take full advantage of the UNIX programming environment. If you want to learn how to work with the operating system and if you want to write programs that can interact with directories, terminals and networks at the lowest level, you will find this book essential. It is impossible to write UNIX utilities of any sophistication without understanding the material in this book.

"A gem of a book. The author's aim is to provide a guide to system programming, and he succeeds admirably. His balance is steady between System V and BSD-based systems, so readers come away knowing both."
—SUN Expert

250 pages, ISBN 0-937175-23-4

Managing Projects with make

2nd Edition
By Steve Talbott and Andrew Oram

Make is one of UNIX's greatest contributions to software development, and this book is the clearest description of *make* ever written. Even the smallest software project typically involves a number of files that depend upon each other in various ways. If you modify one or more source files, you must relink the program after recompiling some, but not necessarily all, of the sources.

Make greatly simplifies this process. By recording the relationships between sets of files, *make* can automatically perform all the necessary updating. The new edition of this book describes all the basic features of *make* and provides guidelines on meeting the needs of large, modern projects.

152 pages, ISBN 0-937175-90-0

Checking C Programs with lint

By Ian F. Darwin

The *lint* program checker has proven itself time and again to be one of the best tools for finding portability problems and certain types of coding errors in C programs. *lint* verifies a program or program segments against standard libraries, checks the code for common portability errors, and tests the programming against some tried and true guidelines. linting your code is a necessary (though not sufficient) step in writing clean, portable, effective programs. This book introduces you to *lint*, guides you through running it on your programs and helps you to interpret *lint*'s output.

"Short, useful, and to the point. I recommend it for self-study to all involved with C in a UNIX environment."—Computing Reviews

84 pages, ISBN 0-937175-30-7